Risk Management

Project success is an elusive goal in every business or technical domain. Project failure usually results from unhandled risks to the technical, cost, and schedule aspects of the project. There are four primary root causes of project failure.

1. Unrealistic performance expectation, with missing Measures of Effectiveness
2. Unrealistic cost and schedule estimates based on inadequate risk-adjusted growth models
3. Inadequate assessment of risk and unmitigated exposure to these risks without proper handling strategies
4. Unanticipated technical issues with alternative plans and solutions to maintain the effectiveness of the project processes and its deliverables

Risk Management provides a comprehensive overview of the people, principles, processes, and practices as the fundamental base upon which an effective risk management system resides. However, this does not guarantee effective risk management and successful projects and businesses. The first half of the book describes risk management processes, as well as a delineation between risk and hazards and how these are connected. The second half of the book provides industry examples of the approach to risk management in a specific context and with specific approaches and artifacts where applicable.

The book focuses on risks created by uncertainty, their identification, and the corrective and preventive actions needed to address these risks to increase the probability of project success. The book's goal is to provide a context-driven framework, developing a foundation for a rational approach to risk management that makes adaptation to circumstances as easy as possible.

Glen B. Alleman has, over the past 25 years, led program management offices, software product development organizations, and ERP deployment projects. His current interests include Integrated Product Team (IPT) deployments of Microsoft Project Server, integration of schedules and costs on enterprise programs, and probabilistic risk assessment integration. As well, Glen consults in the system architecture, business process improvement, and program management office deployment fields. Prior to these activities, Glen was vice president of Program Management, at Rocky Flats Environmental Technology Site (www.rfets.gov), where he directed the programmatic controls aspects of the IT closure activities through the deployment of DCMA-compliant Earned Value Management Systems controlling agile software development processes.

Jon M. Quigley has product development expertise and consults, coaches, and teaches on business, product development, and project management topics (including agile and scrum). This includes embedded systems engineering, with more than 30 years of experience, much of which is in automotive with some industrial control systems. He has done work for PPG, Owens Corning, as well as GM, Plymouth, Harley Davidson, Chrysler, Mack, Volvo, and PACCAR. He has ceded seven U.S. patents to the companies at which he has worked. He has co-authored more than 17 books and contributed to many others, as well as scores of magazine articles, and he is a frequent speaker at technical and project management events.

Risk Management

Glen B. Alleman and Jon M. Quigley

CRC Press
Taylor & Francis Group
Boca Raton London New York

CRC Press is an imprint of the
Taylor & Francis Group, an **informa** business

Designed cover image: Henfrey Murithi

First edition published 2024
2385 NW Executive Center Drive, Suite 320, Boca Raton FL 33431

and by CRC Press
4 Park Square, Milton Park, Abingdon, Oxon, OX14 4RN

CRC Press is an imprint of Taylor & Francis Group, LLC

ISBN: 9781032543215 (hbk)
ISBN: 9781032545646 (pbk)
ISBN: 9781003425465 (ebk)

DOI: 10.1201/9781003425465

Typeset in Garamond
by Newgen Publishing UK

Contents

Acknowledgments

Glen Alleman has many colleagues and mentors to thank for providing advice and ideas resulting in this book. The concept of risk management started with Rick Price of Lockheed Martin Space, beginning with proposals for manned and unmanned systems, where the planning of the proposal writing was risk-adjusted in the same way the deliverables of the program. He wants to acknowledge John Caterham, CIO at Rocky Flats Environmental Technology Site, where he was a program manager for the Information and Communications Technology section, where managing in the presence of uncertainty was the standard daily process. This book, like his other writing efforts, would not have been as straightforward to complete without the support of his wife, Linda Chartier.

Jon M Quigley has many folks to thank throughout his career, everything from the positions he held while working during his undergraduate degree and master's degrees to the many experiences and exchanges with others on product development and project management topics. Through these experiences, they have witnessed many failures that have provided them with learning opportunities that inform the text. He wants to thank those with whom he has worked on many other projects, like Roopa Shenoy, Kim Robertson, Shawn P. Quigley, Kenny Thomas, Rick Bertalan, Rick Byrum, and far too many others to mention. Finally, he would like to thank all he has worked with over time at many organizations, including those through Value Transformation LLC. He prefers to list by name, but that would cover many pages. Lastly and more importantly, he wants to thank his family for providing him with the space for studying, consulting, speaking, and writing.

Introduction

Why This Book

No matter the endeavor, business or personal, there are risks. For-profit businesses are predicated on what is often referred to as taking a risk to earn a reward. That is, there is no guarantee that the undertaking being engaged will produce the desired monetary results. Even when a project is successful in delivery, there is likely uncertainty in the revenue stream generated. Still, there are much worse outcomes than a failed project or perhaps failed business cases; there are possibilities of harm being done to people using the product.

This book provides a comprehensive overview of the people, principles, processes, and practices as the fundamental base upon which an effective risk management system resides. However, this does not guarantee effective risk management and successful projects and businesses. The first half describes risk management processes, as well as a delineation between risk and hazards and how these are connected. The second half of the book provides industry examples of the approach to risk management in a specific context and with specific approaches and artifacts where applicable.

The goal of the book is to provide a context-driven, developing foundation for a rational approach to risk management that makes adaptation to circumstances as easy as possible. This book focuses on risk management in a project context (with heavy product development influence), but the fact of the matter is risk exists beyond projects, and these can have an impact on a project, a series of projects, and the enterprise at large. The method of project execution, conventional or agile, both require a robust risk management system. Effective risk management is essential for any ongoing concern; adequately identifying potential risks and either addressing these possible eventualities or organizing and planning to reduce, or better still, eliminate is required to maintain and grow the business.

A common lexicon (terminology) can go a long way to developing a cohesive approach, and better yet continuously improving that approach over time. A common language and mental models provide a core that the team or organization understands, from which improvement ideas can be contested, tested, and integrated when validated. This book can provide the foundation for an organization.

> Most risk management publications refer to the benefits of having a common language of risk within the organization. Many organizations manage to achieve this common language and common understanding of risk management processes and protocols, at least internally. However, is usually the case that within a business sector, and sometimes even within individual organizations, the development of a common language of risk can be very challenging.[1]

While this book is focused on risk from a project perspective, operations can pose a significant impact on the project as well. Rather than think of the organization as a disparate collection of people and functions, it is really a collection of systems. To be successful, that is, producing the desired outcome, requires working to understand this amalgamation of these systems and identifying and undertaking appropriate actions in response to challenges and risks.

Project success is an elusive goal in every business or technical domain. Project failure usually results from unhandled risks to the technical, cost, and schedule aspects of the project. There are four primary root causes of project failure:

1. Unrealistic performance expectation, with missing Measures of Effectiveness
2. Unrealistic cost and schedule estimates based on inadequate risk-adjusted growth models
3. Inadequate assessment of risk and unmitigated exposure to these risks without proper handling strategies
4. Unanticipated technical issues with alternative plans and solutions to maintain the effectiveness of the project processes and its deliverables

Project managers are constantly seeking ways to eliminate or control risk, variance, or uncertainty. This is a hopeless pursuit. This book will show that the only solution is to *manage in the presence of uncertainties* that create risk.

There are consistent themes that contribute to *less-than-acceptable* outcomes for projects that must be addressed by Risk Management:

- Significant gaps in the risk management practices employed by projects and their organizations.
- Uneven and inconsistent application of risk management practices within the project and across the organization.
- Ineffective integration of risk management with program and organizational management.
- Increasingly complex management environments.

Each of these can be found on troubled projects. The solution to each *theme* and the *four root causes* is obvious in principle but hard in practice.

The outcome of our effort here is to provide the principles, practices, and processes to *increase the probability of project success.* The first step in this path is to acknowledge that all risk only comes from uncertainty. And that uncertainty only comes in two forms:

- **Aleatory uncertainty**: Comes from a random process. Flipping a coin and predicting either HEADS or TAILS is aleatory uncertainty. In other words, *the uncertainty we are observing is random; it is part of the natural processes of what we are observing.*
- **Epistemic uncertainty**: Comes from the lack of knowledge. This lack of knowledge comes from many sources. Inadequate understanding of the underlying processes, incomplete knowledge of the phenomena, or imprecise evaluation of the related characteristics are common sources of epistemic uncertainty. In other words, *we do not know how this thing works, so there is uncertainty about its operation.*

In this book, we will connect risk management with root cause analysis to create a set of processes known to work in a variety of domains. Apply continuous risk management (CRM)

- **Continuously managing** risks produced by uncertainty has shown positive correlations between risk management and increasing the probability of program success.
- **Determining which risks are important** to deal with in a prioritized model, their interactions, statistical interdependencies, propagation, and evolution.
- **Implementing strategies to handle risk** with mitigation, correction, prevention, and avoidance, derived from Root Cause Analysis, to remove and prevent the conditions and actions creating the risks.

Continuous risk management increases the probability of project success by:

- **Preventing problems before they occur** with a *pre*mortem to identify the cause and take corrective and preventive actions to remove the condition and activity of the root cause before the risk becomes an issue.
- **Improving product quality by focusing on program objectives** and consciously looking for risks that affect Cost, Schedule, and Performance throughout the program's lifecycle.
- **Enabling better use of resources** through early identification of problems and providing input to management decisions regarding resource allocation.
- **Promoting teamwork** by involving personnel at all levels of the program and focusing their attention on a shared vision of the mission to provide a mechanism for achieving the needed Measures of Effectiveness and Measures of Performance.

This book focuses on risks created by uncertainty (reducible and irreducible), their identification, and the corrective and preventive actions needed to address these risks to increase the probability of project success.

Uncertainty is the consequence of all complex systems. It is the lack of needed knowledge of the state of the system in the present or in the future that creates risk. [238], [241] Adaptability, flexibility, and other systems "–illities" are devoid of meaning in a deterministic world. In the non-deterministic world, risk management is a critical success factor for increasing the probability of program success.

Risk Never Occurs without a Cause, that Cause Is Always Uncertainty Risk Is the Outcome of Uncertainty

One contributing factor to the probability of a project successfully delivering capabilities needed to accomplish its mission is determined by integrated data and processes used to manage the project.

Each project performance factor informs one or more of the Five Immutable Principles of Project Success in units of measure meaningful to the decision-makers.

1. What does *Done* look like in units of measure meaningful to the decision-maker?
2. What is the *Plan* and *Schedule* to reach *Done* with the needed *Capabilities* at the needed time for the needed cost?
3. What *Time*, *Money*, and *Resources* are needed to reach *Done*, and in what period are they needed?
4. What *Impediments* will be discovered on the way to *Done*, and their *Corrective* or *Preventative* actions?
5. What are the units of measure needed to credibly describe how progress is being made toward *Done*?

Note

1 D. Baccarini. Estimating Project Cost Contingency – Beyond the 10% Syndrome. Australian Institute of Project Management National Conference, Nov 9 2005. Australian Institute of Project Management, 2005.

Chapter 1

Introduction to Risk Management

Doubt is not an agreeable condition, but certainty is an absurd one.
Voltaire, From a letter to Frederick II of Prussia [1]

1.1 Why This Book?

No matter the endeavor, government business or personal, there are risks. There is a business saying to take a risk to earn a reward. The engaged undertaking is not guaranteed to produce the desired monetary results. Even when a project is successful in delivery, there is likely uncertainty in the revenue stream generated. Still, there are worse business outcomes than a single failed project or business case. There are possibilities of harm being done to people using the product, the environment, or the governance of an organization of society.

This book provides a comprehensive overview of the people, principles, processes, and practices as the fundamental base for an effective risk management system. However, this does not guarantee effective risk management and successful projects and businesses. The first half describes risk management processes, delineating between risk and hazards and how these are connected. The second half of the book provides industry examples of the approach to risk management in a specific context and with particular approaches and artifacts where applicable.

The book aims to provide a context-driven, developing foundation for a rational risk management approach that makes adapting to circumstances as easy as possible. This book focuses on risk management in a project context (with heavy product

DOI: 10.1201/9781003425465-1

development influence). Still, the fact of the matter is that risk exists beyond projects, and these can impact a project, a series of projects, and the enterprise at large. The method of project execution, conventional or agile, requires a robust risk management system. Effective risk management is essential for any ongoing concern. Adequately identifying potential risks and either addressing these possible eventualities or organizing and planning to reduce or eliminate risk is required to maintain and grow the business.

A common lexicon (terminology) can go a long way to developing a cohesive approach and continuously improving that approach over time. In addition, a common language and mental models provide a foundation of understanding for the team or organization. This foundation is the springboard for improvement ideas, contesting, testing, and integration when validated. This book can provide this foundation for an organization.

> Most risk management publications refer to the benefits of having a common language of risk within the organization. Many organizations achieve this common language and shared understanding of risk management processes and protocols internally. However, is usually the case that within a business sector, and sometimes even within individual organizations, developing a common language of risk can be very challenging [2].

While this book focuses on the risk from a project perspective, operations can also significantly impact the project. Rather than think of the organization as a disparate collection of people and functions, it is a collection of systems. Producing the desired outcome requires understanding these systems' amalgamation and identifying and undertaking appropriate actions in response to challenges and risks.

1.2 Risk and the Enterprise

Some management consultants make a living off keeping a positive mental attitude and being optimistic. Risk management is not the place for that. A robust objective critique, doing all that possible before relying on hope or luck, is fundamental to any risk management effort. To be practical will require constant review and a clear view of the circumstances and future possibilities. Optimism is helpful, but not when it clouds seeing things for what they are.

When a for-profit company decides to undertake any project, it is a bet, a risk (expenditure) versus a reward (benefit) calculation. The level of sensitivity to things going poorly or risk exposure will influence the size of the bet. To stay relevant and remain in business, a company will likely undertake projects to develop products or services to maintain or grow the company. The organization will identify and evaluate the market state and size and the benefit the company can provide to the customer or clientele. The organization will consider various projects and approaches for this metaphorical bet, prioritizing the most probable success and providing benefits. This evaluation requires generating ideas, and exploring the validity of those ideas, along with cost and risk assessments, including comparative evaluations. Which projects represent the best use of company assets, most likely to produce the needed results? Finding the best possible areas for the company to spend this money on something new requires careful consideration of the direction and actions the company will take. At least this should happen rather than random acceptance of spending and expending of company resources. This analysis will include, for example:

Market size	Market competition
Barrier to entry	Available talent
Cost to bring to market	The material cost of the product
Economic benefit	Cost of quality (good and bad)
Consequences outside the organization for failure	Stability of technology

1.2.1 Risk and Obstacles

In business and almost any endeavor, there are obstacles and risks. The risk may also present obstacles when and if these come to fruition. Obstacles always occur [3]. One of the roles of project management is to differentiate between these two. Perhaps a project strategy can avoid some challenges – however, no matter the chosen project strategy, we will be exposed to risks. Risks are probabilistic; obstacles are to be surmounted by project plans, learning, adapting, and effort (Figure 1.1).

1.2.2 Business Equations

From experience, most businesses perform some business analysis or modeling of the project to understand the "bet." For example, if there is little likelihood of the endeavor, if undertaken, that the project will produce the results the organization requires, it will be terminated before much time, talent, and money has been invested. Knowing this requires some attempt to ascertain the cost (bet required) compared to the reward likely or possible. This comparison often starts with a business case.

1.2.3 Return on Investment (ROI)

One mechanism for understanding the business case for the project is the return on investment (ROI). ROI is a calculation that compares the amount gained against

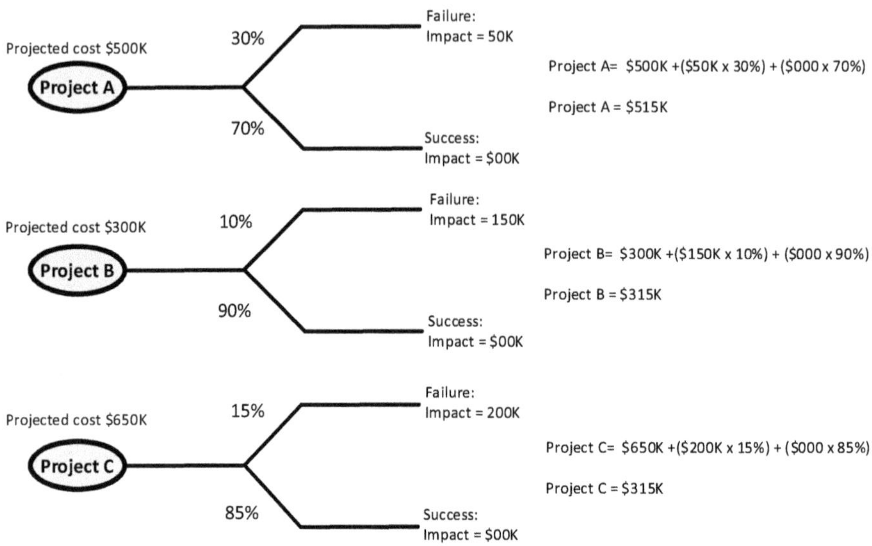

Figure 1.1 Decision tree analysis and project selection.

the amount spent as a percentage. The amount earned minus spent represents the profit generated from the endeavor. The output is a percent representation of the investment.

$$\text{ROI} = \left(\frac{\text{Amount Gained} - \text{Amount Spent}}{\text{Amount Spent}} \right) \times 100$$

or

$$\text{ROI} = \left(\frac{\text{Profit}}{\text{Amount Spent}} \right) \times 100$$

1.2.4 Net Present Value

Net present value is the difference between the present value of the cash inflows and the present value of the cash outflows over time. This comparison is of cash flows now and subsequent cash inflows over time, accounts, or the time value of money, or at least consider it.

$$\text{NPV} = \sum_{t=1}^{t} \frac{C_t}{(1+i)^t}$$

- C_t = net cash inflow during period t
- i = discount rate of return if invested differently
- t = number of compounding periods

1.2.5 Future Value of an Investment

Future value compares what can be brought into the company if undertaking a project with associated risks to another safer proposition.

$$\mathrm{FV} = \mathrm{PV}(1+r)^n$$

- FV = future value
- PV = present value
- r = interest rate
- n = compounding period

1.2.6 Payback Period

The payback period compares the income stream annually to the expenditure. How many years of production will be required to pay the investment? Short payback periods represent a low risk, if valid, as multiple years are not required to repay the investment. Longer durations for the payback may mean an increase in risk. By paying the investment earlier, the exposure to the loss is shorter.

$$\text{Payback Period} = \frac{\text{Investment}}{\text{Annual Cash Inflow}}$$

There is risk in whether and in what manner (strategies and tactics) to undertake a project. Risks continue with cost estimates and duration market size; all may be wrong. A minor variation of these in the individual variables could dramatically impact the project's cost. The value perceived by the customer may not be as significant as our estimates either; there will be variation in that as well. Additionally, the market size may not be grounded or based on tangible evidence but on optimism, wishful thinking, or errant information. The probability of these things being valid and within the range of what we find acceptable adds an element of risk akin to a bet. This assessment of likelihood may explain why only 64% of projects meet their goals.

There is much more to decide what and how a company will invest. The opportunity costs, the cost for not being able to undertake some projects because other projects are worked and consume the available resources and talent. Undertaking a project along with the cost for undertaking the project does not guarantee the outcome the business desires. This risk makes the project undertaking like a bet. The bet on our organization to successfully undertake the project and deliver it successfully. This includes sorting out which project and product are best for the organization to invest. That is at least part of the reason for the business case.

Experience informs that the project team can tell the project manager of potential and imminent risks once they are aware. A significant amount of project management is anticipation (planning), things that can sidetrack our project, and developing actions to address them. Some studies provide a glimpse of project attributes that portend failure. We will review some of these studies and the connection between project strategy and success.

Organizations, projects, and people operate within systems. The organization is a collection of systems, and people work within it. These systems sometimes produce predictable outputs and outcomes, but not always, and the interconnectedness of those systems means the impact is not isolated. Endogenous shocks can disrupt the organization in ways that pose risks if not handled effectively. Miscalculations, errant analysis, poor strategy or tactics selection, and insufficient resources or talent can cause a project and even an organization to fail, at least in part.

Exogenous shocks to the organization, such as natural disasters, accidents, massive supply chain disruption, pandemics, and social unrest, can cause the loss of life, customer loss, business possibilities, and in the worse, incarnation, the business closing permanently. Therefore, the organization's ability to identify and respond to these business challenges is crucial for company longevity.

1.3 Some Examples

Product development endeavors come with external and internal uncertainty to the organization. In addition, they can cost a company considerable money (investment and tooling) and effort (hours and opportunity costs), especially when considering complex multiyear system development. Some examples might help, and we demonstrate these stories via SOARA, often used as an interview technique. We believe it to be a quick and concise approach to articulating a situation.

Situation: Illustrate the event demonstrating key competencies and concepts.
Objective: The goal of the effort.
Action: The description of the steps taken to achieve the objective.
Results: The articulation of the outcomes from the effort.
Aftermath: Summary of learning from the effort.

1.3.1 Product and Technology

The stability of the technology we select for a product development project can present risks to our project schedule and cost.

S	ituation	An instrument cluster for a vehicle is under development. In past projects, the capacity of the microprocessor for the product was soon exceeded as vehicle features were added over the vehicle's life. This required instrument cluster development projects every three to five years. Therefore, the instrument cluster must be able to grow in feature content with a life longer than three to five years and closer to ten years.
O	bjective	Develop an instrument cluster with sufficient resources to meet anticipated vehicle function growth over ten years.
A	ctionable outcome	The team selected an emerging microprocessor underdevelopment from a reputable supplier and planned prototype iterations at a schedule congruent with the product development schedule.
R	esults	Iterations of the microprocessor are delivered throughout the development effort. The iteration is delivered for design verification efforts, and the product passes the testing. After this testing, the supplier indicated they were terminating the further development and manufacturing of the microprocessor due to yield and cost concerns. The product is tooled and designed tested with a microprocessor that will never see the light of day, requiring rework of the PCB, software modification, and subsequent testing.
A	ftermath	The project found a microprocessor version in the same family, meaning sufficient similarities would reduce the development time. However, this change required adding numerous integrated circuits, extending the microprocessor capacity – retesting the redesigned product, including environmental and functional verification. As a result, the project was months late and over budget. The lesson is to be careful when coupling a project to emerging technology. Consider an alternate path should things go errant, and plan accordingly.

1.3.2 Available Talent

Experience, available talent, and level of engagement of that talent can present a significant risk to the project. Even when we believe there to be sufficiently engaged talent, we can be unpleasantly surprised by the results.

S	ituation	A vehicle OEM purchases another OEM and desires to reduce costs and optimize the manufacturing processes, effectively assimilating the newly acquired vehicle brand. The procuring OEM vehicle architecture and manufacturing capability are more sophisticated and adaptable.

O	bjective	Create electrical/electronic (including embedded controllers or ECUs) systems to a common platform based upon procuring OEM without watering down the individual brands.
A	ctionable outcome	Two senior engineers (one lead and one senior) were to define the technical attributes of a specific electronic control module. Since the lead had more experience than the senior, the lead engineer would handle the newly acquired OEM technical definitions. The senior engineer would work with the product variant to procure OEM. The lead engineer was also the project manager of the combined project from a technical perspective. Over time, the lead engineer reviews the senior engineer's specifications. The specifications were not capable. So, the lead engineer creates a template for the senior engineer to do the work. That does not produce the desired results. During a meeting with the senior engineer's manager, the senior informs the manager, and the lead that they never wanted to be part of this project. Now, the project is behind schedule, and no one can fill the senior engineer's role. The lead engineer works longer hours and engages members of the systems engineering group to produce and review the specifications.
R	esults	After long hours and engaging a key member from the systems engineering group, the standards are delivered just in time, produced at the rate of priority of the features in the vehicle, using an agile approach to the work.
A	ftermath	The delivered project was on time but required altering the company's approach to project management (agile) and a herculean effort by the remaining team members (plenty of overtime hours). The lesson is not to wait toward the end but to establish metrics to view the process; more importantly, do never assume that a team member is engaged in the effort. Where talent is concerned, we should have alternate paths available and planned as part of our risk management.

1.3.3 Quality

Sometimes, in the haste of getting a product to the customer, the project takes calculated risks. Making effective decisions requires a balance of the benefits against the potential costs (risks). The level of quality of the product is not a fixed attribute. For example, consider these software applications below; which is riskier?

1. An online video game that does not require nor record your personal information.
2. A video game that is contained on a DVD and is purchased at stores and other outlets.
3. An ABS (antilock braking system) for a vehicle.

S	ituation	A vehicle OEM is making a change to portions of the vehicle systems. The changes are mild or minor, with a reduction in the scope of testing.
O	bjective	Ensure the changes have not brought defects explicitly associated with the changes. Specifically, test only the product's additions or purposely altered portions and ensure the product order book structure is in place to support.
A	ctionable outcome	The specific software components (electronic control units) are altered, with testing at the component level and the simulated systems via hardware in the loop simulator.
R	esults	New vehicle builds come off the manufacturing line with a defect, the unintentional alteration of a software parameter, becoming apparent at vehicle builds.
A	ftermath	The errant parameter is updated. Vehicles already manufactured have the parameter updated using development tools. The software parameter error would have been discovered had the product been tested in regression. Regression testing is a type of software testing performed to ensure that changes or updates to an application or system have not caused any new defects or issues and that existing functionalities still work as intended. It involves re-executing test cases previously run on the application or system to ensure that everything works correctly after any changes. Regression testing was well-known to the team at the start of the project.

1.4 Risk Management Is How Adults Manage Projects – Tim Lister

Projects are unique, time, cost, and often duration bound, with a specific objective to achieve. Projects are not manufacturing or operations where variations in material and processes are often better understood. Projects that undertake activities to produce a particular product, perhaps with new or emergent technology, come with associated uncertainty or risks. Does the organization have the required skills and knowledge to work with the technology? How stable is the technology? Is the technology still evolving? Does the team understand any gap between the product objective and the instability areas of the technology?

Projects set up or change manufacturing lines; even now, a global virus is disrupting the supply chain. Did the organization or project have a response plan or other actions to undertake in eventualities such as this global pandemic? In the example of the worldwide virus, once it has disrupted the environment, it isn't easy to institute actions that can control the business or project. The pressures and the obstruction of the event confound collaboration, clear thinking and response (under stress), and quickly bringing to bear these determined actions. This attempt at resolution is akin to purchasing insurance after a car wreck and the damage done.

It is important to note that the approach to risk will vary by industry and legal impacts and will influence what is deemed risky events. Therefore, there is no one-size-fits-all approach to risk management, though there may be industry themes.

1.5 What Is a Risk?

What is not a risk? Team members on projects have come to us worried about risk and set about describing the situation, and it is not a risk but an event that has happened and has consequences. Risks are events that have some probability and impact on the project and the organization. These events that have already happened are not risks but events that have occurred and have an effect. Risk has two dimensions: probability and severity. The impact or magnitude will vary, but the risks are possible events, not events that have already transpired.

1.6 Origins of Risk

Risk originates from uncertainty. Uncertainty and variation are in everything done. A lack of this understanding or knowledge of variation, cause, and effect amounts to uncertainty in our work. This lack of understanding leads us to errant conclusions and subsequent poor actions like strategy and planning. The approach taken to the project will either increase or reduce the risk. Spontaneous or emergent events can also present a risk that impedes achieving the objective. For example, consider a project undertaken to deliver a specific product with defined functionality. While developing the product, government regulations eliminate the need for the product or the product produced. The risk was that the business opportunity would go away, and that did happen; no longer a risk but a loss. The loss is the invested money in the project.

1.7 Risk and Hazard

There can be confusion about risk and hazard, but these are two very different, albeit often connected, items. A hazard threatens life, health, and the environment; a risk is a possibility that something bad will happen. A hazard couples the risk with exposure. Risk can exist but present no hazard. The classic example is the beach analogy: the water has sharks. While one walks on the beach, they are safe. However, should one wade into the water, that person would be in a hazardous situation, specifically, the risk of being bitten by a shark.

1.8 Aleatory

Aleatory risk, often called "inherent risk" or "uncertainty risk," represents the natural variability and randomness inherent in any project or business endeavor. This type of risk is beyond the control of project managers and typically cannot be eliminated, only managed, or mitigated to some extent. Examples of aleatory risk include market fluctuations, weather conditions, a combination of parameters, and unforeseeable events that can impact project timelines and outcomes. Project risk management strategies for aleatory risk often involve using contingency plans (schedule and budget, management reserve, probabilistic modeling, and risk analysis techniques) to account for the potential impact of these uncertainties on project objectives. By acknowledging and planning for aleatory risk, project managers can better prepare their teams and resources to adapt to unforeseen events and maintain project success despite uncertainty.

> A great challenge in life: Knowing enough to think you are right, but not knowing enough to know you are wrong.
>
> *Neil deGrasse Tyson [4]*

1.9 Epistemic

Epistemology studies knowledge, methods, and validation of things learned. Risks are associated with the unknown or something believed to be known but not. The work, especially project management and burgeoning technology work, requires learning. A lack of knowledge can lead to what seems to be emergent events. Considering the interconnectedness and dependencies, systematic predictions of many of these events are possible.

Making decisions on unsubstantiated opinions or beliefs relies upon the luck of the guess. That might be okay for some low-risk items but not for others. This is not to suggest that responding to emerging events is off the table. Responded in the face of uncertainty, consider the impact of the uncertainty on the project or

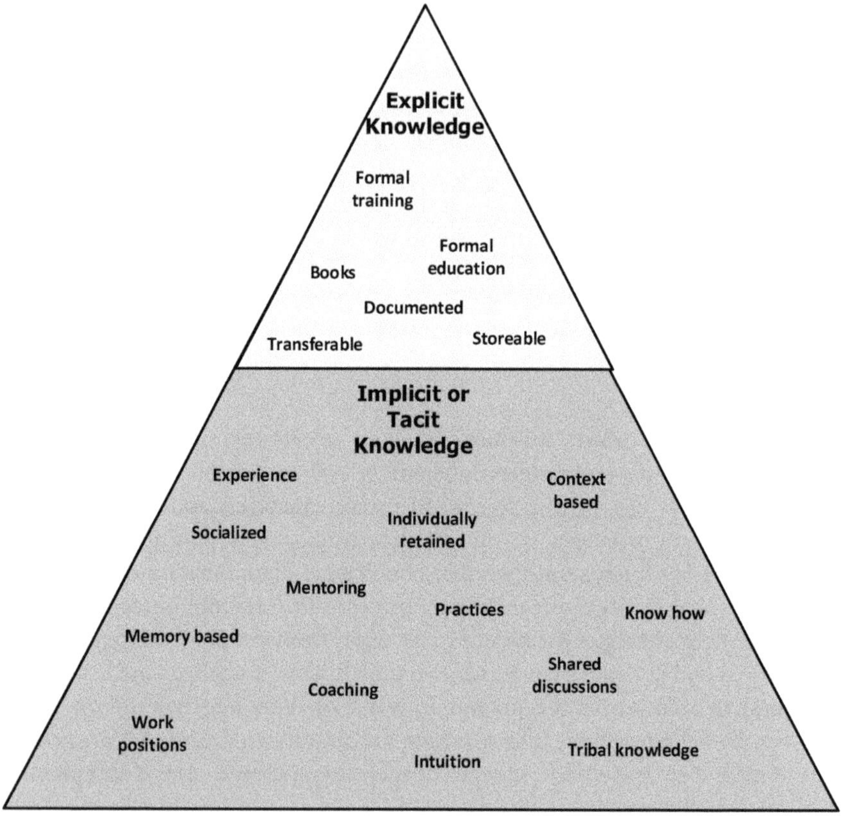

Figure 1.2 Explicit and tacit knowledge examples.

work effort. Risk resides in this uncertainty, which can be reduced by learning and thorough knowledge in general. Ideas unsubstantiated or not vetted to the requisite degree leave the endeavor at risk. Vetting these items is not as easy as it may sound; measurement issues and cognitive biases (discussed in later chapters) confound this effort (Figure 1.2).

1.9.1 Explicit Knowledge

Explicit knowledge is easy to pass in books, magazine articles, work instructions, and other formalized mechanisms. It is written down, easily articulated, and demonstrated or communicated. People who get degrees from universities have explicit knowledge and certifications. The knowledge originates from formalism.

1.9.2 Tacit Knowledge

The value in teams is the various and often disparate experiences and tacit (implicit) and explicit knowledge. Tacit knowledge is born out of experiences, not codified or formalized, and resides in the team members. Unfortunately, it isn't easy to transfer this knowledge quickly and directly.

1.9.3 Implicit Knowledge

Implicit knowledge is intuitive, and experience originates from experiences and incidental activities. This learning may happen even when the individual is unaware of the learning or acquiring knowledge. For example, think about learning to walk, ride a bike, or walk; likely, this did not happen by reading a book or magazine article but is borne from experiments when younger.

1.9.4 Institutional Knowledge

Institutional knowledge is often referred to as tribal knowledge, which is specific to the organization and its processes. This institutional knowledge does not readily transfer to other organizations, though perhaps some may transfer within an industry. Institutional knowledge comes from the actions taken by the team members over time; this includes interactions with the organization's processes and procedures. This is based upon experience, and that experience and any resulting learning from individual to individual team members may, and will likely be different. That is, each person's learning may be different.

1.9.5 Bloom's Taxonomy

One way to assess an individual's knowledge level is through Bloom's taxonomy. Bloom provides a mechanism for evaluating competencies through action words that create a gradation to a specific competency, the lowest level being knowledge or the ability to repeat some truth. As competency grows, the action words move through understanding to the ability to evaluate and create. The ability to take the principles of some domain knowledge and develop new applications is different from recall, for example. These action words make the assessment tangible. This is not a book about learning, but it is essential to understand these striations of knowledge, the competencies required for the project, and the subsequent risk implications. To illustrate, consider the story below (Figure 1.3).

Knowledge and identifying gaps in that knowledge is a step toward reducing risk. From experience, believing something to be true that may not be true is a source of risk and assumptions. These areas require effort to understand in meaningful ways. Part of the risk reduction activities must be about closing the gap between what is known and what needs to be known. The wider this gap, the larger the area of risk.

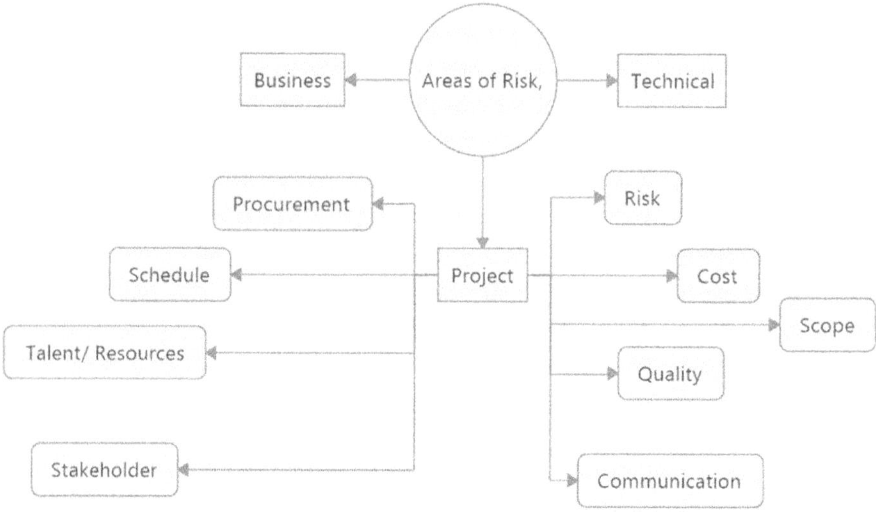

Figure 1.3 An example of areas for risk for a project.

1.10 Ontological

> It is far better to grasp the universe as it really is than to persist in delusion, however satisfying and reassuring.
>
> *Carl Sagan [5]*

Ontology is a branch of philosophy that deals with the nature of existence, the categories of things that exist, and the relationships between them. Ontology refers to a formal description of the concepts and relationships that comprise a particular knowledge domain. It is a way of representing knowledge about a specific domain in a structured and organized manner.

One way ontology relates to risk is through the concept of ontological uncertainty. Specifically, the uncertainty that arises from not knowing the nature of the aspects of a particular situation or scenario. For example, ontological uncertainty might occur at financial risk from not fully understanding the heart of the financial instruments involved in a specific investment.

Another way ontology relates to risk is through the concept of ontological risk. Risks arise from the nature of the entities involved in a particular situation or scenario. For example, in the context of environmental risk, ontological risk might arise from the inherent riskiness of certain substances or activities that are involved in the environment.

Ontology can be a valuable framework for understanding the nature of risk and how it relates to the knowledge areas involved. By understanding the fundamental nature of the world and the entities within it, we can better assess and manage risk in a variety of different contexts.

1.10.1 Central Tendency, Dispersion, and Statistics

Variation exists in everything and refers to the range of presentment of some parameter (such as a length dimension, numeric value, or electric current used). Variation extrapolates to the variations process as well. Project work products and processes also have variations, especially in the performance of people and individuals. Understanding the range of possible outcomes allows us to make a sounder judgment by determining the range of possibilities.

To begin understanding the mathematics of variation, let's look at a measure of central tendencies, specifically the arithmetic mean or average. Mean is the arithmetic sum of a unique attribute, divided by the number of measurements or:

$$\bar{X} = \frac{x1 + x2 + x3 + x4 + x5}{5}$$

Mean can be written in shorthand using the summation symbol:

$$\bar{X} = \frac{\sum_{i=0}^{n} Xi}{n}$$

Another measure of central tendency is the median, the middle value of a number series. For example, consider the sequence of numbers 5.55, 5.45, 5.35, 5.25, and 5.20. The central value of that series is 5.45 for even distributions.

Ascertaining the mode is another form of determining the peak of the distribution. The mode is the value that has the most frequency of occurrence. For example, consider the series 10.3, 10.5, 10.6, 10.7, 10.7, and 10.9. In this series, the mode is 10.7.

While central tendency provides some information on the explored subject, the analysis thus far is limiting. What is often needed to understand are not these single maximum values or most recurring values but to calculate the measure of dispersion.

The peak or average only provides so much information about the measurements; these measures do not inform much. Calculating the range can give a better view of the possible outcomes, mathematically the range is:

$$R = \chi\_\max - \chi\_\min$$

$$R = 30 - 15$$

$$R = 15$$

A better understanding requires a view of the dispersion of the events. Prediction of any sort requires some knowledge of the dispersion. In statistics, sigma (σ) is the symbol used to represent the standard deviation of a dataset. The standard deviation measures the amount of variation or dispersion in a dataset. The standard deviation is helpful because it indicates how much the individual observations in a dataset vary from the norm. A low standard deviation value means that the values in the dataset are close to the mean, while a high standard deviation value means that the values are spread over a broader range.

Understanding sigma is used in various statistical analyses, such as hypothesis testing, confidence interval estimation, and regression analysis. It is also used to define control limits in statistical process control and quality control.

$$\sigma = \frac{\sqrt{\Sigma\left(x_i - \mu\right)^2}}{N}$$

where

σ = population standard deviation.
N = size of the population.
x_i = each value from the population.
μ = the population mean.

From this calculation, we can assess the span of outcomes possible for the parameter under critique.

One standard deviation or one sigma (σ) is then $\bar{x} \pm \sigma$.

Two standard deviations or two sigma (2σ) is then $\bar{x} \pm 2\sigma$.

Three standard deviations or three sigma (3σ) is then $\bar{x} \pm 3\sigma$.

From the standard deviation, it is possible to visualize the dispersion and probabilities based on the deviation (Figure 1.4).

1.10.2 What Is the Source of Variation?

- **Common Cause:** Originates from the essential elements of a manufacturing process, typically the machine, workforce (employees), material, work method, and measurement system (many people also include the environment). These sources are known as the five "Ms" and contribute a fixed amount of variation to a process. Also known as inherent, routine, or predictable variation [6].
- **Assignable Cause:** Unplanned and originates outside of the expected operating conditions for a process. The source of assignable cause variation could be a plugged coolant line, a chip wedged beneath the fixture, a broken tool, or a spike in air pressure. When one of these unpredictable events happens, the process output is usually affected to an unknown degree. The presence of assignable cause variation is often revealed in a control chart [6].

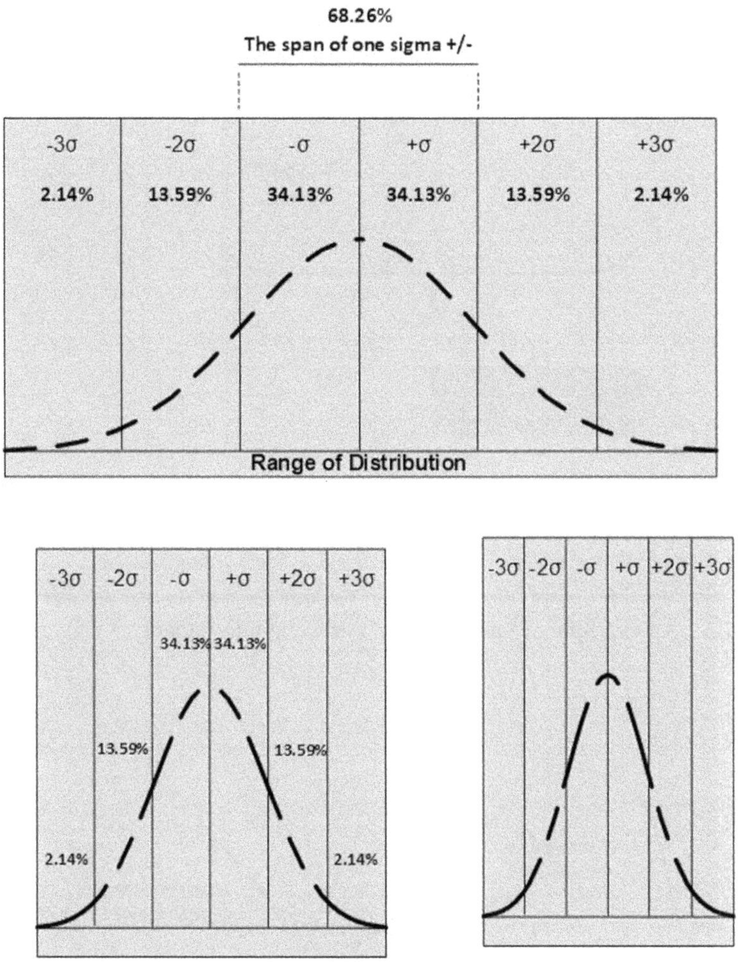

Figure 1.4 An example of the various distributions.

1.10.3 How Is Variation Connected to Risks?

Project schedules provide a great illustration of the consequences of a poor understanding of variation. Consider the schedule build. From experience, the task durations are the minimum or average value duration, not accounting for task variation. As a result, this schedule is almost certain to fail (Figure 1.5).

Task variation, and variation at large, can be understood, to a degree, through good measurement history through statistics or experience. Task variation comprising the schedule and cost are areas of project failure; plans that do not acknowledge this will produce failure. The same is true for the costs of the project. Processes used in the project should be understood and realized where understanding is lacking.

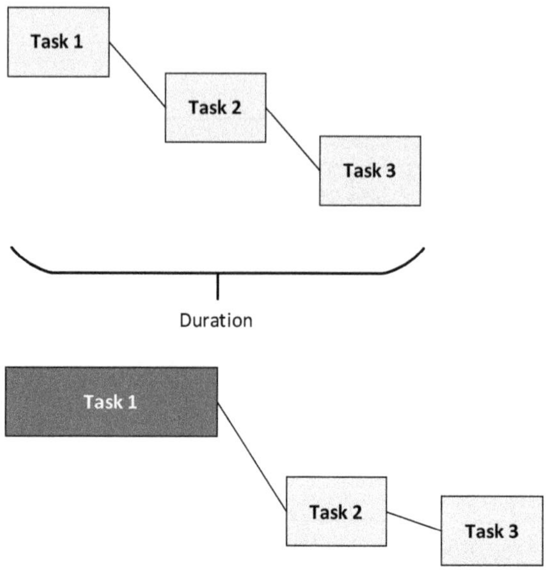

Figure 1.5 An example of task variation and schedule impact.

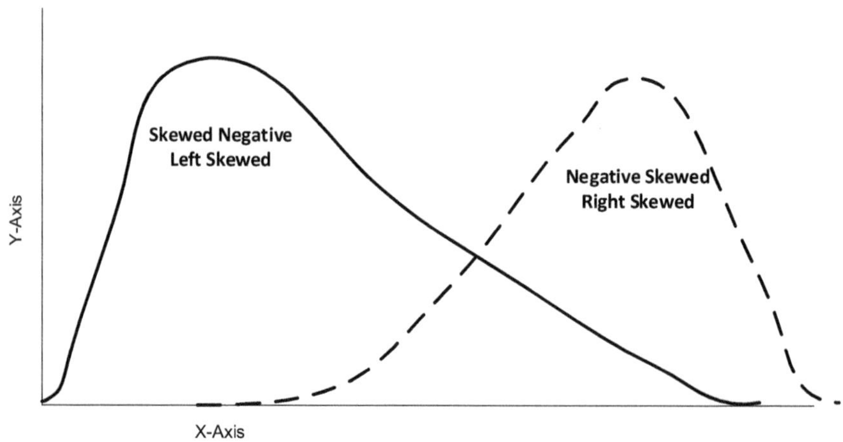

Figure 1.6 Distribution can come with a measure of skewness; it is not always symmetrical.

Understanding variation can be confounded as the distribution is not always normal but can be skewed or log-normal; in fact, when it comes to tasks for schedules, the distribution is not likely to be normal, assuming the normal distribution is not a route to success (Figure 1.6).

1.11 The Six Immutable Laws of Risk Management

Six immutable laws about risk management require understanding to navigate risk, including a suitable way to respond effectively, especially from a system perspective. A better understanding of these laws can help in better analysis, decision-making, recognition of a potential event, and subsequent execution of defined actions.

1.11.1 Uncertainty

As the quote at the beginning of the chapter, doubt may be unpleasant, but certainty is absurd, especially when doing things that have not been done before or in ways that have not previously.

Uncertainty is a lack of knowledge, information, or inability to predict a particular situation or event. Uncertainty can arise from incomplete data, ambiguity, unpredictability, or complexity. Uncertainty is pervasive in many areas of human life, including science, economics, finance, politics, and everyday decision-making.

In science, uncertainty arises from the limitations of our knowledge and understanding of natural phenomena. For example, in quantum mechanics, uncertainty is a fundamental property of particles that occurs from the Heisenberg uncertainty principle, which states that the more precisely the position of a particle is known, the less the momentum is known, and vice versa.

In economics and finance, uncertainty refers to the lack of predictability or reliability of future events, such as market conditions, interest rates, or political developments. Uncertainty can lead to market volatility as investors and businesses adjust their expectations and strategies to account for potential risks and uncertainties.

In decision-making, uncertainty can create challenges for individuals and organizations, as assessing the potential outcomes and consequences of different choices or actions becomes difficult. This exploration can lead to various strategies for coping with uncertainty, such as avoiding or delaying decisions, seeking more information or expert advice, or taking a more cautious or conservative approach.

Things not known are uncertain. Uncertainty comes from a lack of knowledge. The belief that learning solely from experience (anecdotal and uncritiqued) can be a significant source of risk or failure is folly. Cognitive biases can make clarifying and understanding what is known incredibly challenging. For example, it is possible to interpret a pattern where there is no pattern in addition to just not knowing; the degree of knowledge matters. There is variation in everything. Some knowledge is easily acquired and easily understood with time and effort. Some things are going to require additional time spent to learn. It is not just about events that can happen unexpectedly; an understanding of variation. It is not enough to know this can happen but the range of outcomes and associated probabilities.

1.11.2 Level of Risk Aversion

Risk aversion refers to a tendency to prefer a lower-risk option over a higher-risk option with the same expected outcome. For example, a risk-averse person would typically choose a lower-risk investment with a lower potential return over a higher-risk investment with a higher possible return.

The level of risk aversion varies from person to person, project to project, and organization to organization. It can depend on factors such as their financial situation, values, and previous experiences with risk-taking. Some organizations may be more risk-averse than others and prefer avoiding risk altogether, while others may be more willing to take on higher risks for the potential rewards. Risk sensitivity depends upon the industry to some degree. For example, a gaming software company is likely less risk-averse than a company that builds commercial aircraft or automobile manufacturers. Even within a specific industry, risk acceptance or aversion may exist.

1.11.3 Decisions under Duress

Decisions made under duress refer to choices made in high-pressure, stressful situations. These situations may involve physical or emotional threats, time constraints, or limited options.

When faced with a decision under duress, remaining rational and making a well-informed choice can be challenging. The stress and pressure of the situation may lead to impulsive or emotional decisions that may not be in the individual's, project's, or organization's best interest.

It's important to note that decisions made under duress may not always be the best or most rational choices, and it's essential to reflect on the decision once the stressful situation has passed. It may be helpful to seek support from friends, family, or a mental health professional to process the experience and make any necessary adjustments to the decision.

It is easier to think about our approach to the project risk when we are not subject to the immediate consequences of the risk.

1.11.4 Risk and Metrics

Risk and metrics are closely related in that metrics can be used to assess and manage risk. Metrics are quantitative measurements used to evaluate performance, identify potential issues, and track progress toward goals. In the context of risk, metrics assess a risk event's likelihood and potential impact and determine the effectiveness of risk management strategies.

Several types of metrics can be used in risk management, including:

1. **Risk likelihood and impact metrics**: These metrics assess the probability of a risk event occurring and its potential impact on the organization.

2. **Risk exposure metrics**: These metrics evaluate the level of risk exposure for specific areas or processes within the organization.
3. **Risk response metrics**: These metrics assess the effectiveness of risk response strategies and help identify areas for improvement.
4. **Risk mitigation metrics**: These metrics evaluate the effectiveness of risk mitigation measures and help identify areas for improvement.

Using metrics to assess and manage risk, organizations can make more informed decisions and proactively mitigate potential risks. In addition, regular monitoring and evaluation of risk metrics can help organizations identify emerging threats and take appropriate action before they become significant issues.

1.11.5 Risk Response

Risk response refers to the actions individuals, organizations, or projects take to manage, mitigate, transfer, or accept a risk's potential negative consequences or impacts. Ideally, this happens early in the project, where the response is planned out (see Section 1.11.3). However, whether planned or an emerging event requires consideration of the reaction, the project has a range of responses available.

1.11.6 Risks in an Organization May Be Thematic

While all projects are different, projects within an organization often have similarities and, from experience, similar failure modes. It is unnecessary to burn our hands on the same metaphoric stove; we can and should learn from previous work. The work that has gone before is an opportunity for formal learning retention during the project. An organization with a mechanism for capturing and distributing learning can capitalize on this learning. Without this record, reliance upon memory is subject to distances and biases.

We have heard a manager at a vehicle Original Equipment Manufacturer (OEM) lament, "It is okay to make mistakes, but can't we make different ones." Unfortunately, this does not suggest that capturing learning from previous projects will be a panacea for future project efforts. Most project situations are unique, and understanding every parameter and interaction that leads to a specific outcome is often not readily discernable. Gain understanding will require effort.

1.12 The 4P's of Risk Management – People, Process, Principles, and Practices

Risk management is not as simple as technical approaches, statistics, or another formally documented approach to risk. Moreover, effective risk management requires much more than this technical and statistical analysis, though these are likewise important. However, there are 4Ps of Risk Management that are more critical.

1. People
2. Process
3. Principles
4. Practices

1.12.1 People

The external and internal environment of the team impacts the organization's ability to identify and rise to risk challenges. Therefore, the team and competencies regarding effective risk management, especially the early portion, cannot be overstated, specifically identifying things that can go wrong.

Mental Models [7]: are frameworks or structures individuals use to organize, understand, and interpret information in their environment. Mental models are shaped by an individual's experiences, beliefs, and assumptions and can influence how they perceive and respond to risk. We take it a step further, suggesting that the mental models must be revised and critiqued by the team members, referring to them as open mental models [8].

Regarding risk, mental models can help individuals decide how to manage or mitigate risks. For example, a mental model that views risks as opportunities for growth and learning may lead individuals to take risks that they believe will ultimately benefit them. On the other hand, a mental model that views risks as threats to safety or security may lead an individual to avoid risky situations altogether.

Mental models can also influence how individuals assess and respond to different types of risks. For example, individuals with a mental model focusing on short-term gains may be more likely to take risks with immediate rewards, even if the long-term consequences are uncertain or hostile. Similarly, individuals with a mental model that prioritizes social approval may be more likely to take socially sanctioned risks, even if they carry significant risks.

Risk Principles that Influence Culture: the project and organization environment need to be such that the team members are willing and able to articulate their thoughts on risk.

1. The amount and constraints upon the communication within the organization will influence the ability to respond adequately.
2. Anecdotally, the level of politics in the organization can create an environment wherein team members do not feel comfortable contradicting.

3. The industry and level of regulations and impact on the customer – automotive versus gaming software – influence the level of risk tolerance of the company.

Psychological Safety: refers to a work environment of the project and the organization that is such that the team members are not afraid to bring unpleasant information.

Culture Implications: Culture influences the ability to identify and respond appropriately; an overly optimistic culture or a culture that does not hold diligence in any appreciable regard runs contrary to risk management. Politics can suppress the organization's status and information flow, making risk identification and management difficult.

Cognitive Biases: are errors in an individual's thinking that produce poor decisions and judgments, often based on interpretation of the experiences. Cognitive biases left undiscovered can present risks to the organization's endeavor.

Logical Fallacies: are common errors in reasoning that undermine the logic of the argument. Logical fallacies impact communication and articulation of the actual state, shared understanding and discovery, and conflict resolution.

Heuristics: are mental shortcuts helping us make quick decisions (and hopefully accurate). These heuristics can help to move through life quickly and safely quickly. The problem is that heuristics are optimization of speed over accuracy or validity.

Believing untrue things to be accurate or inability to assess information and perspective veracity is another source of risk not easily uncovered. Like biases and heuristics, the things not said by people also bring trouble to the equation. The team may accept a premise, but their understanding of it is inconsistent across all team members.

Value of Diversity of Perspectives: helps identify risks and responses for the project. The experiences of a single person or collection of people with the same experiences are less effective than many experiences and perspectives.

In product development, this diversity of perspective comes from:

- Experience
- Knowledge areas
- Knowledge depth
- Creativity

1.12.2 Principles

1.12.2.1 Definition of Done

Projects have defined objectives or scope, and the definition of done is tangible incarnations of the completion or the completion of the project resulting objectives. An actual description of done provides the specific goals for the project work, but equally important is the metric to compare the project outcome. This comparison will inform the level of completion of the effort. Providing the objective is the starting position for determining the approach (strategies) and specific actions (tactics and execution) to meet the goal.

Obstacles and obstructions to this tangible description of done are fodder for risk discussions, as these potentialities may preclude achieving that objective. Additionally, how the project sets about to achieve the goals will eliminate some risks and encourage others. The strategy and tactics matter, and it is incumbent upon the project team, no matter the manner of execution (agile or conventional project approaches), to devise prudent plans commensurate with the associated risks and the objective.

1.12.2.2 Plan, Schedule, Cost, and Capabilities

> An individual who is observed to be inconstant to his plans, or perhaps to carry on his affairs without any plans at all, is marked at once, by all prudent people, as a speedy victim to his own unsteadiness and folly.
>
> *Alexander Hamilton (1757–1804) or*
> *James Madison (1751–1836) [9]*

There are planning events for a project that starts with the project objectives and approaches (strategies and tactics) undertaken to achieve the project objectives. Then, depending on the organization, various project plans may be produced (for example, scope, cost, and quality). Some of this guidance will come via the organization's policies and other documentation; these documents help reduce risk and improve the accuracy and repeatability of work undertaken.

The planning effort is the opportunity to explore several possible solutions to determine the best approach, whatever that may mean for the project and the organization. The plan will have implications on the schedule; it defines the required deliverables and subsequent tasks and costs to meet these objectives. The manner of articulating the project objectives or goals matters. Poorly defined scope makes optimizing the project challenging, if not impossible. Focusing on the tangible, specific capabilities, with performance metrics, provides a particular target as a baseline, not only focusing on the work but also providing a precise measure taken during the work. Metrics help with predictions, comparing the attributes at any given time in the development and project progress with the target attributes, making predictions and opportunities to alter the method to achieve these goals.

1.12.2.3 Time, Money, Resources, and Done

Knowing the scope and the work required to produce the product or service with the capabilities and performance specifically defined makes possible assessments of the amount of time, money, and resources to achieve completion, also known as estimates. There is uncertainty in the development of estimates and their propagation throughout the company. Sadly, these difficulties are one of the reasons for the no-estimates proponents. No estimates mean going over budget is impossible; there is no over budget and no later deliveries (no estimates of time). Situations and circumstances vary; industry, company, and the scope of the work all require consideration of the risk.

1.12.3 Process

The easiest way to explain how things work can be to see things as a process (Figure 1.7).

1.12.3.1 Overview of Risk Management Processes

Risk management consists of processes to discover, assess, and determine suitable actions in response to the risk. Each technique focuses on specific objectives, the depending methods building upon the previous cycle (Figure 1.8).

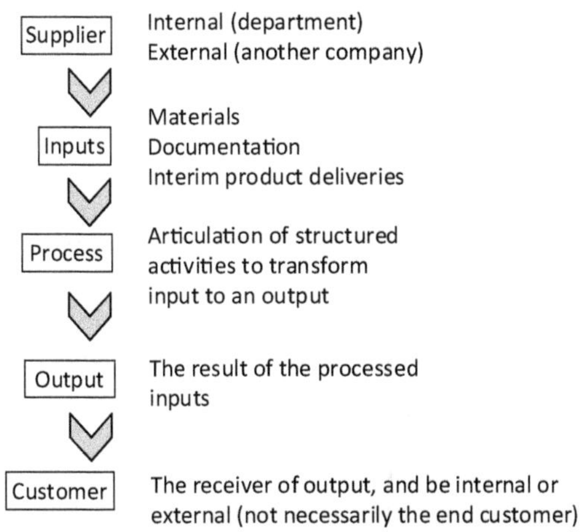

Figure 1.7 An example of the chain of events (Supplier, Input, Process, Output, Customer; SIPOC) that produces output.

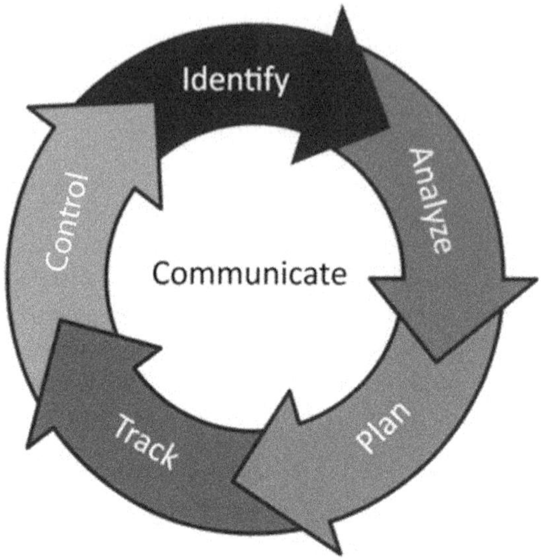

Figure 1.8 Overview of risk management processes.

1.12.3.1.1 Identify

There are a host of techniques used to discover potential maladies. The goal of this process is to uncover those things that can go wrong. A diversity of views, talents, and competencies provides a chance for a comprehensive view of the possible risks and things that can go wrong.

Historical records, including post-project activities such as lessons learned or white book exercises, can provide good fodder; at least, there should be no surprise since these events have happened in the past.

1.12.3.1.2 Analyze

Beyond identifying those things that can go wrong is assessing the impact. Again, there are a variety of ways to attempt understanding. For example, expert opinion can help understand the impact and probability of individually identified risks. Limited time and resources require prioritization of things most likely to cause harm from a severity (how bad this event will harm) and probability (likelihood) perspective.

Process assets or process documentation and recorded metrics can help us understand the range of performance for these processes. This information can help with schedule and cost risks in addition to performance failures from the process and the depending implications.

1.12.3.1.3 Response

After learning what can go wrong and to what degree comes the response. Not only the risk response but to know when to deploy responses, it is prudent to identify parameters and associated metrics with the objective of visibility into the risk item before the risk comes to the fore. In this case, lead indicators that allow prediction are better than lag indicators, which inform that the problem's results have happened.

1.12.3.1.4 Margin

The way to address the various issues is by increasing margins. For example, consider mechanical devices; the margin consists of tolerances on those measurements. For multiple mechanical components in a system, understanding tolerance stack-ups ensure the ability to build the system and for the system to function as desired. To extend the example further, consider a developed product that must work in a wide range of environments; perhaps the maximum temperature expected might be 80°C. Should the product fail at 81°C? This question illustrates the concept of margin, the space between the operation or expectation and the actual.

Similar to product margins are project management margins. Projects focus on scope, cost, and timing. All of these also benefit from margins. In this case, the margins are the end product description, the amount of money available versus estimates of costs, and the estimated delivery date compared to the actual amount of time to accomplish the project objectives.

1.12.3.1.5 Buy Down

In finance and investment, a buy-down is a method to manage risk. By reducing the interest rate on a loan, the borrower can reduce their monthly payments, which can help to reduce the risk of default or nonpayment.

For example, in a mortgage buy-down, the borrower may pay an upfront fee to the lender in exchange for a lower interest rate for a set period, such as the first few years of the loan. A lower interest rate can reduce the borrower's monthly payments during the initial period, making the loan more affordable and reducing the risk of default.

Buy-downs can also be used in other contexts to manage risk. For example, in insurance, a deductible is a form of buy-down in which the policyholder agrees to pay a portion of the loss or damage before the insurance company begins to cover the costs. Buy-down can reduce the insurance company's risk exposure and help lower the policy's price for the policyholder.

Buy-downs can effectively manage risk in various financial contexts by reducing costs and increasing affordability for borrowers or policyholders. However, it is essential to carefully evaluate the costs and benefits of a buy-down strategy and the potential risks and uncertainties involved before deciding to proceed with such a strategy.

1.12.3.1.6 Change the Approach (Avoid)

There are benefits to exploring the risks early in the effort. Continuing with the view of the potential project as a bet, we can elect not to undertake the project with a risk too high and a reward too low. To assess will require some evaluation mechanism – metrics.

1.12.3.1.7 Do Nothing (Accept)

There is a German proverb: "*He who grasps too much lets much fall.*" This saying is true for managing risks. Many things can go wrong in project work or work in general, but these are not all equally weighted. Some risks require more attention than others, making it essential to consider the most severe events and adopt an effective and efficient screening method to select those that need attention.

1.12.3.1.8 The Lie That Is Risk Transfer

The best way to describe risk transfer is to consider automotive insurance. However, paying the automotive insurance does not prevent the accident from occurring; it pays for "fixing" what has been broken by the accident.

Transferring project work to others who may be more skilled or competent; however, what happens when those responsible for this part of the work cannot do work or fails in some way? Transferring may improve the possibility of success, reducing the risk associated with failure but not eliminating it. Other actions may also be prudent depending upon the consequences of the transferred work product.

1.12.3.1.9 Tracking

Measurements and metrics make it possible to predict when risks are imminent. However, these measurements must be carefully identified and collected. Metrics provide indicators of circumstances or status changes. Leading indicators are predictive and lag indicators, which confirm that something has occurred or that the state has changed.

Defining the metrics associated with specific risk events is only as good as the measurements and the attention given to these indicators. Therefore, as with action items, it is essential for those team members closest or responsible for the task or objective to measure and monitor. In addition, defining the level or value metric measurement is to know when to invoke the controlling actions. These metrics are the basis of a closed-loop control system; the sampling rate and the response time of the control system will have impacts on the ability to control.

1.12.3.1.10 Controlling

It is not enough to identify and determine a suitable measurement and manner of acquisition and discover an appropriate risk response. It is also necessary to apply controls. Controls are actions taken to influence the risk, perhaps reduce or eliminate the risk's probability, by quickly enacting the controlling measures the team identified earlier.

1.12.3.1.11 Communicate

Project management requires effective communication; this is especially valid for risk management. Communication is necessary for both identified and previously unidentified or potential risks. Communication is the mechanism for articulating discovery, invoking response plans, and adapting where required. Anecdotally, informal team communication, for example, project discussions at the water cooler that lead the team members to realize something wicked their way comes – to paraphrase a 1983 movie of a similar title. I have had team members stop me at the water cooler, informing me of some emerging situation, a risk that seemed to be coming to fruition. For the team, understanding and responding timely and appropriately requires communication.

1.12.4 Practices

1.12.4.1 Measurements

> What gets measured gets managed.
>
> *Peter Drucker, The Practice of Management [10]*

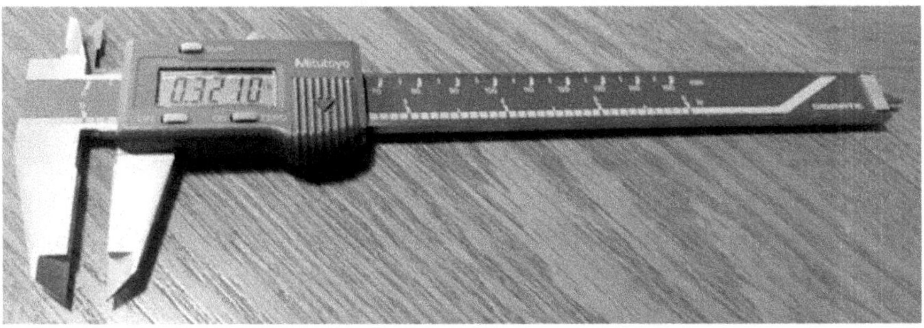

Measurements or metrics are how we understand variation. We can use historical records. Measurements are essential to understanding an event or parameter range of possibilities or outcomes. Data helps with predictions and can aid in planning.

Figure 1.9 Relationship between objectives, strategy, tactics, and work effort.

Metrics connected with historical work or process outputs provide a base from which estimates are possible. Besides historical records via metrics, metrics help to determine the organization's and the project's accomplishment rate, providing a mechanism for assessing the performance (Figure 1.9).

1.12.4.1.1 Strategy

Strategy refers to a plan or approaches that an organization or project uses to achieve its goals and objectives. It involves making choices and decisions about allocating resources and deploying capabilities to create value and gain a competitive advantage.

A good strategy typically involves a deep understanding of the organization's strengths and weaknesses and the external environment in which it operates. Appropriate strategy selection requires careful analysis, including market research, customer feedback, and competitive intelligence. A well-crafted strategy should also be flexible enough to adapt to changes.

A project strategy typically includes the following components:

1. **Project Goals and Objectives**: The project goals and objectives are the primary targets that the project team aims to achieve. These should clearly define and align with the organization's overall business strategy.
2. **Scope and Deliverables**: The project scope outlines what is included and excluded from the project and the deliverables the project team will produce. A delineation of effort ensures that all stakeholders have a common understanding of what will be accomplished by the project.
3. **Project Timeline and Milestones**: The timeline defines the project's completion schedule, including key milestones and deadlines. Project schedules help the project team stay on track, meet critical deadlines, and provide a basis for predicting outcomes.
4. **Resource Allocation**: The project team must identify the resources required to complete the project, including personnel, equipment, and budget. A resource

plan ensures that the necessary talent (skills) and resources are available when needed.

5. **Risk Management Plan**: The project team should identify potential risks and challenges that could impact the project's success and develop a risk management plan to mitigate these risks.
6. **Communication Plan**: A communication plan ensures that all stakeholders are informed about the project's progress and that shared information is correct and at the right time.

1.12.4.1.2 Tactics Selection

Project tactics refer to specific actions, plans, and techniques the project team employs to execute the project strategy and achieve its goals and objectives. These are the particular steps taken to bring the project strategy to life.

Examples of project tactics include:

1. **Task Management**: The project team must manage tasks efficiently to ensure they are completed on time and within budget. Task understanding may involve using project management tools like Gantt charts to track progress and meet deadlines.
2. **Communication**: Effective communication is essential for the success of any project. The project team must communicate clearly and regularly with all stakeholders to ensure everyone knows the project's progress, issues, and follow-up steps.
3. **Risk Management**: The project team must identify potential risks and challenges that could impact the project's success and develop a risk management plan to mitigate these risks.
4. **Resource Allocation**: The project team must allocate resources efficiently to ensure that the necessary personnel, equipment, and budget are available when needed.
5. **Quality Control**: The project team must ensure the deliverables meet the required quality standards defined in the project. These standards may involve using quality assurance tools, such as testing and inspection, to ensure the final product meets the specifications.
6. **Stakeholder Management**: The project team must manage the expectations and requirements of all stakeholders, including customers, sponsors, and team members (Figure 1.10).

Project tactics are the project team's steps to implement the project strategy and achieve the desired outcomes. They are essential for the successful execution of the project and should be careful.

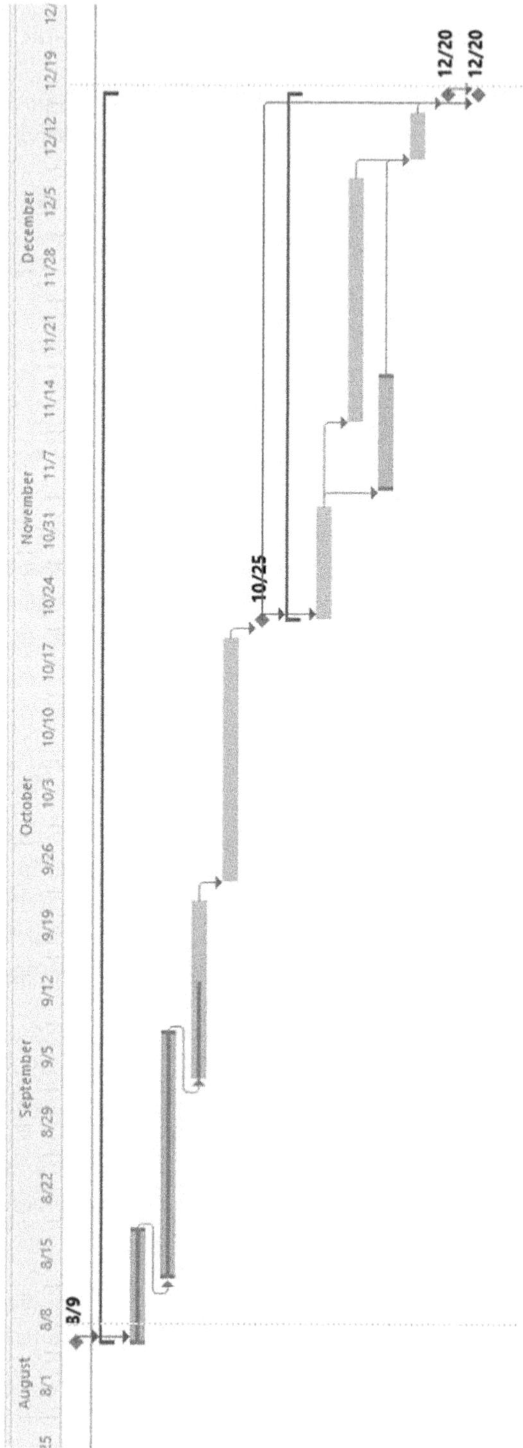

Figure 1.10 An example of a Gannt chart.

1.13 Root Cause Analysis

Root cause analysis and risk management are closely related concepts often used in various fields such as healthcare, manufacturing, and information technology.

Root cause analysis helps to identify the underlying causes of a particular problem or event, which can help to prevent similar issues from occurring in the future. By understanding the root cause of a problem, organizations can take proactive steps to address the issue and prevent it from happening again.

On the other hand, risk management involves identifying, assessing, and mitigating risks that may impact an organization's operations, projects, or goals. It involves systematically identifying potential risks, evaluating their likelihood and impact, and developing strategies to mitigate or avoid them.

The use of root cause analysis has a broader context on the risk management process. For example, suppose an organization identifies a shortcoming in the performance of a particular process or system. In that case, we explore the root cause to understand the underlying factors contributing to that performance. This knowledge provides a basis for improvement and risk reduction.

References

1. Voltaire, *From a letter to Frederick II of Prussia*, 28 November 1770.
2. P. Hopkin with C. Thompson, *Fundamentals of Risk Management; Understanding, Evaluating, and Implementing Effective Risk Management*, Kogan Page Publishers, 2012.
3. E. Verzuh, *Fast Forward MBA in Project Management: The Comprehensive, Easy to Read Handbook for Beginners and Pros*, Wiley, 2021.
4. T. Oppong, 20 January 2023. [Online]. Available: https://medium.com/mind-cafe/neil-degrasse-tyson-a-great-challenge-of-life-ba554fb34f61#:~:text=In%20a%20tweet%2C%20Tyson%20shared%20a%20powerful%20quote,of%20ignorance%20and%20what%20to%20do%20about%20it
5. C. Sagan, *The Demon-Haunted World: Science as a Candle in the Dark*, Ballantine Books, 1997.
6. D. R. Bothe, *Reducing Process Variation Using the DOT Star Problem Solving Strategy*, Landmark Pub, 2002.
7. P. Senge, *The Fifth Discipline: The Art and Practice of the Learning Organization*, Doubleday, 1990.
8. J. M. Quigley, S. P. Q. Quigley, *Continuous and Embedded Learning for Organizations*, Taylor and Francis, 2022.
9. A. Hamilton, J. Madison, J. Jay, J. N. Rakove, *The Federalist: The Essential Series*, 62, St Martins, 1788.
10. P. F. Druker, *The Practice of Management*, Routledge, 2017.

Chapter 2

Risk Identification

> Risk represents any situation where some events (or processes) are not known with certainty.
>
> *Jean-Paul Chavas [1]*

2.1 Thinking (Reasoning) Approaches

The beginning of risk management is the identification of those things that are not known or things that are believed to be accurate but may, in fact, not be. Risk identification begins with asking questions about the work and the end goal of the work. Risk identification requires exploring the scope, the effort needed, and many other early items in the project effort. The quality of the risk management will depend heavily on this effort. Insufficient exploration of what can happen and what is likely to happen will lead to inadequate analysis and preparation.

Approaching the work as if there is a high degree of certainty or belief that there is a perfect understanding of the variation of the variables is not the road to success. There are limits to optimism; in fact, an objective approach is well-founded.

There are several ways of thinking about the work pipeline, which will require more than one thinking approach to be effective. Although these approaches have advantages and disadvantages, an overreliance on a single method will only inform so much. Instead, they match the path to the circumstances and follow-on actions from our reasoning to determine if our thinking and beliefs are accurate.

DOI: 10.1201/9781003425465-2

2.2 Deduction

Deductive reasoning takes a general rule and extrapolates specific, always valid rule conclusions. Use inferential thinking to work through a chain of events starting from a public statement or condition and following that path exploring the possible logical outcome. The approach is fundamental to the scientific method of testing hypotheses and theories. Deductive inference begins with general principles or rules known or assumed to be true [2]. One incarnation of deductive reasoning is the syllogism; for example, birds lay eggs, a goose lays eggs, and a goose is a bird. Syllogisms are effective but sometimes lead to errant results; for instance, birds lay eggs, and platypus lays eggs, and therefore, the platypus is a bird (Figure 2.1).

There are other limits to this approach. It works well enough when things are linear and easily connected from item to event. However, the real world is more complex than that; systems are more complicated. Predicting odd or spurious (emergent) events is not always possible. Even with these limitations, deductive thinking is associated with certainty.

Using deductive reasoning, the company could identify potential risks such as the possibility of making the product with faulty materials, accidents during manufacturing or use, or the case of the product failing or malfunctioning. Then, based on these risks, the company can take appropriate steps to mitigate or eliminate them, such as conducting thorough testing and quality assurance checks, implementing safety protocols during manufacturing, or including warranties or guarantees with the product.

Deductive reasoning is an essential tool for identifying and managing risks, as it allows companies and individuals to identify potential hazards and take proactive steps to mitigate or eliminate them.

2.3 Inductive

Inductive reasoning takes what is known and projects it into areas that are either poorly understood or unknown [1]. Inductive reasoning is the opposite of deductive

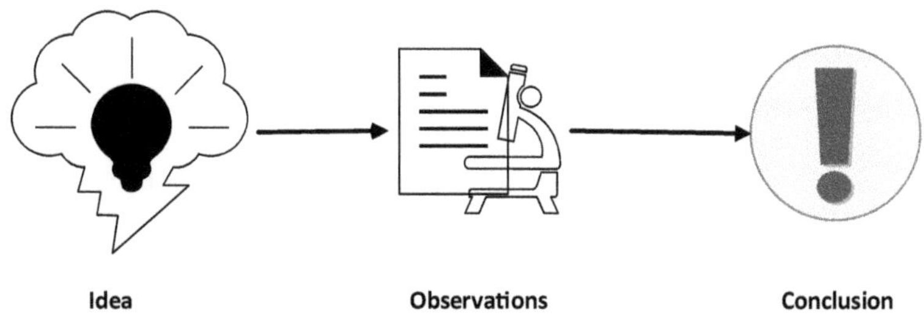

Figure 2.1 The flow of deductive reasoning.

Figure 2.2 An example of inductive reasoning flow.

reasoning in that broad statements is made based on specific observations or data. Inductive thinking relies on pattern recognition and applying that pattern recognition in another context. Inductive reasoning is associated with probability based on observations or historical records (Figure 2.2).

For example, suppose we observe that a company's sales have consistently decreased over the past year. In that case, we may conclude that there is a risk of financial instability, the conclusion based upon specific observations of declining sales, and we can use this information to identify potential risks and take proactive measures to mitigate them.

Similarly, if we observe that a company's production processes are prone to errors or defects, we may conclude there is a risk of quality issues and customer dissatisfaction. Again, by examining specific observations and examples, we can identify potential risks and take steps to prevent or mitigate them.

Overall, inductive reasoning can be a valuable tool for risk identification because it allows us to draw general conclusions based on specific observations, helping us to identify and address potential risks before they become significant problems.

2.4 Abductive

Abductive reasoning is a type of logical reasoning that involves using available information and evidence to draw a reasonable conclusion or hypothesis. For example, in the context of risk identification, it can identify potential risks by considering all the available evidence and making an educated guess as to what could go wrong.

For example, suppose a company is planning to launch a new product. In that case, they may use abductive reasoning to identify potential risks by considering the product's intended use, the materials used, and any potential hazards associated with those materials. They may also consider the risks associated with manufacturing, distribution, and product use.

Using abductive reasoning for risk identification allows companies to proactively address potential risks and take preventive measures to mitigate them before they occur. It can also help organizations to be more proactive in identifying and addressing emerging threats, as it allows them to consider all the available information and draw logical conclusions based on that data.

2.5 Analogical

Analogical reasoning uses similarities between two or more things, perhaps things that appear to have nothing to do with each other on the surface. Analogical reasoning is another pattern recognition approach. We spot a pattern in one place and can see how that pattern might apply in another context. Or, we use the analogy to consider our topic from a different perspective. A supermarket has served as an analogical source for many businesses. When planning a new business, evaluating how to serve customers better, or planning a new line, many business strategists reach for a supermarket analogy to ask if they can provide everything a customer may need when shopping for items in their category [3].

Analogical reasoning for risk identification involves comparing a current situation or problem to a similar situation or difficulty encountered in the past. This process involves identifying similarities and differences between the two conditions and using that information to anticipate potential risks or hazards that may arise.

Analogical reasoning is a valuable tool for risk identification because it allows companies to draw upon past experiences and knowledge to anticipate and mitigate potential risks. By comparing their current situation to similar situations in the past, they can identify patterns and trends that can help them identify potential risks and take steps to mitigate them. This juxtaposition of experiences to current situations can help to prevent costly mistakes and improve the chances of success for their products or projects.

2.6 Cause and Effect

The human mind finds patterns. This pattern recognition saved us from predators. The problem is that our brains see patterns even where there may be no pattern. Discerning an actual pattern (if there is one) in the data or understanding the cause-and-effect limits is not trivial. For example, past experiences influence daily decisions and actions; some perceived patterns may not be patterns.

Cause and effect reasoning is a common approach used in risk identification as it helps identify the root cause of potential risk and its consequences. For example, if a company is considering implementing a new technology, it may use cause-and-effect reasoning to identify the potential risks.

The first step in using cause-and-effect reasoning for risk identification is to identify the potential cause of the risk. These possible causes could be a change in company policy, a new technology, or the business environment. Upon identification of reasons, the next step is to consider the potential effects of this cause. These effects could include financial losses, operational disruptions, or reputational damage.

Upon connecting the cause and effect of a potential risk, the project can then take steps to mitigate or eliminate the threat. The actions could involve implementing new controls or procedures or conducting additional analysis or testing to understand better the potential risks and how to manage them.

Cause and effect reasoning is a valuable tool for risk identification. It helps identify the root cause of potential risk and its consequences, allowing companies to take proactive steps to mitigate or eliminate these risks.

> We should be careful to get out of an experience only the wisdom that is in it and stop there lest we be like the cat that sits down on a hot stove lid. She will never sit down on a hot stove lid again and that is well but also she will never sit down on a cold one anymore.
>
> *Mark Twain [4]*

2.7 Critical Thinking

Critical thinking comes with technical fields, or at least it should, such as the variety of engineering domains (for example, software, electrical, and electronics). Modern systems can be complex, consisting of constituent components, and these interactions require understanding, especially when things are not going as desired.

Critical reasoning is a valuable tool in the process of identifying risks. It involves analyzing and evaluating information and arguments logically and objectively.

To use critical reasoning for risk identification, one must first gather all relevant information about the situation or project. The preparation may include data on past performance, industry trends, and external factors impacting the project.

The gathered information is critically evaluated by asking questions about the validity and reliability of the data, examining the assumptions and biases that may influence it, and weighing the evidence for and against different hypotheses.

The final step is to use this critical evaluation to identify potential risks. This evaluation may involve identifying areas of uncertainty, possible threats or vulnerabilities, and domains where the project may be at risk of failure.

By using critical reasoning to identify risks, individuals and organizations can take proactive steps to mitigate potential threats and increase the chances of success for their projects.

> When you know thing, to hold that you know it; and when you do not know a thing, to allow that you do not know it – that is knowledge.
>
> *Confucius [5]*

2.8 Knowledge

Knowledge is domain specific. The manner we acquire that ability varies greatly. At any point in our careers, what we know about particular domains changes (breadth of knowledge). In the medieval days, this gradation of knowledge was in the form of Apprentice, Journeyman, and Master (depth of knowledge). Perhaps this gradation is outdated, but the fact remains that knowledge is depth and domain-dependent. Demonstrated strength in one area does not mean strength in all areas.

2.9 Explicit

Explicit knowledge comes from formalized efforts, for example, education and formal training. Explicit knowledge is easily transferable and consistent. Direct knowledge can be isolated from actual application.

• Standards and documentation	• Books
• Formal training	• Videos
• Manuals	• Measurements and Data

2.10 Team

To adequately explore risk, there must be a team environment wherein it is safe to do so. An environment where team members cannot or will not present their perspectives is not helpful when exploring risks. In fact, from experience, a company that focuses on a positive mental attitude as a euphemism for accepting the strategy or tactics will likely find serious failures.

A team with a diversity of perspectives can ensure a comprehensive view of the area under scrutiny,

> Perhaps you have heard the parable of the blind men and the elephant. The story starts with blind people that have never seen or touched an elephant. They travel to touch an elephant, but everyone can only feel one part of the animal. After each touch on the animal, they take what they have learned and describe the great beast. For example, the person touching the trunk says the animal is like a great snake. Everybody has

> a perspective of what the animal is, though their limited experience results in no agreed or cohesive description, and instead, the discussion descends into chaos. Nevertheless, sharing experiences reveals the true nature of the animal [11].

2.11 Organizational Culture

It does not matter the team constituency if the organization's culture is not compelling for team development. To demonstrate one of the cultural maladies, we relate a story to present about mitigated speech [5].

> A lower-tier supplier pressures the manager of a test department to shortcut product testing. The lower tier supplier must acquire miles on the systems at their beta customers. There is pressure to verify the vehicle systems in 2 days. There are 2 vehicle platforms, not identical, and the base platform requires an estimated 3000 test cases. The second platform will require an additional 1500 test cases. The test manager informs that the tier 1 – supplier will require 4 weeks to conduct the most critical test cases and 6 weeks to complete the 4500 test cases. Essential cases of testing would be those features that can either cause danger to the customer or other vehicles and drivers or could potentially leave the vehicle driver stranded. During the meeting to determine the best approach to meet the tier one supplier's demands, the Chief Project Manager for the project tells the supplier, "We will do the best we can to meet their need for the vehicle going to Beta testing customers." **No chance of concluding testing in 2 days**, but the Chief Project Manager gave the supplier the illusion that perhaps 2 days was possible.

This book is not about organizational culture, but to deny that this has no impact on the organization's ability to address risk adequately is grossly negligent. It is also true that there is no single approach to organizational culture, as in, do this, and success is guaranteed. There are many dimensions to the stew that we refer to as corporate culture. One model of the dimensions of organizational culture is that of Gert Hofstede [6]:

1. Power distance – the degree to which people accept the unequal distribution of power in the organization
   a. relatively equal – low power distance
   b. extremely unequal – high power distance

2. Individualism versus collectivism is the degree to which people in an organization prefer to act as individuals or group members
3. Quantity versus quality
4. Uncertainty avoidance
5. Long-term versus short-term

2.12 Historical Record

Operating from processes and recording the results over time can provide a historical record from which a measure of understanding the possibilities, specifically the performance of the process. However, experience suggests a significant source of project failures associated with errant schedule development. Specifically, the schedule has no tangible connection to process data and variation; the plan is overly optimistic and driven by external events without understanding what is possible.

> Progress far from consisting in change, depends upon retentiveness. When change is absolute there remains no being to improve and no direction is set for possible improvement: and when experience is not retained, as among savages, infancy is perpetual. Those who cannot remember the past are condemned to repeat it. In the first stage of life the mind is frivolous and easily distracted; it misses progress by failing in consecutiveness and persistence. This is the condition of children and barbarians, in which instinct has learned nothing from experience.
>
> *George Santayana, The Life of Reason, Volume 1, 1905 [7]*

Understanding the history of our work can be done with some essential tools. A short list is provided below:

1. Control charts
2. Histograms
3. Checklists
4. Brainstorming
5. Thought experiments and pre-mortems
6. Expert
7. Delphi technique
8. Ishikawa

2.12.1 Control Charts

Control charts are closely associated with manufacturing processes. Control charts are a statistical tool used to monitor a process over time and identify any deviations or changes. These deviations may indicate the presence of risks or problems in the process.

Control charts are used to identify and track trends or patterns in a process, specifically changes in the mean or variability of the process. If the data points on the control chart fall outside the control limits, it may indicate a risk or problem.

Control charts can identify risks in various processes, including manufacturing, healthcare, and financial management. For example, our team can use control charts to monitor the accuracy of project financial reports or the rate of defects in a manufacturing process.

By identifying and tracking potential risks through control charts, organizations can take proactive measures to address and mitigate those risks, ensuring the overall quality and effectiveness of the process.

2.12.2 Histograms

Dispersed data represent variables [8]. Not understanding dispersion, specifically the dispersion of critical attributes related to the project, product, or processes, is a significant source of risk. The histogram allows us to visualize the data distribution, which at least makes better decisions possible. The visualization is via count data (for example, event occurrence); thus, this cannot be easily obtained last minute, but will require the organization to think forward about the key metrics and manner of collecting those key parameters count data:

1. Gather data
2. Calculate
3. Range
    a. Range of thickness (product)
    b. Range of durations (process and project)
4. Calculate class width
    a. Range/# classes
    b. Example product 100 mm/30 samples = 3.3 mm
    c. Example project
5. Set up class boundaries
6. Create the graph

A story often explains and demonstrates the principles in an easily assimilated way. For example, a project manager approaches the testing manager about setting up the testing of the systems on the vehicle. The project manager indicates the vehicle will arrive at the testing facility at the end of a specific week and that the testing will start at the beginning of the following week. The project manager does not know that prototype vehicles from this location require rework to make the vehicle adequate for systems-level testing. Test preparation will need time to explore the car and determine the gap between the design intent and the actual state. Test preparation ensures

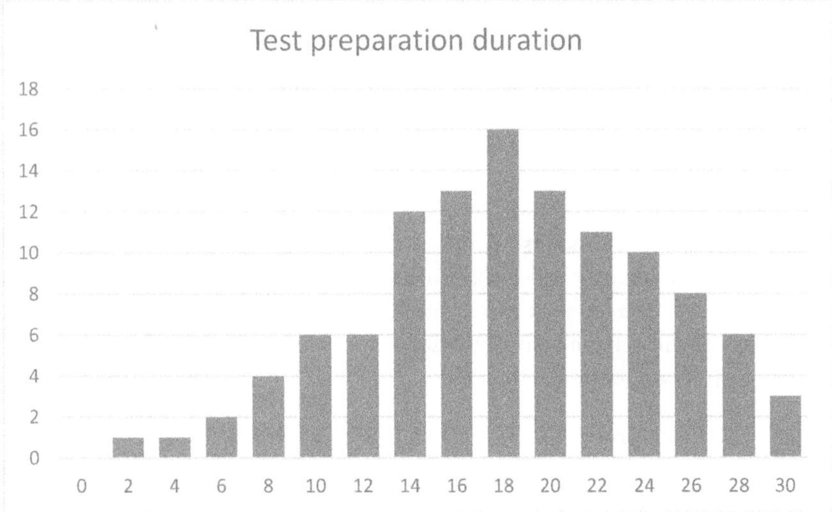

Figure 2.3 Histogram demonstrating the range of durations for test preparation.

that all of the electronic control units (ECUs), wire harnesses, and other components represent a configuration in hardware and software of the design iteration of the system. Otherwise, testing the vehicle system will amount to testing disparate system components of various iterations and configurations that have nothing to do with the production or iteration intent. The manager had been recording the time it takes to identify and rework these vehicles to the point where the vehicle is fit for testing. The resulting histogram allowed the testing manager to articulate the historical performance record and allow for a measure of prediction based on probability and past experiences. Based on the data, this estimate made it possible to alter the plan to adapt to this past performance or find another way to do the work (an experiment) to improve the probability of success (Figure 2.3).

2.12.3 Checklists

Checklists are double-edged swords. On the one hand, checklists can help us not forget or exclude steps in the effort. On the other hand, checklists can lead our team only to consider the checklist as just a sheet of paper and box-checking. The result can be a lack of critical thinking on the work context or approach.

Checklists can be a valuable tool for identifying risks in a given situation. Some risk identification uses of checklists are:

1. **Pre-event checklist**: At the start of a significant event or project, use a list to identify potential risks and assess their likelihood and impact. This exploration includes weather conditions, equipment failure, and unexpected delays.

2. **Process checklist**: When conducting a new process or activity, use lists to identify potential risks. For example, a manufacturing process may have specific hazards that must be identified and managed.
3. **Safety checklist**: Safety checklists are commonly used in many industries to identify potential risks and hazards. These checklists may include adequately using protective equipment, emergency procedures, and handling hazardous materials.
4. **Risk assessment checklist**: A risk assessment checklist is a more detailed tool that helps to identify and evaluate risks in a specific situation. This assessment may include factors such as the likelihood of a risk occurring, the potential impact of the risk, and the potential controls or mitigation measures that can be put in place to reduce the risk.

A specific checklist approach to risk management is the risk assessment form. Risk assessment forms are documents to identify and assess potential risks associated with a particular activity, project, or process. The forms can vary depending on the specific needs of the organization, but they typically include the following elements:

1. **Description of the activity or project**: This section should briefly overview the assessed activity or tasks.
2. **Identification of hazards**: This section should identify any potential hazards or sources of risk associated with the activity or project. This identification could include physical threats, such as machinery or equipment, or environmental hazards, such as weather or location.
3. **Assessment of risk**: This section should assess the likelihood and severity of each identified hazard and assign a risk rating based on the level of risk. Using a numeric or color-coded scale can act as a risk rating.
4. **Control measures**: This section should identify counteractions to mitigate or eliminate the identified hazards. These counteractions could include administrative controls, such as training or supervision, or engineering controls, such as protective equipment or barriers.
5. **Responsibility and action plan**: This section should identify who is responsible for implementing the control measures and outline a method for monitoring and reviewing the effectiveness of the efforts.

2.13 Experience

Everybody has experiences, and some people may have similar experiences with different perspectives or prioritize learning from that experience. Diversity of thought and perspectives is the true benefit of diversity in a team setting, setting up the symbolic blind spot, which represents risk. Drawing from team experience and going outside the team are ways to learn.

Several techniques of varying degrees of formalism help evoke these perspectives. These explorations need to happen at the beginning and ongoing to some extent in projects.

2.13.1 Brainstorming

Using brainstorming is a technique to identify potential risks in a project. It is a group problem-solving method that involves generating many ideas and solutions in a short period. Conduct brainstorming sessions with project team members, stakeholders, or experts.

In risk management, use brainstorming to identify potential risks that may impact the project objectives. The team can brainstorm on different aspects of the project, such as schedule, budget, scope, quality, and resources. The group can also brainstorm the potential causes and effects of the identified risks and possible mitigation strategies.

One way to conduct a brainstorming session for risk identification is to overview the project goals, objectives, and constraints briefly. Then, the facilitator can ask open-ended questions that prompt the group to think about potential risks and hazards. The facilitator can also ask the team to brainstorm on possible causes and effects of the identified risks and potential mitigation strategies.

Brainstorming is a valuable technique for risk identification as it allows for generating many ideas quickly. It also encourages participation from all team members and can lead to identifying previously overlooked risks by individuals working alone. Additionally, brainstorming allows us to find multiple solutions and alternatives for the identified risks, which can be helpful in risk management and decision-making:

1. Defer judgment – no critique of the ideas presented during the event
2. Encourage ideas
3. Intermingle ideas
4. Maintain focus on the topic
5. Not a free-for-all
6. Quantity of ideas

2.13.2 Mind Mapping

Mind mapping is a technique to identify and organize risks in a project. It involves creating a visual diagram representing the relationships between ideas or concepts related to the project. Mind maps do not require particular expertise and tools. Paper and pen or on a whiteboard will suffice.

Mind mapping identifies potential risks and their relationships to other project elements in risk management. For example, mind mapping illustrates the project's different components and identifies potential risks associated with each one. As a result, mind mapping can lead to the discovery of probable cause-and-effect relationships and the development of mitigation strategies.

One way to use mind mapping for risk identification is to start with the project goal or objective in the center of the map and then branch out to different areas of the project, such as the schedule, budget, or scope. You can then identify potential risks associated with each site and connect them to the relevant components on the map.

Mind mapping can be a valuable tool for identifying and organizing risks in a project, as it allows for a visual representation of the relationships between different risks and project elements. It can also help uncover hidden dangers and enable the team to identify and prioritize the most critical threats quickly.

2.13.3 Ishikawa Diagram

One of my favorite total quality management tools is the Ishikawa fishbone diagram. Ishikawa is typically used to explore failures and generate ideas of things that either make the loss happen or may be contributing factors. The Ishikawa diagram is often used in manufacturing and includes measurements, materials, people, environment, processes, and machines. The ultimate structure is hierarchical, with minor bones describing specific causes of the visible failure effect at the head of the fish. Underneath these particular causes are bones that explain the reason for the cause and subsequent failure (Figure 2.4).

Typically, for quality, the diagram would use an actual failure or defect. However, waiting for a failure to use the tool is not a proactive approach but reactive to the observed anomaly. Therefore, applying the Ishikawa diagram in this way is not good

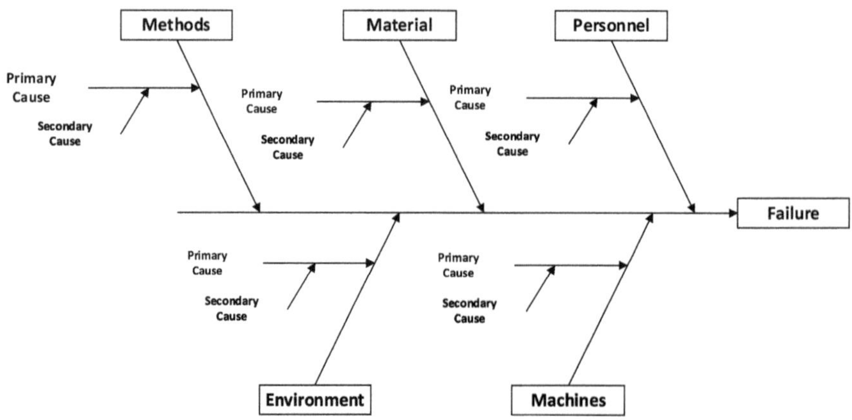

Figure 2.4 An example of an Ishikawa diagram for manufacturing.

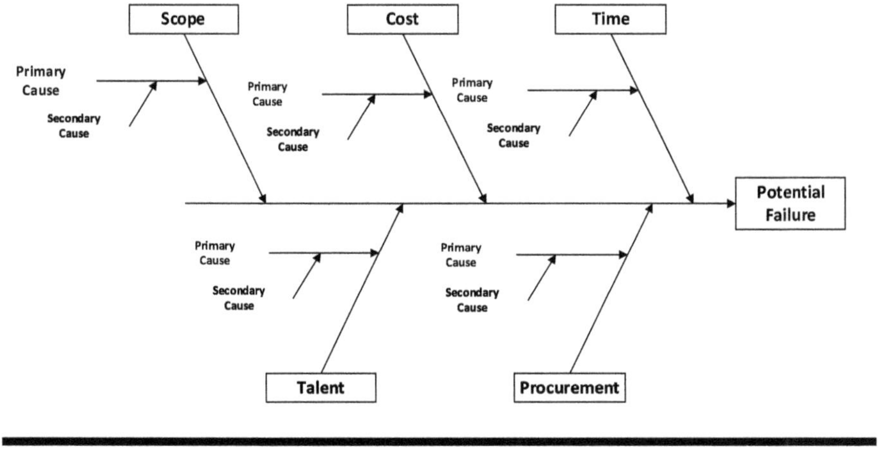

Figure 2.5 Ishikawa diagram applied to project management.

for risk management. However, a minor modification can provide this forward-looking approach, that is, put the typical or imagined failure mode at the head of the fishbone. Think of what can go wrong in the project; in this way, this approach becomes akin to a structured brainstorming or pre-mortem approach to the project potentialities.

As an exercise in project management classes, I use the Ishikawa diagram with a specific failure at the head, for example, budget overrun. Then, make the large bones of typical project management failure areas, such as scope, budget, talent, and procurement. Then, work through the knowledge management areas to ascertain causes that may allow failure mode to occur (Figure 2.5).

Performing this exercise provides a good illustration of the dynamics of the project and subsystems. In truth, while the knowledge areas are separate, these are subsystems that interact. For example, it is possible to have a scheduling failure, but the root of that failure may have no basis in the schedule management but available talent.

Then, the team will prioritize the likely failures and derive experiments and other ways to explore the possibilities.

2.13.4 Thought Experiments and Pre-mortems

To borrow from Albert Einstein and his thought experiments, we explore risk and the potential consequences of our actions by asking questions and thinking things through [9]. Thought experiments investigate the probable or possible results of actions we consider taking. Thought experiments allow for a measure of exploration without taking action. However, it should take a critical review to be of any value. For example, rather than physics, we should perform our thought experiments on the range of possibilities in the project. Then, it is possible to evaluate the implications of that decision on the desired objective of the project. Does this help? Could this work? It is appropriate to meditate on unintended consequences; perhaps a short critique of strategy, tactics, or technical solution results in an undesired outcome because of a lack of systematic analysis.

Pre-mortems are like thought experiments but are typically associated with projects and project management to uncover failure modes to which a project may succumb. The objective is to discover potential project missteps in planning to allow the team to consider different steps or paths. Thus, the strategies and tactics are fodder for critique and adaptation.

2.13.5 Interviews and Expert

Expert opinion is a method of risk identification that involves seeking the input of individuals with specialized knowledge or experience in a particular area. It can effectively identify potential risks in a project, but there are also some potential drawbacks.

Pros:

- Expert opinion can provide valuable insights and perspectives on potential risks that may not be immediately obvious to others.
- Experts can identify risks specific to a particular industry or domain, which may not be apparent to those without that specialized knowledge.
- Experts can guide the likelihood and potential impact of identified risks, which can help prioritize and manage them.

Cons:

- Expert opinion can be costly and time-consuming to gather, especially if experts are not readily available within the organization.
- Experts may have biases or limited perspectives that can affect their assessment of risks.
- Experts may not always be aware of the latest research or developments in their field, which can affect the accuracy of their risk assessments.

To improve the knowledge of the range of topics, disciplines, and domains that may require exploration outside of the present experiences of the team members. Diverse backgrounds lead to diverse perspectives. Team members can be on the same project, experience the same failure, and come away with different views on the reasons for the losses.

This experience may be inside the organization and outside; for example, the organization may have internal communities of practice (CoP), or external organizations, such as SAE International or the Automotive Industry Action Group for vehicle development and automotive product manufacturing.

Expert opinion can be a valuable resource for risk identification, providing valuable insights and perspectives on potential risks. However, it can also be costly and time-consuming, and experts may have biases or limited perspectives that can affect their assessment of risks. Therefore, it is essential to consider these pros and cons when deciding whether or not to use expert opinion as a method of risk identification.

2.13.6 Expert Judgment – Unstructured

Unstructured expert opinion is a risk identification method that involves seeking the input of individuals with specialized knowledge or experience in a particular area without a pre-determined set of questions or criteria. This approach allows experts to provide their insights and perspectives on potential risks without being constrained by a specific list of hazards or a structured process.

Unstructured expert opinion can help identify risks that may not be immediately obvious or previously considered. It can also provide valuable insights and perspectives on the likelihood and potential impact of identified risks. However, there are also some potential drawbacks to consider when using unstructured expert opinion for risk identification.

One drawback is that unstructured expert opinion can be difficult to quantify and compare. Without a structured process, it can be challenging to determine the reliability and validity of the expert's opinion. Additionally, experts may have biases or limited perspectives that can affect their assessment of risks.

Another drawback is that unstructured expert opinion can be time-consuming and costly, especially if experts are not readily available within the organization. Moreover, experts may not always be aware of the latest research or developments in their field, which can affect the accuracy of their risk assessments.

2.13.7 Delphi Technique and Planning Poker

This technique has roots in the RAND Corporation for technological forecasting; the Delphi Technique is a group decision process about the likelihood that certain events will occur [10]:

1. Identify facilitator.
2. Identify experts to send the queries.
3. Send a questionnaire or item under consideration to the experts.
4. Experts answer the questionnaire with their unique perspectives.
5. The facilitator gathers these answers and compiles so the result is anonymous.
6. The facilitator sends this updated compilation to the experts again.
7. Repeat until convergence of questionnaire responses.

Wide-Band Delphi (WBD) is a structured expert opinion method for risk identification. It is a consensus-based approach involving multiple rounds of anonymous questionnaires, feedback, and expert discussions, to reach a consensus on the likelihood and potential impact of identified risks.

The WBD method is a systematic and iterative process that can help to overcome some of the limitations of unstructured expert opinion. It allows for the quantification and comparison of expert opinions and encourages the experts to revise their views in light of feedback from other experts. This exploration can help reduce biases and ensure the final results are more accurate and reliable.

The WBD method can help identify risks that may not be immediately obvious or previously considered. It can also provide valuable insights and perspectives on the likelihood and potential impact of identified risks. However, there are also some potential drawbacks to consider when using the WBD method for risk identification.

One drawback is that the WBD method can be time-consuming and costly, especially if experts are not readily available within the organization. Additionally, the WBD method may not be suitable for identifying risks that require a rapid response, as the process may take several rounds to reach a consensus.

A modern version of this in the agile environment is known as planning poker. Planning poker works similarly, but rather a distributed team, the assessment happens in an open environment mitigating undue influence through the process. This team interactive discussion right there and then makes this a quicker method than the Delphi Technique and encourages team discussions:

1. A facilitator distributes a series of cards to each team member.
2. The facilitator then describes the topic or area of review; the team will estimate the time, degree of difficulty, and size of the work in the agile results.
3. The team will place down a card with the value that the team member believes represents the degree of difficulty or the size (depending upon what is being presented by the facilitator).
4. When all team members have selected the card, they believe represents their perspective, the cards are all flipped, revealing the team members' answers.
5. Then, a discussion of the range of answers and why people selected what was selected.
6. Keep doing this until the answer converges – discussing the results after each event (Figure 2.6).

2.13.8 Nominal Group Technique

The Nominal Group Technique (NGT) is a structured method for group problem-solving and decision-making for risk identification. It is a process that involves a series of steps, such as generating ideas, discussing and clarifying them, and then prioritizing them.

Figure 2.6 Planning poker cards for estimating.

To use NGT for risk identification, one can follow these steps:

1. **Define the problem or potential risk:** Clearly define the problem or potential threat to address.
2. **Generate ideas**: Individually, participants generate a list of potential risks, causes, and effects.
3. **Discussion and clarification**: Participants share and discuss their ideas to reach a common understanding of the potential risks and causes.
4. **Prioritization**: The group prioritizes the risks based on their likelihood and potential impact on the project objectives.

NGT can be an effective method for risk identification as it allows for generating many ideas quickly. It also encourages participation from all team members and can lead to the identification of overlooked risks. Additionally, NGT allows for finding multiple solutions and alternatives for the identified risks, which can be helpful for risk management and decision-making.

However, one of the potential drawbacks of using NGT is that it may be time-consuming and require a high level of participation and commitment from all team members. Additionally, reaching a consensus on the priority of risks among the group may be challenging.

Exploration of strategies, tactics, and especially uncovering risks in work is fodder for NGT. This technique applies some level of formalism without undue burden by moderating those strong verbal and assertive personalities allowing space for those less vocal on the team.

Present the problem, and then take the following steps [6]:

1. Members meet as a group after each member independently writes down their ideas on the problem.
2. After this silent period, each member presents one idea to the group. Then, each member takes their turn, giving a single thought until all concepts have been introduced and recorded. No discussion takes place until recording all statements.
3. The group now discusses the ideas for clarity and evaluates them.
4. Each group member silently and independently rank-orders the ideas. The idea with the highest aggregate ranking determines the final decisions.

2.14 Root Cause Analysis

RCA can be an effective method for risk identification as it allows for a comprehensive understanding of the problem or potential risk and its underlying causes. It can also help to identify potential risks that may have been overlooked by focusing on the symptoms rather than the underlying causes. Additionally, use RCA to determine the causes of a problem, which can help prevent it from happening again.

2.15 Bow-Tie Analysis

Bow-tie analysis is a risk management technique to identify and visualize potential hazards and their associated consequences in a process or system. It involves creating a diagram with two parallel lines (the "bow tie") representing the hazard and consequence and connecting the two lines with control measures or barriers in the middle. This analysis identifies the steps taken to prevent or mitigate the effects of the hazard. Bow-tie analysis identifies and assesses risks leading to effective risk management strategies.

2.15.1 The Steps Involved In Bow-Tie Analysis

1. **Identify the hazard**: The first step is to identify the hazard that needs to be analyzed. This identification could be a physical hazard, an operational hazard, or any other type of risk.
2. **Determine the consequence**: Next, determine the consequence or impact of the hazard if it were to occur.
3. **Identify the control measures**: Identify the control measures that are in place or that can be put in place to prevent the hazard from occurring or to mitigate its consequences.

4. **Create the bow-tie diagram**: Draw the diagram by connecting the hazard and consequence with the control measures in the middle.
5. **Evaluate risk**: Evaluate the risk by considering the likelihood of the hazard occurring and the potential consequences.
6. **Implement risk management strategies**: Based on the risk evaluation, implement the appropriate risk management strategies, such as implementing additional control measures, modifying existing criteria, or reducing the likelihood of the hazard occurring.
7. **Review and update**: Regularly review and update the bow-tie analysis to ensure it remains relevant and effective in managing risks.

2.15.2 Pros of Bow-Tie Analysis

1. **Visualization**: Bow-tie analysis represents hazards and their associated risks, making it easier to understand and communicate.
2. **Risk identification**: It helps to identify potential hazards and the consequences of those hazards, which is a critical step in risk management.
3. **Prioritization**: By evaluating the likelihood and consequences of hazards, bow-tie analysis helps to prioritize risk management strategies.
4. **Comprehensive**: The bow-tie analysis considers all hazard aspects, including the causes, control measures, and consequences, providing a thorough risk assessment.

2.15.3 Cons of Bow-Tie Analysis

1. **Complexity**: Creating a bow-tie diagram can be complex and time-consuming, especially for complex systems or processes.
2. **Limited flexibility**: The bow-tie diagram is a static representation and does not allow for dynamic risk assessment or changes in risk over time.
3. **Limitations in data availability**: The bow-tie analysis's accuracy depends on the data's availability. In some cases, obtaining the data required for an accurate analysis may be challenging.
4. **Limited to certain hazards**: Bow-tie analysis is best suited for real and well-defined hazards and may not be appropriate for more complex or intangible risks.

2.16 Project Management Tools

2.16.1 Risk Register

A risk register is a document or database used to track and manage potential risks in an organization. The risk register follows the steps in the risk management process in the ideal layout. It typically includes a list of identified threats, their likelihood, potential impact, and the risk management strategies to address them. The purpose of a risk register is to provide a centralized location for tracking and managing risks and ensure that identified risks are addressed systematically and consistently. A risk register typically includes the following information for each risk:

1. **Risk identification**: A clear and concise description of the risk, including its cause and potential consequences.
2. **Risk assessment**: An evaluation of the likelihood and potential impact of the risk.
3. **Risk management strategies**: A description of the measures in place or planned to address the risk, including risk mitigation, transfer, and acceptance.
4. **Owner**: The person or group responsible for managing the risk.
5. **Status**: The current status of the risk and any updates or changes.
6. **Monitoring and review**: A plan for regularly monitoring and reviewing the risk and updating the risk register as needed.

A risk register is a valuable tool for risk management because it provides a comprehensive view of all the risks facing an organization, enables the prioritization of risk management efforts, and facilitates effective communication about risks and risk management strategies.

Pros of a Risk Register:

1. **Centralized risk management**: A risk register provides a central location for tracking and managing all risks, making identifying and prioritizing risk management efforts easier.
2. **Improved risk assessment**: By documenting risks, their likelihood and impact, and risk management strategies, a risk register can help organizations to assess and manage risk more accurately.
3. **Improved communication**: A risk register provides a clear and concise summary of risks and risk management strategies, making it easier to communicate this information to stakeholders.
4. **Improved decision-making**: A risk register helps prioritize risk management efforts by highlighting the most significant risks and the strategies to address them.

Cons of a Risk Register:

1. **Time-consuming**: Creating and maintaining a risk register can be time-consuming, especially for organizations with many or complex risks.
2. **Limited flexibility**: A risk register can become outdated quickly, and it may be difficult to update it in real time as risks change.

3. **Dependence on data quality**: The accuracy and usefulness of a risk register depend on the quality of the data used to populate it. Inaccurate or incomplete data can lead to incorrect risk assessments and ineffective risk management strategies.
4. **Limited ability to assess dynamic risks**: A risk register is a static document and may not be able to keep up with rapidly changing or evolving risks.
5. **Potential for complacency**: If a risk register is not regularly reviewed and updated, organizations may become complacent about risks and fail to address emerging risks promptly.

2.16.2 Tracking Gantt Chart

Risk identification through tracking a Gantt chart involves monitoring project tasks, progress, and deadlines in the chart and identifying potential risks or issues that may impact the project schedule or completion. This risk identification comes through regularly reviewing the Gantt chart, comparing actual progress to the planned progress, and identifying any delays or deviations from the plan. The identified risks are then evaluated and managed proactively to minimize their impact on the project.

2.16.3 Simulation

Simulation can be a valuable tool in project management. It involves creating a model or virtual environment replicating real-world conditions and allowing users to test and evaluate different scenarios before implementing them. As a result, simulation can help project managers identify potential problems, explore solutions, and make informed decisions.

Various stages of the project can be simulated, for example, planning, design, and implementation. For instance, in the planning phase, simulation can help project managers evaluate the feasibility, estimate costs, and identify potential risks. In the design phase, simulation can help project managers optimize the project's design and identify improvement areas. Finally, in the implementation phase, simulation can help project managers to test different scenarios and identify the most efficient and effective way to implement the project.

Simulations can train project team members and stakeholders by providing them with a virtual environment where they can practice different scenarios and test their skills; simulation can help to improve the team's performance and reduce the likelihood of errors.

Several project management simulation tools can help managers model and analyze different scenarios. Here are some popular project management simulation tools:

1. **Simul8**: This simulation software allows project managers to model and analyze complex processes and systems, including healthcare, logistics, and manufacturing.

2. **AnyLogic**: This is a simulation software that allows project managers to model and analyze different types of systems, including supply chains, transportation systems, and manufacturing processes.
3. **Promodel**: This is a simulation software that allows project managers to model and analyze different processes and systems, including production lines, call centers, and supply chains.
4. **Arena**: This is a simulation software that allows project managers to model and analyze different types of systems, including manufacturing processes, supply chains, and service systems.
5. **iGrafx**: This is a simulation software that allows project managers to model and analyze different processes and systems, including business processes, supply chains, and quality management systems.
6. **FlexSim**: This is a simulation software that allows project managers to model and analyze different processes and systems, including manufacturing processes, supply chains, and service systems.

A specific example of simulation tools would be Monte Carlo. Monte Carlo simulation is a technique used in project management to model the uncertainty and risks associated with a project. The method involves running multiple simulations using random variables to estimate the probability of different outcomes.

In the Monte Carlo simulation, the disaggregated project is divided into smaller tasks or activities, each with dependencies as applicable. For each activity, define the range of possible outcomes based on the input variables and a probability distribution for each input variable. The simulation then randomly selects values for each input variable based on its given probability distribution and calculates the resulting outcome for the activity.

The Monte Carlo simulation technique can help project managers to:

1. **Identify potential risks**: By running multiple simulations, project managers can identify the most likely risks and uncertainties associated with the project.
2. **Estimate project costs and schedule**: Monte Carlo simulation estimates the project's expected duration and budget, considering the various risks and uncertainties.
3. **Evaluate different scenarios**: Project managers can use Monte Carlo simulation to evaluate other methods and determine the best action.
4. **Develop contingency plans**: Monte Carlo simulation can help project managers to develop contingency plans for dealing with potential risks and uncertainties.

2.17 SWOT Analysis

SWOT analysis and risk identification are two related concepts in business and management. SWOT analysis is a strategic planning tool to identify an organization's strengths, weaknesses, opportunities, and threats. Risk identification is the first step in the risk management process, where potential risks to an organization's capital and earnings are identified and documented.

The SWOT analysis can support risk identification by helping organizations identify potential risks arising from their internal and external environment. For example, recognizing the organization's weakness is identifying the threats or potential risks that may impact its operations. On the other hand, opportunities identify potentially unrecognized growth possibilities.

In conclusion, the SWOT analysis can be a valuable tool in the risk identification process. By using the SWOT analysis to identify potential risks, organizations can improve the efficiency and effectiveness of their risk management processes. Additionally, by integrating the SWOT analysis and risk identification, organizations can ensure the alignment of risk management efforts with their overall strategic goals and objectives.

References

1. J. P. Chavas, *Risk Analysis in Theory and Practice*, Elsevier Butterworth-Heinemann, 2009.
2. M. A. Anleitner, *The Power of Deduction*, Amsterdam University Press, 2010.
3. I. E. Team, "Indeed," 13 December 2022. [Online]. Available: www.indeed.com/career-advice/career-development/types-of-reasoning
4. M. T. (L. Clemens), Following the Equator, Vol. 1 (Vol. 5 of The Writings of Mark Twain), Chapter 11, epigraph, 1897, reprinted 1968.
5. "Quotes," 05 March 2020. [Online]. Available: www.goodreads.com/quotes/296096-when-you-know-a-thing-to-hold-that-you-know
6. M. Gladwell, *Outliers: The Story of Success*, Little, Brown and Company, 2019.
7. S. P. Robbins, *Organizational Behavior: Concepts, Controversies, Application* (8th ed.), Prentice-Hall, 1998.
8. G. Santayana, *The Life of REason: Or, the Phases of Human Progress*, Pantianos Classics, 2018.
9. K. Ishikawa, *Introduction to Quality Control*, London: Chapman and Hall, 1993.
10. W. Isaacson, *Einstein: His Life and Universe*, Simon & Schuster, 2017.
11. T. Wax, "The Gospel Coalition Org," 2016 August 2016. [Online]. Available: www.thegospelcoalition.org/blogs/trevin-wax/3-ways-the-blind-men-and-the-elephant-story-backfires/

Chapter 3

Risk Analysis

> The primary objective of Risk Analysis is the assessment of the uncertainties to produce risk-informed decision-making needed to increase the probability of project success [1,4].
>
> Risk analysis is the process of systematically evaluating each identified, approved risk to estimate the probability of occurrence (likelihood) and consequence of occurrence (impact) and then converting the results to a corresponding risk level or rating [64,66].

Traditional Risk Analysis starts with identifying, evaluating, and prioritizing risk, assessing the probability of risk occurrence for epistemic uncertainties creating reducible risk and the stochastic behaviors of the aleatory uncertainties and the impact of the risk on project success, then placing this information in a Risk Register, so decisions can be made about the response to risk should it become an issue [7,67].

This approach starts with qualitative analysis that fails to recognize there are phenomena not addressed by classical project risk management methodologies, including loops, reaction chains, and non-linear couplings of interrelationships between risks creating other risks, propagation of risks between interrelationships creating further risk, analysis of alternatives and their risk assessment, the premortem analysis needed to remove the uncertainties, and the dynamic evolving connections between risk to cost, schedule, and technical performance [15,24,35].

Quantitative Risk Analysis is then needed to determine the root cause(s) of the uncertainties (reducible and irreducible) that create risk. *Risk Handling* strategies are then developed to correct or prevent the occurrence of the root causes of the

DOI: 10.1201/9781003425465-3

risk created by the uncertainties, which can then increase the Probability of Project Success (PoPS).[1]

With these principles in place, Risk Analysis addresses the gaps in traditional Risk Analysis by:

- Starting with the root cause analysis of the characteristics of uncertainties that create risk.
- Identifying possible consequences of risk to the Measures of Effectiveness (MOE) and Measures of Performance (MOP) of delivered project capabilities.
- Determining the qualitative and quantitative risk level needed to develop effective risk handling strategies in Chapter 4.
- Identifying corrective and preventive actions needed to *handle* the causes creating the risks created by uncertainties.

The approach in this chapter to Risk Analysis moves beyond analyzing the contents of the Risk Register and applies a Systems Engineering approach to Risk Management [64,70,71].

This approach to Risk Analysis develops an understanding of [3]:

- Information on the risks in the risk register – source, type of uncertainty, the root cause.
- Effectiveness and reliability of the controls used to *manage* the uncertainties creating risk.
- Probabilistic and statistical data needed to analyze the risk.
- Critical knowledge of the impact of risk on the probability of project success.

Risk analysis quantitatively and qualitatively assesses each risk created by uncertainties, the reason for its occurrence and consequences, the likelihood of that occurrence, derives the level of risk from determining the risk handling strategy, and the effectiveness and performance of that handling strategy in reducing risk and increasing the probability of project success.

With this foundation, Risk Analysis enables the Risk Management actions to reduce the impact of risk to an acceptable level throughout the project lifecycle with continuous, forward-looking actions applied to risks and their interrelationships – treated as an integrated system of systems, for cost, schedule, and technical performance elements of the project.

Epistemic and Aleatory uncertainties create risks that propagate through the project producing dependencies and interdependencies between these risks on complex projects, which can be modeled as a network structure [49,50].

With this approach, the risk is defined as …

> … the likelihood (qualitative or quantitative) that an undesirable event, created by Aleatory (irreducible) or Epistemic (reducible) uncertainty, from the identified Root Causes, creates an undesired Effect that lowers the probability of project success [62].

Using this definition, Risk Analysis is the process of examining each uncertainty creating the identified risk item or process, refining the description of the risk, isolating the root cause(s) creating the risk, to determine the effects of the risk should it occur and become an issue [31] by:

- Rating risk and prioritizing risk events defined in terms of their probabilistic and statistical (stochastic) processes, the severity of consequence or impact, and relationship to other risk items or processes.[2]
- Considering the root causes of the risk's reducible and irreducible uncertainties.
- Identifying the possible effects on the project's cost, schedule, and technical performance.
- Determining the risk level with qualitative and quantitative measures.
- Documenting the consequences in preparation for risk-handling processes to correct or prevent the root causes of the uncertainties that create reducible and irreducible risks described in Chapter 4.

We'll discuss *reducible* and *irreducible* uncertainties and the risks they create later in this chapter. For now, it's important to separate these during analysis and have handling strategies for any risk management process to be successful, as well as recognizing *all risk comes from uncertainty* – epistemic and aleatory.

3.1 The Story of Risk Analysis Can Be Told Using the SOARA Framework[3]

> A core principle of risk management is the recognition that all risk comes from uncertainty.[4]

These uncertainties come in two forms: (1) uncertainties that can be reduced, (2) uncertainties that cannot be reduced. ISO 31000 (with a slight modification) tells us Risk Analysis is based on determining the impact of these two types of uncertainty on the probability of project success (Table 3.1).

Table 3.1 The SOARA Paradigm Tells the Story of Risk Analysis

S	ituation	With the contents of the Risk Register developed in Chapter 2, in the presence of uncertainties – reducible and irreducible, we need an assessment of the impact of the risks created by uncertainty on technical performance, cost, and schedule of the project to make risk-informed decisions about the effectiveness of risk handling plans needed to increase the probability of project success.
O	bjective	Develop an analysis of risks, their classification, assessment of the efficacy of the handling strategies needed to increase the probability of project success.
A	ctionable Outcome	For each identified risk or collection of risks, develop a risk handling plan and assess the plans effectiveness on increasing the probability of project success.
R	esults	For each risk or collection of risks, with the risk handling plan, and an assessment of the increased probability of project success is available to the decision-makers.
A	ftermath	Risk-informed decisions of effective handling strategies, risk control mechanisms, and reduced risk results of those strategies are available to the decision-makers.

> Risk is the effect of uncertainty on project objectives.
>
> Uncertainty is a state or condition that involves a deficiency of information (probabilistic or statistical) and leads to inadequate or incomplete knowledge of understanding.
>
> In the context of risk management, uncertainty exists whenever the knowledge or understanding of an event, consequence, or likelihood is inadequate or incomplete, or a naturally occurring random process – a stochastic process, impacts cost, schedule, or technical performance of the project.
>
> *ISO 31000:2009, ISO 17666:2016, and ISO 11231:2101*

Risk analysis starts with examining project outcomes and objectives impacted by the uncertainties creating risk. Once risks are identified and categorized as reducible or irreducible, they are analyzed to identify qualitative and quantitative impacts of risk on project success. With this information, appropriate steps can be taken to *Handle* the impact of risk(s) [10].

Risk Handling describes the process of identifying, evaluating, selecting, and implementing corrective or preventive actions to remove or reduce the uncertainties creating risk to assure acceptable levels of risk, given constraints and objectives of the project.[5]

With the specific corrective or preventive actions, Risk Handling defines when these actions should be performed, who is accountable for performing the actions, and associated cost and schedule for the handling actions. With this information, the appropriate handling strategy can be selected from the handling options [1,10].

This risk management approach differs from the Project Management Institute's. The approach in this book is based on *Risk-Informed Decision Making* in high-risk/high-reward organizations and domains [24]. Risk-Informed Decision-Making addresses:

- Uncertain future risk impacts are created from reducible and irreducible uncertainties and the impacts of these risks on the PoPS.
- The likelihood those events from epistemic uncertainties will come for and the corrective or preventive actions needed to reduce the impact of this epistemic uncertainty.
- The characteristics of risk created by *natural randomness* (Stochastic) produce aleatory uncertainties and the *margin* needed to protect the project's deliverables' cost, schedule, and technical performance from these stochastic processes.
- The application of corrective and preventive actions needed to increase the probability of on-time, within-budget, on-specification delivery of capabilities required for mission success or business strategy fulfillment.

> Poor risk management … is one of the significant causes of project collapse … [8].

The first step to increase the PoPS is to make risk-informed decisions based on identified sources of uncertainty, creating the risk, and taking corrective and preventive actions to reduce or remove these uncertainties and handle risks in Table 3.2.

With these example sources, Risk Analysis determines the probabilistic properties for reducible risks and stochastic properties for irreducible risks and the impact of these risks on achieving project objectives. Risk analysis addresses the uncertainties and their resulting consequences by:

- Considering the probability distribution function of the Epistemic uncertainty, the event-based uncertainty, creating a reducible risk and the Aleatory, the natural stochastic variability of the uncertainties creating an irreducible risk.
- Identifying reducible and irreducible impacts on technical performance, schedule, and cost.

Table 3.2 Sources of Risk to Be Addressed with Corrective or Preventive Actions Needed to Increase Probability of Project Success

• Schedule risk without sufficient schedule margin or risk buy-down activities.	• Organization or Mission risk without alternatives for delivering needed Capabilities.	• Contractual risk with no Plan B for planned cost, schedule, and technical performance.
• Cost risk without sufficient Management Reserve, Cost Contingency, or Schedule Margin.	• Technical feasibility risk, with no Analysis of Alternatives for Plan B.	• Project performance risk (i.e. planned Return on Investment if a system doesn't materialize).
• Lack of hazard analysis and removal creates health and safety risk to users of service or product.	• Technical mismatch of obsolescence of equipment of processes creating risk with no upgrade or replacement plan.	• Reputational risk without handling plans to address stakeholder impacts.
• Unrecognized dependencies of risks internal or external to project.	• Unrecognized business or market behaviors for products or services of the project.	• Unrecognized risk propagation within or external to project without a model of impacts or handling plans.

- Identifying dependencies between risks and the propagation of risks through their dependencies across the project.
- Considering the likelihood of each risk's impact on the project success.
- Identifying possible consequences of this occurrence on the technical performance, schedule, and cost of the project.
- Identifying the risk level, each risk handling strategy, and how these strategies will be assessed for their effectiveness in reducing of the risk's impact.

3.1.1 What Is Risk Analysis?

Risk analysis evaluates the properties of the uncertainties creating risk and assesses the range of possible project outcomes [28]. Risk Analysis identifies which risk probabilistic events or naturally varying processes warrant handling strategies. It is important to understand the stakeholders' risk tolerance to analyze risk. This involves ascertaining the scope, schedule, budget, and quality tradeoffs. In addition, stakeholder risk tolerance may change as the project progresses. The six steps for making risk-informed decisions to increase the PoPS are [24]:

1. Understanding of stakeholder expectations regarding risk and deriving risk-adjusted project performance measures.
2. Developing feasible alternatives of project deliverables in the presence of uncertainties that create risk.
3. Defining frameworks for managing in the presence of uncertainty and choosing the analysis methods.
4. Conducting the Risk Analysis and documenting the results.
5. Developing risk-informed project performance commitments.
6. Selecting alternatives and document decision rationale.

With these six steps, the Risk Analysis process produces the [1]:

- Estimates of the probability of occurrence for Epistemic uncertainty and the stochastic distribution functions for Aleatory uncertainty create risk.
- Estimates of cost, performance, and schedule consequence created by risk.
- Determination of the risk level of the project.
- Estimates of the frequency of occurrence, timeframe, and inter-relationship of other risks.
- Determination of risk prioritization given a risk level and other considerations.

Risk Analysis identifies the assessment parameters for each risk. When completed, it provides the necessary information for further handling of risk, accomplished by evaluating both the probability of occurrence and impact of risk against established criteria. Risk determination is performed using quantitative and qualitative techniques, dependent upon complexity and preference. In either case, a risk factor is calculated to determine the level of risk.

Information relative to risk factors and risk levels is contained in each project's specific management plan developed in Chapter 4. With detailed analyses contained in the lifecycle documentation – the *Project Management Plan*.

The tools and techniques of Risk Analysis include [11]:

- Expert opinions from qualified individuals or groups.
- Analysis of relevant historical data and comparison to similar projects or systems [13].
- Uncertainty, sensitivity, and scenario analysis of cost, schedule, and technical performance.
- Probabilistic Risk Assessment (PRA), Fault Tree Analysis (FTA), Failure Modes Effects Analysis (FMEA), and similar techniques used in conjunction with performance risk analysis, safety analysis, etc.
- Decision analysis with decision tree and Expected Monetary Value (EMV).

- Decision-making under uncertainty and risk, using payoff matrices [12].
  - Real Options with risk-adjusted variables for cost and value decision-making [14].
  - Design Structure Matrix and Risk Structure Matrix [15].

3.1.2 How Does Risk Analysis Provide Information to the Decision-Makers?

For project success, management must make risk-informed *decisions* using:

- Information supporting decisions regarding project direction and setting schedule and cost targets and contingencies.
- Identified corrective or preventive actions that can be taken to improve technical, schedule, and cost performance.
- Known and knowable causes of poor project performance.
- Monitored the status of the project as it proceeds.
- Demonstrated compliance with procedural requirements for project risk management.

The results from Risk Analysis include:

- Quantitative and qualitative results, including uncertainty, for tasks, and the total project.
- Identification of essential contributors to uncertainty by task and total project.
- Identification of potential risk reduction actions.
- Identification of key boundary conditions.
- Fulfillment of project risk management requirements.

3.1.3 Information Provided to Decision-Makers Needed to Increase the Probability of Project Success

> Risk Analysis determines which risks warrant a response by determining the level of the risk, the information needed to analyze the risk – both qualitative and quantitively – to produce a priority ranked list of risks, their handling strategies, and expected outcomes required to reduce the uncertainties creating risk needed to increase the probability of project success.
>
> Risk Analysis results in data to make Risk-Informed Decisions.

Risk Analysis assesses the underlying uncertainties creating risks identified in the Risk Register developed in Chapter 2 and assesses the impact of those risks on the probability of the project success. Risk analysis starts with determining the *source* of risk – the risk's *Root Cause* – at the project's planning stage, continuing through the project's life into production or use of the produced capabilities.

The principal outcome of Risk Analysis is the Technical Basis for Deliberation (TBfD), a document that catalogs the set of candidate alternatives, summarizes the analysis methods used to quantify the performance measures, and presents the results.[6] The TBfD is the input that risks informs the deliberations that support decision-making. This information does not necessarily mean that a decision is risk-informed; instead, without this information, a decision cannot be risk-informed [25,27].

All projects operate in the presence of uncertainty that creates risk. In the presence of these uncertainties, three core questions need to be answered by the Risk Analysis process through the assessment of the impacts of risk on the probability of project success.

These questions are what the probability is:

1. Of completing the project *on or before* the needed date?
2. Of completing the project *at or below* the planned cost?
3. That the delivered technology satisfies the required capabilities needed for project success.

Analyzing risk and creating handling plans provides information to answer the questions in Table 3.3. The answer to each of these is contained in the handling plan developed in Chapter 4. Each plan element is then traceable to the root causes of the uncertainty – the conditions and actions that create the cause of the risk.

The Technical Basis of Deliberation contains the following section:

- **Technical Summary**: The problem to be solved by this effort and each of the general contexts of each of the alternatives.
- **Top Level Requirements and Expectations**: Top-level requirements for cost, schedule, and technical performance parameters subject to risk.
- **Derivation of Performance Measures**: MoE, MoP, Key Performance Parameters (KPP), Technical Performance Measures (TPM), and Critical Success Factors (CSF).
- **Decision Alternatives**: Trade studies, analysis of alternatives, imposed constraints on performance measures, mapping to top-level requirements
- **Risk Analysis Framework and Methods**: Each analyzed alternative shows how discipline-specific models are integrated into an analysis process that preserves correlations among performance parameters.
- Risk Analysis Results, including:
  - **Scenario Descriptions**: For each alternative, the main scenarios are identified by the Risk Analysis.

- **Performance Measure Probability Distribution (PDF)**: For each alternative, the marginal performance measure PDFs, along with a discussion of any significant correlation between PDFs.
- **Imposed Constraint Risk**: For each alternative, the risk with respect to imposed constraints, along with a discussion of significant drivers contributing to that risk.
- **Supporting Analyses**: For each alternative, uncertainty analyses, and sensitivity studies are summarized.
- **Risk Analysis Credibility Assessment, in Table 3.3**: Questions asked and answered during the Risk Analysis process.

> Cost, Schedule, and Technical Performance quantification, when properly done, increases the probability of project success by reducing the probability of project failure [6].

Poor Risk Analysis is a major cause of cost overruns, late deliveries, and poor return on investment for the stakeholders.

Risk analysis in this chapter supports the Risk Management processes in this book by providing information to the decision-makers:

- **Empirically Valid:** Demonstrated to work to produce actionable outcomes.

Table 3.3 Questions Asked and Answered during the Risk Analysis Process

• What is the root cause (condition and action) or triggering event for uncertainties creating the risk?	• Does this risk impact business, or just the project or a portion of the project?
• How will we recognize when the risk has occurred? • What is the physical evidence of this occurrence?	• What will happen when the risk occurs and turns into an issue?
• How effectively are we currently handling risk? • What are the units of measure of this effectiveness?	• What steps can we take to better manage this risk? • How is effectiveness of these actions measured?
• What should we do if we fail to handle this risk effectively?	• How are risks analyzed for probabilistic events and statistical processes?
• How are the probabilistic and statistical properties elicited for the risk?	• How are analysis decisions made with this information?

- **Practical**: For all projects, no matter the domain, context, size, type, phase, or quality of the requirements or planning processes that operate in the presence of uncertainty.

3.2 The Risk Analysis Process

Analysis of risk focuses on informing the decision-making process in the presence of uncertainty at two levels [1]:

- At the macro-level, uncertainty impacts decisions about the produced capabilities, products, services, systems, processes, technical and financial performance, and business success.
- At the micro-level, uncertainty impacts decisions about cost, schedule, and technical performance, with micro-level decisions driving the macro-level decisions.

Risk analysis examines sources of uncertainty, root causes of the uncertainties, outcomes, and impacts of reducible (Epistemic) and irreducible (Aleatory) uncertainties creating risk to project success.

This analysis starts by identifying qualitative and quantitative risk attributes – at the project's micro- and macro-level – held in the Risk Register. During Risk Analysis, for probabilistic processes, these attributes the probability of occurrence for epistemic uncertainty and the probability of impact of that risk on project outcomes. For stochastic processes, the statistical properties of aleatory uncertainty are assessed for their impact on cost, schedule, and technical performance from irreducible uncertainty.

Risk analysis then develops a model for the occurrence and impact of the risk and an analysis of the effectiveness of the correction or prevention of the risk. The result is actionable information needed to develop risk-handling plans that can increase the probability of project success.

3.2.1 Uncertainty Is the Source of All Risks

With identified risks from the Risk Register, the next step identifies the root cause(s) of the uncertainties that create risk. Operationally, a risk driver can be a single performance parameter (Cost, Schedule, and Technical Performance), a single event (release date, upgrade, and contractual deliverable), or a set of performance parameters or events that, when varied over their range of uncertainty, cause the planned performance of that parameter to change from tolerable to intolerable (or marginal).

Identifying risk drivers focuses on conditions that create opportunities for risk reduction. Risk drivers may affect more than one risk, impact more than one project element, and cross multiple organizational units. Risk drivers are communicated at multiple levels of the risk model, with the lowest level a risk driver expressed as the possibility that an individual performance parameter will be (or are) outside the range of tolerable performance.

When a risk impacts a driving project performance parameter, the risk driver is expressed as the possibility that an undesirable outcome will occur. This effect can be from reducible or irreducible uncertainties. Both create risk that impacts the probability of project success.

Risk drivers identified during Risk Analysis are used during Risk Handling Planning (Chapter 4) to create effective increases in the probability of success.[7] Risk response options to be considered for a given risk driver depend upon the nature of the uncertainty that creates the risk.

> If it occurs, an uncertain event, process, or situation may have no beneficial or detrimental effect on a project's objectives [20].
>
> Managing in the presence of uncertainty is "the" Critical Success Factor for increasing the probability that the project achieves its objectives.

Risk analysis assesses the impact of identified risks created by uncertainty on the probability of project success. The type of Risk Analysis performed depends on the uncertainty that creates the risk.

This approach differs from other risk management processes, where the probability of occurrence and impact are the starting points. Here, we start with the *driver* of that probability, the *uncertainties* that are the basis of the probabilities – the *root cause of the uncertainty.*

Without finding the cause of the uncertainty, we will always be treating the *outcomes* of risk after it has occurred, rather than the *reason* for the risk, where prevention or corrective actions can be taken. In this book, we'll use definitions of uncertainty shown in Figure 3.1 [16].

Let's look in more detail about the uncertainties that create risk.

3.2.1.1 Epistemic Uncertainty Creates Reducible Risk

Epistemic Uncertainty – from the Greek επιστημη (episteme) – is the uncertainty created by the lack of knowledge of the quantities or processes of a system or an environment. Epistemic uncertainties are reducible with better knowledge, better models, experiments to test the behavior of a system. Epistemic uncertainty creates *reducible* risk, handled with *risk buy down* activities funded from the project baseline. Epistemic uncertainty is represented by ranges of values for project parameters (Cost, Schedule, and Technical Performance), a range of workable models, the level of model detail, multiple expert interpretations, and statistical confidence levels.

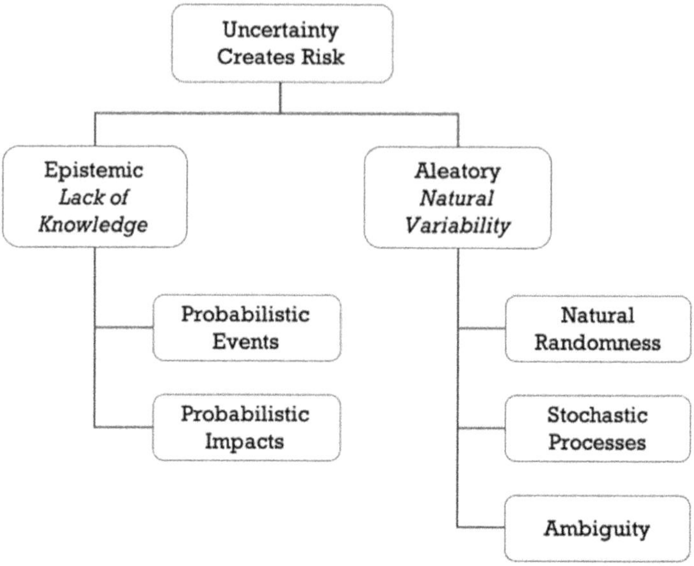

Figure 3.1 Two classes of uncertainty that create a risk to project success in this chapter. Epistemic uncertainty is reducible with information about the source of the uncertainty. Aleatory uncertainty is irreducible since it is due to probabilistic variability.

The accumulation of information and implementation of actions from this information reduces epistemic uncertainty needed to eliminate or reduce the likelihood and/or impact of risk. This uncertainty is modeled as an assessment of the probability of our knowledge and the probability of occurrence of an undesirable event.

Epistemic uncertainty creating risk can be used in a narrow or broad sense. Here it is used in its broad sense, to encompass any risk created by epistemic uncertainty created by lack of knowledge – *a mistaken belief.* [17]

3.2.1.2 Aleatory Uncertainty Creates Irreducible Risk

Aleatory Uncertainty – from the Latin *Alea* (a single die) – is uncertainty present in the natural variation of a system or the environment the system operates. Aleatory uncertainty comes from inherent randomness, natural stochasticity, environmental or structural variation across space and time in the properties or behavior of the system under observation – in this case a project.

Unlike Epistemic uncertainty, the accumulation of more data or additional information does not reduce Aleatory uncertainty. The result is an *irreducible* risk that can only be handled with cost, schedule, or technical performance parameter margin.

When a schedule margin is needed, it is released and assigned to protect a delivery date. When the cost margin is needed, it is used to cover the cost overage. When a Technical Performance margin is needed, the design of the product is improved to cover the risk of technical performance shortfalls.

The determination of how much margin is needed to protect the project, the reduction of risk by assigning the margin, the improvement in the probability of meeting the planned dates for the planned cost, with the planned technical performance is the foundation of Risk Analysis.

3.2.1.3 Distinguishing Between Epistemic and Aleatory Uncertainty

A primary failure of traditional risk management is not recognizing all risk comes from uncertainty and that uncertainty comes in two forms, each requiring distinctly different Risk Analysis processes:
Epistemic uncertainty:

- Is represented by a single value of the probability of occurrence of a risk.
- Is focused on the extent to which the event is or will be true or false, that is, the risk will occur or not occur with some probability.
- Is measured by the confidence in the knowledge or model of the causal system determining the outcome.
- Is attributed to missing or inaccessible information or expertise.
- Is due to information that in principle could be known, but in practice are not known because a measurement is not accurate, because the model neglects certain effects, or because data is hidden.

Aleatory uncertainty:

- Is represented as a class of possible outcomes created by an underlying stochastic process.
- Is focused on assessing an event's propensity to occur.
- Is measured as the naturally occurring by the relative frequency of occurrence.
- Is attributed to stochastic behavior of the underlying processes of the system.

Table 3.4 summarizes the key features between Epistemic and Aleatory uncertainties found on projects [50].

3.2.1.4 Handling Risks Created by Aleatory and Epistemic Uncertainty

When Aleatory uncertainty creates risk (originating from natural variability in the system and/or its environment), the handling strategy must reduce or eliminate the

Table 3.4 Distinguishing Epistemic Uncertainty from Aleatory Uncertainty, Both Create Risk that Reduces the Probability of Project Success

	The Model of the System or Project Elements	*Parameters of the System or Project*
Epistemic	Uncertainty about the model of the system or project elements appropriately represents the actual system behavior or project elements. This uncertainty allows for the possibility of alternate models or the weighted average of several models describing the project elements and their interaction in the presence of epistemic uncertainty.	Uncertainty about the shape and content of the probabilistic distribution functions (PDF) of possible project parameter values. Sources of this uncertainty include data quality and data completeness and is improved as more knowledge becomes available.
Aleatory	There is a misfit between the project model predictions and the actual observations from naturally occurring variability. This uncertainty can contain an epistemic component that considers missing variables or variables left out of the model.	The irreducible randomness of the possible outcomes, given an assumed distribution. It is understood variability and is propagated through the project when the uncertainties are connected in a physical or logical network.

variability and its source or provide sufficient *margin* to protect the project from the consequences of the risk.

When Epistemic uncertainty creates risk (originating from lack of knowledge), the handling strategy must determine the root causes of the uncertainty and applying a corrective or preventive action to remove the lack of understanding or increase the understanding to reduce the risk.

> In the presence of both classes of uncertainty, estimates are required to handle the resulting risk [22].

Information produced by this Risk Analysis is used to develop the Risk Handling Plans developed in Chapter 4. For both reducible and irreducible risk, Root Cause Analysis answers the question:

> Why is this uncertainty (either reducible and irreducible) present, where did it come from, what are the conditions and/or actions that created the

uncertainty, what are the corrective, preventive actions, or margins to remove or reduce the uncertainty, and what is the effectiveness of these actions on the probability of project success?

Three root causes of Aleatory and Epistemic uncertainty creating risk to project success are:

- **Physical**: Uncertainty in the tangible or material properties or behaviors.
- **Humans**: Behaving in an uncertain manner causing undesirable outcomes impacting the project or its deliverables or processes by lowering the probability of success.
- **Organizational**: Systems, processes, or policies use to make decisions operating in uncertain or inconsistent manner.

Applying Root Cause Analysis to Risk Management and the analysis of risk includes [32]:

- **Safety-Based**: Developed in the field of accident analysis and occupational safety and health.
- **Production-Based**: With origins in quality control and quality management.
- **Process-Based**: Follows production root cause analysis, but with expanded scope to include product processes and business processes.
- **Failure-Based**: Rooted in the practice of failure analysis employed in engineering and maintenance.
- **Systems-Based**: Emerged from the previous areas along with change management, risk management, systems management, and analysis.

For these project domains and any others, the risk handling activities (Epistemic buy down and Aleatory margin) are planned, scheduled, and funded by the project, measured, and assessed by their ability to *reduce* uncertainties that create the risk.

Analysis of the two risk types of uncertainty provides an understanding of the level of risk. It guides the Risk Managers to develop the corrective and preventive actions needed to handle the risk through a variety of means:

- Avoiding risk by eliminating the cause of uncertainty eliminates the risk.
- Mitigating risk with direct actions to correct or prevent the uncertainty from occurring or removing the naturally occurring variances in the underlying processes
- Transferring the risk to another party for handling. The issue here is that the other party may need to handle the risk properly, or the risk will return.
- Accepting the risk leaves the corrective or preventive action for the future to be handled by implementing contingency plans if and when the risk becomes an issue.

Identifying the consequences of risk to the performance, schedule, and cost is based on identified risk levels in a Risk Reporting Model, using data in a Risk Register (RR), and a model of the risk interactions and their propagation of the risk in a Risk Structure Matrix (RSM).

3.2.2 Why Is Risk Analysis Needed?

> Risk Analysis is shown to identify and assess factors that negatively affect the success of a business or project [34].

The topic of *Risk Analysis* is applicable to all stages of any project – from initial capabilities and requirements planning to project development, deployment, to use.

During Risk Analysis, a critical success factor is separating Qualitative and Quantitative Risk Analysis [18,19]:

Qualitative Risk Analysis prioritizes risks for further analysis or action by assessing their subjective probability of occurrence, impact, and other characteristics.
- The risk of an engine failure during takeoff of our Wright Flyer is larger than an engine failure during sustained flight. Let's focus on developing an engine that can sustain the rigors of high loads with lower cooling air flowing over the cylinder heads during takeoff.

Quantitative Risk Analysis provides an objective numerical rating of the risk [23].
- We have an 80% confidence that the total payload weight of the Wright Flyer will be under the target weight of 350 pounds on or before our first test flight at Kitty Hawk, the 1st week of August 1908.

Qualitative Risk Analysis prioritizes risks for analysis or action by *subjectively* determining the risk's likelihood or probability of occurring and *subjectively* rating its impact on the project.

Quantitative Risk Analysis prioritizes risk for analysis or action by *objectively* analyzing the effect of risks on the project, with a quantified risk exposure to determine the confidence interval of the project parameter of interest. Quantitative Risk Analysis is the preferred approach to all but the simplest projects and their risks.

Quantitative Risk analysis starts by identifying the sources of risk:

- What is the source of Aleatory uncertainties that create irreducible risk?
- What is the source of Epistemic uncertainties that create reducible risk?

Quantitative Risk analysis continues by separating reducible (Epistemic) risks from irreducible (Aleatory) risks and then separating Qualitative Risk Analysis from Quantitative Risk Analysis [40].

To receive benefits from Risk Analysis, we need to examine each identified risk to refine its description, isolate the cause, determine the effects, and set the risk handling priorities. Refining each risk starts with assessing its probabilistic likelihood or stochastic behavior, its consequence, and its relationship to other risk areas or processes. This is done through a detailed study of the risks that have been identified to gather enough information about future risks to judge the root causes, the likelihood, and the consequences if the risk occurs.

With this framework, the Risk Analysis sequence is straightforward:

- Develop a probability or statistical (Epistemic or Aleatory) and consequence model by allocating consequence thresholds against the Work Breakdown Structure (WBS) or product or process another breakdown structures and their criteria.
- Assign the probability of occurrence for each Epistemic uncertainty to each risk using the criteria in the Risk Reporting Matrix.
- Determine the statistical properties of the Aleatory uncertainty for each risk.
- Determine the consequences of the risk, where it becomes an issue, in terms of Performance, Schedule, and/or Cost impact using defined criteria.
- Document the results in the project Risk Register or Risk Structure Matrix.

3.2.3 Benefits of Risk Analysis with This Approach

> Risk Management is How Adults Manage Projects.
>
> *Tim Lister*[8]

Risk is any potential shortfall that may impact future outcomes needed for project success, with three general project elements impacted by risk §6.4 of [29]:

- **Cost**: Budget, funds, and expenditures of funds (actual cost).
- **Schedule**: Duration, resource consumption, milestones, and deliverables are all subject to risk.
- **Technical Performance**: Performance, effectiveness, all the … *ilities* of a project.[9]
- **Scenarios**: A sequence of credible events describing the evolution of cost, schedule, and technical performance from a given state to a future state.
- **Interactions and Interdependencies**: Modeled to reveal propagation of risks across projects.

The analysis of risk is characterized through a set of triplets:

- The *named scenarios* leading to degraded performance in one or more of these project elements.
- The *Likelihood*(s) of those scenarios.
- The *Consequence*(s), *Impact*, or *Severity* of the impact on project performance that results if the scenarios were to occur.

Each of these uncertainties is the basis of the analysis of risk using the likelihoods and consequences to inform the decision-makers on:

- **Cost Risk**: The risk associated with the ability of the project to achieve its lifecycle cost objectives using the appropriate funding.
- **Schedule Risk**: Associated with the adequacy of the estimated time allocated for the development, production, implementation, and operation of the project's deliverables.
- **Technical Risk**: Associated with the evolution of the design and the production of the project's deliverables affecting the level of performance needed to meet the stakeholder expectations and technical requirements.

With the risk impacts identified, the PoPS can be determined. When there is a cost impact the project's Management Reserve will be used to cover this cost overrun.[10] When there is a schedule impact, schedule margin will be used to absorb the schedule overrun or additional work performed, funded by the Management Reserve to correct or prevent the risk from impacting the project.

With these two assessments, handling methods for cost and schedule risks can be developed. The third impacted item is Technical Performance of the project's deliverable. These can be impacted by Epistemic or Aleatory uncertainties as well. The handling strategies for the Technical Performance impacts can range from changes in the technical design, redesign, to increasing design margins.

3.2.3.1 Cost Risk Analysis

By defining cost risks, their handling strategies, and assessing their impact on cost performance, a project cost life-cycle assessment can be produced. The Life-Cycle Cost (LCC) can then be integrated with schedule and technical assessment of the technical performance risk handling processes.

Cost Risk Analysis provides project management with early estimates of potential cost overruns and the cost elements with probability distributions that most greatly influence these outcomes.

With cost assessment, the funding supporting the technical development and acquisition approaches can be determined to assure the adequacy and phasing of funding to produce a project LCC cost analysis with known variances from near-term budget execution impacts and external budget changes and constraints, documenting the cost basis and risk impacts.

The Cost Risk analysis is performed with these 11 steps [26]:

1. Acquire the point estimate for the cost.
2. Develop statistical and probabilistic uncertainty distributions.
3. Identify the Risk Register uncertainties, reducible and irreducible, associated with the cost estimate.
4. Identify the framing assumption for each uncertainty.
5. Perform simulations of the uncertainty processes on the cost risk.
6. Apply correlation factors between the Cost Estimating Relationships (CER).
7. Apply any other influences on the cost Risk Analysis.
8. Interpret the results of the cost Risk Analysis against the planned budget for the project.
9. Consider possible cost risks outside the project.
10. Allocate and phase risk funding to match risk profile.
11. Report the results to the decision-makers for acceptance or correction.

Cost Risk Analysis is expressed by the sensitivity of how the estimated project cost might differ from the actual project cost. With this information, decision-makers can assess how much cost risk they are willing to assume, and how much cost margin and Management Reserve will be needed to protect the project from cost overruns [36].

Common cost-estimating techniques include:

- **Parametric**: Using regression or other statistical methods from Cost Estimating Relationships (CERs).[11]
- **Analogy**: Estimate cost based on historical data for an analogous system or subsystem.
- **Engineering Estimates**: The system is decomposed into lower–level components, each cost separately for direct labor, direct material, and other costs.
- **Actual Past Costs**: From experience or trends used to estimate future costs for the same system – Reference Class Forecasting

3.2.3.2 Schedule Risk Analysis

Schedule Risk Analysis (SRA) uses uncertainties in the task duration and project risks affecting schedule execution with a statistical simulation technique (most often the Monte Carlo method) to analyze the confidence level in meeting selected project deliverables dates.

Schedule delays come from [42]:

- **Internal factors**: Portfolio and project commercial contexts, project development, project delivery, interdependencies, risk propagation, and other systemic uncertainties.
- **External factors**: Causes related to regulatory, local, state, federal, and geopolitical challenges.

The first question for Schedule Risk Analysis is, *do these risk factors impact first-order performance?*

When schedule risk impacts the critical path – it is a first-order impact – and both schedule and cost will have negative outcomes. This risk should be carried as a schedule risk, and the schedule delay models the cost impacts.

The evaluation of schedule delay starts with the duration of the delay and network logic that is *pushed to the right* by the delay. The next step is to incorporate impacts on the technical development of deliverables from schedule uncertainties created from the delay. Finally comes the quantifying schedule excursions reflecting the effects of cost risks, including resource constraints.

3.2.3.3 Technical Performance Risk Analysis

To evaluate the Technical Performance of a deliverable, Technical Risk Indicators (TRI) are needed to provide the Effectiveness and Performance measures of the feasibility of a technology to provide the capabilities needed for Mission or Business success. This analysis considers the risk to the capabilities provided by the project [43].

While the TRI provides an early indication of areas of risk, the Technical Risk Assessment (TRA) of the TPM assesses the technical risks and issues associated with each option in the capability proposal. TPM involves predicting the value of a key technical performance parameter of the higher-level product under development based on current assessments of products lower in the system structure. The TPM assesses how well the system produced by the project is achieving its performance requirements.

The TRI is a quantitative metric, developed from the TRA, indicating how risky a project activity will impact technical performance will be in future. TRA informs stakeholders of risks and issues to the TPM's and develops effective risk handling and issue resolution strategies to assure the technical performance of the project's produced capabilities meet the planned performance goals.

When there is an impact on the technical performance of the project's deliverables, there is risk to the product's or service's efficacy and performance. These risks also have schedule and cost impacts since lowered performance needs to be corrected or prevented, requiring time and money.

This type of risk is carried as a technical performance risk for these project components and described in project documents, including:

- **Operational**: Initial Capabilities Document (ICD), Capability Development Document (CDD), Capability Production Document (CPD), threats, suitability, and effectiveness.
- **Technical**: Systems Engineering Plan (SEP), Technology Readiness Levels (TRL), specifications, TEMP, technical baselines, standards, materiel readiness.
- **Management**: Organization, staffing levels, personnel qualifications/experience, funding, management processes, planning, documentation, logistics.

Analysis of Technical Performance Risk is characterized by three components [22]:

- The scenarios leading to one or more degraded performance parameters
- The likelihood(s) – qualitative and quantitative – of these scenarios occurring
- The consequences – qualitative and quantitative severity – of resulting performance degradation resulting from the scenarios if they were to occur

3.3 Analyzing Probabilistic and Statistical Uncertainty That Create Risk

The Only Certainty is Uncertainty.

Pliny the Elder, Historia Naturalis, Bk ii [7]

There are simple and sometimes simple-minded ways of analyzing risk, starting by ignoring the root cause of risk. Identifying the root cause of the uncertainty is the starting point for successful risk management. *Why is this uncertainty present on our project?*

Actions taken to resolve a risk often only address the problem itself, not the underlying cause of the risk created by the uncertainty. Root cause analysis of the uncertainty-creating risk deals with identifying the conditions and actions that cause the uncertainty-creating risk. Root Cause Analysis identifies common sources of risk and leads to a wide range of risk responses. Attention must be paid to distinguishing between risks whose impact has an unspecified cause and those with a specific cause.

Each Risk created by a probabilistic event or an underlying stochastic process has three components:

1. The root cause for the probabilistic event or the underlying stochastic process. This root cause has a condition and an action to create the cause.
   - Each cause has a probability or stochastic process of occurrence represented by the root cause. This underlying process must be addressed with a corrective or preventive action in the handling plan for managing the risk.
   - The consequence if the root cause occurs is a process as well.

2. The uncertainty associated with the creation of the risk that comes in one of two forms:
   — Reducible Uncertainty – a probabilistic process – event based
   — Irreducible Uncertainty – a statistical process – stochastic
3. The impact on the project when that uncertainty turns into an *issue*
   — This impact itself has an uncertainty that must be determined. It could be event based, or it could be a change in a statistical process.

This approach starts with identifying sources of risk from:

- **Concept of Operations (ConOps)**: Describes the characteristics of a proposed system from the viewpoint of the system's users.
- **Systems Engineering Models**: A set of related system models that define, design, analyze, and document the system under development.
- **UML Models**: Modeling language for software engineering that provides a standard way to visualize the design of a system.
- **IDEFØ Models**: A functional modeling approach for systems and an engineering approach for needs analysis.

With these models, the sources of uncertainty can be revealed, and reducible and irreducible risks identified.

The strengths of starting with Root Cause Analysis, include [33]:

- Enabling identification of additional or subsidiary risks.
- Enabling identification of risks that may be linked because of their common cause.
- Establishing basis for the development of preventive and comprehensive responses.

3.3.1 Eliciting Probabilistic and Statistical Properties of Project Risks

With the Risk Register, developed in Chapter 2, we can analyze individual risks, interdependencies between risks, and propagation of these risk across the project that create other risks.

These uncertainties have a range of values derived from the probability of occurrence for Epistemic uncertainty and a statistical distribution of the aleatory uncertainties.

Eliciting this information means:

- Starting with each project deliverable, assessing the uncertainties impacting the success of the work.

- For each uncertainty – reducible and irreducible – developing the range of values of probability and statistical processes based on the most likely value and the upper and lower ranges, from Reference Classes, or models of a deliverable's behavior as the basis of estimate (BOE).[12]

With this information behavior and impact of the risk can be developed. The source of the risk starts with the WBS containing the products and the services produced by the project in accordance with some WBS standard:

- MIL-STD-881D applied in U.S. government.
- 33R-15 from AACEI for construction.
- Project Management Institute's WBS Practice Standard.
- ISO 21511 Work Breakdown Structures for project and program management.
- IEEE 1058-2001 WBS standard.

There are also sources of risk not in the WBS, to be identified in other documents:

- **Project Management Plan (PMP)**: That defines how a project is going to be carried out.
- **Statement of Work (SOW)**: Narrative description of a project's work requirement.
- **Statement of Objectives (SOO)**: Describing the broad, basic, top-level objectives of the project, acquisition, or procurement.
- **ConOps**: Describes the characteristics of a proposed system from the viewpoint of an individual who will use that system.
- **Integrated Master Plan (IMP) and Integrated Master Schedule (IMS)**: The IMS is an integrated and networked multilayered schedule of project tasks required to complete the work effort captured in a related IMP assessed with measures of increasing maturity of delivered Capabilities.

The results of these activities increase our understanding of the impact of risk on the PoPS represented in a model of the epistemic and aleatory uncertainties that create risk. With the models, questions can be asked about reducing the risk and the impact of that reduction on the probability of project success. Using the models of the individual risk, we can build a network model of the risk to assess the drivers of risk on other risk – using a Design Structure Matrix described in Chapter 8.

This leaves behind a measurable confidence level of the risk and its impact on the probability of success of the project.

- We have an 80% confidence of completing *on or before* the needed date.
- We have a 75% confidence of completing *at or below* the needed cost.
- We have a 95% confidence the delivered technical performance will complete the needed mission or fulfill the needed business case.

This quantifiable risk reference model is the basis of a quantitative risk management process. The reference model can be reused in the future, when similar conditions exist on other projects, creating a *reference class* database.[13]

3.4 Challenges for Risk Analysis

There are many challenges to the work needed for risk-informed decisions to be effective in reducing risk and increasing probability of project success. These challenges are not *standalone* but come in combinations, over different time frames, and may repeat once corrected or prevented.

Constant assessment of these and other challenges is needed with the corrective or preventive action shown in Table 3.5, applied to increase the probability of project success:

3.5 Eliciting Probabilistic and Statistical Uncertainties

PRA is a collection of techniques to provide a range of likelihood's for risks, hazards, and exposures to activities or outcomes that reduce the PoPS using quantitative methods [57].

Since all risk comes from uncertainty, event-based risks are modeled probability distributions of the Epistemic uncertainty to quantify the likelihood of occurrence of a risk event. For natural variability created by Aleatory uncertainty, statistical distributions represent the relative frequency of a given state of the system and the degree of belief or confidence that a given state of the system exists.

A narrow definition of PRA means a statistical or thought process used to analyze and evaluate the variability of availability of data or the uncertainty across data sets. In this chapter, PRA describes a process using probability to assess the variability in the behavior of systems, and the uncertainty of the information about these systems, and using this analysis to support Risk Informed Decision Making used to Increase the Probability of Project Success.

PRA is used here to include both quantitative and qualitative methods for dealing with scenarios, models, and uncertainties in the inputs to risk models. Probabilistic techniques are used with benefit–cost analysis, regulatory impact analysis, and engineering performance standards and, for a variety of applications in many disciplines.

We can start looking for these probabilistic and statistical uncertainties and their impacts on the Probability of Success in the Risk Register and other project documents, but first we must acknowledge …

> Risks Identified are rarely realized, risks realized were rarely identified.
> All unidentified risks are acceptable risks [48].

Table 3.5 Challenges to Effective Risk Analysis and their Corrective or Preventive Actions

<table>
<tr><th>Challenges to Effective Risk Analysis</th><th>Corrective or Preventive Actions to These Challenges</th></tr>
<tr><td>Not recognizing all Risk is the effect of uncertainty on the objectives of the project.</td><td>Analysis of risk in the Risk Register starts with classifying the risk into Aleatory or Epistemic uncertainties.</td></tr>
<tr><td>Incomplete evaluation of the sources of risk.</td><td>Determine the root cause of all risks. The condition and or action that creates the uncertainty that in turn creates the risk.</td></tr>
<tr><td>Missing knowledge of the overall impact on the project objectives, like scope, time, cost, and quality.</td><td>Develop a model of risk with causal dependencies and risk propagation.</td></tr>
<tr><td>Failure to identify secondary or new risks arising from the already identified risks.</td><td rowspan="3">Develop a risk propagation model to reveal impacts of each risk and propagation of these impacts across the project.</td></tr>
<tr><td>Lack of transparency of the sources of risk and their impacts on the project.</td></tr>
<tr><td>Failure to model the propagation of risk.</td></tr>
<tr><td>Biases in Risk Analysis processes.</td><td>Use analytical processes to assess risk properties.</td></tr>
<tr><td>Lack of risk decision-making structure and lack of accountability for risk decisions in an organization, once decisions have been made.</td><td>Build a risk management process model with risk, impacts, corrective and preventive actions, and accountabilities.</td></tr>
<tr><td>Lack of meaningful risk assessment process.</td><td rowspan="8">Develop and deploy an end-to-end risk management process to assure all steps are applied consistently across all phases of the project.</td></tr>
<tr><td>Lack of an open, risk-aware culture.</td></tr>
<tr><td>Risk assessment is viewed as barrier to day-to-day business activities.</td></tr>
<tr><td>Lack of a common definition of critical risk terms.</td></tr>
<tr><td>Lack of executive management support for risk management.</td></tr>
<tr><td>Failure to use appropriate risk metrics.</td></tr>
<tr><td>Mismeasurement of risks and its impact on probability of project success.</td></tr>
<tr><td>Hidden Cost, Schedule, and Technical Performance risks.</td></tr>
</table>

It is critical to separate Aleatory uncertainty from Epistemic uncertainty. In aleatory uncertainty, we model risk with statistical processes of the uncertainty. What is the range and frequency of possible values of a parameter that create the risk. In Epistemic uncertainty, we model risk with a probability of occurrence of an uncertainty value. What is the probability the risk will turn into an issue.

3.5.1 Eliciting Uncertainties to Inform Risk Decisions

For risk management to be successful, we must elicit the probability of occurrence of a risk from risk created by reducible uncertainties and assess the statistical properties of the underlying processes created by aleatory uncertainties.

To successfully elicit these uncertainties, we need to:

- Define a formal elicitation process based on uncertainty, not on the PMI or similar processes.
- Write a Risk Management Plan stating how the elicitation processes are to be performed.[14]
- Install tools and processes to use them to elicit the risk and hazards.

The result of this effort is a model of the epistemic and aleatory uncertainties and the risk they produce used to model the performance of the Integrated Master Schedule. This effort produces data used to develop the probabilistic Estimate to Complete (ETC) and Estimate at Completion (EAC) needed to make risk-informed management decisions.

3.5.2 Elicitation of Aleatory and Epistemic Uncertainty Needed to Model Risks

Risk Management is the basis of good project management. To assess the severity of a risk and its impact on the success of the project, we need to know the nature of the risk and its characteristics. A critical success factor in risk management is the distinction between epistemic (probabilistic) and aleatory (stochastic) uncertainties.

Model of risk are developed to provide guidance to the types of questions asked of experts in capturing aleatory and epistemic uncertainties [51,52]. The uncertainties underlying a quantity may be classified (aleatory or epistemic) according to the goals of the risk process. The nature of such classification affects the probability elicitation process and implementation of the resulting judgments on where Risk Analysis is made.

In distinguishing between aleatory variability and epistemic uncertainty, it is helpful to describe the parameter under consideration – the cost, task duration, or technical performance. If the parameter has one value and then has another value, then it is an aleatory uncertainty. The variability is random. If the parameter is either one value or another, but we are not sure which it is, then the parameter has epistemic uncertainty.

All risk comes from uncertainty, and these uncertainties impact all project management activities. We need to determine the needed margin to protect the project from Aleatory uncertainties and determine the *risk reduction* activities for Epistemic uncertainties:

- **Cost**: We need sufficient budgeting in the project baseline, Management Research, and budget margin to protect the impact of risk in the baseline budget.
- **Schedule**: We need sufficient schedule margin to protect the deliverables for the natural variances in the work and work duration extensions due to rework and resource-lowered performance.
- **Technical Performance**: We need technical margin to protect the product service performance measures or under specification of those measures to meet the Effectiveness and Performance requirements.

For all project risks, models of the uncertainties are built to connect these models with the development of risk.

Using models, we can identify the *value at risk* and the impact of uncertainty on this Value at Risk and determine the needed Management Reserve, Cost and Schedule Margin, risk buydown budget, and Management Reserve for emergent requirements and their associated risk.

The starting point for collecting the uncertainties is the Work Breakdown Structure and related project documents, where it is determined if the uncertainties are Aleatory and Epistemic for each risk.

With the Epistemic and Aleatory uncertainties identified and connected to named risks in the Risk Register analysis can start by identifying the sources of the uncertainty.

3.6 Analyzing Sources of Risk Created by Uncertainty

All risk comes from uncertainty and that uncertainty comes in two forms – reducible uncertainty and irreducible uncertainty.[15] With the risks identified, categorized into their sources – aleatory or epistemic uncertainty – prioritized with qualitative ranking, we need the source of the uncertainties creating the risk.

Only by knowing the risk source can corrective and preventive actions be taken to *handle* the risk before it turns into an issue. When analyzing the risk sources, we'll use one or more of these methods below summarized here and detailed in Chapter 9 – *Advanced Topics.*

- Root Cause Analysis [32,54,55].
- **Monte Carlo Simulation** – a computational algorithm, using repeated random sampling to obtain numerical results [75,76].
- **Bayesian Analysis** – is a statistical inference method to estimate parameters on an underlying distribution based on observed distributions [74].
- **Fault Tree Analysis** – is a graphical tool to model causes of system-level failures.
- **Reference Class Forecasting** – a method predicting the future by looking at similar past situations and their outcomes [77].
- **Design Structure Matrix and Risk Structure Matrix** – a method of focusing on the elements of a complex systems and how they related to each other [78].

In this chapter, we'll visit the concepts of Root Cause Analysis and Monte Carlo Simulation as two effective means of analyzing the impact of risk on the Probability of Project Success.

In Chapter 8, we'll revisit those in more depth, as well as the four methods of Risk Analysis.

3.6.1 Categories of Project Risk

Before applying any method to analyzing risks, we need to categorize the risks and the root causes of the uncertainties that create risk, to assure the right method is applied to the category. Many types of project risks lead to unfavorable cost, scheduling, or performance [56]:

- Cost risk, usually escalating project costs due to low accuracy costs estimation and scope increase.
- Project risk (calendar), is the risk that the activities will take longer than expected. The reductions of the project usually increase the costs and delay the receipt of the project's benefits, with a possible loss of the competitive advantage.
- Performance risk, is the risk that the project will not produce results in accordance with the project specifications.
- Governance risk refers to the performance of the administration regarding the company's ethics and reputation.
- Strategic risks result from errors in strategy, such as choosing a technology that cannot be operated.
- Operational risk includes risks due to poor implementation and process problems, such as procurement, production, and distribution.

- Market risks include competition, foreign exchange, commodity markets, and interest rate risk, as well as liquidity and credit risks.
- Legal risks arise from legal and regulatory obligations, including contractual risks and litigation against the organization.
- Risks associated with external hazards, including storms, floods, and earthquakes; vandalism, sabotage, and terrorism; labor strikes; and civil unrest.

3.6.2 Root Cause Analysis of Sources of Uncertainty That Create Risk

> Root cause analysis (RCA) is a systematic process for identifying "causes" of problems or events and the approach for responding to them.
>
> RCA is based on the basic idea that effective management requires more than merely "putting out fires" for problems that develop but finding ways to prevent them.[16]

Conventional risk management considers risks to have a probability of success and a probability of impact, when that risk become an issue. The basic approach to problem solving in the presence of risk, from Buddha[17] is *causal observation* [54]. This is the basis of Qualitative Risk Analysis.

> Go ask the Chief Engineer, she'll know what happened the last time the feedwater pump for the cooling tower failed and brought down the production of product.

This is the basis of *linear thinking* a simple, and simple-minded *cause and effect* process, again the basis of Qualitative Risk Analysis.

Buddhist writings tell us *as a net is made up of a series of knots, so everything in the world is connected by a series of knots*. This approach is based on Categorization of the risk and the creation of risk from these categorical actions. The *fish–bone* diagram or *Management Oversight and Risk Tree (MORT)* are examples of *Categorical Thinking.*

All uncertainty that creates risk has a cause for that uncertainty. This cause may be reducible – the probabilistic failure of a piece of equipment, or it may be irreducible – the weather or an earthquake.

Risk analysis starts determining the Root Cause of the uncertainties (reducible and irreducible) that creates the risk. With this understanding, handling strategies can be developed to address the Conditions and/or the Actions that create the root cause from the uncertainty [47,54,55].

Everything we do in risk management is fundamentally focused on finding the *cause* for the risk and discovering the *corrective* and *preventive* actions needed to *handle* the risks produced by the cause. The conditions can be the uncertainties (reducible and irreducible) and the actions can be activities that create the risk in the presence of these uncertainties.

There are four basic principles of root cause analysis when applied to assessing risk:

1. Cause and Effect are the same thing. Every cause creates an effect, which becomes the cause of the next effect.
2. Cause and effect are part of a continuum of cause and effect (there is NO risk-free project).
3. Every effect has at least two causes in the form of actions and conditions.
4. An effect exists only if its causes exists at the same point in time.

Risk management starts with searching for the Cause of the uncertainty. Once found – and there are likely many cause – correction or prevention of the condition and/or actions that creates risk is stated in the handling plan developed in Chapter 4.

For every risk in the Risk Register, we need to conduct RCA of the uncertainties that are the source of risk. By starting on RCA, the source of the uncertainties can be "handled" in a logical manner that can be modeled with RCA tools and described in more detail in Chapter 8.

3.6.3 Monte Carlo Analysis of Cost, Schedule, and Technical Risk

The Monte Carlo Simulation method is named after the city of Monte Carlo in the principality of Monaco. In the casinos of Monet Carlo, a roulette wheel is a simple random number generator. The wheel has numbers 1 through 36 and 0 and 00. Monte Carlo methods' name and systematic development date from about 1944 and the Manhattan Project.

Monte-Carlo simulation uses random simulation or random sampling technique whose principles are:

- To solve these problems of mathematics, physics, engineering technology, and production management, a probability model or random process should be established first, making its parameters equal to the solution of the problem.
- Then, based on this model or process, through sampling test is to calculate the statistical characteristic of the parameters.
- Finally, give out the approximation of the problem, and the solution accuracy can be expressed in the form of the standard error of the approximation or other statistical characteristics.

The MCS method inverts the approach by solving the deterministic problem by generating random numbers used to model project duration, cost, and other parameters. The Monte Carlo Simulation (MCS) method provides approximate solutions to various mathematical problems by performing statistical sampling experiments from a population of samples matching the range of samples of the possible values found on a project parameter. With a statistical distribution of the possible samples of a parameter – a cost or duration – the MCS draws samples from this distribution, places them in the schedule, cost, or technical performance model, and determines the resulting outcomes.

3.7 Analyzing Impact of the Risk on Project Success

The result of Risk Analysis is to inform decision-makers of the Probability of Project Success. Analysis of risk starts with the identified risks in the Risk Register. Risk impact assessment is the process of assessing the probabilities and consequences of risk events if they are realized [70].

3.7.1 Qualitative versus Quantitative Risk Analysis

> It is important to distinguish between qualitative Risk Analysis and quantitative Risk Analysis.

Qualitative Risk Analysis is *subjective*, with ordinal measures from *low* to *high*, focused on identifying risks with a relative measure both the likelihood of a specific risk event occurring during the project life cycle and the impact it will have on the cost, schedule, and technical performance.

Quantitative Risk Analysis is *objective*, using cost, schedule, and technical performance data from models to analyze the effects of risk on the cost, schedule, and technical performance.

The purpose of these two methods is the same, but with different effectiveness. The quantitative approach signs a numerical value to the risk, while the qualitative approach assigns a relative measure of risk defined on a scale from low to high. Using quantitative data, Risk A has a 23% chance of occurrence, with a 15% chance of causing a 4-week delay in the deliverable impacted by the risk, with a 75% confidence.

The results of the qualitative risk assessment are used to prioritize risks, on a defined scale, if they were to be realized. Ranking risks in terms of their criticality or importance provides insights to the project's management on where resources may be needed to manage or mitigate the realization of high probability / high consequence risk events for the Epistemic uncertainties creating risks.

Qualitative Risk Analysis can be performed are some common approaches for eliciting the relative ranking of the risks shown in Table 3.6:

Table 3.6 An Example of the Approaches at Our Disposal to Exploring Risks

• Interviewing	• Brainstorming
• Delphi Technique	• SWOT Analysis
• Root Cause Analysis	• Assumption Analysis
• Probability and Impact Matrix	• Expert Judgment
• Schedule Risk Modeling	• Cost Risk Modeling

Quantitative Risk Analysis is the process of analyzing risks numerically with the goal of identifying their effects on the project outcome using relevant and verifiable data to produce a numerical value to predict the probability of a risk event outcome.

For Quantitative Risk Analysis, modeling and simulation, Monte Carlo is one approach to use project's uncertainties to produce estimates of values of cost, schedule, and technical performance operating in the presence of those uncertainties [63]. Monte Carlo simulation provides estimates of the *true most likely value* of the output distribution of the modeled variable. Sensitivity analysis, from the Monte Carlo Simulation, of all project work described in a Design Structure Matrix showing connectivity between all the work elements and the propagation of risk through this network.

Monte Carlo Simulation, using risk uncertainties and their impact, produces estimates of values of cost, schedule, and technical performance operating in the presence of those uncertainties. Monte Carlo Simulation estimates the *Most Likely value* of the output distribution of the modeled variable.

The objective of quantitative and qualitative analysis of these approaches to Risk Analysis includes:

- Revealing risk and develop corrective and preventive actions to reduce or remove the root cause of the uncertainties that create risk.
- Qualitative Risk Analysis is subjective, while quantitative risk assessment is objective.
- There can be a subjective bias in case of qualitative analysis. This is not the case with quantitative analysis.
- Another fundamental difference between quantitative and qualitative Risk Analysis is the quantitative analysis considers the overall project risks while qualitative risk assesses the specific risks to the project.
- The overall project risks are due to the correlations and interdependencies of different risks and applies to the overall project instead of individual activities.

3.7.2 Qualitative Risk Analysis

Qualitative Risk Analysis is the consideration of a range of characteristics such as probability of occurrence, degree of impact on the objectives, manageability, timing of possible impacts, relationships with other risks, and common causes or effects. — PMI Standard for Risk Management in Portfolios, Programs, and Project [73].

Qualitative Risk Analysis prioritizes a list of undifferentiated risks using a predefined risk rating scale. PMI tells us the consideration of a range of characteristics such as probability of occurrence, degree of impact on the objectives, manageability, timing of possible impacts, relationships with other risks, and common causes or effects.[18]

Qualitative Risk Analysis involves identifying risks, how likely they are to happen, and the potential impacts if they do [72,44].

The results are shown using a Probability versus Impact ranking matrix. This type of analysis can also categorize risks, either by source or effect.

A qualitative Risk Analysis prioritizes the identified project risks using a predefined rating scale. Risks will be scored based on their probability or likelihood of occurring and the impact on project objectives should they occur.

The Risk Owners provide the basis for Probability of Occurrence and Probability of impact(s). The Risk Owner may cite recent trends or Baseline Change Proposals, risks realized on other projects, or a quick estimate. The use of professional judgment is acceptable if no other information is available.

Identified risks are broken into two groups in the risk register, those identified as existing project risks that are being managed, and potential risks that are listed on a watch list that is reviewed on a regular basis. Those risks on the watch list may be moved to the priority risk register as their particular situational assessment determines (Table 3.7).

The development of the Qualitative Risk Analysis values is domain and project dependent. The probability of occurrence and the impacts, are domain specific, depending on technology, business, governance, or other system paradigms. The definition of the meaning of the five scales, and their ranges is project dependent. These ranges are developed by those accountable for risk management. This starts with the Project Manager, and usually flows to the Risk Manager, reporting to the Project Manager.

3.7.3 Quantitative Risk Analysis

A quantitative Risk Analysis is the analysis of risks, using numerical analysis a quantitative rating is used to develop a probabilistic analysis of the project's risk [41].

Measures the uncertainties of qualitative Risk Analysis defines achievable targets for the work to be performed for risk reduction from epistemic uncertainties and needed margin for irreducible uncertainties, that produce a *probability of success* for the project.

Table 3.7 A Sample Likelihood Determination of Qualitative Risk Using a Five-level Scale

Likelihood (L)	*Level*	*Definition*
Nearly Certain to Occur	5	The event is expected to occur in most circumstances as there is a history of regular occurrence for similar projects/programs/facilities. Complex process or new technology and/or facilities that may exceed the state of the art. Impacting factors outside the control of organization. **Greater than a 90% chance of occurrence.**
Highly Likely to Occur	4	There is a strong possibility the event occurs as there is a history of frequent occurrence for similar projects/programs/facilities. Probably occurs in most circumstances. Major facility and/or equipment development. Impacting factors outside the control of organization. **75–90% chance of occurrence.**
Likely to Occur	3	The risk might occur at some time as there is a history of casual occurrence for similar projects/programs/facilities. Modification of a technology or process at a site; new technology with moderate facility and/or equipment modifications. The "broad middle group." **25–75% chance of occurrence.**
Unlikely to Occur	2	Not expected, but there is a slight possibility of occurrence. Routine processes, suitable facilities exist with minor equipment modifications. **10–25% chance of occurrence.**
Very Unlikely to Occur	1	The risk may occur in exceptional circumstances. It could happen but probably never will occur. Routine process with existing technologies. No previous incidence of occurrence. **Less than a 10% chance of occurrence.**

A quantitative analysis:

- Quantifies the possible outcomes for the project and assesses the probability of achieving specific project objectives.
- Provides a quantitative approach to making decisions when there is uncertainty.
- Creates realistic and achievable cost, schedule, or scope targets.

Quantitative risk management uses verifiable data to produce a numerical value used to predict the probability of a risk event outcome. For each risk, the likelihood of the risk occurring, assuming successful mitigation, and what the impact of the risk would be under the best case, most likely case, and worst case, in terms of dollars and impact on the critical path is documented in a Risk Management report. The Results of the Quantitative Risk Analysis with input from the Risk Register determines Management Reserve and Contingency Reserve values to be included in the project's cost estimate.

Qualitative Risk Analysis estimates the impact of risks on project cost and schedule and is a numerical or more objective analysis of the probability and consequence of risks to the overall project through the use of statistical modeling techniques. The most important objectives of the project risk management implemented by Quantitative Risk Management include:

- Decreasing to the maximum extent practicable the number of high and moderate risks by identifying project risks, establishing meaningful and measurable handling strategies and actions, and tracking the actions to closure.
- Maximizing the return on investment to the project by identifying, enhancing, and exploiting opportunities results in meaningful cost and schedule savings for the project.

The post-handling strategy likelihood and impacts represent the residual risk. The residual risk impact is zero when employing an "avoid" or "transfer" handling strategy, and ultimately results in no cost or schedule contingency. In general, when the handling strategy is "mitigate," the worst-case residual impact is the same as the unmitigated impact in case the handling strategy fails; however, the worst-case impact may be reduced if the Risk Owner is certain of the success of the mitigation actions. The residual risk remains the same as the original evaluation when employing the "accept" handling strategy.

The residual risk parameters (likelihood, cost impacts, and schedule impacts) are input to Risk Analysis software and the necessary cost and schedule contingency is determined at a confidence level determined by the Project Manager. The risks, residual risk parameters, and calculated cost and schedule contingency is published in a risk assessment, prior to Critical Decisions, or as deemed necessary by the Project Manager (e.g., when a significant project change occurs).

For each risk, the Risk Manager documents the likelihood of the risk occurring, assuming successful mitigation, and what the impact of the risk would be under the best case, most likely case, and worst case, in terms of dollars and impact on the critical path. The Results of the Quantitative Risk Analysis with input from the Risk Register determines Management Reserve and Contingency Reserve values to be included in the project's cost estimate.

The post-handling strategy likelihood and impacts represent the residual risk. The residual risk impact is zero when employing an "avoid" or "transfer" handling strategy, and ultimately results in no cost or schedule contingency. In general, when the handling strategy is "mitigate," the worst-case residual impact is the same as the unmitigated impact in case the handling strategy fails; however, the worst-case impact may be reduced if the Risk Owner is certain of the success of the mitigation actions. The residual risk remains the same as the original evaluation when employing the "accept" handling strategy.

The Risk Manager provides the Project Manager a monthly update to the total project risk exposure based on risks closed (avoided or mitigated), new risks opened, and changes in status, probabilities, or impacts for existing risks, and an assessment of the project contingency remaining against the project's current risk exposure.

3.7.4 Cost Risk Analysis and Contingency Assessment

Cost overruns are common on all projects – commercial and government. The cost Risk Analysis and contingency assessment processes provide estimates and management processes by answering the following questions [69]:

- What is the most likely cost?[19]
- How likely is the baseline cost estimate to be overrun?
- How much contingency is required on the project to guarantee that the total project cost is not to be exceeded, with a certain confidence level?

Cost risk and uncertainty exist through all phases of a project's life cycle [68]. The cost estimator must identify the uncertainties that create risk. The cost analyst must defend the uncertainty and risk assessments built into the cost estimate and ensure that it is appropriately applied to the estimate.

Projects require budgets to set the sponsor's financial commitment and provide the basis for cost control and measurement of cost performance. A key component of a project budget is cost contingency.

There are six activities associated with developing a cost-risk assessment in order to understand the current confidence level of the project and estimate the amount of Unallocated Future Expense (UFE) necessary to achieve a desired confidence level [68]:

1. Determine the project's cost drivers and risks created by those with input from the project staff-technical and project staff.
2. Develop probability distributions for the technical and schedule cost drivers.
3. Develop probability distributions for the cost model uncertainty.
4. Run the risk model.
5. Identify the probability that the actual cost is less than or equal to the point estimate for the cost.
6. Recommend sufficient cost margin to achieve desired confidence level for budgeted cost for work performed.

The following best practices are used to increase the probability of cost success. The overarching principles of cost Risk Analysis is the analysis must be transparent, traceable, defendable, and timely.

Cost and Schedule baseline estimates must have a clear BOE that identifies the logic, data, methodology and calculations used to estimate the resources required to perform a specific task or group of related tasks. BOEs detail the thought process and calculations used to arrive at the estimate. BOEs are used to provide proposal evaluators with a reasonable, credible, and defendable technical and cost narrative that supports the proposed effort for the estimated resources.

- Include all the cost elements and schedule activities.
- Be supported by relevant data, all possible risks, threats, liens, uncertainties, mitigation strategies, and opportunities must be explicitly quantified, including their probability of occurring, their estimated cost and/or schedule consequences, and the analysis must address available annual resources.
- The analysis must incorporate impacts of cost and schedule performance to date.
- Risks must be transparently incorporated into cost, schedule, and/or both

3.7.4.1 Monte Carlo Simulation of Cost Risk

Monte Carlo Simulation provides a technique to understand the impact of uncertainties on the cost of a project.[20]

Monte Carlo Simulation can estimate the cost contingency and management reserve needed to *protect* a budget or delivery date, from the reducible and irreducible risks in the Risk Register.

In the absence of a Monte Carlo Simulation of cost, a simple but naïve approach is to add a fixed percent for Management Reserve to the cost baseline. This ignores the realities of the structure of the project, the dependencies of the risks, and the changing risk profiles as the project progresses.

Using *expert judgment* is the next step in the naïve path for Management Reserve, since that judgment is unlikely to be based on qualitative assessments rather than quantitative assessments derived from past performance or parametric models of the project's structure. The same issues are for heuristic methods.

The more accurate and precise method of the cost estimate is to develop a Monte Carlo Simulation of the cost model for the project, risk-adjusted for reducible and irreducible uncertainties, and use those values to assess the need for Management Reserve and Cost Margins.

This starts by dividing the project into major sections – by technology – and develop the base model of the ranges of values used for the Monte Carlo Simulation from the Risk Register.

The Monte Carlo simulation method has many benefits in project management:

- It helps evaluate the risk of the project.
- It helps predict the chances of failure, and schedule and cost overrun.

- It converts risks into quantifiable data to assess the impact on the project's probability of cost, schedule, and technical success.
- It helps build a realistic budget and schedule.
- It helps gain management support for risk management.
- It helps in decision-making with objective evidence.
- It helps to find the chances of achieving project milestones or intermediate goals.

Monte Carlo Simulation provides identification of how likely we are to meet project milestones, deliverable dates, and deadlines. This information is used to create a more realistic budget and schedule that:

- Predicts the likelihood of schedule and cost overruns.
- Quantifies risks to assess impacts better.
- Provides objective data for decision-making.
- The Monte Carlo simulation can show the overall probability for the entire project or a large subset of it (such as a phase), down to the analysis of individual activities or risks.

There are limitations of Monte Carlo Simulation as well:

- There must be three estimates for every activity or factor being analyzed.
- The analysis is only as good as the estimates provided.

3.7.5 Schedule Risk Analysis to Assess Needed Margin

Schedule Risk Analysis uses statistical modeling to predict the margin needed, and the level of confidence in that margin, to meet the project's deliverables and completion date. This analysis focuses on critical and near-critical path activities, since those activities are the primary affecting the project's completion date. Like the cost estimate risk and uncertainty analysis, a schedule Risk Analysis starts the collection of project risk data such as [45]:

- Risks that may jeopardize schedule success, found in the risk register prepared before the Risk Analysis is conducted.
- Probability distributions specified by a point estimate of activity durations – the *Most Likely* value of the task duration.
- Probability of a risk in the Risk Register occurring and the probability distribution of impact of the risk, if it were to occur and become an issue.
- Probability that a cascading branch of activities may occur (for example, a test failure could lead to several recovery tasks).
- Correlations between these activity durations, including any loops in the network of risks.[21]

The outcome of the simulation is a probability distribution for each modeled completion date and the confidence levels of those dates. Since all schedules have reducible and irreducible uncertainties in their work elements and the relationships between these elements, assessment and analysis of the risk created by these uncertainties is needed to increase the probability of project success.

The steps to setup and perform the Monte Carlo Simulation are as follows:

- **Baseline Schedule**: Construct an activity timetable.
- **Define Uncertainty**: Define activity time and cost probability distributions.
- **Run Monte Carlo Simulations**: Run multiple project progress simulations.
- **Interpret the Simulation Results**: Interpret the sensitivity measures and construct.

With the outcomes of the simulation, we can determine some important aspects of the schedule:

- **Criticality Index (CI)**: Measures the probability that an activity is on the critical path.
- **Significance Index (SI)**: Measures the relative importance of an activity.
- **Schedule Sensitivity Index (SSI)**: Measures the relative importance of an activity taking the CI into account.
- **Cruciality Index (CRI)**: Measures the correlation between the activity duration/cost and the total project duration/cost.

The result of the simulation is an actionable outcome meaningful to the decisions makers.

> Increased visibility to the probability of completing on or before the needed delivery date.

With this understanding, those paying for the work does not have a higher confidence in the schedule through:

- Reduced resource costs.
- Reduced labor costs.
- Identified high-risk areas.
- Increased confidence in the schedule's completion date.
- Actionable information to take corrective and preventive actions to *stay on schedule*.

3.7.5.1 Monte Carlo Simulation of Schedule and Cost Risk

Monte Carlo Simulation for schedules is the technique used to understand the impact of risk and uncertainty in the schedule for a project. The project schedule

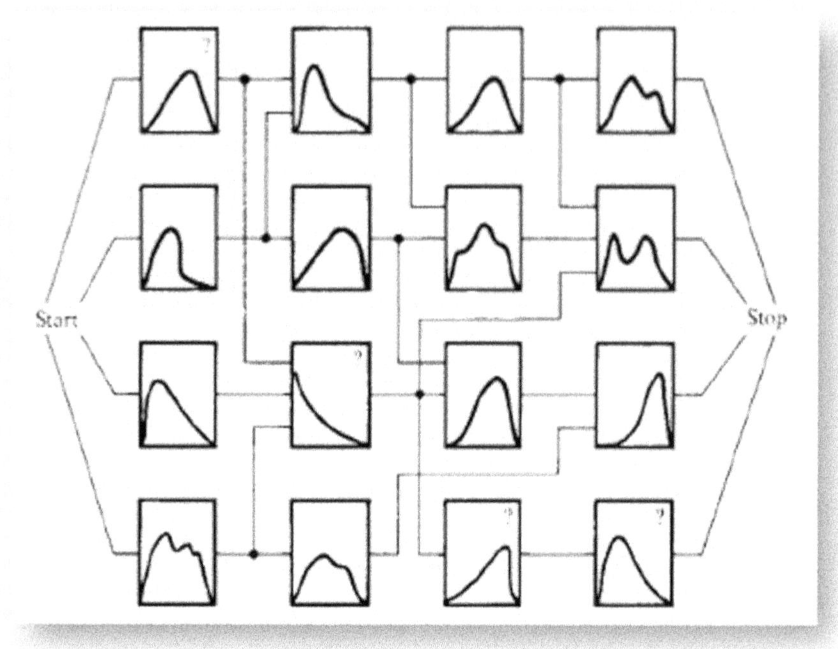

Figure 3.2 Each task has a probability distribution for the aleatory uncertainties of duration of the work. These PDFs can be identical, or they can be individual, but each creates a risk to the completion of the work defined by the most likely duration.

contains work effort with durations for the work. These durations are the Most Likely values for the task durations.

Schedule risk assessment starts with the Risk Register. Both aleatory and epistemic uncertainties will have impact on the duration of tasks. The primary driver for schedule Risk Analysis are aleatory uncertainties in the duration of the work (Figure 3.2).

With the assigned Most Likely Durations for the work, and the upper and lower limits from the probability distribution for the uncertainties in the work durations, we can produce an assessment of the probability of completing *on or before* a date and *at or below* a cost as shown in Figure 3.3.

3.7.5.2 Schedule Margin Analysis, Assignment, and Management

With the confidence information from the Monte Carlo Simulation, Schedule Margin can be applied to Protect the delivery date of the total project or individual elements within the project. Schedule analysts use it to help ensure that either a

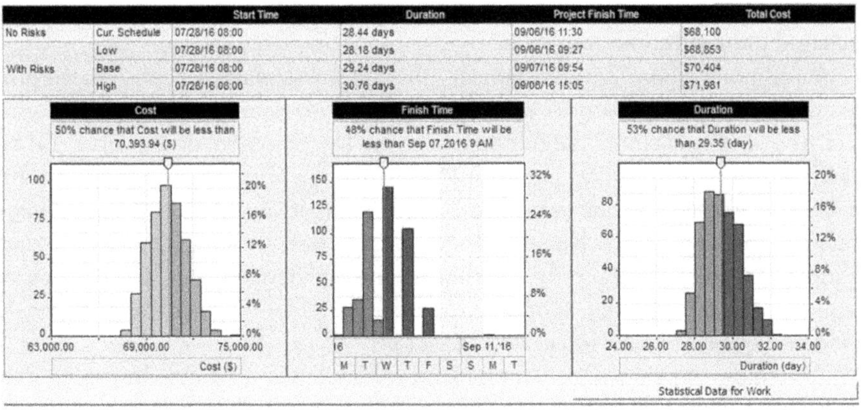

Figure 3.3 Using the most likely durations for task activities and their possible ranges of duration, the Monte Carlo simulation can show the confidence of completing *on or before* a date, *at or below* a cost, and the probability of the total duration of the project.

certain milestone or an overall schedule's completion is protected. Margin is defined as the allowance carried in the budget, projected schedules to account for uncertainties and risks, NASA NPR 7120.5E.

All projects work is subject to uncertainties, both Aleatory uncertainty that creates irreducible risk and Epistemic uncertainty that creates reducible risk.

For the risk created by aleatory uncertainty, only margin can be used as the handling strategy, since aleatory uncertainty is *irreducible*.

This margin can come in three forms:

- **Schedule Margin**: Tasks with duration, but no cost, or work activities to deal with schedule inconsistencies as a *buffer* to protect delivery dates.
- **Cost Margin**: Management reserve set aside for management control purposes (known unknowns) rather than designated for the accomplishment of one or more tasks. The MR is not part of the cost baseline but is held in the total contract budget.
- **Technical Margin**: Design margin to protect the needed performance from

Identifying, defining, and assigning margin is a critical success factor for all projects.

3.7.6 Analysis of Technology Readiness Levels

Many costly and complex projects require the development of advanced technologies and their integration into large and complex systems. Project efforts may also use existing technologies, but in new applications or environments. The question is not whether to take risks, but rather where and how to take them so they can be managed more effectively.

A Technology Readiness Assessment (TRA) is a systematic, evidence-based process that evaluates the maturity of technologies and services critical to the performance of a larger system or the fulfillment of the key objectives of a project. TRAs, which measure the technical maturity of a technology or system at a specific point in time, do not eliminate technology risk, but when done correctly, illuminate concerns and serve as the basis for discussions on how to mitigate potential risks as projects move from the early stages of technology development, where resource requirements are relatively modest, to system development and beyond, where resource requirements are often substantial [58].

Technology development is the process of developing and demonstrating new or unproven technology, the application of existing technology to new or different uses, or the combination of existing and proven technology to achieve a specific goal. Technology development associated with a specific acquisition project must be identified early in the project life cycle and its maturity level should have evolved to a confidence level that allows the project to establish a credible technical scope, schedule, and cost baseline. Projects that perform concurrent technology development and design implementation run the risk of proceeding with an ill-defined project baseline. A successful project is a project that satisfies its intended purpose in a safe, timely, and cost-effective manner that would reduce LCCs and produce results that are defensible to expert reviewers [60].

TRL are a type of measurement system used to assess the maturity level of a particular technology. Each technology project is evaluated against the parameters for each technology level and is then assigned a TRL rating based on the projects progress [58,59].

There are nine TRL. TRL 1 is the lowest and TRL 9 is the highest. TRL's answers the question – are the requirements attainable? NASA researcher, Stan Sadin, conceived the first scale in 1974. It had seven levels, which were not formally defined until 1989. In the 1990s, NASA adopted a scale with nine levels, which gained widespread acceptance across the industry and remains in use today.

Applying TRL's for risk management starts with a metrics-based process assesses the maturity of, and the risk associated with, critical technologies and an assessment of project technology risks and readiness. It also provides TRL definitions, descriptions, and supporting information.

For project success, TRL's must increase while risk decreases as the project progresses. Deploying a product or service with TRL's. Criteria that consider both the technology and the sponsor's ability to assimilate it are more likely to succeed than those that consider only the technology (as in the use of TRLs).

Moore identified types of sponsors and procurers of products and services as: Innovators; Early Adopts; Early Majority; Late Majority; and Laggards [61]. Each sponsor or procurer has their own tolerance for risk defined through some form of assessment.

TRL are a measurement system to assess the maturity level of a particular technology. Each technology project is evaluated against the parameters for each technology level and is then assigned a TRL rating based on the projects progress. There are nine TRLs. TRLs guide the selection of technology alternatives to reduce project risk. The lower the TRL, the lower the maturity and the higher the risk. Determining the impact of the risk is part of Risk Analysis. The nine levels of TRL guide this assessment:

1. **Basic principles observed and reported**: Lowest level of technology readiness. Scientific research begins to be translated into applied research and development.
2. **Technology concept and/or application formulated**: Once basic principles are observed, practical applications can be invented. Applications are speculative, and there may be no proof or detailed analysis to support assumptions.
3. **Analytical and experimental critical function and/or characteristic proof-of-concept**: Active research and development is initiated. This includes analytical studies and laboratory studies to physically validate analytical predictions of separate elements of the technology.
4. **Component and/or breadboard validation in a laboratory environment**: Basic technological components are integrated to establish that the pieces will work together. This is relatively "low fidelity" compared to the eventual system.
5. **Component and/or breadboard validation in relevant environment**: Fidelity of breadboard technology increases significantly. The basic technological components are integrated with reasonably realistic supporting elements so that the technology can be tested in a simulated environment.
6. **System/subsystem model or prototype demonstration in a relevant end-to-end environment**: Representative model or prototype system, which is well beyond that of TRL 5, is tested in a relevant environment. Represents a major step up in a technology's demonstrated readiness.
7. **System prototype demonstration in an operational environment**: Prototype near, or at, planned operational system. Represents a major increase in maturity from TRL 6, requiring demonstration of an actual system prototype in an operational environment.
8. **Actual system completed and qualified through test and demonstration**: Technology has been proven to work in its final form, integrated into the overall system, and under expected operational conditions. In almost all cases, this TRL represents the end of system development. Examples include development test and evaluation during system verification in its intended use and operational environment to determine if it meets the requirements.
9. **The actual system has proven through successful operations**: Actual application of the technology in its final form and under operational conditions, such as those encountered in operational tests and evaluation during system validation.

3.7.6.1 Where Are Technology Readiness Levels Applicable?

Technical deliverables, including technology development, are produced as the project evolves from early requirements discovery to design to operation. The technology development process is not limited to the conceptual development stages but also transitions throughout the project's life.

The process of the project management, the evolution, and iterations are necessary to continue support of the design. It also addresses emerging issues related to the technology-driven by the design process, including risk management functions.

Throughout the project lifecycle analysis of risk can be guided by the assessment of the current TRL and the needed TRL.

3.8 Integrating Technical Performance, Cost, Schedule Risk Analysis

All Project Risk belongs to one or more of three categories:
Cost, Schedule, and Technical Performance.

Projects are many times managed by measuring cost and schedule adherence to a plan. Having looked at the Cost and Schedule impacts of risk in previous sections and their impacts on the delivery the needed Capabilities of the project, we're missing the critical connection between cost, schedule, and technical performance risk and the mechanisms to protect from that risk (Figure 3.4).[22]

3.8.1 Risk Analysis of Project Performance Measures

These TPM have uncertainties that create risk, which requires analysis of the risks to:

- Cost
- Schedule
- Technical Performance Measure (TPM)
- Measures of Performance (MOP)
- Measures of Effectiveness (MOE)
- Key System Attributes (KSA)

For these measures, there are metrics used to assess impacts on the probability of project success, starts with Plans

- Key TPM Plans
- Deliverables Plans
- Summary level Integrated Master Schedule and proposed spend plan

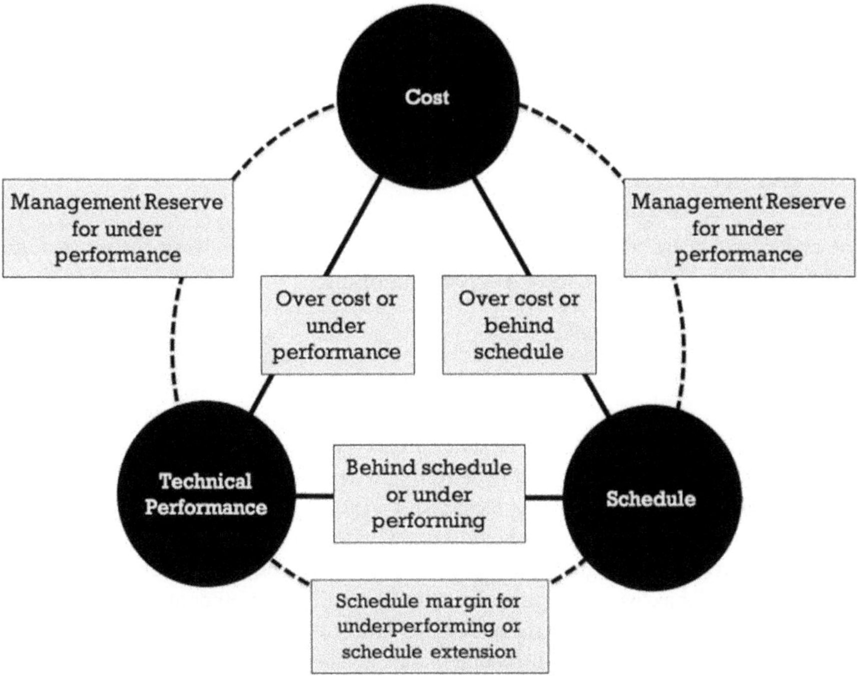

Figure 3.4 Risk to cost, schedule, and technical performance create a risk to the probability of project success.

- Labor Full Time Equivalent (FTE) plan
- Risk registers and handling actions
- Computation of initial Management Reserve
- Risk Burn Down Plan
- Computation of planned schedule margin
- Schedule health and performance check

With project data, the actual performance is compared against the actual performance

- TPM plan versus estimates actuals versus cost and schedule performance metrics.
- Deliverables plan versus actual deliverables versus cost performance and schedule performance measures.
- FTE versus actuals.
- Cumulative budget spends and actuals against plan.
- Risk Burn Down Plan versus actual.
- Cost and Schedule informed by Risk Burn Down actuals.

- Schedule health and schedule performance versus planned performance.
- Management Reserve usage and remaining balance.
- Updated Risk Register.
- Forecast of EAC and Estimates Completion Date (ECD).
- Confidence levels of meeting contractual best case, worst case, and most likely EAC and ECD.

The analysis of these measures is the basis of *Continuous Risk Management* and will be described in detail in Chapter 4 – Risk Handling.

Notes

1 The Probability of Project (or Program) Success (PoPS) is a framework for determining the ability of a project to succeed in delivering systems or capabilities. PoPS standardizes the reporting of selected project factors and areas of risk as described in "Acquisition Management Metrics," Systems Engineering Guide, MITRE Corporation.

2 It is important to distinguish aleatory uncertainty from epistemic uncertainty. Aleatory uncertainty (objective, stochastic, or irreducible) arises from randomness or unpredictability due to stochasticity of the underlying processes. It includes variability over time, across space or among individual components in a system. Epistemic uncertainty (subjective, state-of-knowledge, or reducible) arises from imperfect knowledge, ignorance and limitations to information.

3 Originally SOARA was an interviewing process. It is used here and other chapters to tell the story of the chapter and guide the reader through the chapter contents, by stating what the outcomes from reading the chapter will be before reading the chapter.

4 This is different from the current Project Management Institute approach to risk management. Recognizing that risk comes from uncertainty is the foundation of risk management at NASA, Department of Energy (NNSA), and seismic risk management, medical analysis, and other government agencies.

5 "Risk & Safety Management: Risk Handling," *AcqNotes*, 2020.

6 The TBfD specifies the minimum information needed to risk-inform the selection of a decision alternative. The content of the TBfD is driven by the question, "What information do the deliberators and decision-makers need in order for their decision process to be fully risk-informed?" The TBfD provides specific risk information to understand the uncertainties associated with each alternative. The TBfD serves as the technical basis for risk-informed selection of alternatives within the program or project [24].

7 In this book we speak of risk handling as the basis of increasing the probability of success. Risk handling is the choice of a strategy to reduce the likelihood the occurrence of the risk and/or the magnitude of the negative impact of the risk is measurably effective [21].

8 Tim Lister is a Principal of The Atlantic Guild and author of the design, risk management and human aspects of software systems.

9 … ilities are characteristics or quality of a system applied across a set of functional and system requirements like maintainability, reliability, serviceability.

10 Management Reserve is an amount of contract budget set aside for management control purposes (known unknowns) and used when risk is realized for identified work without the contract scope of work, rather than designated for the accomplishment of one or more tasks.
11 A CER is an equation used to estimate a given cost element using an established relationship with one or more independent variables. The relationship may be mathematically simple, or it may involve a complex equation (derived from regression analysis of historical systems or subsystems).
12 Basis of Estimate identifies the logic, data, methodology, and calculations used to estimate the resources required to perform a specific task or group of related tasks. BOEs detail the processes and calculations used to arrive at the estimate.
13 Reference class forecasting is a method of predicting the future by looking at similar past situation and their outcomes.
14 The Risk Management Plan defines the scope and processes for the identification, assessment, and management of risks which could impact the implementation of the program and/or its relevant projects. Risk Management Plan includes the processes for assessing risks that potentially jeopardize successful completion of projects and addresses risks that potentially jeopardize human health and the environment. The plan defines the strategy to manage program-related risks throughout the project life cycle so there is an acceptable minimal impact on cost and schedule, and technical and operational performance.
15 As stated, before there is a third form of uncertainty – ontological uncertainty. But we'll not consider that in this chapter.
16 Washington State Department of Enterprise Services.
17 Luang Prinyayogavipulya, Concise Principles of Buddhism, second edition (1957)
18 Project Management Institute Standard for Risk Management in Portfolio, Programs, and Projects, 2019.
19 Statistical distributions have three attributes. Mean (Average), Median (middle most value), and Mode (most recurring value). In risk management we want to use the Mode, or Most Likely number. The Average of 0 and 100 if 50. The average of 48 and 52 is 50, so average cost is of little use. The Median between 0 and 100 is 50. The most likely is the number that we'd expect to see over time and is the basis of making decision in the presence of uncertainties.
20 Details of the Monte Carlo Simulation process and its application in risk management are described in Chapter 8 – Advanced Topics.
21 In the Integrated Master Schedule (IMS), loops between work tasks are not possible. In the network model of risk propagation, they are and are common. The Design Structure Matrix (DSM) described in Chapter 8, can be used to model risk propagation and the loops they form. A causes B, B causes C, C causes A can be modeled with Monte Carlo Simulation and in several tools.
22 Management Reserve can cover newly identified work, necessary rework, work transfers, adjustments to overhead rates.

References

1. Charles Yoe, *Principles of Risk Analysis: Decision Making Under Uncertainty*, CRC Press, 2012.

2. Palash Dutta, "An Approach to Deal with Aleatory and Epistemic Uncertainty within the Same Framework: Case Study in Risk Assessment," *International Journal of Computer Applications*, Volume 80, No 12, October 2013.
3. "Risk Assessment and Risk Treatment," Broadleaf, Resource Materials, June 2014
4. T. Nilsen and Terje Aven, "Models and Model Uncertainty in the Context of Risk Analysis," *Reliability Engineering and System Safety*, Volume 79, No 3, March 2003.
5. "*Risk Management Guide for DOD Acquisition*," 7th ed. (Interim Release), Department of Defense, December 2014. https://apps.dtic.mil/sti/pdfs/ADA470492.pdf
6. John K. Hollman, *Project Risk Quantification: A Practitioner's Guide to Realistic Cost and Schedule Risk Management*, Probabilistic Publishing, 2016.
7. *Practices Standard for Project Risk Management*, Project Management Institute, 2009. www.pmi.org/-/media/pmi/documents/public/pdf/certifications/practice-standard-project-risk-management.pdf?v=1e0b5985-74af-4c57-963c-b91a9af6fecb
8. Rashad Yazanifard and Kaizer Boikany Ratsiepe, "Poor Risk Management as One of the Major Reasons Causing Failure of Project Management," in *Management and Service Science (MASS), 2011 International Conference on Management and Service*, Wuhan China.
9. Preston G. Smith and Guy M, *Proactive Risk Management: Controlling Uncertainty in Product Development*,, Merritt, CRC Press, 2002.
10. N. Lavanya and T. Malarvizhi, "Risk Analysis and Management a Vital Key to Effective Project Management," *PMI Global Congress*, 2008.
11. Space and Missile Systems Center (SMC), "Risk Management Process Guide," Version 2.0, 5 September 2014.
12. Helena Gaspars-Wieloch, "The Impact of the Structure of the Payoff Matrix on the Final Decision made Under Uncertainty," *Asia-Pacific Journal of Operational Research*, Vol. 35, No. 01, 1850001, 2018.
13. Bent Flyvbjerg, "From Nobel Prize to Project Management – Getting Risks Right," *Project Management Journal*, Vol. 37, No. 3, August 2006, pp. 5–15 .
14. Johnathan Mun, *Real Options Analysis: Tools Techniques for Valuing Strategic Investments and Decisions*, Wiley Finance, 2002.
15. Frank Merle, "Using DSM Approach to Manage Interactions between Project Risks," *12th International Dependency and Structure Modelling Conference*, DSM' 10, 22–23 July 2010.
16. Farzaneh Farhangmehr and Irem Y. Tumer, "The Capture, Assessment and Communication Tool for Uncertainty Simulation (CACTUS) in Complex Systems," *Proceedings of IMECE 2008.*
17. Justin B. Biddle and Rebecca Kukla, "The Geography of Epistemic Risk," in *Exploring Inductive Risk: Case Studies of Values in Science*, edited by Kevin C. Elliot and Ted Richards, pp. 215–237, Oxford University Press, 2017.
18. Thomas J. Altenbach, "A comparison of Risk Assessment Techniques from Qualitative to Quantitative," *ASME Pressure and Piping Conference*, 23–27 July 1995.
19. David McCullough, "*The Wright Brothers*," Simon & Schuster, 2015.
20. "Risk and Uncertainty in Project Portfolio Management, *Lecture Notes in Electrical Engineering*, Shiwang Yu and Na Guo, Vol. 218, pp. 815–822, 2013.

21. "Choosing a Project Risk-Handling Strategy: An Analytical Model," Miao Fan, Neng-Pai Lin, Chwen Sheu, *International Journal of Production Economics*, 112, pp. 700–713, 2008.
22. "NASA Risk Management Handbook," NASA/SP–2011–3422, Version 1.0, November 2011.
23. "Uncertainty Quantification Using Evidence Theory," William L. Oberkampf, *Advanced Simulation & Computing Workshop*, Sandia National Laboratory, 22–23 August 2005.
24. "Risk-Informed Decision Making Handbook," NASA/SP-2010-576. https://ntrs.nasa.gov/api/citations/20100021361/downloads/20100021361.pdf
25. "S3001: Guidelines for Risk Management," Independent Verification and Validation Program, Version G, 16 October 2017. www.nasa.gov/wp-content/uploads/2015/10/s3001_guidelines_for_risk_management_-_ver_g_-_10-25-2017.pdf
26. "Cost Risk/Uncertainty Analysis Overview," Defense Acquisition University, October 2016. https://docplayer.net/55510320-Cost-risk-uncertainty-analysis-overview.html
27. "Risk-informed decision-making processes: An Overview," Enrico Zio and Nicola Pedroni, Foundation pour une culture de sécurité industrielle FONCSI, No 2012-10. www.icsi-eu.org/en/publication/risk-informed-decision-making-processes
28. "Uncertainty Characterization in Risk Analysis for Decision-Making Practice," Enrico Zio and Nicola Pedroni, Foundation pour une culture de sécurité industrielle FONCSI, No 2012-07. www.foncsi.org/en/publications/collections/industrial-safety-cahiers/uncertainty-QRA/CSI-uncertainty-QRA.pdf
29. "Expanded Guidance for NASA Systems Engineering, Volume 1: System Engineering Practices, NASA/SP-2016-6105-SUPPL.
30. "Classifying Risk Uncertainty for Decision Making," Don Port and Joel Wilf, *Proceedings of the 52nd Hawaii International Conference of System Sciences*, 2019. https://scholarspace.manoa.hawaii.edu/server/api/core/bitstreams/4aa2cd09-4a32-4438-b26e-08b563616c95/content
31. "Technical Probabilistic Risk Assessment (PRA) Procedures for Safety and Mission Assurance for NASA Programs and Projects," NPR: 8705.5A, June 7, 2015.
32. "Root Cause Analysis as Part of Enterprise Risk Management," Wendell Bosen and Kristina Narvaez, Risk Management Society, Utah Chapter, Sprint 2012 Workshop, Utah Department of Transportation. www.erm-strategies.com/presentations/root-cause-analysis-as-part-of-enterprise-risk-management/
33. "Project Risk Management: Comparative Analysis of Methods of Project Risk Management," Mira Mileusnić Škrtić and Karolina Horvatinčić, *Collegium Antropologicum*, Volume 38, Suppl. 1, pp. 125–134, 2014.
34. "Probabilistic Risk Assessment to Inform Decision Making Frequently Asked Questions," Office of Science Advisor, EPA/100/R-14/003, July 2014
35. "Eados: A Prioritization Analysis and Risk Assessment Capability," NASA Cost and Schedule Symposium, Tuesday, August 14 – Building 8 Auditorium, 2018.
36. "Estimating Cost Uncertainty Using Monte Carlo Techniques," P. F. Dienemann, RM-4854-PR, Rand Corporation, January 1966.
37. "Project Risk Analysis: How Ignoring It Will Lead to Project Failures," Lev Virine, *Risk Management Conference*, PMI Global Conference, 26 October 2014.

38. "Opportunity Management: Be Careful What You Ask For," Edmund H. Conrow and Robert N. Charette, *Defense AT&L*, March–April 2008.
39. Ian Stewart, *Do Dice Play God? The Mathematics of Uncertainty*, Basic Books, 2019.
40. "Risk Analysis 101: How to Analyze Project Risk," Jennifer Bridges, Project Manager, www.projectmanager.com/training/how-to-analyze-risks-project
41. "Quantitative Risk Analysis Support to Decision-Making for New Systems," Robert W. Youngblood III, Homayoon Dezfuli, Idaho National Laboratory, INL/CON-18-52121-Revision, May 2019.
42. "Study on the Main Causes of Project Schedule Delays," Saleh Al-Wadei, PMI, Central Italy, Chapter, 29 May 2020.
43. *Technical Risk Assessment Handbook*, Defence Science and Technology Organization, Department of Defence, Australian Government, 2010.
44. "Risk Assessment – Qualitative Methods," *Corps Risk Analysis Gateway Training Module*, Institute for Water Resources, US Army Corps of Engineers.
45. *GAO Cost Estimating and Assessment Guide*, GAO-09-3SP.
46. David Hulett, *Practical Schedule Risk Analysis*, Gower, 2009.
47. Werner G. Meyer "Quantifying Risk: Measuring the Invisible,", *PMI Global Congress*, EMEA, London, 2015.
48. "Technical Risk Identification at Program Inception Product Overview," Bill Frazier, John McBride, Andrew Hsu, and Amy Weir, U.S. Space Program Mission Assurance Improvement Workshop (MAIW), Aerospace Corporation, Dulles, VA, 8 May 2014.
49. "Dealing with Project Complexity by Matrix-Based Propagation Modeling for Project Risk," Chao Fang and Franck Marle, *Journal of Engineering Design*, Vol. 24, No. 4, 2012. doi: 10.1080/09544828.2012.720014
50. "Distinguishing Two Dimensions of Uncertainty," Craig R. Fox and Gülden Ülkumen, in *Perspectives on Thinking, Judging, Decision Making*, Universitetsforlagetet, 2011.
51. Sergio Gerosa, Nicola Di Placido, and Corrado Lo Storto, "Using Knowledge Elicitation Techniques in the Risk Assessment of Space Projects," *PMI Global Congress*, 2006.
52. "Risk-Informed Decision-Making in the Presence of Epistemic Uncertainty," Didier Dubois and Dominique Guyonnet, *International Journal of General Systems*, Volume 40, No 2, pp. 145–167, 2011.
53. "*The Owner's Role in Project Risk Management*," Committee for Oversight and Assessment of U.S. Department of Energy Project Management, National Research Council, 2005
54. *Seven Steps to Effective Problem-Solving and Strategies for Personal Success*, Dean L. Gano, Apollonian Publications, LLC, Richland Washington, 2011.
55. *Apollo Root Cause Analysis: Effective Solutions to Everyday Problems Every Time*, 3rd ed., Dean L. Gano, Apollonian Publications, Richland, WA, 2007.
56. "Risk management process in projects," Elena Doval, *Review of General Management*, Volume 30, Issue 2, 2019.
57. "Increasing the Probability of Program Success with Continuous Risk Management," Glen Alleman, Tom Coonce, and Rick Price, *The Measurable News*, College of Performance Management, pp. 27–46, 2018.14
58. "Technology Readiness Assessment Guide," GAO-16-410G, August 2016.

59. "Technology Readiness Assessment (TRA) Guidance," Assistant Secretary of Defense for Research and Engineering (ASD(R&E)), 13 March 2011.
60. "Technology Readiness Assessment Guide," DOE G 413.3-4A, 10-22-2015.
61. *Crossing the Chasm*, G. A. Moore, Capstone Publishing, 1998.
62. "*Perspectives on Risk in Space System Development*," Jesse Leitner, NASA Goddard Space Flight Center, Safety and Mission Assurance Directorate, Code 300, 2018.
63. *Modeling and Simulation Fundamentals: Theoretical Underpinnings and Practical Domains*, edited by John A. Sokolowski and Catherine M. Banks, John Wiley and Sons, 2010.
64. "Risk Management," in *Guide to the Systems Engineering Body of Knowledge*, INCOSE, IEEE Systems Council, Stevens Institute of Technology, www.sebokwiki.org/wiki/Risk_Management
65. "*Mitigating Cognitive Biases in Risk Identification: Practitioner Checklist for the Aerospace Sector*," Debra L. Emmons, Thomas, A Mazzuchi, Shahram Sarkani, and Curtis Larsen, www.dau.edu/library/arj/ARJ/arj84/ARJ84%20Article%203%20-%2016-770%20Emmons.pdf
66. "*Risk Analysis in Theory and Practice*," Jean-Paul Chavas, Elsevier, 2004.
67. "*Managing Project Risk and Uncertainty: A Constructively Simple Approach to Decision Making*," Chris Chapman and Stephen Ward, John Wiley & Sons, 2002.
68. "NASA Cost Estimating Handbook, Version 4.0, Appendix G: Cost Risk and Uncertainty Methodologies," February 2015.
69. "Using Monte Carlo Simulation to Mitigate the Risk of Project Overruns," Z. Bouayed, *International Journal of Safety and Security Engineering*, Volume 6, Issue 2, 2016.
70. "Risk Impact Assessment and Prioritization," Systems Engineering Guide, MITRE Corporation.
71. "Risk Management," Systems Engineering Guide, MITRE Corporation.
72. "An Introduction to Qualitative Risk Analysis," SAFRAN, www.safran.com/content/introduction-qualitative-risk-analysis
73. "*The Standard for Risk Management in Portfolios, Programs, and Projects*," Project Management Institute, 2019.
74. "*Bayesian Methods for Hackers: Probabilistic Programing and Bayesian Inference*," Cameron Davidson-Pilon, John Wiley & Sons, 2016.
75. "*Essential of Monte Carlo Simulation: Statistical Methods of Building Simulation Models*," Nick T. Thomopoulos, Springer, 2012.
76. "*The Monte Carlo Simulation for System Reliability and Risk Analysis*," Series Editor, Hoang Pham, Springer, 2013.
77. "From Nobel Prize to Project Management: Getting Risks Right", Bent Flyvbjerg, *Project Management Journal*, Volume 37, No. 3, pp. 5–15.
78. "*Design Structure Matrix Methods and Applications*," Steven D. Eppinger and Tyson R. Browning, The MIT Press, 2012.

Chapter 4

Risk-Handling Plan

> An individual who is observed to be inconstant to his plans, or perhaps to carry on his affairs without any plan at all, is marked at once. By all prudent people, as a speedy victim to his own unsteadiness and folly.
>
> *Alexander Hamilton in Federalist Papers*

Risk Planning is like other project planning or problem-solving activities. In this chapter, the Planning for Risk-handling starts with translating risk information developed in Chapter 3 into decisions and handling actions and the plans to implement those actions.[1]

Every project or business initiative has objectives and goals it seeks to accomplish. These are the project or initiative's Critical Success Factors (CSF). Risk threatens the successful completion of these CSF [1].

With the risks identified in Chapter 2 and analyzed in Chapter 3, plans are needed for developing the handling strategies.

The identified uncertainties – both reducible and irreducible – create a risk to the success of achieving the objectives or goals of the project. With these uncertainties:

- Risk has an effect that deviates from the expected – positive and/or negative.
- Objectives have different aspects (financial, health and safety, and environmental goals) and apply at different levels (strategic, organization-wide, project, product, and process).
- Risk refers to potential events and consequences or a combination of these.
- Risk is expressed in terms of combinations of consequences of an event (including changes in circumstances) and associated likelihoods of occurrence.
- Uncertainty as to the state, even partial, of deficiency of information related to, understanding or knowledge of, an event, its consequence, or likelihood.

DOI: 10.1201/9781003425465-4

> Risk planning is the least practiced risk management process but the most important one. Little or no formal risk planning typically exists on many projects. This can weaken risk management process effectiveness by causing risk issues to be missed, analyses to be inaccurate or inconsistent, poor risk-handling approaches, and subjective risk monitoring. Formal risk planning should be a performance on most projects and will aid overall risk management process effectiveness [1].

This Chapter is a checklist-focused description of what should be in the *Risk-handling Plan* (RHP) based on the contents of the Risk Analysis.[2]

4.1 Reviewing the Risk-Handling Process – An Overview

For risk-handling processes to be credible and effective, we need the following activities.

4.1.1 Risk Identification

- Define the uncertainties creating risk and the *Triggers* that occur to cause those uncertainties to be present on the project and planning processes for handling the risks created by the uncertainties:
  - Changes to Baseline or overall solution approach.
  - Discovery of new information affecting the solution. Typically found while accomplishing the work or discussion in related meetings.
- Planned Process for Risk Handling:
  - Regularly held meetings to identify and review upcoming risks based on current work.
  - Periodic full review of the risk register with the team.
  - Both Stakeholder and Project Team participation.
  - Results report produced after each meeting.
  - While risk identification is not the focus of each risk meeting, it is always pursued.

4.1.2 Risk Analysis and Impact Modeling

- Modeling the expected impact of the risk on cost, schedule, and technical performance:
  - Assess the feasibility of meeting cost and schedule.
  - Tie risk events to a timeframe/baseline.
  - Typically done for Baseline Change Processes.

- Processes and methods to respond and manage *in the presence of uncertainty* that creates a risk:
  - Recurring focus on time frames sufficiently short to take corrective or preventive action to control the impact of the risk.
  - Track and record the progress on handling outcomes for each risk.
  - Modeling consequences or likelihood of occurrence of the risk and connecting those actions with the handling plans.
- Develop a Risk Model
  - Incorporate current baseline information in risk management, cost, and schedule tools.
  - Assign general uncertainty distributions for task durations in the schedule and their impacts on cost and technical performance.
  - Define event risk from the Risk Register with the probability of occurrence and probability of impact on cost, schedule, and technical performance.
  - Quantify and connect event-based risks to work activities in the Integrated Master Schedule (IMS).
  - Identify the stochastic variability of naturally occurring (Aleatory) uncertainties and their creation of risk to cost, schedule, and technical performance.
  - Validate this data and run a Monte Carlo Simulation to forecast the cost Estimate to Complete (ETC), Estimate at Completion (EAC), and Estimated Completion Date (ECD).

4.1.3 Risk-Handling Planning

- Define the Roles and Responsibilities of the participants in the risk management process. Who owns the risk, who captures the risk in the Risk Register, and who connects the risks with the cost and schedule models?
- Define the frequency of updates of the Risk Register and related risk documents.
- Define the step-action processes for performing all risk management work.
- Identify process improvement opportunities and work toward automating the connection between the scheduling tool, Risk Register, and the risk Modeling tools.

4.1.4 Risk Tracking and Control

- Track and Control project cost, schedule, and technical performance and report this in weekly status meetings:
  - For Stakeholders and Providers.
  - Conduct joint identification and problem-solving sessions.
  - Use the Risk register and its model to facilitate all tracking and control processes.

  - Assure tracking and control are focused on current work, recent developments, and future work.
- Management's role is to make sure risk process work focused on institutionalizing risk management process across all aspects of the project – cost, schedule, and technical performance management.
  - Make risk management the basis of project *governance* by incorporating it as a regular part of daily, weekly, and monthly business rhythm.
  - Reinforce with full support demonstrated by Project Team and Stakeholder management.

4.1.5 Avoiding Decision Traps While Managing Risk

A fundamental failure of Risk Planning and the Management of Risk is to assume *it will improve if we wait long enough.*

> The odds are six to five that the light at the end of the tunnel is the headlight of an oncoming train.
>
> – *Paul Dickson [1]*

- **Anchoring**: The tendency of the decision-makers to give disproportionate weight to the first information they receive. It is related to a preference for people to reason in terms of perturbations from a "baseline" perception, and to formulate their baseline quickly and sometimes baselessly.
- **Status Quo Bias**: The tendency to want to preserve the status quo in weighing decision alternatives. In many decision situations, there are good reasons (e.g., financial) to maintain the status quo, but the bias cited here is a fundamental tendency of how people think. The reference [16] notes that early designs of "horseless carriages" were firmly based on horse-drawn buggies, despite being sub-optimal for engine-powered vehicles. There is a tendency for managers to believe that if things go wrong with a decision, they are more likely to be punished for having taken positive action than for having allowed the status quo to continue to operate.
- **Sunk-Cost Fallacy**: The tendency to throw good money after bad: to try to recoup losses by continuing a course of action, even when the rational decision would be to walk away, based on the current state of knowledge. This bias operates in the perpetuation of projects floundering by any objective standard to the point where additional investment diverts resources that would be better spent elsewhere. A decision process should generally be based on the current situation: what gain is expected from the expenditure being contemplated.
- **Confirmation Bias**: The tendency to give greater weight to evidence that confirms our prior views and even to seek out such evidence preferentially.
- **Framing Assumptions**: A class of biases that relate to the human tendency to respond to how a question is framed, regardless of the objective content of the

question. People tend to be risk-averse when offered the possibility of a sure gain and risk-seeking when presented with a certain loss. However, it is sometimes possible to describe a given situation either way, leading to very different assessments and subsequent decisions.

- **Overconfidence**: The widespread tendency to underestimate the uncertainty inherent in the current state of knowledge. While most "experts" will acknowledge the presence of uncertainty in their assessments, they tend to do a poor job of estimating confidence intervals. The truth lies outside their assessed bounds much more often than would be implied by their stated confidence in those bounds. This is particularly true for decisions that are challenging to implement, as many decisions at NASA are. In the face of multiple sources of uncertainty, people tend to pay attention to the few with whom they have the most experience and neglect others. It is also particularly true for highly unlikely events, where limited data is available to inform expert judgment.
- **Recall ability**: The tendency to be strongly influenced by experiences or events that are easier to recall, even if a neutral statistical analysis of experience would yield a different answer. This means that dramatic or extreme events may play an unwarrantedly prominent role in decision-making based on experience.

The RHP must address each of the biases with corrective or preventive actions on the part of the decision-makers if any improvement in the probability of success is to occur.

4.2 Planning for Handling Risk

Planning – Wikipedia tells us – is thinking about the activities required to achieve the desired goal. It is the critical first activity for achieving any desired result for any activity. Planning involves creating and maintaining a plan, which is a fundamental property of intelligent behavior in the presence of uncertainties that create risk.

Risk-handling Planning develops and documents an organized, comprehensive, and interactive strategy for identifying and tracking root causes, developing Risk mitigation Plans, performing continuous risk assessments, and assigning adequate resources.

In project management, the planning phase is when project plans are documented, project deliverables and requirements are defined, and project schedules are created. Planning involves creating a set of plans to guide the project team through the project's definition, implementation, and delivery phases. Plans created during this phase define how to manage schedule, cost, quality, change, risk, and related issues.

Risk itself is part of the planning process; by asking the question, *what could go wrong with this Plan?*

4.2.1 What Is a Risk-Handling Plan?

> Risk-handling is the process that identifies and selects options to reduce or handle the reducible and irreducible uncertainties that create risk [33].

RHPs state what corrective or preventive actions must be taken to address a project's cost, schedule, or performance risk. In this process, decisions and handling strategies are developed based on knowledge of project risks.

Risk planning translates risk information developed in Chapter 3 into management decisions and the risk-handling decisions needed to reduce risk and increase the probability of project success. The RHP is a document stating the details of the risk management process.

The first step in managing risk is identifying and analyzing those risks, as described in Chapters 2 and 3. Next is the planning of the handling strategies for each risk or a set of risks. Planning is deciding what should be done about *handling* the risk. Do we prevent the risk from occurring or correct the underlying cause of the uncertainty that created the risk?

Once the initial risk analysis is complete (Chapter 3), the risk enters a planning phase where the risk is further analyzed to ensure the consequence and likelihood scores are correct for qualitative risk analysis. The stochastic processes are correctly defined for the quantitative risk analysis, and risk has been assigned to the proper owner.

Four basic activities take place during the risk planning phase:

1. Generate a set of candidate risk response alternatives for corrective or preventive actions.
2. Conduct a risk analysis of each alternative.
3. Assess and select an alternative for implementation.
4. Implement the chosen alternative.

Developing a mitigation plan includes defining the leading risk driver(s). These drivers are the uncertain elements in risk with the most potential to contribute to a performance shortfall. A risk driver can be a single performance parameter, a single event, a set of performance parameters collectively, or a group of events collectively that, when varied over their range of uncertainty, causes the performance risk to change from tolerable to intolerable (or perhaps marginal). A risk driver intends to focus risk management attention on those potentially controllable situations that present the most significant opportunity for risk reduction. The type of risk response options to be considered for a given risk depends on the nature of the uncertainty that makes it a driver. Risk reduction is typically accomplished via mitigation when the uncertainty is primarily caused by variability in the system or the environment. Suppose the uncertainty is primarily due to a lack of knowledge. In that case, the response often begins with research to better understand the facts of the matter. It proceeds to mitigation if, after the investigation is complete, the risk is still intolerable.

The risk planning process has the following inputs, functions, and outputs. The result is a Risk Plan that defines the following:

- Roles and Responsibilities of the participants in the risk management process. Who owns the risk, who captures the risk in the Risk Register, and who connects the risks with the cost and schedule models?
- Frequency of updates of the Risk Register and related documents.
- Step-action processes for performing the risk-handling work.
- Process improvement opportunities toward automating the connection between the scheduling tools, Risk Register, and risk Modeling tools.

4.2.1.1 Which Risks Should Be Handled?

Not all risks identified and analyzed need to be handled. Determining which ones to *handle* is a process defined in the Risk Action Plan [5]:

- **Research Plan:** Defines the strategy, actions, responsibilities, and schedules for conducting the research on the source of uncertainties, the root causes created by these uncertainties, properties, and impacts of the risk. Evaluate and report the results of this research to the decision-makers.
- **Acceptance Rationale:** States which risks are accepted *as is*. The reasons for accepting the risk, including the current conditions and assumptions that support the decision, are defined.
- **Tracking Requirements:** Defines the indicators, thresholds, and tracking requirements for *watching* the risk.
- **Handling Plan:** Defines handling strategies, actions taken during the strategy, due dates for outcomes of the strategies, responsibilities for performing these tasks, for handling the risk.

The risk review process determines which risks to handle once the risk analysis is complete from Chapter 3. This risk analysis is presented to the Risk Review Board (RRB) to consider:

1. Does the risk statement and context statement communicate the possible sequence of probabilistic events or stochastic processes leading from the root cause of the uncertainty creating the risk through to the impacted project element and the consequences of that impact?

2. Is the risk based on documentation, individual, or group knowledge?
3. Does the risk involve a change from the project baseline plan for which an adequate contingency plan does not exist? If this affects an existing contingency plan that is believed to be inadequate, the failure of that contingency plan must be addressed in the impact portion of the risk statement.
4. Is the uncertainty (reducible or irreducible) creating the risk factually correct and supported by objective evidence?
5. Is the impact of the risk credible and possible?
6. Does the risk impact at least one project activity requirement that can be objectively measured, described, and characterized?
7. Is the consequence of the risk written without regard to potential handling strategies?
8. Can something be done to prevent, correct, or reduce the likelihood of the impact and severity of the consequence of the risks? If the risk is actionable, a determination is based on current programmatic constraints.

4.2.1.2 Developing Risk-Handling and Contingency Plans

Once the initial risk review is complete, the risk enters a planning phase. During this phase, the risk shall be further analyzed to ensure that the consequence and likelihood scores are correct and the risk has the correct owner. Four basic tasks take place during this phase.

These tasks are:

1. Generate a list of candidate-handling activities.
2. Conduct a risk analysis of each handling alternative.
3. Select the best handling activity for implementation.
4. Implement the selected handling activity.

The RHP includes defining the leading risk driver(s). These drivers are created by the uncertainties that create the risk with the most potential to contribute to a performance shortfall.

For risk created by Epistemic uncertainty, the risk driver can be a single performance parameter, a single event, a set of performance parameters collectively, or a set of events collectively, when varied over their range of uncertainty, causing the performance risk to change from tolerable to intolerable (or perhaps marginal).

For risk created by Aleatory uncertainty, the risk driver is the natural uncertainty in the underlying cost, schedule, or technical processes [9].

A risk driver intends to focus the management risk on potentially controllable situations that present the greatest opportunity for risk reduction. The type of risk response options to be considered for a given risk depends on the nature of the uncertainty that makes it a driver. When uncertainty is primarily caused by system or environment variability, risk reduction is typically accomplished through the correction or prevention of natural variability. Suppose the uncertainty is primarily due to a lack of knowledge. In that case, the response begins with research to better understand the lack of knowledge and proceeds to handling if, after research is complete, the risk is still intolerable.

This Risk assessment produces criteria for determining response options. When the Risk Score is less than or equal to 7, there is no specific requirement to generate a mitigation plan.

4.2.2 Determining the Approach to Handling Risk

All project work is subject to uncertainty that creates risk. The first step the determining the approach to risk-handling is to identify the risks and place them in a Risk Register. Risks are composed of three elements:

1. The risk created by epistemic or aleatory uncertainty.
2. The consequences to the project from the risk.
3. The probability of occurrence for an epistemic uncertainty or the natural variability for an aleatory uncertainty associated with the risk.

With these elements, risks have three types:

1. A known risk is evidenced in the project planning process.
2. An unknown risk that needs to be recognized in the project planning process.
3. An unknowable risk that is possible to be recognized.

The primary role of the risk management process is to identify *known* and *unknown* risks. Risk Planning is the key to establishing a shared understanding of the project's cost, schedule, and performance risks, the sensitivity of the project's probability of success to these parameters, management's tolerance to these risks, and the processes to establishing practical processes to correcting or preventing the risks from impacting the project's probability of success.

In the planning process, key evaluation criteria need to be established, with their assessment of impact on cost, schedule, and technical performance of the project. The characterization of these impacts is highly dependent on the project, the technical domain, the business domain, management's tolerance for risk, regulatory guidance, and other external and internal processes.

Table 4.1 provides a template for assessing potential risks and determining the approach to handling the risk. The Project Team and Stakeholders use this table as a *discussion capture* document to come to agreement on what is meant by *impact on the project of a risk were it to become an issue.*

Table 4.1 The Project Risk Criteria Must Be Determined during the Project Planning Process to Guide the Collection of Project Risks, Assessment of their Impacts and Effectiveness of the Risk-handling Plans on the Probability of Project Success for Any Project Risk Planning to Be Credible

Sample Project Risk Criteria to be Determined During Project Planning Process			
Likelihood of the Occurrence of a Risk	*Low Likelihood*	*Medium Likelihood*	*High Likelihood*
The probability of occurrence or statistical impact of the risk	Define the meaning of low likelihood for the product or service	Define the meaning of medium likelihood for the product or service	Define the meaning of high likelihood for the product or service
Consequences	Define the consequences and their units of measure for each likelihood class		
Business impact – cash flow, profit margin, market acceptability	Using a financial model of the project, the *Net Present Value* adjusted for risk triggers, events, and naturally occurring processes (rain), the that the remaining project work will perform as needed can be assessed and corrective or preventive actions taken to *keep the project GREEN*.		
• Net present value • Product or project support costs • Product or project cost increase • Product sell price reduction	Financial impact covered by *margin* or *management reserve*	Financial impact requires reassessment of project plans or contract performance requirements with a re-planning process	Financial impact requires a replanning of the contractual performance or possibly a new contract or supplier
Service or customer impact – recognized or felt by the end user of the product or project	The defined Capabilities produced by the project in terms of Effectiveness and Performance need Upper and Lower limits		
• Operational performance of product or service • Warrant returns • Maintenance and support of installed products or services	Margins for performance variances can handle variances in product or project deliverables performance	Adjustments to project or service performance with updates or changes in stated capabilities	Redesign or redevelopment of product or service needed to meet needed customer capabilities

(*Continued*)

Table 4.1 (Continued) The Project Risk Criteria Must Be Determined during the Project Planning Process to Guide the Collection of Project Risks, Assessment of their Impacts and Effectiveness of the Risk-handling Plans on the Probability of Project Success for Any Project Risk Planning to Be Credible

Sample Project Risk Criteria to be Determined During Project Planning Process			
Likelihood of the Occurrence of a Risk	*Low Likelihood*	*Medium Likelihood*	*High Likelihood*
Project performance impact recognized as a shortfall by the customer	Project performance is defined by Measures of Effectiveness (MOE), Measures of Performance (MOP), Technical Performance Measures (TPM), and Key Performance Parameters (KPP)		
• Project completion delays • Product delivery delays • Performance shortfalls	Slight shortfall in cost, schedule or technical perform can be protected by margin	Replanning of product or service delivery dates or performance parameters	Redefining of product or service delivery dates or performance parameters
Production impacts	Production flow cane be modeled as a flow process where work is *pushed* through the system or Kanban queues where work or products are *pulled* through the system		
• Changes in production volume creating shortfall in inventory or delivery commitments	Safety stock or buffers for production flow	Replan production runs or expanded buffers (Theory of Constraints)	Redesign production processes
Product or service quality	Quality standards are defined with upper and lower control limits for cost, schedule, and technical performance		
• Product or service efficiency loss • Product or service effectiveness loss • Product or service performance loss	Margins used for standard variances	Safety margins for out of bounds items	Redesign to restore protective margins

With the contents of Table 4.1, the project team and stakeholders can arrive at an agreed assessment of the impacts of risk and the handling strategies to correct or prevent the risk, or actions to be taken when the risk turns into an issue.

4.2.3 Defining the Scope and Actions of Risk-Handling

The risk-handling strategy includes the handling options or combination of options and the specific implementation approach. It answers the question, *what is the plan to address the risk?* or *Should the risk be accepted, avoided, transferred, or mitigated?* After analyzing the risks (in Chapter 3), project management personnel should develop a strategy to manage risks by evaluating the four risk-handling options. The project chooses the best option or hybrid of options based on the risk analysis, prioritization, and potential for risk reduction.

The selected handling plan for project risks should be reflected in the project's Business and Technical Strategy for the relevant decision points and milestones. It should include the specifics of:

- *What* should be done to handle the risk?
- *When* it should these activities be accomplished?
- *Who* is responsible for performing these activities and what is resulting cost, schedule for the work, and what is the expected performance impact to the project after they are performed?
- What *Resources* are needed to implement the RHP?

When selecting the handling option(s) and developing the implementation approach, the risk owner and risk management process should address the following:

- Is the risk-handling strategy (the option[s] and implementation approach) feasible?
- Is the risk-handling strategy affordable regarding funding and any needed additional?
- Resources (e.g., personnel, equipment, facilities)?
- Is adequate time available to develop and implement the risk-handling strategy?
- What impact does the risk-handling strategy have on the overall project schedule?
- What impact will the risk-handling strategy have on the system's technical performance?
- Are the expectations realistic given project circumstances, constraints, and objectives?

Projects and their management can easily fail to identify project risk-handling activities without impacting the planning, requirements, or project budget and resource allocation.

4.3 Implementing the Risk-Handling Plan (RHP)

The primary objective of risk-handling planning is to optimize future project performance concerning risk. The risk-handling planning process described above develops specific actions. It assigns responsibilities to deal with individual risks, capitalize on opportunities cost-effectively, and then collectively deal with the remaining risks through contingency (reserve and recovery plans). The RHP is the output of that process [35].

The RHP describes:

- The specific actions to reduce risks with buydown activities for reducible risks and margin for irreducible risks, focusing on higher-priority risks first.
- The management of contingency to address residual risks and other uncertainties; and
- Recovery plans when the established contingency or margin is inadequate (i.e., to cover the rest of the residual risks and other uncertainties).

4.3.1 Execution of the Risk-Handling Plan

There are two primary approaches to risk-handling described in the RHP:

- Individually and proactively through risk reduction processes of *buy down* or *margin.*
- Collectively and reactively through *contingency* and *management reserve* to execute recovery plans.

In the risk management model, Risk-handling is a proactive process of performing effective actions to reduce risks (e.g., through avoidance or transfer, including risk allocation, by contractually assigning residual risks to a party in the contract) [35].

When the risk-handling processes are ineffective, Contingency management is applied using adequate resources when the residual risk occurs. Recovery plans involve ways to continue the project (possibly changed) if the contingency is exceeded. The RHP documents these activities.

Like all plans, the RHP must be executed successfully to increase the probability of project success. To be successful, the RHP must be executed by staff based on:

- **Responsibility**: Assignment of a risk manager and "owners" of significant individual risks.
- **Commitment**: The organization must commit to the plan.
- **Resources**: Adequate resources (funding and staff) must be provided to carry out the plan.
- **Authority**: Specific individuals have to be given adequate authority and resources for carrying out their assigned plan responsibilities.

4.3.1.1 Successfully Executing the Risk Reduction Plan

Reducing risk starts with a documented *plan* stating the expected outcomes from the handling activities described in the plan. The success of the execution of the plan is based on assessing the impact of the activities as defined through the:

- Planned handling of the uncertainties that create risk. The progress of these handling activities is monitored, and actual impacts are assessed.
- For reducible uncertainties that create probabilistic risk, they may or may not happen during the period of opportunity. Changes to the probability of occurrence and the period in which that probability might occur are assessed and updated.
- When conditions change for both reducible and irreducible uncertainties that create risk, changes to the RHPs are needed.
- When a risk is realized, contingency or margins are consumed to *handle* the risk.

This process of implementing the RHP (including monitoring, updating, and implementing processes of making project decisions regarding contingency, margins, and recovery) needs to be effective, efficient, and compatible with the organizational and project operating principles.

4.3.1.2 Successfully Executing the Risk Allocation Plan

Risk allocation is a specific way to reduce project risks. The contract is the vehicle for risk allocation. Risk allocation affects cost, time, quality, and the potential for disputes, delays, and claims.

The objectives of Risk Allocation address four goals:

- Allocate risk to the party or project participants best able to manage the risk.
- Allocate the risk in alignment with project goals.
- Share the risk when appropriate to accomplish the project goals.
- Seek to allocate risk to encourage team alignment with the project performance goals.

4.3.1.3 Successfully Executing the Risk Contingency Management Plan

Risk contingency, also called *management reserve*, is money included in the Performance Measurement Baseline to *handle* residual risk. If a risk occurs, and its impacts realized, the Performance Measurement Baseline is be adjusted, with costs transferred from Management Reserve to the Performance Measurement Baseline.

Contingency must be carefully managed to ensure it is not misused or wasted and is available when needed. Like any project expenditure, authorizing the use of contingency is subject to Change Management approval.

4.3.1.4 Executing the Risk Recovery Plan

Risk Recovery plans contain specific options available during each phase of project developed to recover project cost or schedule. Each option is available during a particular phase of project development. Examples of recovery plans include:

- Overtime or additional staffing, resources, or equipment to accelerate remaining schedule.
- Reduction, or deferral of project scope to reduce cost.

4.4 Example Risk-Handling Plan

> A Risk-handling Plan (RHP) is prepared by a project manager to addresses risks, their potential impact to a program and consists of way to reduce these risks. The RHP tells the government and contractor team how they plan on reducing risks to a certain level by a certain time. A RHP should be structured to identify, assess, and mitigate risks that have an impact on overall program life-cycle cost, schedule, and/or performance. It should also define the overall program approach to capture and manage root causes.[3]

The RHP describes how the tasks of risk management will be performed, recorded, and monitored throughout the life cycle of the project. The RHP is used by Stakeholders and Project Managers to access risks using the analysis data from Chapter 3, the impacts of these identified and analyzed risks, and responses or measures to deal with these risks. A RHP includes the risk-handling strategies and how those strategies will be applied, when they will be applied, and the expected outcomes from their application. There are four basic strategies being used by managers to deal with the risks to projects like: accept the risks, avoid the risks, mitigate the risks, and transfer the risks. Content of RHP will depend on the nature of the strategy selected. Some of the common contents of the RHP will include list of risks, impacts of risks, times of risks, key personnel and decided responses to the risks.

With the guidance presented in previous section, here are the notional steps in developing a credible RHP. For each event-based risk and each naturally occurring variability in the Risk Register:

1. Develop and document a risk management strategy and show how this strategy is applied to the project to reduce risk in a measurable manner.

2. Establish the purpose and objective of risk management and how performance of *managing in the presence of uncertainty* will be assessed.
3. Establish the cost, schedule, and technical performance risk processes and working structure to identify, analyze, handle with preventive and corrective actions, monitor, and assess the improvement in the probability of project success in the presence of uncertainties that create these risks.
4. Assign responsibilities for each cost, schedule and technical risk, for managing the risk-handling activities – the preventive and corrective action tasks – the period of exposure to the risk, and the measures of effectiveness (MOE) and performance of their outcomes.
5. Document sources of information for risk models to cost, schedule, and technical performance and the data produced from those models.
6. Develop handling strategies for each risk or classes of risk in accordance with the risk source type – Epistemic or Aleatory
7. Establish the reporting and tracking procedures to assess the performance of the risk-handling strategies and take corrective actions with those strategies are not effective.

4.4.1 Risk-Handling Plan Introduction

4.4.1.1 Risk Management Process Overview

Throughout the life of a project, risk management reduces potential risks to an acceptable level before they occur. Risk management is a continuous, forward-looking process applied to anticipate and avert risks that may adversely impact the project and can be considered both a project management and a system engineering process.

When the balance between Systems Engineering and Project Management is achieved, through overall risk management ownership, implementation, and day-to-day responsibility the probability of project success is increased.

The top-level processes for Risk Management needed to achieve this goal include [33].

4.4.1.1.1 Risk Planning

- Clearly define the Roles and Responsibilities of all participants in the risk management process. Who owns the risk, who captures and maintains the risk in the Risk Register, who connects the risks with the cost, schedule models, and technical performance models?
- Define the frequency of the updates of the Risk Register and related documents. This should be no less than every mount. But answer the question: *how long are you willing to wait before you find out you are late?* Asses the progress of handling at one-half the interval
- What are the step-action plans for performing the risk-handling work?

4.4.1.1.2 Risk Identification

- Identify the risk *Triggers* or *Drivers* and the outcomes from the planned sessions for Risk Management.
- Make changes to the Baseline or overall solution approach as a result of identifying new and updating existing risks.
- Discover new risk information affecting the project's delivered capabilities. These discoveries are typically found while accomplishing the work or discussion in related meetings.
- Conduct regularly held meetings, on fine-grained boundaries, to identify and review upcoming risks based on current work.
- Conduct periodic end-to-end full reviews of Risk Register contents with Stakeholders and Project Team to assure existing risks are still applicable and any new risks are properly assessed.
- Formally report results produced after each meeting in the form of an updated *Probability of Project Success.*
- While risk identification is not main focus of each risk meetings, it is always the starting point – *what new risks have been discovered since our last meeting?* This is the basis of Continuous Risk Management.

4.4.1.1.3 Risk Analysis and Impact Modeling

- Modeling of expected cost and schedule using Monte Carlo simulation or some probabilistic analysis algorithm.
- Assess feasibility of meeting cost and schedule to a confidence level defined in the RHP.
- Connect risk events to a timeframe in the baseline plan, to show *period of impact* on the overall project.
- Response Management Plan.
- Recurring attention.
- Tracking and recording of progress on eliminating or reducing risks.
- Consequence or likelihood of occurrence.
- Develop Risk Model.
- Incorporate current baseline information in Acumen and P6.
- Assign general uncertainty distributions for task durations.
- Add event risk from Risk Register.
- Quantify and tie event-based risks to work activities.
- Validate data and run Monte Carlo Simulation.

4.4.1.1.4 Risk Monitoring and Control

The risk monitoring and control evaluates the effectiveness of risk-handling activities against metrics and provide feedback to the other risk management process steps.

Risk monitoring results may also provide a basis to update RHP, develop additional risk-handling options and approaches, and re-analyze risks. The monitoring of the risk-handling results is used to identify new risks, revise an existing risk with a new facet, or revise some aspects of risk planning. This is accomplished through:

- Regular meetings to assess the progress of the risk-handling processes as they are applied to increase the probability of project success.
- Stakeholder or Owner participation in this process to assure the risk communication processes are effective.
- Joint identification and problem solving.
- Facilitated with Risk register.
- Risk-handling activities focused on current work or recent development and assessed for their effectiveness on future developments.
- All process work focused on *institutionalizing* the risk management process.
- Regular part of daily business rhythm.

4.4.1.2 Separating Reducible and Irreducible Uncertainties That Create Risks

The Reducible and Irreducible uncertainties were introduced in Chapter 3. These uncertainties create two forms risk. Reducible risk is where direct actions can lower the probability of occurrence and probability of impact. Irreducible risk where only margin can be applied to protect the outcomes of the risk from impacting the project. This RHP addresses both these types. Since risk is the outcome of Uncertainty, distinguishing between the types of uncertainty in the definition and management of risk on complex systems is useful when building risk assessment and management models.

Risk management success requires we separate these uncertainties to not only increase the clarity of risk communication, making it clear which type of uncertainty can be reduced and which types cannot be reduced, but also establish the basis for the processes of handling the risk. For the risk created by reducible uncertainty (Epistemic) we can develop handling plans to develop the knowledge needed to reduce the risk. For risk created by irreducible uncertainty (Aleatory) only margin can be used to protect the project from the impacts of this uncertainty.

- **Reducible risk:** Risk is due to a lack of knowledge of quantities or processes of the system or the environment. Reducible uncertainty is represented by the ranges of values for parameters, a range of workable models, the level of model detail, multiple expert interpretations, and statistical confidence. Reducible uncertainty derives from a lack of knowledge about the appropriate value to use for a quantity assumed to have a fixed value in the context of a particular analysis. The accumulation of information or actions taken to reduce reducible the uncertainty that eliminates or reduces the likelihood and/or impact of risk. This uncertainty is modeled as a subjective assessment of the knowledge and the probability of occurrence of an undesirable event from that lack of knowledge.

- **Irreducible risk:** A risk from the inherent variation associated with the physical system or the environment. Irreducible uncertainty arises from inherent randomness, natural stochasticity, environmental or structural variation across space and time in the properties or behavior of the system under study. The accumulation of more data or additional information cannot reduce aleatory uncertainty. This uncertainty is modeled as a stochastic process of an inherently random physical model. The projected impact of the risk produced by Aleatory uncertainty can only be addressed through cost, schedule, and/or technical margin.

4.4.1.3 Roles and Responsibilities for the Risk Management of Project

Every member of the Project Team has risk management responsibilities and adheres to the risk management process. Specifically, those responsibilities include:

- Program Manager, Program Management Office, Owner, or Lead Stakeholder(s)
  - Manages contingency risks and applies CR funds accordingly.
  - Supports the overall risk management process through risk integration, identification, and review with the UCEP and Advanced Sources and Detectors (ASD) Project Teams.
  - Ensures the sponsoring project office continues to be informed of the status of project risks with potentially large cost and schedule impacts as soon as they are identified.
  - Approves mitigation/avoidance plans for federal risks and enhancement/exploitation plans for federal opportunities.
  - Formally accepts or rejects the transfer of any risks from the contractor to the federal government.
  - Oversee acceptance and closure of risk owned by the FPD.
  - Serve as the single point of contact between Federal and Contractor staff for all risk-related questions and concerns.
  - Develop an environment in which risk identification is encourages and lessons learned are identified and documented.
- Project Manager
  - Maintain this RHP.
  - Applies a continuous iterative risk management process.
  - Ensure development of Risk Assessments at significant project milestones and as requested by Program Management, Owners, or Stakeholders.
  - Ensure configuration control of the Risk Register.

 - Serve as the Risk Manager or appoints a Risk Manager, as appropriate.
 - Documents and manages risks in the project risk register.
 - Develop, maintain, and provide required risk documentation and reports to appropriate project and project management personnel.
 - Ensure the sponsoring project office continues to be informed of the status of project risks with potentially large cost and schedule impacts as soon as they are identified.
 - Oversee acceptance and closure of risks owned by the Project Manager.
 - Oversee the roles and responsibilities of each Project Team member with respect to risk management.
 - Coordinate with the project's Contracting Officer early in the acquisition process and throughout the project for contract-related risks.
 - Serve as the focal point of communication between the contractor and the project office for all risk-related questions and concerns.
 - Develop an environment in which risk identification is encouraged and lessons learned are identified and documented.
 - Ensure the Owner or Stakeholder is apprised of high-impact risks and any significant changes in risks.
- Risk Manager
  - Maintains this RHP.
  - Plans and schedules risk management priorities and activities.
  - Ensures development of risk assessments at significant project milestones and as requested by the Project Manager.
  - Monitors and assesses implementation of the RHP.
  - Participates in monitoring and addressing project risks.
  - Ensures configuration control of the Risk Register.
- Produces risk metrics and reports, as required.
- Project Team Members, other Subject Matter Experts, and Risk Owners
  - Support the Project Manager throughout the project life cycle in identifying, analyzing, managing, monitoring, and reporting risk.
  - Recommend handling strategies and actions for assigned risks.
  - Develop mitigation/avoidance plans for risks and enhancement/exploitation plans for opportunities.
  - Report status of action items for mitigation and avoidance plans.
  - Recommend closure of assigned risks when the risks have been eliminated or avoided.
  - Provide the Project Manager with documentation in support of closing risks.
  - Maintain continuous awareness of risk status and report significant changes to the Project Manager or Risk Manager.
  - Analyze assigned risks for probability of occurrence and potential impacts.

4.4.2 Managing Project's in the Presence of Uncertainty

With risks identified and analyzed in Chapter 3, the plan(s) to manage the project in the *presence* of uncertainties that create risk, requires a step-by-step process.

4.4.2.1 Risk Management Process

The risk management process starts with the Risk Breakdown Structure (RBS) modeled after the Work Breakdown Structure (WBS). The RBS is an ordered list of the risks – internal or external, anticipated or unforeseen – that can impact the project's scope, schedule, and budget. It's hierarchical and graphical in nature.

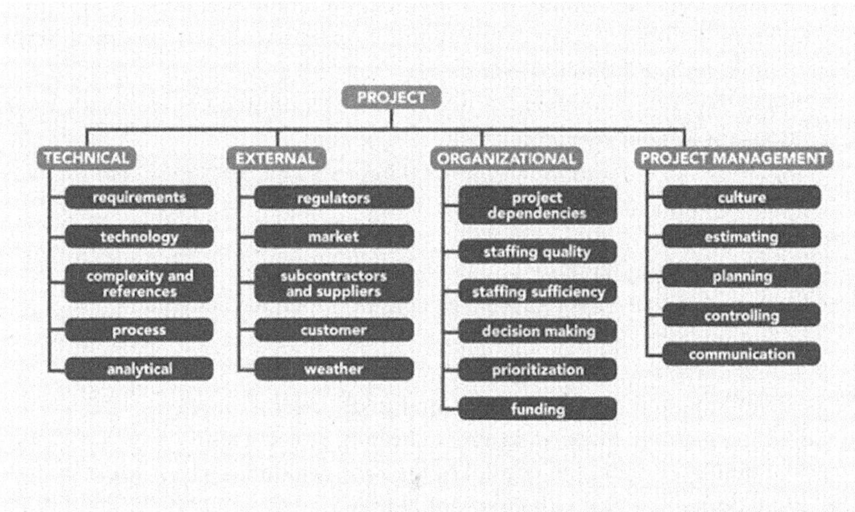

The RBS categorizes project risk into:

- **External risks**: Outside control of the project.
- **Internal risks**: Risk that can be addressed.
- **Technical risks**: Risk to scope or requirements definition and technology.
- **Project management risks**: Risks impacting planning, communication, project control, cost, and scheduling.

With the RBS, project risk management has the following steps:

- **Risk-handling planning**: Prior to the initiation of risk management, activities in the proposed baseline (scope, schedule, and cost) are evaluated to determine their potential for risk. This evaluation (risk screening) assesses all work activities against a set of screening categories in the areas of construction, interface control, safety, regulatory and environmental, security, design, resources, space migration etc. Work activities identified as project risks are tracked within the RSB RHP.

- **Risk identification**: Risks are identified that impact the successful completion of the project. Risks are identified for the entire life cycle of the project. Risk associated with project work scope, cost, and schedule are identified by challenging the assumptions, logic, and scope of the project and examining the identified uncertainties associated with each stage of the project.
- **Risk assessment**: Risks are assessed to determine their Probability of Occurrence and Probability of Impact on the project's cost, schedule, and/or work scope. This includes a qualitative and quantitative assessment of the consequences of the risks and the probability of Occurrence, the period of exposure to the risk, and any residual risk after mitigation activities.
- **Risk-handling**: The risk-handling strategy determines if the risk (in order of preference) it is to eliminate, transfer, prevent, mitigate, or assume (accept the risk).
- **Risk management impact and control actions**: A risk impact assessment is performed on the project and the effect of the risk-handling strategies. Risk-handling strategies are reflected in the project's baseline, and residual risks are reflected in the project contingency.
- **Risk reporting and tracking**: Risk reporting and tracking is the documentation of the risk management process.

4.4.2.1.1 Managing Reducible and Irreducible Risk

Reducible and Irreducible risk creates an overall risk to project success. Separating these risks is a critical success factor for defining how to manage each risk and the possible opportunities that are encountered during the risk management elicitation process shown in Figure 4.1.

4.4.2.1.2 Identifying Programmatic and Technical Risk

The following steps will be used to identify the programmatic and technical risks:

1. Define the reducible and irreducible technical and programmatic risks. These include event-based technical and programmatic risks (reducible) and the naturally occurring variances for work efforts and technical performance (irreducible).
5. Place these risks in a Risk Register. For the Reducible Risks, define the Probability of Occurrence, activities to Mitigate the risk, and the Residual risk after mitigation. For Irreducible Risk, define the Probability Distribution Functions (PDF) for the naturally occurring variance.

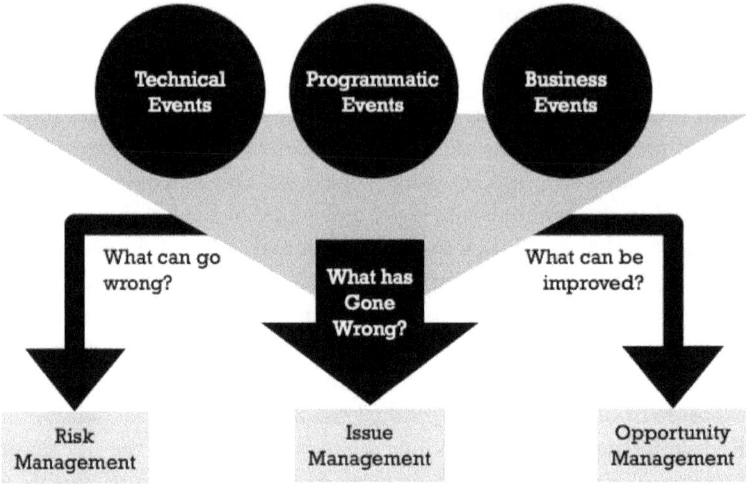

Figure 4.1 Separating technical, programmatic and business (changes in government guidance) risks.

6. Connect these risks to the products and processes in WBS and IMS. For reducible risks with mitigations, define work in the
7. IMS to reduce them or assign budget to Management Reserve to cover the probability the risk will occur. For irreducible risks, with their probability distribution model and resulting variances, assign Schedule Margin to protect schedule delays.
8. Identify when, where, and how to inform Earned Value (BCWP) using the reducible and irreducible risk at the work performance level using project performance per the Earned Value Management System Description.
9. Status the risk reduction plans for reducible risks using the risk Buy Down Plan and use this to inform BCWP with variance between planned and actual risk reduction.
10. Status the performance of irreducible risk (work duration variance) in Margin Burn Down Chart and its impact on future irreducible risk and any adjustments to the PDF from past performance.[4]

4.4.2.2 Risk-Handling Planning

The Project Manager, working with the Project Team, ensures the RHP is implemented to actively identify, assess/analyze, handle, monitor/review, and report risks throughout the life of the project. Risks are identified as early as possible in the project so as to minimize their impact. The steps for accomplishing this are outlined in the following sections. The Project Manager serves as the Risk Manager or may delegate this responsibility. Project risks are reviewed regularly and coordinated with both the Project Team and the project stakeholders.

Risk management funds are established as:

Total Reserve = Contingency Reserve (CR) + Management Reserve (MR)

The stakeholder controls the project CR funds. The Project Manager controls the MR funds.

4.4.2.3 Risk Identification

Identification of risk is an organized approach for determining which events may affect the project and for documenting the characteristics of the events that could happen. Risk identification is the most important phase of the project risk management process.

Risk identification is a continuous process throughout the project's lifecycle. Any change to the cost, schedule, or technical scope of the project triggers an assessment of the current risks and any possible new risks. A RBS is derived from the WBS, assessing each project deliverable for any possible risk to the success of the project.

The risk identification process relies on the experience, insight, and input of the Project Manager and project team members. Risk identification is conducted in advance of critical decision milestones, when a major project risk is unexpectedly realized, or when analyzing significant contract or Baseline Change Proposals.

Risk identification starts by breaking the project elements into a RBS. The RBS is structures and organizes project risks, in one or more hierarchical manners, to demonstrate the most likely source of the risk. The RBS provides an organized list of risks that represents a coherent portrayal of project risk and leads to a broader risk analysis.

4.4.2.4 Root Cause Analysis

Risk management anticipates what could happen in the future with *handling plans* to minimize undesirable consequences of the risk where it to *come true*. Root cause analysis looks incidents in the past to understand how and why the risk turned into an issue. Root Cause Analysis is the method of problem solving that identifies the root causes of failures or problems. A root cause is the source of a problem and its resulting symptom, that once removed, corrects or prevents an undesirable outcome from recurring.

Providing a thorough explanation of why an incident did happen is the prerequisite for mitigating a risk in the future. Most organizations do a poor job investigating their problems. A complex problem can get condensed in an executive summary which provides the truth – but not the whole truth. When important details are omitted an incident gets distorted. Action plans are then developed from

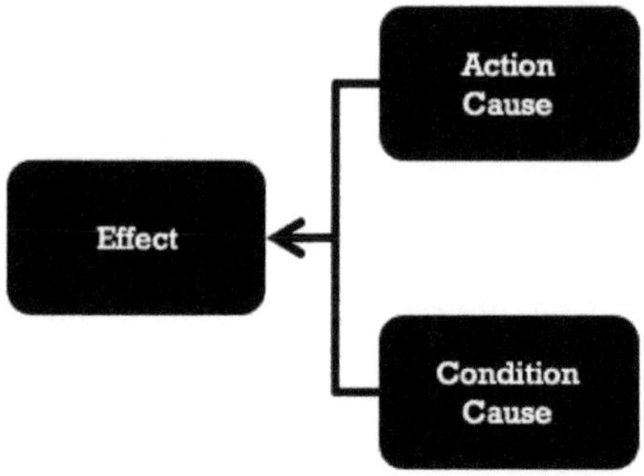

Figure 4.2 The cause-and-effect relationship are the core principle of effective problem solving. Effective problem solving is the core of effective risk management.

an analysis that did not adequately represent the issue. Many people, but not all, are then surprised when a previously unrecognized scenario materializes.

The framework for Root Cause Analysis has three basic elements, connected through causality. Each Effect has two classes of *cause* (Figure 4.2).

A common approach to problem solving categorized causes or identify causal factors and looks for root causes within the categories. These *causes* are the sources of Risk. Categorization schemes do not reveal the cause-and-effect relationships needed to find effective solutions needed to identify and handle risks. It is the effective solution, to *prevent the risk from* occurring, we are after.

We need a structured approach to investigating and analyzing significant adverse events or system deficiencies and their required improvement – not based on Story Telling. We need an approach that provides information and tools to be incorporated into risk management, quality management, independent verification and validation and improvement procedures in order to:

- PREVENT future occurrence of adverse events resulting from a risk *coming true* that *causes* or *can cause* undesired performance of our systems.
- CORRECT the practices, processes, or technical behaviors that lead to identified risks.

This approach to Root Cause Analysis, and the corrective and preventive actions needed to handle the *cause* of risk is the basis of Risk Management of the project.

Direct causes many times result from another set of causes – the intermediate causes – and these may be the result of still other causes. This chain of cause and effect must be revealed in a way that clearly points to the corrective or preventive action need to remove or eliminate a risk. When a chain of cause and their effects is followed from a known end-state (time now), back to an origin or starting point, root cause is revealed, and corrective or preventive actions can be applied. A root cause is an initiating cause of the causal chain which leads to an outcome or effect of interest.

4.4.2.4.1 Principles of Cause and Effect Applied to Risk Management

For each Primary Effect ask *why the Effect Occurs*? Nothing happens without a cause. Every time it is asked *why* two causes must be found – an Action Clause and a Condition cause.

Causes are never part of a Linear Chain found in standard Fishbone diagram or narrative approach. Look for causes to create the effect. Two causes are needed for each Effect. Causes are never part of a Linear Chain found in standard Fishbone diagram or narrative approach.

Look for causes to create the effect. Two causes are needed for each Effect.

- **A condition cause**: May exist prior to the Effect. Or conditions may be in motion or active during the Effect. Conditions are the causes often ignored or beyond our knowledge.
- **An action cause**: Momentary causes that bring conditions together to cause an effect. Actions are causes most easily recognized.

Connect all Actions and Conditions with a Caused By phrase to either an Action or a Condition. Support each Cause with evidence or an answered question. Connect all causes (Actions and Conditions) with a Caused By phrase to either an action or a condition. Support each Cause with evidence or an answered question (Figure 4.3).

4.4.2.4.2 Four Steps in Root Cause Analysis

1. Define the problem:
   - What is the problem that creates the Risk?
   - When did it happen in the past and when might it happen in the future?
   - Where did it happen did it happen in the past and where might it happen in the future?
   - What is the significance of the problem and its impact on a future outcome (impact)?
2. Create the cause-and-effect chart:
   - For the primary effect, ask why did this happen.
   - Look for causes in actions and conditions.
   - Connect all the causes with caused by for the next cause and its effect.
   - Support causes with evidence or an open question.
3. Identify effective handling plans that must be put in place to prevent or corrective the condition or action:
   - Prevent the occurrence or recurrence.

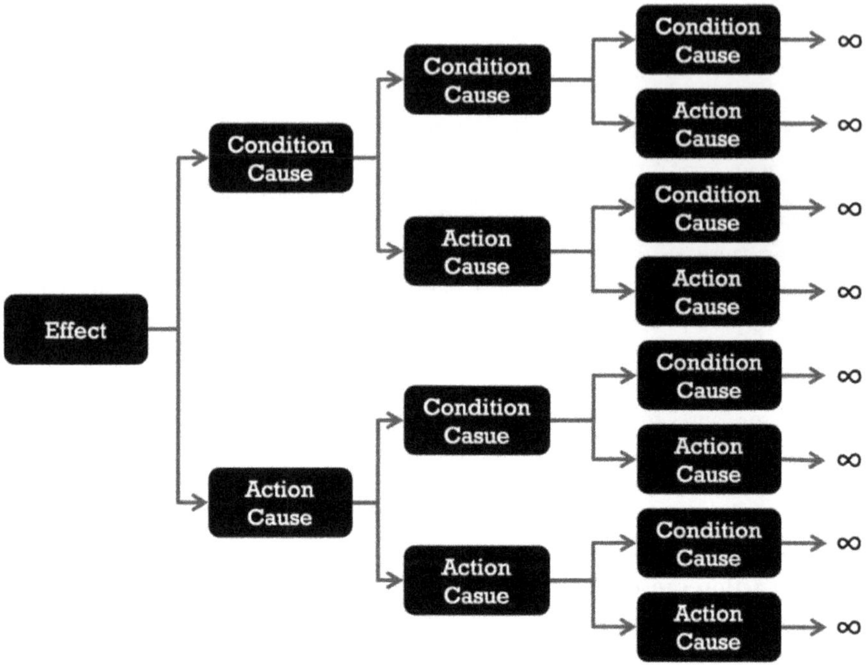

Figure 4.3 Causes are not linear. They branch out into two causes each time it is asked why of an effect and if asked why for each of these causes, there is a never expanding set of causes. For each cause, there is a following action cause and condition cause. Both an action and a condition are needed to create a cause, that creates the effect.

- Be within the control of the project.
- Meet the goals and objectives of the project.

4. Implement the best solutions (handling plan):
   - Measure the effectiveness of these handling plans in units defined in the Action and Condition causes.

4.4.2.4.3 The Culture of Effective Risk Management Using Root Cause Analysis

The culture of Effect Risk Management is based on the following steps:

- Critical Elements – The Work Force should:
  - Be exposed to the principles of causation to understand that "stuff" does not just happen.
  - Should know that we can find effective solutions to event-based problems.

  - Understand that different perspectives are a key to effective solutions and easily accommodated when you use the Reality Charting process.
  - Know their role in defining problems and finding effective solutions to prevent recurrence.
  - Know that management is behind this initiative.
- Infrastructure – Have a plan to implement Root Cause Analysis based Risk Management:
  - Top-level management support.
  - A Program Champion.
  - Dedicated Incident Investigation Facilitators.
  - Incorporation of the Reality Charting process into existing procedures and protocol.
  - Involve every employee in this effective problem-solving initiative.
- Management buy – in and support:
  - Show the effective problem-solving processes to managers so they know the principles of effective problem-solving.
  - Show overview of root cause analysis processes so managers know what the outcomes are and why it is effective for risk management.
  - Provide a workshop on managing effective problem-solving. Discuss applications to Risk-handling strategies and Continuous Improvement to correct or prevent risks
- Create a program champion:
  - **Qualifications**: An experienced incident investigator and facilitator.
  - **Training**: Familiar with RCA concepts
  - **Role**: The *Go To* persons for all things RCA and be able to effectively facilitate incident investigations
- Dedicated risk management employing root cause analysis:
  - **Identify stakeholders**: Who have to solve problems as part of their daily work scope.
  - **Mentoring**: The Program Champions and Risk Manager mentor practitioners and support them to develop skills for conducting Root Cause Analysis in search for the sources of risk, their prevention and correction.

4.4.2.5 Risk Analysis

Once a risk or opportunity has been identified, it is assessed and analyzed two ways: (1) qualitatively – to assist the Project Manager and Risk Owner in establishing the priority for handling, monitoring, and reporting the risk; and (2) quantitatively – to assist the Project Manager and Risk Manager in understanding the impact the risk could have on the project and the adequacy of the contingency available if the risk is realized.

This analysis is performed with the Monte Carlo Simulation tool with its standard processes, independent cost modeling, and Excel to capture risk parameters and general data manipulation.

With selected tool, the Monte Carlo Simulation examines all paths not just the deterministic Critical Path in the schedule, to assess the impact of each risk on cost, schedule, and deliverables.

4.4.2.5.1 Qualitative Risk Analysis

The likelihood and impact of occurrence for each identified risk is assessed by the project team and recorded in the project risk register.

The Risk Owners provide the basis for Probability of Occurrence and Probability of impact(s). A detailed cost estimate or schedule FRAGNET is not necessary at this point. The Risk Owner may cite recent trends or Baseline Change Proposals, risks realized on other projects, or a quick estimate. The use of professional judgment is acceptable if no other information is available.

Identified risks are broken into two groups in the risk register, those identified as existing project risks that are being managed, and potential risks that are listed on a watch list that is reviewed on a regular basis. Those risks on the watch list may be moved to the priority risk register as their particular situational assessment determines.

A matrix determines the impacts of a risk. Each likelihood ranking used in the matrix has a description/score as shown in Tables 3.6 and 3.7 of Chapter 3, and risk levels determined, as shown in Figure 3.7 of Chapter 3.

4.4.2.5.2 Quantitative Risk Analysis

Qualitative risk analysis estimates the impact of risks on project cost and schedule and is a numerical or more objective analysis of the probability and consequence of risks to the overall project through the use of statistical modeling techniques. To this point, this RHP has discussed the most important objectives of the project risk management:

- Decreasing the number of high and moderate risks by establishing meaningful and measurable handling corrective and preventive actions and tracking these actions to closure.
- Maximizing the return on investment to the project by identifying, enhancing, and exploiting opportunities results in meaningful cost and schedule savings for the project.

Quantitative risk analysis determines the amount of cost and schedule contingency needed by the Stakeholder to establish a Total Project Cost at the desired confidence

level, and to inform the likelihood of completing the project on time and on budget. This quantitative risk analysis is usually done with a Monte Carlo-based tool.
For each risk, the Risk Manager documents the likelihood of the risk occurring, assuming successful mitigation, and what the impact of the risk would be under the best case, most likely case, and worst case, in terms of dollars and impact to the critical path. The Results of the Quantitative Risk Analysis with input from the Project Risk Register determines Management Reserve and Contingency Reserve values to be included in the project's cost estimate.

The post-handling strategy likelihood and impacts represent the residual risk. The residual risk impact is zero when employing an *avoid* or *transfer* handling strategy, and results in no cost or schedule contingency. When the handling strategy is *mitigate*, the worst-case residual impact is the same as the unmitigated impact in case the handling strategy fails. The worst-case impact may be reduced if the Risk Owner is certain of the success of the mitigation actions. The residual risk remains the same as the original evaluation when employing the *accept* handling strategy.

The residual risk parameters (risk likelihood, cost, and schedule impact) are inputs to risk analysis and the cost and schedule contingency is determined at a confidence level determined by the Stakeholder. The risks, residual risk parameters, and calculated cost and schedule contingency is published in a risk assessment, prior to Critical Decisions, or as deemed necessary by the Project Manager, when a significant project change occurs.

The Risk Manager provides the Project Manager with a monthly update to the total project risk exposure based on risks closed (avoided or mitigated), new risks opened, and changes in status, probabilities, or impacts for existing risks, and an assessment of the project contingency remaining against the project's current risk exposure.

4.4.2.6 Risk-Handling Strategies

Risk-handling strategies include:

- **Acceptance**: Nothing will be done.
- **Avoidance**: Eliminate the cause of a risk by not encountering the uncertainties.
- **Transfer**: Make another party responsible for the risk (subcontractor, outsource, etc.).
- **Mitigation**: Identify ways to reduce the likelihood or the impact of the risk.

As well as these four primary handling strategies, risks can be *handled* with the following:

- **Exploit**: Convert the cause of the risk into an opportunity [2].
- **Enhance**: Identify ways to increase the likelihood or the impact of the opportunity.
- **Share**: Apportion the benefits of a risk.

4.4.2.6.1 Risk Acceptance Handling Plan

When the risk is accepted, the project acknowledges that the risk event or condition may be realized. Accepting a risk does not mean it should be ignored. It should continue to be tracked through continuous monitoring to ensure the accepted consequences do not change for the worse. The monitoring process should establish knowledge points that provide reevaluation opportunities. Before accepting the risk, the project should identify the resources and schedule that would be needed should the risk be realized. Occasionally, executives and managers must seek relief from the next higher headquarters. Undoubtedly, in constrained environments, programs and executive managers occasionally must accept risk due to competing priorities. However, programs should make every attempt to understand the risk so future efforts are fully informed and strategically planned.

4.4.2.6.2 Risk Avoidance Handling Plan

Through risk avoidance, the project reduces or eliminates the risk event or condition by taking an alternate path. Simply stated, it eliminates the source of the risk and replaces it with a lower-risk solution. Analyzing and reviewing the proposed system in detail provides insight into the drivers for each technical requirement. Examples might be changing operating procedures or using a low-risk mature technology. Risk avoidance may provide the PM with an understanding of what the real needs are and ways of circumventing the risks that are not critical to project cost, schedule, and/or performance. This may require changes to the allocation of project resources, or requirements and specifications that reduce risk to an acceptable level. The avoidance handling option should be used only if the selected implementation approach truly results in the desired effect and reduced risk likelihood and/or consequence.

4.4.2.6.3 Risk Transfer Handling Plan

Risk transfer includes reassigning the risk responsibility to another entity. This approach may involve reallocating a risk from one project to another, between the government and the prime contractor, within government agencies, or even across two sides of an interface managed by the same organization. However, programs should recognize that transference of risk does not eliminate all responsibility and risks must be monitored for potential consequences. A prerequisite for transferring risk is the acknowledgment from the receiving entity that it now owns the risk. For example, a performance risk can be transferred to an external project that is managing the external side of the risk.

4.4.2.6.4 Risk Mitigation Handling Plan

The risk mitigation option seeks to actively reduce risk to an acceptable level before it becomes an issue. Mitigation takes action to reduce the likelihood (probability of occurrence for an epistemic uncertainty or stochastic properties for Aleatory uncertainties), and on occasion the consequence, of a risk to as low as possible in order to minimize potential project impacts. Programs should avoid the tendency to readily select mitigation as the risk-handling option without seriously evaluating the acceptance, avoidance, and transfer options. The mitigation approaches include but are not limited to:

- **Multiple development efforts**: Develop competing systems in parallel that meet the same performance requirements.
- **Alternative design**: Identify an off-ramp design option that uses a lower-risk approach.
- **Trade studies**: Create a balance of engineering requirements in the design of a system.
- **Early prototyping**: Build and test prototypes early in the system development.
- **Incremental development**: Deliver capabilities in incremental releases.
- **Technology maturation**: Technology will replace an existing technology.
- **Robust design**: Apply advanced design and manufacturing techniques to promote quality through design.
- **Reviews, walk-throughs, and inspections**: Reduce the probability and likelihood and potential consequences and impacts of risks with assessment of actual or planned events.
- **Design of experiments**: Identify critical sensitive design factors that create potentially high risk to achieve a particular user requirement.
- **Open systems, standard Items, or software reuse**: Use commercial specifications and standards. Use existing, proven hardware and software where applicable.
- **Mockups**: Explore design options using mockups, especially for man–machine interface.
- **Models and simulation**: Investigate various design options and system requirement levels.
- **Key parameter control boards**: Establish a control board for a parameter when a particular feature (such as system weight) is crucial to achieving the overall project requirements.
- **Test, analyze, and fix**: Plan a period of dedicated testing to identify and correct deficiencies.
- **Demonstration events**: Establish knowledge points that demonstrate whether risks are being abated.
- **Process proofing**: Simulate actual production environments and conditions to ensure repeatedly conforming hardware and software.

The selected handling strategy; action items; and responsible person, due date, and basis for closure of each action item are recorded for each risk in the project risk register.

Examples of mitigation and avoidance strategies that can be used for some of the typical project risks include:

- **Unanticipated field conditions, including contamination, debris, and groundwater**: Take multiple borings and surveys early in the design process, and establish and implement dewatering plans prior to the start of excavation.
- **Changes in sponsoring project requirements**: Ensure a project requirements document has been prepared by the project sponsors, ensure project sponsors participate in all project reviews, and ensure implementation of project requirements are jointly reviewed by the sponsors and the project team on a periodic basis.
- **Delays caused by adverse weather**: Include potential weather delays in schedule uncertainty analysis; plan work on a 4-day-a-week, 10-hour-a-day basis using the fifth day-in-a-week basis in case of bad weather.
- Availability of vendors and materials due to natural disasters consuming availability of electric-related contractors and supplies – coordinate early procurement of long lead materials.
- Project cash flow changes and disruptions due to budget shortfalls and continuing resolutions – plan the project anticipating a continuing resolution at the start of each fiscal year; brief decision-makers on a routine basis, emphasizing milestones and progress made toward achieving milestones; ensure that stakeholders are aware of the impact of potential funding shortfalls; and ensure that contractor meets or exceeds expectations.

4.4.2.7 Risk Monitoring and Reporting

Integrated risk monitoring will conduct risk management metric monitoring integrated with other standard project metrics. This monitoring and reporting begin with the root cause of any negative or positive impact upon a metric to include a determination as to whether it involved a risk including whether it involved the positive benefit-risk known as an opportunity. The output of the reporting process can be the input to the risk management process for further risk identification, analysis of consequence and impact ratings, and the analysis of the handling strategy as planned or as being implemented.

If the project is subject a standard for integration of safety into the design, key risks should be tracked and reported per the requirements of the standard and in relation to the maturity of the project and technical studies that are ongoing. The safety standard provides for developing risk and opportunities assessments relative to safety in design issues and decisions. Given the potentially significant costs associated with safety decisions, the integration of safety into the design process needs to include also a strong link between the development of Safety-in-Design and the identification of project technical and programmatic risks. With anticipated risks, early identification of possible opportunities to address potential risks allows the project to define appropriate cost range estimates. Comprehensive risk identification, coupled with an appropriately conservative safety design posture, affords the project the opportunity to execute within the range estimate with a higher degree of reliability. The project's risks and opportunities assessments are intended to be inputs to its RHP and to be managed accordingly.

Risk monitoring involves the systematic tracking and evaluation of the effectiveness and appropriateness of the risk-handling strategy, techniques, and actions established for each risk. Monitoring is performed on individual risks, and the overall project risk status. Risk discussions are a necessary element of risk communication and feedback and, as much as possible, should become a routine part of standard project progress meetings. Information to be captured in the risk register from the monitoring and reporting phase include the following key element:

- The Comments Section is updated whenever the risk is modified or discussed for the purpose of providing historical information on the evolution of the risk. Any details provided in this section aids project personnel in seeing the evolution of the risk over time. Lessons learned information is captured in this section – when a risk occurs or closes, when handling actions succeed or fail, etc.

The monitoring process is performed by the Risk Manager and Risk Owners to:

- Monitor trigger events.
- Ensure that the Risk Owner shown for each risk is current, and that Risk Owners are performing their responsibilities.
- Ensure that risks, especially low-impact risks, risks on the watch list, and risks with an "accept" handling strategy, have not changed since they were first evaluated.
- Ensure that handling strategy action items are being completed on time and are effective.
- Ensure that information is being updated in the project risk register.
- Ensure that changes made to one risk do not impact other risks or create other potential risks.

All risks with a high impact should be reviewed and reported at regularly scheduled UCEP weekly team meetings. The status of risks with a high impact is provided to the FPD. All risks with a medium impact are reviewed and reported at least quarterly at regularly scheduled project risk meetings. All risks with a low impact should be reviewed and reported at least semiannually at regularly scheduled project risk meetings. Upon closure of a risk, the following information is captured:

- What events led to risk closure?
- If the risk occurred, how did it manifest?
- What lessons learned could be gathered from the way in which the risk unfolded?

This information is captured as a final update to the Comments Section in the risk register.

4.4.2.8 Management and Contingency Reserve

Management Reserve (MR) is budget and part of the Contract Budget Baseline (CBB) and traces to the Performance Baseline.

Contingency Reserve (CR) are funds needed to cover potential cost increases stemming from a variety of project risks. According to best practices, the difference in cost between the project team's estimate and the desired confidence level should determine the required contingency amount.

How much contingency should be allocated to a project beyond the 50% confidence level depends on the project cost growth an agency is willing to risk. While no specific confidence level is considered a best practice, experts agree that project cost estimates should be budgeted to at least the 50% confidence level, but budgeting to a higher level (for example, 70–80%, or the mean) is now common practice.

4.4.2.8.1 Management Reserve Process

MR is the amount of the total contract budget withheld for management control purposes by the provider. MR is not part of the Performance Measurement Baseline nor represented in the IMS. MR is handled in accordance with a Management Reserve, Instruction. A formal Management Reserve assessment is conducted and communicated as described in a Provide guide, based on the thresholds established by Program Management of the project.

4.4.2.8.2 Contingency Reserve (CR) Process

CR is part of the Contract Price, which is associated with possible future events or conditions arising from causes the precis outcomes is indeterminable at the time of the estimate. CR is the portion of the project Performance Base (PB) that is available for risk uncertainty with the project scope, but outside the scope of contract. CR is not to be used to absorb the impacts of cost or schedule overruns. CR is not part of the Performance Measurement Baseline nor represented in the IMS. CR is controlled by Stakeholder personnel as delineated in the Project Execution Plan (PEP).

4.4.2.9 Risk Reporting and Feedback

Risk discussions are a necessary element of risk communication and feedback and, as much as possible, should become a routine part of standard project progress meetings. The Risk Manager reports status of the following risk metrics at weekly Integrated Project Team Risk Management status meetings:

- Risks opened, closed, or realized within the last month.
- Handling strategy action items closed in the last month.
- Overdue handling strategy action items.
- Total risk exposure.

New or emerging risk are added to the Risk Register through the Project Change Control process, on an as-occurrence basis and reviewed during the IPMR review and approval process.

4.5 Risk Register

The risk register is an information repository for each identified risk on project. It provides a common, uniform format to present the identified risks. The level of risk detail may vary depending upon the complexity of the project and the overall risk level presented by the project as determined initially at the initiation phase of the project in accordance with project's business management process.

The fields stated here are those that should appear in the risk register, whether the risks presented are a threat or an opportunity [23].

- **Risk**: Risk as identified and should include the cause, the risk likelihood, and the effect (consider separate sub-fields for each to allow search capabilities on common causes of risks). The preferred statement should be in the affirmative to gain the most effective risk-handling responses or strategies.
- **Risk identification number** : Unique identification number for the risk. WBS, identification number.
- **Risk owner**: Person responsible for tracking, monitoring, documenting, and ensuring the handling response or strategy is implemented and reported upon.
- **Risk category** : Category assigned for grouping or from RBS analysis. Risk Status: Open or closed.
- **Risk assumptions** : Any assumptions pertaining to the risk itself. The identification of assumptions may be clues to other risks.
- **Risk probability and basis**: Likelihood of this event occurring. Use the appropriate qualitative risk analysis matrix.

- **Risk consequence and basis**: Outcome of this event. Use the appropriate qualitative risk analysis matrix.
- **Risk level**: The intersection of the probability and consequence on the appropriate qualitative risk analysis matrix, which determines the overall potential risk impact to the project.
- **Risk monitoring trigger**: Early warning signs that this risk is about to occur.
- **Success metric**: Measure by which the Federal Project Director or Contractor Project Manager will know that the avoidance strategy or handling response or strategy has been successful.
- **Avoidance strategy**: If there is an avoidance strategy to eliminate risk completely it should go in this field. Avoidance is a type of risk-handling strategy.
- **Risk-handling strategy**: Step-by-step (similar to a project plan) approach to eliminating or reducing the risk if no avoidance strategy is immediately available; includes the dates for completion. Include the probability of success for the risk-handling strategy and consider probabilistic branching to account for the handling strategy failing.
- **Cost for Risk-handling strategy**: Necessary cost for implementing the handling strategy.
- **Cost assumptions**: Assumptions that relate to the cost contingency values.
- **Schedule for handling strategy**: Necessary schedule for implementing the risk-handling strategy.
- **Schedule assumptions**: Assumptions that relate to the schedule contingency values.
- **Residual risk**: Remaining risk once the risk-handling strategy is completed.
- **Risk-handling strategy for residual risk**: This may be filled in depending upon the level of risk perceived by the Federal Project Director or the Contractor Project Manager.
- **Residual risk probability and basis**: Likelihood of this event occurring. Use the appropriate qualitative risk analysis matrix.
- **Residual risk consequence and basis**: Outcome of this event. Use the appropriate qualitative risk analysis matrix.
- **Residual risk level**: The intersection of the probability and consequence on the appropriate qualitative risk analysis matrix, which determines the overall potential risk impact to the project. Secondary Risk: Risk arising as a direct result of the implementation of a risk-handling strategy. Secondary Risk Probability and Basis: Likelihood of an event occurring. Use the appropriate qualitative risk analysis matrix.
- **Secondary risk consequence and basis**: Outcome of an event. Use the appropriate qualitative risk analysis matrix.
- **Secondary risk level**: The intersection of the probability and consequence on the appropriate qualitative risk analysis matrix, which determines the overall

potential risk impact to the project. Trigger Date: Early warning sign of the date that this risk is about to occur.
- **Trigger metric**: Event, occurrence, or sequence of events that indicates the risk may be about to occur, or the pre-step for the risk indicating that the risk will be initiated.

The risk register may also include back-up strategies for primary risks, risk-handling strategies for residual and secondary risks, the dates of upcoming or previous risk reviews, and a comment section for historical documentation, lessons learned, and subject matter experts' input.

4.5.1 Risk Capture and Reporting

Risks are captured and recorded using the form shown in the *Risk Detail Sheet*. Each Risk is characterized by the following:

- A unique Risk ID, risk name, description and consequences.
- Risk Owner and the Subprojects affected if that is the case.
- Estimated risk probability, inputs on the cost and schedule, and activity ID's for the work items that are impacts by the Risk Event.
- The risk ranking derived by a combination of risk probability and impacts.
- Risk-handling strategies to reduce the probability and impacts of the risks and to decrease the probability of impact from the risk.
- Risk response plans to be executed if the risk were to happen.
- An evaluation of residual risk with the probability of occurrence and consequences.
- Any comments associated with the Risk.
- A Risk Closure assessment.

4.5.2 Schedule Margin Process

Schedule margin is allowed before project events or key project deliverables. Schedule is a *buffer* to protect from schedule slippage with no assigned resources or budget.

Any significant changes in the IMS requires a narrative of the reasons for these changes. This may include the results of a Schedule Risk Assessment, schedule duration assumptions, and status of the schedule margin. Schedule Margin is used to cover the inherent schedule variances due to naturally occurring processes that cannot be handled. These are Irreducible uncertainties and placed in front of contract events or end item deliverables.

"Activity durations should be estimated under most likely or "normal" conditions, not under optimal, "success-oriented" conditions or with padded durations. Most likely conditions for estimated durations imply that duration estimates do not contain padding or margin for risk. Rather, risk margin should be introduced as separate schedule contingency activities to facilitate proper monitoring by management, as discussed in Best Practices, Durations also should not be unrealistically short or arbitrarily reduced by management to meet a project challenge."[5]

4.5.3 Cost and Schedule Best Practices

Guidance for Cost and Schedule Best Practices form the basis for credible Risk Assessments of two of three elements of the project. Technical Risk Assessment is the third.

A poorly formed, inconsistent, and Illogical Schedule and Cost Baseline and corresponding WBS is a Risk in itself since these documents fail to identify reducible and irreducible risks that impact the contractual deliverables identified in the WBS and WBS Dictionary.

4.5.4 Schedule Ten Best Practices

The schedule for the project will be assessed against the following Ten Best Practices [31]. Effective scheduling depends on 10 characteristics. Any schedules created for the project need to confirm these characteristics are present with tangible evidence. In the absence of this evidence, there is a risk that the schedule is not credible, and this will impact the probability of success of the project.

1. **Capturing all work activities** in the schedule to reflect all deliverables defined in the program's WBS, defining in detail the work necessary to accomplish a project's objectives, including activities both the Federal and Contractors staff and suppliers are to perform.
2. **Sequencing all activities in a manner planned** so that critical project dates can be met. These work activities must be logically sequenced and linked – that is, listed in the order in which they are to be carried out and joined with logic. Any predecessor activity must start or finish before its successor (Finish to Start relationships). Date constraints and lags should be minimized and justified. This ensures that the interdependency of activities collectively leads to the completion of activities or milestones that can be established and used to guide work and measure progress.
3. **Assigning resources to all activities** to reflect labor, materials, travel, facilities, equipment, and the like needed to do the work, whether they will be available when needed, and any constraints on funding or time.
4. **Establishing the duration of all activities** to realistically reflect how long each activity will take. When the duration of each activity is determined, the same rationale, historical data, and assumptions used for cost estimating should be used. Durations should be reasonably short and meaningful and should allow

for discrete progress measurement. Schedules that contain planning and summary planning packages as activities will reflect longer durations until broken into work packages or specific activities.

5. **Verifying the schedule can be traced horizontally and vertically**. The schedule should be horizontally traceable, linking products, deliverables, and outcomes associated with other sequenced activities. These links show the handoffs between tasks and their deliverables and verify that activities are arranged in the correct order for achieving aggregated products, deliverables, and outcomes. The schedule should also be vertically traceable with data are consistent between different levels of a schedule. When the schedule is vertically traceable, lower-level schedules are consistent with upper-level schedule milestones, providing total schedule integrity and enabling different teams to work to the same schedule expectations.
6. **Confirming that the critical path is valid** by identifying the program's critical path – the path of longest duration through the sequence of activities. Establishing a valid critical path is necessary for examining the effects of any activity's slipping along this path. The program's critical path determines the program's earliest completion date and focuses the team's energy and management's attention on the activities that will lead to the project's success.
7. **Ensuring reasonable total float by** identifying the amount of time a predecessor activity can slip before the delay affects the program's estimated finish date – so that the schedule's flexibility can be determined. The length of delay that can be accommodated without the finish date's slipping depends on the number of date constraints within the schedule and the degree of uncertainty in the duration estimates, among other factors, but the activity's total float provides a reasonable estimate of this value. As a general rule, activities along the critical path have the least total float. Unreasonably high total float on an activity or path indicates that schedule logic might be missing or invalid.
8. **Conducting a schedule risk analysis** starts with a good critical path method schedule. Data about project schedule risks are incorporated into a statistical simulation to predict the level of confidence in meeting a program's completion date; to determine the contingency, or reserve of time, needed for a level of confidence; and to identify high-priority risks. Programs should include the results of the schedule risk analysis in constructing an executable baseline schedule.
9. **Updating the schedule** using actual progress and logic to provide a realistic forecast of start and completion dates for project activities. Maintaining the integrity of the schedule logic is necessary to reflect the true status of the program. To ensure that the schedule is properly updated, people responsible for updating should be trained in critical path method scheduling.

10. **Maintaining a baseline schedule** as the basis for managing the project scope, the time period for accomplishing it, and the required resources. The baseline schedule is designated the target schedule and is subjected to a configuration management control process. Program performance is measured, monitored, and reported against the baseline schedule. The schedule should be continually monitored to reveal when forecasted completion dates differ from baseline dates and whether schedule variances affect downstream work. A corresponding basis document explains the overall approach to the program, defines custom fields in the schedule file, details ground rules and assumptions used in developing the schedule, and justifies constraints, lags, long activity durations, and any other unique features of the schedule.

4.5.5 Characteristics of Credible Cost Estimates

Effective cost estimating depends on nine characteristics [32]. Any cost estimates created for the project need to confirm these characteristics are present with tangible evidence. In the absence of this evidence, there is a risk that the cost estimate is not credible, and this will impact the probability of success of the project.

	Characteristic	*Description*
1	Clear Identification of Task	The estimator must be provided with the system description, ground rules, and assumptions, and technical and performance characteristics Estimate's constraints and conditions must be identified to ensure the preparation of a well-documented estimate.
2	Broad participation in preparing estimates	All stakeholders should be involved in deciding mission needs and requirements and in defining system parameters and other characteristics Data should be independently verified for accuracy, completeness, and reliability.
3	Availability of valid data	Numerous sources of suitable, relevant, and available data should be used Relevant, historical data should be used from similar systems to project costs of new systems; these data should be directly related to the system's performance characteristics.
4	Standardized structure for the estimate	A standard WBS, as detailed as possible, should be used, refining it as the cost estimate matures and the system becomes more defined the WBS ensures that no portions of the estimate are omitted and makes it easier to make comparisons to similar systems and programs.

	Characteristic	*Description*
5	Provision for project uncertainties	Uncertainties should be identified, and allowance developed to cover the cost effect Known costs should be included and unknown costs should be allowed for.
6	Recognition of inflation	The estimator should ensure that economic changes, such as inflation, are properly and realistically reflected in the life-cycle cost estimate.
7	Recognition of excluded costs	All costs associated with a system should be included; any excluded costs should be disclosed and given a rationale.
8	Independent review of estimates	Conducting an independent review of an estimate is crucial to establishing confidence in the estimate; the independent reviewer should verify, modify, and correct an estimate to ensure realism, completeness, and consistency.
9	Revision of estimates for significant project changes	Estimates should be updated to reflect changes in a system's design requirements. Large changes that affect costs can significantly influence project decisions.

4.5.6 Steps for Developing a High-Quality Risk-Adjusted Cost Estimate

These 12 steps, when followed, increase the probability of a credible cost estimate. Without these steps, there is a risk that the cost estimate will not be credible. This risk, along with the credibility of the Schedule, have the same impact as other risks to the success of the project.

	Description	*Associated Tasks to Create a Credible Cost Estimate*
1	Define estimate's purpose and schedule	• The estimate's purpose • The level of detail required • Who will receive the estimate • The overall scope of the estimate
2	Develop estimating plan	• The Cost Estimating team • Outline the cost estimating approach • The estimated timeline • Who will do the Independent Estimate? • The Team's master schedule

	Description	*Associated Tasks to Create a Credible Cost Estimate*
3	Obtain data and information	• Identify in a technical baseline description document: • The relationship to Stakeholder's priority projects and capabilities produced by the project • System and performance characteristics • Technology implications • Acquisition schedule and strategy • Risk items • System quantities for development, test, and production • Operation and maintenance plans • Predecessor or similar legacy systems for analogous estimate comparison • Create a data collection plan with an emphasis on collecting current and relevant technical, programmatic, cost, and risk data • Investigate possible data sources • Collect data and normalize them for cost accounting, inflation, learning, and quantity adjustments. • Analyze information for cost drivers, trends, and outliers; compare results against know rules of thumb and standard factors derived from historical data • Investigate/Interview data sources and assess pedigree (reliability, accuracy, completeness, etc.); document all pertinent information
4	Identify ground rules and assumptions	• Clearly define what is included and excluded from the estimate • Identify project-specific assumptions such as the estimate's base year, including time-phasing and life cycle cost assumptions • Schedule information by phase including any schedule or budget constraints • Escalation/inflation assumptions • Equipment and/or materials that the government is to furnish • Use of existing facilities or newly modified facilities. Technology assumptions and new technology to be developed • Commonality with legacy systems • Effects of new ways of doing business

	Description	*Associated Tasks to Create a Credible Cost Estimate*
5	Determine Estimating approach	• Work Breakdown Structure (WBS) • Best estimating method for each WBS element • Potential cross-checks for likely cost and schedule drivers • Develop a cost-estimating checklist
6	Develop Estimate	• Develop the cost model by estimating each WBS element, using the best methodology from the data collected • Include all estimating assumptions in the cost model • Express costs in constant year dollars • Time-phase the results by spreading costs in the years they are expected to occur, based on the master schedule • Sum the WBS elements to develop the overall point estimate • Validate the estimate by checking for errors such as double counting, omitting costs, or factors • Compare estimates against the baseline to identify variances • Perform cross-checks on cost drivers to see if results are similar • Update the model as more data become available or as changes occur; compare results against other and/or previous estimates
7	Conduct Sensitivity and Risk Analysis	• Determine the level of cost, schedule, and technical risk associated with each WBS element and discuss it with technical experts • Analyze each risk for its severity and probability of occurrence • Develop minimum, most likely, and maximum ranges for each element of risk • Use an acceptable statistical analysis model (Monte Carlo simulation) to develop a confidence interval around the point estimate • Determine the type of risk distributions and the reason for their use • Identify the confidence level of the point estimate • Identify the amount of contingency funding and/or management reserve to determine the risk-adjusted estimate • Recommend that the project or project office develop an RHP to track and mitigate risks

	Description	*Associated Tasks to Create a Credible Cost Estimate*
8	Draft Basis of Estimate (BOE) Document	• Document the estimate rules and assumptions • Document all steps used to develop the estimate so that it can be recreated quickly by a cost analyst unfamiliar with the project and produce the same result • Document the purpose of the estimate, the team that prepared it, who approved the estimate, and on what date • Describe the project, including the schedule and technical baseline used to create the estimate • Present the time-phased life-cycle cost of the project • Include auditable and traceable data sources for each cost element • Describe estimating methodology and rationale • Document all data sources on how the data were normalized
9	Perform QA and QC and Peer reviews	• Thoroughly review BOE to avoid errors and omissions • Validate that standard policies and procedures have been followed, that and requirements have been met to ensure a high-quality estimate • Ensure that Stakeholder cost estimating goals have been achieved
10	Present Estimate for Approval	• Ensure BOE has an executive summary • Develop a briefing that presents the documented life cycle cost for management approval including: • An explanation of the technical and programmatic baseline and any uncertainties • Comparison to prior and analogous projects, prior estimates, and baselines • Enough detail to present and defend the estimate by showing its completeness, accuracy, and high quality • Act on and document management feedback. • The cost estimating team should request acceptance/approval of the estimate
11	Check/Validate and update estimate to reflect actual cost data and conduct variance analysis	• Update the estimate to: • Reflect changes in project scope and/or assumptions • Keep current as the project passes through key milestones and critical points • Replace estimates with EVM and actual costs at completion • Assess variances from actual and estimated costs and document lessons learned

	Description	Associated Tasks to Create a Credible Cost Estimate
12	Store Estimate data in a database	• Document estimate, costs, parameters, drivers, and changes that occurred that affected the estimate

Notes

1 Many risk management texts speak about *mitigation* of risk. Mitigation is one risk-handling strategies.Others include: Avoid, Control, Accept, Transfer (ACAT).

2 The Risk-handling Plan is not the same as a Risk-handling Plan, which documents how risk are identify, impacts estimated, and responses defined. This chapter speaks only to the risk response aspect of the Risk Management process.

3 "Risk & Safety Management: Risk-handling Plan (RHP)," http://acqnotes.com/acqnote/tasks/risk-management-plan

4 This is a critical success factor for the Management of Risk. *Learning* from Reducible Risk and Irreducible Risk performance to inform future risk management performance is part of the Risk Management processes using Monte Carlo Simulation.

5 From GAO Cost Estimating and Assessment Guide, "Estimate Durations," pp. 64.

References

1. "*Effective Risk Management: Some Keys to Success*," 2nd ed., Edmund H. Conrow, American Institute of Aeronautics and Astronautics, 2003.
2. "Opportunity Management: Be Careful What You Ask For," Edmund H. Conrow and Robert N. Charette, *Defense Acquisition Technology & Logistics*, Defense Acquisition University, March–April 2008.
3. "The Official Rules: 5,427 Laws, Principles ad Axioms to Help You Cope with Crises, Deadlines, Bad Luck, Rude Behavior, Red Tape, and Attacks by Inanimate Objects," Paul Dickson, Courier Corporation, p. 76, Dover Publications, 21 November 2003.
4. "Chief Executives Define Their Own Data Needs", John F. Rockart, *Harvard Business Review*, pp. 81–93, 1979.
5. "Guidelines for Risk Management: S3001," Version G, NASA Independent Verification & Validation Program, 16 October 2017.
6. "Risk and Risk-Handling Strategies in Construction Projects," Manpreet Kaur and Rajwinder Singh, *International Journal of Management Studies*, Volume V, Issue-1(4), January 2018.
7. "Managing Project Uncertainty: From Variation to Chaos," Arnoud De Meyer, Christoph H. Loch, and Michael T. Pich, *Singapore Management University, Institutional Knowledge at Singapore Management University*, 12-2002.
8. "Choosing a Project Risk-Handling Strategy: An Analytical Model," Miao Fan, Neng-Pai, and Chwen Sheu, *International Journal of Production Economics*, Volume 112, pp. 700–713, 2008.

9. "*Risk Analysis: Uncertainty Characterization in Risk Analysis for Decision-Making Practice*," Enrico Zio and Nicola Pedroni, FonCSI, Securite Industrielle, 2012–2007
10. Management of Risk in Information Technology Projects," David Baccarini, Geoff Salm and Peter E. D. Love, *Industrial Management & Data Systems*, Volume 104, Number 4, 2004
11. "The Effectiveness of Risk Management: An Analysis of Project Risk Planning Across Industries and Countries," Ofer Zwikael and Mark Ahn, *Risk Analysis*, Volume 31, No. 1, 2011.
12. "Planning Deconstructed: 5 Types of Planning Crucial to Delivering on Strategy with a Dynamic and Continuous Approach," Plan View, info.planview.com
13. "Planning Effort as an Effective Risk Management Tool," O. Zwikael and A. Sadeh, *Journal of Operations Management*, Volume 25, Issue 4, pp. 775–767, 2007.
14. "Software Risk Management: Principles and Practices," Barry W. Boehm, *IEEE Software*, Volume 8, Issue 1, January 1991.
15. "*The Owner's Role in Project Risk Management*," Committee for Oversight and Assessment of U.S. Department of Energy Project Management, National Research Council, 2005.
16. "Deliberate Ignorance in Project Risk Management," Elmar Kutsch and Mark Hall, *International Journal of Project Management*, 28, pp. 245–255, 2010.
17. "*Management of Novel Projects under Conditions of High Uncertainty*," Arnoud De Meyer, Christoph H. Loch, and Michael T. Pich, Judge Business School, University of Cambridge, 2006.
18. "*Department of Defense Risk Management Guide for Defense Acquisition Systems*," 7th ed. (Interim Release), December 2014.
19. "*Department of Defense Risk, Issue, and Opportunity Management Guide for Defense Acquisition Programs*," January 2017.
20. "Risk Management: Current Issues and Challenges," Edited by Nerija Banaitiene, InTech, 2016.
21. "*Risk Management and Simulation*," Aparna Gupta, CRC Press, 2014.
22. "*Fundamentals of Risk Management: Understanding, Evaluating, and Implementing Effective Risk Management*," 4th ed., Paul Hopkin, IRM, 2017.
23. "Risk Management Guide," DOE G 413.3-7A Chg 1, 22 October 2015.
24. "*Department of Defense Risk Management Guide for Defense Acquisition Programs*," 7th ed., December 2014.
25 "*Tutorial: Risk Analysis and Monte Carlo Simulation*," Dan Fylstra, *International Solver*, July 2017.
26 "*Fundamentals of Risk Management*," 5th ed., Paul Hopkin, IRM, Kogan Page.
27. "The Effectiveness of Risk Management: An Analysis of Project Risk Planning Across Industries and Countries," Ofer Zwikael and Mark Ahn, *Risk Analysis*, Volume 31, Issue 1, 2011.
28. "*Quantitative Risk Analysis Support to Decision-Making for New Systems*," Robert W. Youngblood III, Homayoon Dezfuli, Idaho National Laboratory, May 2019.
29. "*A Comparison of Risk Assessment Techniques from Qualitative to Quantitative*," Thomas J. Altenbach, Lawrence Livermore National Laboratory, 1995.

30. "*An Introduction to Team Risk Management*," R. P. Higuera, et al., CMU/SEI-94-SR-1, Software Engineering Institute, May 1994.
31. GAO-16-89G, Schedule Assessment Guide, Best Practices for Project Schedules.
32. GAO-09-3SP GAO Cost Estimating and Assessment Guide.
33. "*Risk Management*," Guide to the Systems Engineering Body of Knowledge.
34. "IEC/FDIS 31010 – Risk Management – Risk Assessment Techniques," 2009.
35. "*Guide for the Process of Managing Risk on Rapid Renewal Projects*," National Academies of Sciences, Engineering, and Medicine, The National Academies Press, 2012.

Chapter 5

Risk Tracking

Measure what is measurable, and make measurable what is not so.

- Galileo Galilei [1]

Up to this point, potential risks, symptoms of those risks should these come to fruition, and the proposed response are all identified, leading us to track and monitor these potentialities. Project risk tracking is essential for project success. The project will not likely achieve success by gathering this information to ignore. One could easily argue that the project manager's significant role in developing a focus on the project and risk management throughout the project lifecycle.

5.1 Risk Tracking

Project risk tracking is monitoring the potential risks associated with a project throughout its lifecycle. This is not to suggest that identifying and assessing risk are terminated once the project is underway; it is not so. Those previous identification activities continue with the project; however, without comparing the risks considered against those observed, the actions considered effective responses to each specific risk identified are contrived.

Risk tracking helps ensure project success; by tracking risks throughout the project lifecycle, organizations can initiate those risk response actions quickly, reducing the severity of impact and helping ensure that the project stays on track, on budget, and meets its objectives.

Risk tracking is part of proactive risk management, allowing organizations to take a proactive and continuous approach to project risk management. Risk tracking facilitates better decision-making, but by better understanding the risks associated

 DOI: 10.1201/9781003425465-5

with a project, organizations can make more informed decisions about allocating resources, prioritizing tasks, and managing timelines. Much of this happens long before the potential risk can occur.

Risk tracking improves communication, facilitating communication and collaboration among project team members by keeping everyone informed about potential risks and their status via the risk management log. The recording and tracking of these potential difficulties, recorded, make the dissemination of a shared understanding when coupled with a common lexicon. Every team member has access to the list of risks, with some team members, those closest to specific individual risks, often part of the monitoring. These team members monitor specific attributes or parameter states. This input informs the project of the proximity to risk occurrence [2].

Risk tracking reduces cost by making it possible for the organization to avoid costly and time-consuming problems down the line or time taken to determine the approach required in the throes of the impact of the risk on the project and the team. This avoidance planning helps save money and resources spent on remediation efforts.

5.1.1 Triggers

A risk trigger is an event or condition that, when it occurs, indicates that a particular risk has materialized or become more likely to occur. In other words, a risk trigger is a signal that alerts you to the fact that a risk event has either occurred or is about to happen and that you need to take action to mitigate or manage that risk.

For example, a risk trigger for a construction project might be severe weather, which could delay the project timeline and increase costs. The project schedule will account for an average number of work days lost due to weather, ten days per year. For example, in the first year of a two-year project, halfway through that first year, the team lost six days due to the weather. This project plan may identify six days lost in 6 months as excessive stops due to weather. In project risk planning, this might be a trigger threshold to invoke other actions to prevent schedule violations.

Identifying risk triggers is essential to risk management, as it allows you to mitigate risks before they become actual problems proactively. By monitoring risk triggers, you can take appropriate action to prevent or minimize the impact of troubles on your project or organization. In addition, identifying symptoms (trends or specific attributes) can be the telegraph of an emerging (risk) event.

5.1.2 Contingency

A contingency in project risk management is a reaction plan to an untoward event; in short, we plan for the failure and specific response in the event we see that event emerging. The threshold at which we will decide to initiate action, or enact our contingency efforts, is referred to as a trigger. For a catalyst to "fire," we must set a threshold value that activates our response in such a way as to meet the risk successfully. Firing early or late is not a practical approach.

Thresholds are set based on financial, schedule, and quality anomalies. For example, if our project is running more than a pre-decided percent of the budget at a specific milestone, we would expect to trigger corrective action up to and including executive involvement. Budgetary deviations are bad enough, but it is common for projects to run into scheduling issues. We want the schedule triggers to fire as early as possible for the following reasons:

- Immediate corrective action.
- Inform the customer or project sponsor, even if internal.
- Bring in upper management (escalation plan) to remove identified barriers.

Unfortunately, quality issues and their associated triggers are often unfired until late in product development. Part of the explanation lies in the fact that we typically rely on testing to ascertain the quality, and we generally cannot test until we have at least a prototype version of the product.

It is insufficient to have a trigger when we pass a threshold – we should also plan for the reaction explicitly and in detail. Even better is to use failure mode and effects analysis (FMEA) to assess our tasking and see if we can anticipate the failure and remedy the issue, thereby preventing the loss from ever occurring.

5.2 WBS, Schedule, and Cost

5.2.1 WBS

A Work Breakdown Structure (WBS) is a tool used in project management that breaks down a project into a hierarchy of deliverables, each of which can be estimated and assigned to a team member or a group for completion (Figure 5.1). This disaggregation helps:

1. **Provides a clear project scope**: The WBS defines the scope and size of the project, breaking it down into smaller, more manageable components. This breakdown ensures that everyone involved in the project understands the organization's expectations of them and the project goals.
2. **Facilitates communication**: The WBS provides a common language for all stakeholders, making it easier to communicate the project status, progress, and issues. It also helps to ensure everyone is on the same page, working toward the same goal.

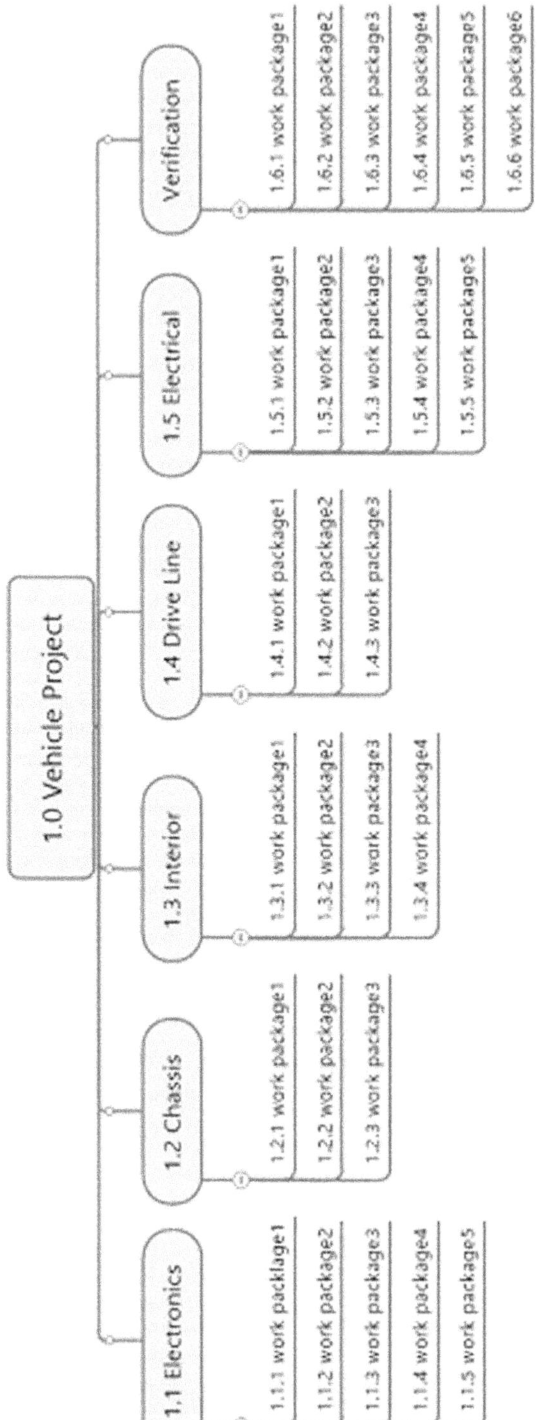

Figure 5.1 An example of a work breakdown structure (WBS).

3. **Simplifies project planning**: The WBS simplifies project planning by breaking the project into smaller, more manageable components. Disaggregation makes estimating project timelines, assigning resources, and managing risks easier.
4. **Helps with resource allocation**: The WBS makes allocating resources to specific tasks easier based on the project's needs. Disaggregation ensures that resources and talent are efficiently employed, reducing waste, and unnecessary costs.
5. **Enables better cost management**: The WBS allows for more accurate cost estimation and tracking, helping to ensure that the project stays within budget.
6. **Facilitates project tracking and monitoring**: The WBS provides a clear roadmap for the project, making tracking progress, and monitoring performance against the project plan easier.
7. **Improves risk management**: The WBS helps identify and manage project risks by breaking the project into smaller components, making it easier to identify potential risks and develop mitigation strategies.
8. **Enhances project quality**: The WBS enables better project quality management by breaking the project into smaller components, allowing for more focused quality control efforts.

The WBS is a tree diagram that breaks the project into progressively smaller and more manageable components; it illustrates the disaggregation of project scope. The top level of the WBS is the overall project, subdivided into smaller and more specific elements. Each level of the WBS is further broken down into more specific and manageable pieces until each part is small enough to be assigned to a team member or group.

The WBS helps project managers identify all the work products required to complete a project, reducing the risk of missing items associated with the project's scope. In addition, the WBS helps with estimating due to the disaggregation of the project scope and can connect individual work products to individuals or departments. This connection of talent to work products ensures we have at least considered the talent required, thus reducing associated risks. Finally, the WBS and this connection of work products to cost and duration estimates, and ultimately the work as performed, provides metrics and a baseline for tracking performance. Changes to the scope, cost, or schedule objectives will require changes to the project baselines.

5.2.2 Baselines

There are three areas for the project's baselines: scope, schedule, and cost (project artifacts). The baseline is a fundamental component of project management that ensures that the latest approved version of the scope, cost, and schedule plans and constraints is available. Projects are subject to changes, and the change control system of the project ensures that only approved changes impact the scope, schedule, and cost, and these plans are updated accordingly.

Controlled updates to these critical documents ensure the team works toward the latest objective according to cost and schedule. In addition, document updates provide a reference point throughout the project's life cycle. For example, when it is necessary to alter or adapt the project schedule, an approval process will result in an updated schedule, the new schedule baseline. From experience, lack of project change controls and scope, schedule, and cost baselines are sources of project failures.

Here are some ways in which the schedule baseline is essential to project management:

1. **Provides an updated plan**: The schedule baseline establishes an approved (valid) plan for the project, outlining the tasks and the timeline for completion. The baseline is the latest version of the project artifact; the team has confidence in the schedule reflecting the latest project circumstances and approved changes.
2. **Enables project tracking**: The schedule, cost, and schedule baseline provide a reference point for tracking progress. By comparing the project progress to the baseline, the project manager can identify any delays or deviations and take corrective action as necessary.
3. **Facilitates project communication**: The schedule baseline provides a common understanding of the project's timeline and progress, enabling effective communication among the project team, stakeholders, and sponsors.
4. **Enables project forecasting**: These baselines allow forecasting of the project's completion date, budget, scope, and resource requirements. Forecasting helps the project manager to anticipate any potential issues and plan accordingly.
5. **Supports project control**: The schedule baseline enables effective project control by providing a framework for measuring and managing project performance. Baselines allow the project manager to monitor progress, identify issues, and take corrective action to keep the project on track.

The baseline concept is a critical component of project management, providing a clear plan for the project's execution, enabling effective tracking and communication, and supporting project change control and forecasting. When things change, external or internally initiated, a response is required. The WBS and these project baselines are part of the earned value management (EVM; Figure 5.2).

5.2.3 Earned Value Management

EVM [3] is a project management technique that integrates project scope, schedule, and cost objectives. It helps project managers assess project performance by comparing a project's planned and actual progress regarding its size, scope, schedule, and cost. EVM provides a comprehensive framework for measuring project progress,

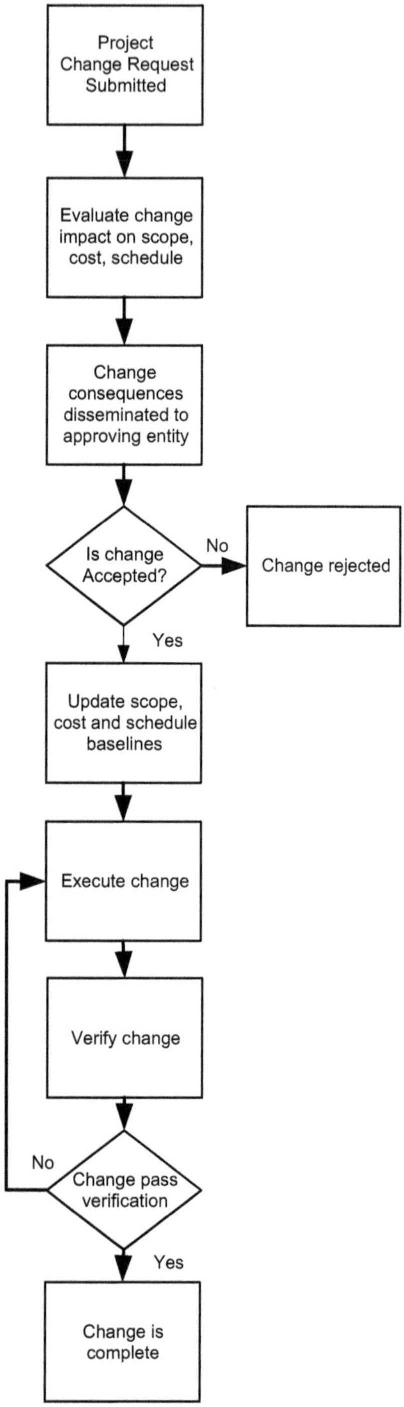

Figure 5.2 An example of a change management process.

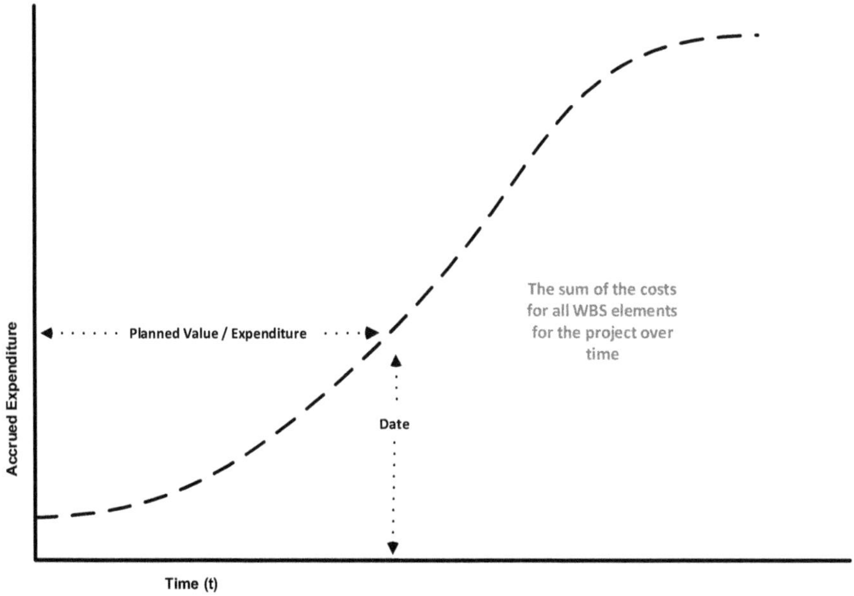

Figure 5.3 An example of a planned value curve.

identifying variances from the baseline plan, and taking corrective actions to ensure project success (Figure 5.3).

There are three key elements to EVM:

1. **Budgeted Cost of Work Scheduled (BCWS)**: Represents the authorized budget allocated for the work scheduled at a given time.
2. **Budgeted Cost of Work Performed (BCWP)**: Represents the value of the work completed at a given time.
3. **Actual Cost of Work Performed (ACWP)**: Represents the actual cost incurred for completing the work scheduled and performed (Figure 5.4).

Using these three elements, project managers can calculate various performance metrics, such as Schedule Performance Index (SPI), Cost Performance Index (CPI), and Estimate At Completion (EAC). These metrics provide insight into the project's overall health and help project managers identify potential problems early, allowing for timely corrective actions.

CPI is a ratio that describes the effectiveness of the project via dollars; the closer to \$1, the closer the project is to performing as expected relative to cost.

$$\text{CPI} = \frac{\text{EV}}{\text{AC}}$$

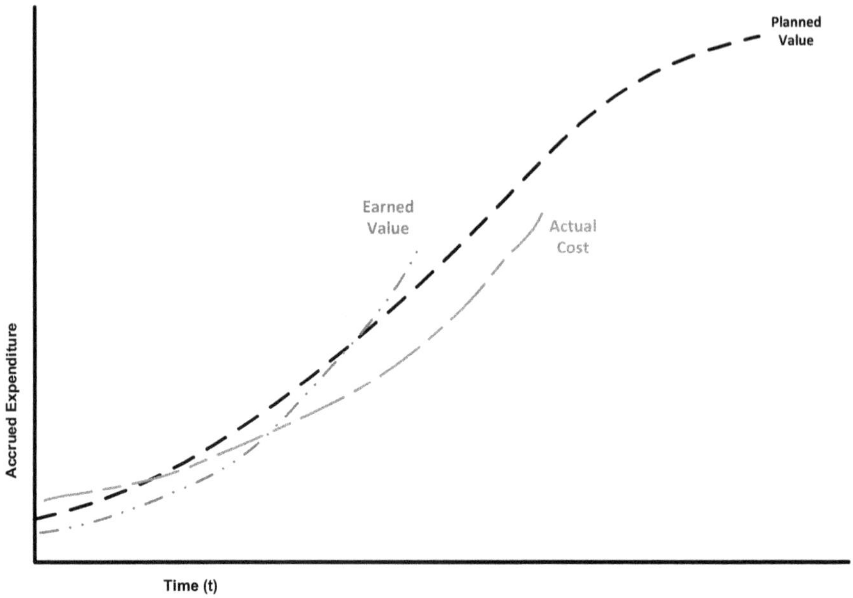

Figure 5.4 An example of earned value curves.

SPI describes the effectiveness of the work progress; unity means execution is in line with the project plan, greater than unity implies the project is performing better than planned, and less than agreement means the work is progressing slower than planned.

$$\text{SPI} = \frac{\text{EV}}{\text{PV}}$$

Cost variance (CV) describes the project's budget performance. A negative CV, the project is over budget; a positive CV, the project is under budget 0, the project is performing per the plan.

$$\text{Cost variance} = \text{EV} - \text{AC}$$

Schedule variance (SV) describes the project's performance against the planned schedule. A negative SV, the project is behind schedule; a positive SV, the project is ahead of schedule.

$$\text{Schedule variance} = \text{EV} - \text{PV}$$

The results of these equations make it possible to make predictions about the project. For example, consider a project one million dollar Budget at Completion (BAC) with a CPI of 0.85. It is then possible to calculate an Estimate A Completion (EAC).

$$\text{EAC} = \frac{\text{BAC}}{\text{CPI}}$$

Prediction is a significant role of the project manager and is part of identifying emerging risks. Like the estimate at completion (EAC), the Variance at Completion (VAC) provides an estimate of the delta or difference in cost to complete the project from the present baseline.

$$\text{VAC} = \text{BAC} - \text{EAC}$$

The To-Complete Performance Index (TCPI) is a key metric used in EVM to assess the projected efficiency required for the remaining work to achieve specific project goals or targets. It helps project managers evaluate how efficiently they can utilize the remaining budget to complete the project within the planned cost.

$$\text{TCPI} = \frac{(\text{BAC} - \text{EV})}{(\text{BAC} - \text{AC})}$$

- **TCPI > 1**: Indicates that the project needs to be more cost-efficient in the remaining work than it has been to achieve the budgeted goal. It implies that cost savings or efficiencies are necessary to complete the project within the planned budget.
- **TCPI = 1**: Suggests that the project needs to continue at the same cost-efficiency level to complete within the planned budget.
- **TCPI < 1**: Implies that the project execution has been more cost-efficient than planned. This better execution condition provides a margin for the remaining work; it can be completed less cost-effectively and perhaps still achieve the budgeted goal.

By monitoring the TCPI throughout the project, project managers can gain insights into the cost performance required in the remaining work to meet the budgeted objectives. It helps them make informed decisions and take corrective actions to ensure the project is completed within the allocated budget and on schedule. Setting up the project in a way to be able to track the performance, identify key metrics, and continuously monitor it can warn the project team of the project schedule and cost risks.

EVM is used mainly in the construction, engineering, and defense industries. It is a powerful tool for assessing project performance and ensuring project success. However, there are many prerequisites and difficulties, and one of the reasons for Agile approaches.

5.2.4 Difficulties

There are a few difficulties when using EVM; for example, the planned performance is compared against the estimates, and the EVM information, therefore, is only as good as the veracity of the forecast. Comparing the actual performance to poor estimates will not be very informative to the project manager. Therefore, it is prudent for the project manager to question even the positive performance indicators, as this could be an estimated problem.

The project EVM metrics tracked should have defined boundary areas similar to margins in mechanical tolerances. Mechanical tolerances refer to the allowable variation or deviation from a specified dimension or characteristic in a mechanical component or system. Tolerances are essential in manufacturing and engineering to ensure that parts fit together, perform their intended function, and meet the required quality standards. Rather than expecting perfect performance or a single point of performance, for example, 1.0 SPI or CPI, express this as tolerances. For example, set a range of performance with boundaries where actions in response may be required.

Before implementing EVM, there are a few prerequisites that must be in place to ensure the successful application of this technique:

1. **A clear project scope**: A clear understanding of the scope is essential to apply EVM. The project scope should be detailed and broken down into manageable work packages.
2. **A well-defined WBS** is a hierarchical decomposition of the project scope into manageable work packages. It provides a framework for organizing and managing the project work and is a prerequisite for implementing EVM.
3. **Clear metrics** associated with the progress of the project work, for example, metrics related to percent completion, to objectively assess the completion.
4. **A detailed project schedule**: A detailed project schedule should include all the activities and their planned start and end dates. The project schedule is broken down into smaller periods (such as weeks or months) to facilitate EVM analysis.
5. **A baseline plan**: A baseline plan is the approved plan for the project scope, schedule, and cost. It serves as the reference for measuring project performance and is a prerequisite for implementing EVM. All of these plans should fall under change management controls.
6. **A project management information system (PMIS)**: A PMIS software tool provides project managers with the necessary information to manage the project effectively. It should be capable of tracking project progress, costs, and schedule information.
7. **Trained project team**: The project team should be trained in EVM concepts and techniques to ensure a common understanding of the method and to facilitate its implementation.

8. **Commitment from stakeholders**: Stakeholders should be committed to using EVM as a project management tool and willing to invest the necessary resources for its implementation.
9. **Reporting systems**: The effort should include a repeatable time reporting system; specifically, time and material reporting must be traceable to specific work products.

5.3 Metric Gathering

Project management and metric gathering are closely related, as metrics provide the data that project managers need to monitor and evaluate the progress of a project, including the cost, scope, and schedule metrics, as well as the status of potential risk items. Metrics are quantitative measures that can assess various aspects of a project, such as schedule performance, budget performance, quality, and customer satisfaction. Here are some examples of metrics that project managers may gather:

1. **Schedule performance**: This metric tracks the actual progress of the project against the planned schedule. The schedule is measured in terms of completed tasks or completion percentage and calculated using EVM. However, individual task completion and associated hours.
2. **Cost performance**: This metric tracks the project's actual cost against the planned budget.
3. **Quality**: This metric tracks the quality of the project deliverables in terms of defects or errors. This set of metrics might include reviews of product artifacts or interim deliverables and product performance attributes.
4. **Customer satisfaction**: This metric tracks the fulfillment of the project's customers or stakeholders through surveys or feedback.

Project managers can use metrics to monitor performance, identify improvement areas, and make data-driven decisions. Gathering metrics can also help project managers to identify potential risks and take corrective action to avoid project delays or failures.

To effectively gather metrics, project managers must identify the key performance indicators (KPIs) relevant to their project and establish a system for collecting and analyzing data. Metric gathering can involve using project management software or tools to track real-time metrics and generate reports that provide insights into project performance.

5.3.1 Consequences of Poor or Lack of Measurements

Measurements can be significant to the project risk exposure. Correctly identified, sampled, and interpreted provide feedback on the actions taken. Poorly conducted or lack of measures can have severe consequences for organizations, including:

1. **Inaccurate decision-making**: Poor measurements can result in incorrect data, leading to flawed decision-making. Suppose a project uses incomplete, outdated, or unreliable data. In that case, it may make decisions not in its best interest, including changing strategies or tactics and promptly responding to emerging conditions.
2. **Wasted resources**: If a project is not measuring the right things or mismeasuring things, they may waste valuable resources on objectives not aligned with their strategic goals. This waste can lead to wasting time, money, and other resources, being over budget, and being late to deliver.
3. **Poor performance**: If a project is not measuring the right things or is measuring things poorly, it may be unable to identify areas where performance lags and possible improvements. Lack of measures can result in poor overall performance, negatively impacting customer satisfaction, employee morale, and profitability.
4. **Missed opportunities**: Poor measurements can also result in missed opportunities for growth and improvement. If a project is not tracking the right metrics, it may not be able to identify risks and the nature of those risks on the project.
5. **Loss of credibility**: If a project's measurements are inaccurate or unreliable, that project's credibility is lost. This creditability loss can damage the reputation and make attracting customers, investors, or other stakeholders more difficult.

Poor measurements can have significant consequences for the project, including inaccurate decision-making, wasted resources, poor performance, missed opportunities, and loss of credibility. Conversely, successful projects establish clear metrics and measurement processes to collect accurate and reliable data to drive informed decision-making and continuous improvement.

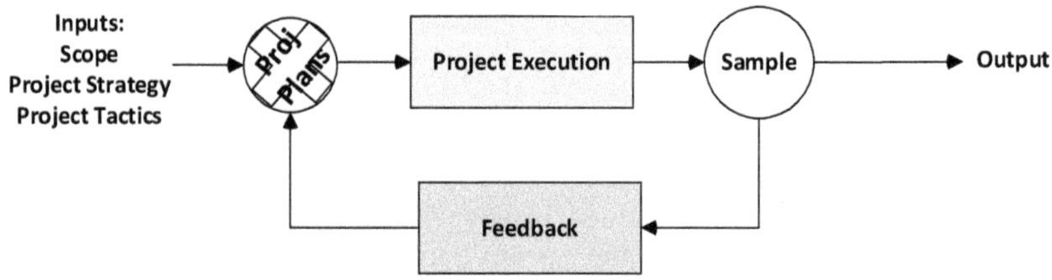

5.3.2 Identify What Matters

> The essence of strategy is choosing what not to do.
>
> *Michael Porter [4]*

Strategy, tactics, and metrics are interrelated and interdependent concepts. Projects use these concepts to achieve project goals and objectives. Projects select strategies and tactics to achieve the purposes of the project. A start with a common lexicon:

1. Strategy is an organization's overall plan to achieve its long-term goals and objectives. A well-defined strategy provides a clear direction for the organization, outlining the key objectives, target customers, and the value proposition that the organization offers.
2. Tactics are an organization's specific actions and initiatives to execute its strategy. Tactics focus on achieving short-term goals and objectives to support the strategic plan.
3. Metrics are the project's quantifiable method of tracking progress and performance toward specific goals and objectives. In addition, metrics provide feedback on the effectiveness of the tactics used to execute the strategy and help organizations evaluate the success of their strategic plans.

Metrics are quantifiable measures to track progress and performance toward specific goals and objectives. In addition, metrics help to evaluate the effectiveness of the tactics being used to execute the strategy and provide feedback on the success of the overall strategic plan. This way, metrics provide feedback to assess the project's selected strategy and tactics.

Strategy, tactics, and metrics are interconnected concepts to achieve the project's goals and objectives. A well-defined strategy provides the overall direction for the project, tactics are the specific actions used to execute the strategy, and metrics are the quantifiable measures used to track progress toward achieving the goals outlined in the strategy (Figure 5.5).

Selecting a poor strategy and tactics can lead to failure, and some of those failures can be painful. Using metrics to help the team assess the selected project approaches will lead to the desired results. Metrics provide a basis for evaluating actions taken against desired or expected results.

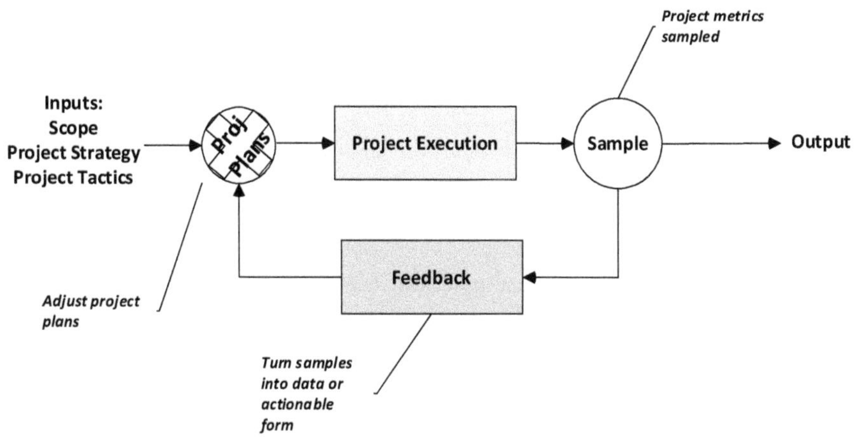

Figure 5.5 Closed loop system example connected to risk management and metrics.

5.3.2.1 Metric Gathering

How we gather the metrics, precisely how and what is measured, will impact the project results. Much like poor measurements from a carpenter building, a cabinet will result in a poorly constructed structure, rework, high costs, and ultimately failure. Determining what to measure and how to take those measurements can be complicated. Those taking the measurements influence the result of the measurements, the tools used, and the sampling approach determined [5]. Variations in each of these elements will impact the measurement. In equation form, the variation in the data:

$$\sigma^2 = \sigma_p^2 + \sigma_s^2 + \sigma_m^2$$

where:

σ_s = variation due to sampling;

σ_p = variation due to process; and

σ_m = variation measurement reproducibility.

Consistency in the approach to measurements will help with repeatability. An example of the process for gathering metrics involves the following steps:

1. **Define the objective**: Clearly define what needs to be measured and why.
2. **Identify the key metrics**: Determine which will best help you achieve your objective.
3. **Choose the data sources**: Decide where the data will come from and who and how it will be collected.
4. **Develop a data collection plan**: Specify the method, frequency, and duration of data collection.
5. **Collect and store the data:** Ensure that the data is collected accurately and stored in a secure and accessible location.
6. **Clean and analyze the data:** Remove any inaccuracies or outliers and perform necessary analyses.
7. **Communicate the results**: Present the analysis results clearly and clearly.
8. **Continuously monitor and update**: Regularly review and update the metrics to ensure they remain relevant and accurate.

It's important to note that, where practical, the measurement process should be well-documented, repeatable, and scalable to ensure that the metrics are reliable and meaningful.

5.3.2.2 Metric Gathering Gone Wrong

There is likely not much difference in consequences between not measuring or measuring poorly. However, several types of errors can occur when gathering metrics.

Since there is a strong connection between metrics and the ability to predict, it is incumbent upon the project manager and project team to understand how to gather metrics and what commonly goes wrong.

Some of the things that can, exploration of the things that can go wrong in metrics gathering:

1. **Sampling error** occurs when the sample used for measurement does not accurately represent the population studied.
2. **Measurement error** occurs when the data is collected inaccurately or with an errant or poorly calibrated measurement tool.
3. **Observer bias** occurs when the person collecting the data influences the results (one of many biases plaguing project management).
4. **Data coding error** occurs when data is improperly recorded or coded during data entry.
6. **Confounding variables**: This occurs when other factors besides the one being measured influence the results.
7. **Data integrity** issues occur when the data is altered or deleted during storage or transmission.
8. **Selection bias** occurs when the sample is not randomly selected, leading to a biased representation of the population studied.

Not tracking or errantly tracking, from experience, will probably lead to the same outcome, failure.

5.3.2.3 Minimize Errors in Metrics Gathering

Knowing what can go wrong is only partly helpful. So here are some ways to minimize errors in metric gathering:

1. **Define clear objectives**: Clearly define what needs to be measured and why so that the correct data is collected.
2. **Choose appropriate data sources**: Select data sources that are reliable and relevant to the objective.
3. **Use random sampling**: Ensure that the sample used for measurement is randomly selected to represent the studied population.
4. **Validate measurement tools**: Ensure that all measurement tools, such as questionnaires or instruments, are validated and adequately calibrated.
5. **Train data collectors**: Provide training to data collectors to minimize observer bias and ensure consistent data collection practices.
6. **Use double data entry**: Implement double data entry to minimize coding errors and ensure data integrity.
8. **Control for confounding variables**: Consider and control for potential confounding variables to minimize their influence on the results.

9. **Perform quality control**: Implement a rigorous process to ensure accurate and error-free data.
10. **Continuously evaluate and improve**: Continuously evaluate and improve the metrics-gathering process to ensure that the results are reliable and meaningful.

Metrics provide information for decision-making. Making decisions based on poor or missing information are different roads with a common destination based upon luck.

5.4 Developing a Risk Tracking Plan – 413.3b-7

Part of an effective risk management process is the risk tracking plan. This plan serves as a repository of the identified risks, the symptoms, and the planned response. The risk register or risk tracking plan is the repository for the identified risks and actions we intend to take should the risk be encountered.

The US Department of Energy's Risk Management Guide (413.3-7A) is a comprehensive description of the content of a risk register [6]; see below:

- Project title and code (denotes how the project is in the tracking system used by the site office and contractor, often via alphanumeric designator and name).
- Unique risk identifier (determined by the individual site).
- Risk statement (consider separate sub-fields to capture cause/risk/effect format to facilitate automated search capabilities on common causes of risks).
- Risk category (project, technical, internal, external, and any sub-category that may be deemed unique to the project, such as safety or environment).
- Risk owner.
- Risk assumptions.
- Probability of risk occurrence and basis.
- The consequence of risk occurrence and basis.
- Risk cause/effect.
- Trigger event.
- Handling strategy (type and step-wise approach with metrics, who has the action, planned dates, and actual completion dates). Include the probability of success for the risk-handling strategy and consider probabilistic branching to account for the handling strategy failing.
- Success metric for overall handling strategy.
- Residual risks.
- Secondary risks.
- Status (open/closed) and basis.

5.4.1 Recurring Risk Tracking Meeting

A recurring risk tracking meeting reviews and updates the status of risks and the effectiveness of the risk management strategies. The meeting aims to ensure continuous monitoring and that the risk management process remains effective. The following are some of the critical elements of recurring risk-tracking discussions:

1. **Agenda**: Establish an agenda that clearly outlines the purpose and goals of the meeting.
2. **Participants**: Invite critical stakeholders responsible for risk management and have relevant information to share.
3. **Review of risks**: Review the current status of each threat, including any new dangers that have arisen, and assess the effectiveness of the risk management strategies.
4. **Discussion of risk management strategies**: Discuss any necessary changes to the risk management strategies based on the status of the risks.
5. **Reporting**: Prepare and distribute a report that summarizes the outcomes of the meeting, including any updates to the risk management strategies.
6. **Action items**: Assign action items to participants to ensure the record of meeting decisions. Consider keeping the action items posted in an easily updated area where updates are quickly done (for example, SharePoint)
7. **Follow-up**: Schedule a follow-up meeting to review the progress of the action items and continue monitoring the risks.

Having regular risk-tracking meetings helps keep the risk management process on track and ensures addressing the risks promptly.

5.4.2 Setting Up a Risk Register

A risk register is a document or tool to manage organizational or project risks. The risk register is a log of the risk items discovered in the identification portion; this includes the specific metrics (symptoms), who is responsible, when to articulate, and identified actions to initiate when breaching the trigger. In addition, the risk register will be part of the project review meetings. This register will include reviews of the items on the risk register and identifying emergent issues that may become a risk.

The following are the steps to set up a risk register:

1. **Determine the scope**: Of the risk register, identifying the risks to include and the level of detail.
2. **Identify the risks**: That could impact the organization or project, done through brainstorming sessions, risk assessments, or reviewing project plans.

3. **Assess the risks**: And the potential impact of each identified risk to prioritize and focus on the most damaging risks.
4. Prioritize the risks based on their likelihood and impact.
5. **Document the risks**: In the risk register, include a description of the risk, the likelihood and impact, and the current status.
6. **Develop risk management strategies**: To mitigate, transfer, or accept each risk based on its priority.
7. **Assign responsibility**: For implementing the risk management strategies and monitoring the risks.
8. **Regularly update**: The risk register to reflect changes in the status of the risks and the effectiveness of the risk management strategies.

A well-structured and comprehensive risk register helps ensure effective management and that the risk management process is well-informed and efficient. From experience, it is good to have the entire team access the risk register; this includes updating it as deemed appropriate.

5.4.3 Establishing Risk-Tracking Metrics

Establishing risk-tracking metrics is a crucial part of the risk processes. Use metrics to measure the effectiveness of the risk management strategies and identify improvement areas. The following are some of the critical steps to establish risk-tracking metrics:

1. **Define the objectives**: Clearly define the risk management process's objectives and intended metrics to provide.
2. **Identify potential metrics**: Identify the possible metrics used to assess the risk management strategies' effectiveness and the risks' status.
3. **Evaluate the metrics**: Evaluate the potential metrics based on their relevance, accuracy, and ease of measurement.
4. **Select the metrics**: Select the most relevant and useful metrics for the risk management process.
5. **Define the measurement criteria**: Define the measurement criteria for each metric, such as the data sources and the methods for collecting the data.
6. **Establish a reporting process**: Establish a reporting process for the metrics, including who will receive the reports and how often they will be produced.
7. **Implement the metrics**: Implement the selected metrics and establish a process for collecting and analyzing the data.
8. **Continuously evaluate and improve**: Continuously evaluate and improve the metrics based on their effectiveness and relevance, and update them as needed.

Having effective risk-tracking metrics helps in predicting. These also ensure that the risk management process is well-informed, efficient, and effective. Metrics are what allow differentiation between opinion and occurrence.

5.4.4 Designing Risk-Tracking Reports

Designing risk-tracking reports is part of the risk management process; how are we articulating these metrics? The reports help to communicate the status of risks and the effectiveness of the risk management strategies. The following are the steps to design risk-tracking reports. Who needs to know what and how do we display in ways that are quickly understood?

1. Define the purpose of the risk tracking report, including the information the report intends to provide and the audience for the info.
2. Select the information to include reports, such as the status of each risk, the likelihood and impact of each risk, and the effectiveness of the risk management strategies.
3. Determine the report format, such as a table, graph, or dashboard.
4. Choose the visualizations used to present the information, such as bar charts, pie charts, or heat maps.
5. Establish a regular reporting schedule, such as monthly or quarterly, to ensure that the risk management process remains well-informed and efficient.
6. Review and test the report to ensure the information is accurate and the message is easy to understand.
7. Continuously improve the report based on feedback from stakeholders and changing requirements.

Having effective risk-tracking reports helps to ensure that risks are effectively managed and that the risk management process is well-informed and efficient.

5.4.5 Ensuring Risk-Tracking Stakeholders Are Engaged

Engaging stakeholders is an essential aspect of the risk-tracking process as it helps to ensure that the process is well-informed, efficient, and effective. The following are some critical steps to ensure that risk-tracking stakeholders are engaged:

1. **Identify stakeholders**: Who will be involved in the risk management process, including internal and external stakeholders?
2. **Define their roles**: What are the roles and responsibilities of each stakeholder in the risk management process?
3. **Communicate the process**: The risk management process and the information provided to each stakeholder, including the risk tracking reports and metrics.
4. **Involve stakeholders in risk assessments**: Involve stakeholders in risk assessments to ensure the identification of all relevant risks and the risk management strategies are well-articulated throughout the project team.

5. **Provide regular updates**: Provide regular updates on the status of risks and the effectiveness of the risk management strategies to keep stakeholders informed.
6. Encourage feedback from stakeholders on the risk management process and the risk tracking reports and metrics.
7. **Continuously evaluate and improve**: Continuously evaluate and improve the risk management process based on feedback from stakeholders and changing requirements.

Engaging stakeholders helps ensure the risk management process is well-informed, efficient, and effective and that the risk-tracking reports and metrics provide relevant information.

> Nothing will ever be attempted if all possible objections must be first overcome.
>
> *Samuel Johnson [7]*

5.5 Implementing a Risk Tracking System

Project size and the organization's risk sensitivity will influence the approach to risk management. For de minimis projects, tracking risks may not require formalized methods. On the other hand, costly projects or projects that can have severe consequences on the customer are good candidates for a more formal risk management approach.

5.5.1 Choosing the Right Risk-Tracking Tool

Choosing the right risk-tracking tool is an important decision that can significantly impact the efficiency and effectiveness of the risk management process. The following are some key factors to consider when choosing a risk-tracking tool:

1. **Purpose**: Clearly define the purpose of the risk tracking tool, including the information it needs to provide and the stakeholders who will use it.
2. **Features**: Consider the features of the risk tracking tool, including the ability to identify and prioritize risks, assess likelihood and impact, and manage risk mitigation strategies.
3. **Ease of use**: Ensure that the risk-tracking tool is easy to use and does not require extensive training or technical skills.
4. **Integration**: Consider the ability of the risk-tracking tool to integrate with other systems and tools, such as project management or financial management tools.
5. **Security**: Consider the risk tracking tool's security and data protection measures, primarily if it will be used to store confidential information.

6. **Cost**: Consider the cost of the risk tracking tool, including upfront costs, recurring costs, and any additional services or support.
7. **User feedback**: Consider user feedback and reviews from other organizations that have used the risk tracking tool to ensure that it meets the needs of similar organizations.
8. **Support**: Consider the level of support and customer service provided by the vendor of the risk tracking tool, including access to documentation, training, and technical support.

Choosing the right risk-tracking tool can help to ensure that the risk management process is well-informed, efficient, and effective and that the risk-tracking reports and metrics provide relevant information.

5.5.2 Integrating Risk Tracking with Project Management Software

Integrating risk tracking with project management software can be a valuable way to improve the efficiency and effectiveness of the risk management process. The following are some critical steps to integrate risk tracking with project management software:

1. **Identify the project management software**: Choose the software used to integrate with the risk tracking tool.
2. **Assess compatibility**: Assess the compatibility of the risk tracking tool and the project management software, including the ability to exchange data and perform automated tasks.
3. **Establish a common data structure**: Establish a standard data structure, such as a risk register, to be easily exchanged between the two tools, or ideally, one tool that spans the project lifecycle and domains.
4. **Automate workflows**: Automate workflows between the risk tracking tool and the project management software, such as automatically updating the risk status in the project management software when updating the risk in the risk tracking tool.
5. **Define reporting requirements**: Define the reporting requirements for the integration, including the information provided in risk tracking reports and the format.
6. **Test the integration**: To ensure the accurate data exchange between the tools and domains and the automated workflows function correctly.
7. **Train users**: Train users on the integration and ensure they understand how to use the tools effectively.
8. **Continuously improve**: Evaluate and improve the integration based on user feedback and changing requirements.

Integrating risk tracking with project management software can help to ensure that the risk management process is well-informed, efficient, and effective and that the risk tracking reports and metrics provide relevant and useful information.

5.5.3 Setting Up a Risk-Tracking Dashboard

Setting up a risk-tracking dashboard can be a valuable tool for monitoring and managing risks in a project or organization. Besides the identification, analysis, and assessment, the following steps to set up a risk tracking dashboard:

1. **Choose a dashboard tool**: Many tools help you visualize your risk data. Choose a tool that is easy to use by the team and allows you to customize the dashboard to meet your project needs.
2. **Define the dashboard metrics**: Determine the key metrics that you want to track on your dashboard. These might include the number of risks identified, the likelihood and impact of each risk, the status, and any actions taken to mitigate the risk.
3. **Build the dashboard**: Once you have determined the metrics, it's time to build it. First, use your chosen tool to represent your risk data visually. Next, ensure your dashboard is easy to read and understand and provides a clear overview of your risk management status.
4. **Update the dashboard regularly**: Keeping your dashboard updated with the latest risk information is essential. Update it regularly to ensure that you are aware of any changes in risk status and can take appropriate action.

Reviewing the risk dashboard as part of the project team meetings is prudent. A risk register that goes unreviewed is similar to not performing risk management.

5.5.4 Implementing Risk-Tracking Workflows

Implementing risk-tracking workflows is an essential step in ensuring the efficiency and effectiveness of the risk management process. The following are the steps to implement risk-tracking workflows:

1. **Define the risk management process**, including the steps involved in identifying, assessing, managing, and monitoring risks.
2. **Identify the stakeholders** involved in the risk management process, including risk owners, managers, and team members.
3. **Define the roles and responsibilities** of each stakeholder, including who is responsible for identifying risks, who is accountable for assessing likelihood and impact, and who is responsible for managing risk mitigation strategies.
4. **Choose a risk tracking tool** to manage the risk management process, including identifying, assessing, managing, and monitoring risks.

5. **Establish a standard data structure**: such as a risk register and data from measurement, to ensure all stakeholders can access the same risk information.
6. **Automate workflows**: Automate workflows between the risk tracking tool and other tools, such as project management software, to ensure the data is accurate and up-to-date.
7. **Train users**: Train users on the risk tracking tool and ensure they can use it effectively.
8. **Continuously improve**: Evaluate and improve the risk management process and the risk tracking workflows based on user feedback and changing requirements.

Implementing risk-tracking workflows can help to ensure that the risk management process is well-informed, efficient, and effective and that the risk-tracking reports and metrics provide relevant information.

5.5.5 Documenting Risk-Tracking Procedures

To document risk-tracking procedures, follow these steps:

1. **Identify and define the risks**: Start by identifying the risks associated with your project or organization. Then, describe each risk in detail and assign a priority level.
2. **Develop a risk tracking matrix**: Create a matrix that outlines the risks, their likelihood of occurrence, and their potential impact. This matrix will be the basis for tracking and monitoring risks over time.
3. **Establish risk response plans**: Develop a plan outlining the steps to take if the threat materializes for each identified risk. The response may include risk mitigation, avoidance (strategy or tactic change), or acceptance.
4. **Assign responsibility**: Assign responsibility for monitoring and updating the risk matrix and risk response plans to a specific individual or team.
5. **Establish a schedule for risk reviews**: Regular risk reviews are essential to ensure that the risk matrix and response plans are up-to-date and reflect any changes to the project or organization.
6. **Document procedures**: Document all risk tracking procedures, including the matrix, response plans, and schedule for risk reviews, and make sure that all relevant stakeholders have access to the documentation.
7. **Continuously monitor and update**: Continuously monitor and update the risk matrix and response plans as needed to reflect changes in the project or organization.

5.6 Monitoring and Adjusting Risk Tracking

The control system is as good as the monitoring and administering of controlling actions. Monitoring includes the discovery of emergent issues. Those risks identified at the beginning of the project may not come to pass, and the team makes progress, specifically newly identified threats. Constant monitoring applies to the identified risks, and eyes are open for emergent events.

5.6.1 Regularly Reviewing Risk-Tracking Data

To regularly review risk tracking data, follow these steps:

1. **Schedule regular risk reviews**: Establish a schedule for regular risk reviews, such as monthly or quarterly, depending on the nature and complexity of your project or organization.
2. **Review the risk matrix**: Review the risk matrix to assess any changes in the likelihood or impact of each risk.
3. **Evaluate risk response plans**: Evaluate the effectiveness of the risk response plans and determine if any changes are needed.
4. **Identify new risks**: Look for any previously unknown threats that have arisen since the last review and add them to the risk matrix.
5. **Update documentation**: Update and share the risk matrix and response plans to reflect any changes and ensure the updated documentation with all relevant stakeholders.
6. **Assess overall risk level**: Assess the general risk level of the project or organization and determine if any additional risk management measures are necessary.
7. **Communicate findings**: Communicate the risk review results to relevant stakeholders, including any changes to the risk matrix and response plans.
8. **Incorporate feedback**: Incorporate stakeholder feedback into the risk management process and make any necessary changes.
9. **Repeat the process**: Review risk tracking data regularly to ensure that your risk management efforts are practical and up-to-date.

5.6.2 Updating Risk-Tracking Metrics

To update risk-tracking metrics, follow these steps:

1. **Review the risk matrix**: Regularly review it to ensure that it accurately reflects the risks' current status and the likelihood of occurrence.
2. **Update risk likelihood and impact**: Update the probability and effect of each risk based on new information or changes in the project or organization.
3. **Evaluate risk response plans**: Evaluate the effectiveness of the current risk response plans and determine if any changes are needed.
4. **Add new risks**: Add any unknown risks that have arisen since the last review to the risk matrix.

5. **Update risk matrix**: Update the risk matrix to reflect changes in each risk's likelihood, impact, and response plans.
6. **Document updates**: Document all updates to the risk matrix and response plans and ensure all relevant stakeholders can access the updated documentation.
7. **Communicate changes**: Communicate any changes in the risk matrix and response plans to relevant stakeholders.
8. **Repeat the process**: Regularly update risk tracking metrics to ensure your risk management efforts are practical and up-to-date.

5.6.3 Refining Risk-Tracking Processes

To refine risk-tracking processes, follow these steps:

1. **Evaluate current processes**: Evaluate the current risk-tracking processes to determine their effectiveness and identify areas for improvement.
2. **Solicit feedback**: Solicit feedback from stakeholders, including project team members, management, and other relevant parties, to gain a better understanding of their perspectives and needs.
3. **Analyze data**: Analyze data collected from risk-tracking efforts to identify trends, patterns, and areas for improvement.
4. **Identify best practices**: Research and identify best risk tracking and management practices to incorporate into the current processes.
5. **Develop an action plan**: Develop an action plan outlining the steps to improve risk-tracking processes, including specific goals and timelines.
6. **Implement changes**: Implement the changes to the risk tracking processes, incorporating feedback and best practices as appropriate.
7. **Monitor progress**: Regularly monitor progress to ensure that the changes have the desired effect and that risk-tracking processes are becoming more effective.
8. **Continuously refine**: Continuously refine risk-tracking processes over time to ensure that they remain effective and aligned with the needs of the project or organization.
9. **Document processes**: Document the refined risk-tracking processes to ensure consistency and make training new team members easier.

5.6.4 Communicating Risk-Tracking Information

From experience, prompt responses are critical to a successful response during risk exposure. However, this requires communication, and depending upon the distribution of the team, this can be a challenge. To communicate risk-tracking information effectively, follow these steps:

1. **Determine audience**: Identify the stakeholders who need to receive the risk-tracking information and determine their level of interest and expertise.
2. **Choose the correct format**: The most appropriate format for communicating the information, such as a report, presentation, or dashboard.
3. **Present information clearly**: Present the information clearly and concisely, using visual aids such as charts and graphs to help explain complex information.
4. **Emphasize key points**: Emphasize the critical issues of the risk tracking information, including the likelihood and impact of each risk and the steps taken to manage them.
5. Provide context for the risk tracking information by explaining how it relates to the overall project or organization.
6. **Encourage questions**: Encourage questions and discussion from stakeholders to help ensure everyone understands the information clearly.
7. **Follow-up**: Follow up with stakeholders after communicating the information to ensure they understand the risks and the steps to manage them.
8. **Update information**: Regularly update the risk tracking information to ensure stakeholders have the most current information.
9. **Document communication**: Document the communication of risk tracking information, including the format, content, and audience, to ensure consistency and to make it easier to review and analyze the communication efforts.

5.6.5 Adjusting Risk Mitigation Strategies

Adjusting risk mitigation strategy is an essential element of effective risk management. Adjusting is required, or initial strategies or tactics may be unproductive; new risks can emerge throughout the project.

1. **Conduct regular risk assessments**: Regular risk assessments are essential to identifying changes in the risk landscape and determining whether existing risk mitigation strategies are still effective. Therefore, organizations should conduct risk assessments regularly or respond to significant organizational or external environment changes.
2. **Re-evaluate risk appetite**: Organizations should periodically re-evaluate their risk appetite to ensure it remains aligned with their overall business strategy and goals. If the risk appetite changes, risk mitigation strategies may need to be adjusted to reflect this change.
3. **Review and adjust risk mitigation strategies**: Organizations should regularly review and adapt their risk mitigation strategies to ensure they remain effective. Reviews include evaluating existing strategies' effectiveness and identifying new approaches to address emerging risks.
4. **Involve relevant stakeholders**: It is vital to involve pertinent stakeholders in adjusting risk mitigation strategies. Appropriate personnel includes those

responsible for managing the risks, senior management, and the board of directors.

5. **Monitor and track progress**: Organizations should monitor and track progress in implementing risk mitigation strategies to ensure they are effective. Monitoring includes tracking metrics related to risk management and conducting regular reviews to assess progress.
6. **Communicate changes in risk mitigation strategies**: Projects learn and adapt, including changes in risk strategies communicated throughout the organization to ensure everyone understands the changes and how they may impact their work.

Organizations can adjust their risk mitigation strategies to ensure they manage risks effectively. Organizations can avoid potential risks by regularly assessing risks, evaluating risk appetite, reviewing and adjusting strategies, involving relevant stakeholders, monitoring progress, and communicating changes.

5.7 Best Practices for Project Risk Tracking

Best practices are a slippery slope. The best specific practice is situation and circumstance dependent. In addition, projects encounter various challenges and constraints, making one approach to the letter difficult. Therefore, the best process will be project-specific and require adapting. However, there are fundamental practices that will prove valuable to the organization. These practices apply to the organization's culture regarding risk management; from experience, the culture of the organization will either support effective risk management or detract.

5.7.1 Building a Risk-Aware Culture

Building a risk-aware culture is essential for any organization looking to manage risks effectively. This section will discuss some best practices for building a risk-aware culture within an organization.

1. **Establish clear risk management policies**: It is essential to establish clear policies and guidelines for managing risks. These policies should define risks, the organization's risk appetite, the process for identifying and assessing risks, and the roles and responsibilities of those involved in managing risks.
2. **Communicate the importance of risk management**: Communicate the importance of risk management throughout the organization. Communication includes educating employees on the organization's risks and how they can contribute to managing those risks.

3. **Encourage transparency and open communication**: Encourage transparency and open communication throughout the organization. Transparency includes creating an environment (psychological safety) [8] where employees feel comfortable reporting risks and discussing potential issues.
4. **Involve employees in risk management**: Involve employees in the risk management process. Employee engagement includes providing training and resources to help employees identify and assess risks and encouraging them to report any concerns.
5. **Recognize and reward risk-aware behavior**: Recognize and reward employees who demonstrate risk-aware behavior. Recognition can include incentives for reporting risks or taking proactive steps to mitigate risks.
6. **Continuously evaluate and improve the risk management process**: Continuously evaluate and improve the risk management process to ensure it is adequate and relevant. Evaluation includes reviewing policies and procedures, conducting regular risk assessments, and seeking employee feedback.

By implementing these best practices, organizations can create a risk-aware culture that enables them to manage risks proactively and make informed decisions. A risk-aware culture can help to identify potential risks early, mitigate them before they become significant issues, and ultimately improve the overall performance and success of the organization.

5.7.2 Ensuring Risk Tracking Data Is Accurate

Effective risk management is crucial for any project's success, and accurate risk-tracking data is essential. Some best practices for ensuring the accuracy of risk-tracking data are below.

1. **Define and standardize your risk tracking process**: Establishing a standard process for tracking risks across the organization is essential. Standardization includes defining the risks to follow, the metrics and how to measure them, and the frequency of updates. This standardization will help ensure consistency and accuracy in the data.
2. **Use a centralized system for tracking risks**: Implement a centralized approach to track risks across projects and the organization. This system should be accessible to all relevant stakeholders and provide an accurate picture of the organization's risk profile. The system should also allow for easy tracking and reporting of risks.
3. **Ensure data input is accurate**: Accurate data input is crucial for ensuring the accuracy of risk-tracking data. Training staff responsible for entering data ensures they understand the process and know how to enter information correctly.

4. **Regularly review and update data**: Reviewing and updating risk-tracking data is essential to ensure accuracy. This review includes identifying incomplete or incorrect data and taking steps to correct it. Regular updates also help ensure the organization's risk profile remains up-to-date and relevant.
5. **Validate data with relevant stakeholders**: It is vital to validate risk-tracking data with relevant stakeholders, including those responsible for managing the risks. This validated data ensures that the team is using meaningful data that reflects the project's risk profile and that the project takes any necessary corrective actions.
6. **Conduct regular audits**: Regular audits of the risk-tracking process can help identify any weaknesses or gaps in the system. These reviews include reviewing data inputs, the tracking process, and the accuracy of the data. Conducting audits by an independent party to ensure a measure of objectivity.

5.7.3 Encouraging Stakeholder Participation

Encouraging stakeholder participation in risk tracking is essential for effective risk management, as stakeholders can provide valuable insights and perspectives on a project's risks. Here are some steps to encourage stakeholder participation in risk tracking:

1. **Communicate the importance of risk tracking**: Communicate to stakeholders and project team members the importance of risk tracking and how their participation can help ensure that risks are effectively identified and managed.
2. **Provide training and resources**: Provide stakeholders with training and resources to help them understand the risk tracking process, including the risks they can help identify and how to report them.
3. **Encourage open communication**: Encourage open communication between stakeholders and risk management teams to ensure that all relevant information is captured and considered.
4. **Make the process accessible**: Make the risk-tracking process accessible to stakeholders by using clear and straightforward methods for reporting and tracking risks, such as online tools and forms.
5. **Provide feedback and recognition**: Provide regular feedback to stakeholders on their contributions and recognize their efforts to participate in the risk-tracking process.
6. **Confidentiality**: Ensure stakeholders feel confident that any information they provide will be kept confidential and used appropriately.

Encouraging stakeholder participation and sponsor participation in risk tracking requires effective communication, accessible processes, and a commitment to involving stakeholders in the risk management process. Stakeholder participation can help organizations better identify, understand, and manage their risks when done effectively.

5.7.4 Staying Current with Industry Trends and Developments

Staying current with industry trends and risk-tracking developments is essential for effective risk management. Here are some steps to keep up-to-date with the latest developments:

1. **Attend conferences and events**: Attend conferences, workshops, and other events focused on risk management and tracking to hear from experts, network with peers, and stay current with the latest trends and developments.
2. **Read industry publications**: Read industry publications, such as journals, magazines, and online articles, to keep up-to-date with the latest thinking and risk-tracking developments.
3. **Join professional organizations**: Join professional organizations, such as trade associations, focused on risk management and tracking to access resources and connect with other professionals in the field.
4. **Participate in online forums and discussions**: Participate in online forums and discussion groups focused on risk management and risk tracking to exchange ideas and insights with other professionals.
5. **Stay informed on new technologies**: Stay knowledgeable on new technologies and tools used for risk tracking. Then, consider implementing these tools to improve the efficiency and effectiveness of your risk-tracking process.
6. **Learn from other organizations**: Learn from organizations within and outside your industry that have successfully implemented risk-tracking processes and practices.

Staying current with industry trends and risk-tracking developments requires a proactive approach and a commitment to continuous learning and improvement. However, staying up-to-date with the latest developments can help projects better understand and continuously improve [9].

References

1. I. Gordon and S. Sorkin, *Quoted in the Armchair Science Reader*, Simon and Schuster, 1959.
2. E. Derby and D. Larsen, *Agile Retrospective: Making Good Teams Great*, The Pragmatic Bookshelf, 2006.

3. E. Verzzuh, "The Fast Forward MBA in Project Management," in *Measuring Progress*, John Whiley & Sons, 1999, pp. 245–258.
4. J. Magretta, "Jim Collins, Meet Michael Porter," *Harvard Business Review*, 15 December 2011 [Online]. Available: https://hbr.org/2011/12/jim-collins-meet-michael-porte. [Accessed 19 March 2023].
5. K. Ishikawa, Introduction to Quality Control, 3A Corporation, 1997.
6. Management Office of Department of Energy, "DOE G 413.3-7A Risk Management Guide," 12 January 2011 [Online]. Available: www.directives.doe.gov/directives-documents/400-series/0413.3-EGuide-07a/@@images/file. [Accessed 18 March 2023].
7. S. Johnson, *The History of Rasselas, Prince of Abissinia*, R. and J. Dodsley, and W. Johnson, 1759.
8. P. Naper and A. Rao, *The Power of Agency: The 7 Principles to Conquer Obstacles, Make Effective Decisions and Create Life on Your Own Terms*. St. Martin's Press, 2019.
9. J. M. Quigley and S. Patrick Quigley, *Continuous and Embedded Learning for Organizations*, Taylor and Francis, 2022.

Chapter 6

Communication and Risk

Communication plays a critical role in managing risk in organizations. Effective communication can help identify and assess risks, develop strategies to mitigate risks, and communicate risk information to stakeholders to inform decision-making.

One of the main ways communication can help manage risk is by facilitating information sharing and collaboration across different parts of the organization. For example, when team members communicate regularly and openly, they can share information about potential risks and work together to develop strategies to mitigate them. Communication helps ensure everyone is on the same page when managing risk, which can help prevent errors and oversights that could lead to adverse outcomes.

To explore the difficulty of getting everybody on the same page, consider the formula for calculating the total number of lines of communication.

$$\text{Total Lines of Communication} = \frac{N\ x\ (N-1)}{2}$$

where N = the total number of project team members (Figure 6.1).

Effective communication can also help ensure the articulatio risk information to the right people at the right time. This articulation allows stakeholders to make informed decisions about risk management strategies and take appropriate actions to mitigate risks. For example, suppose a project team identifies a potential threat. In that case, they may communicate this information to senior management, who can then decide how to address the risk, such as allocating additional resources or changing the project timeline.

On the other hand, poor communication can increase the likelihood of risks going unnoticed or unaddressed, leading to adverse outcomes. For example, if team

DOI: 10.1201/9781003425465-6

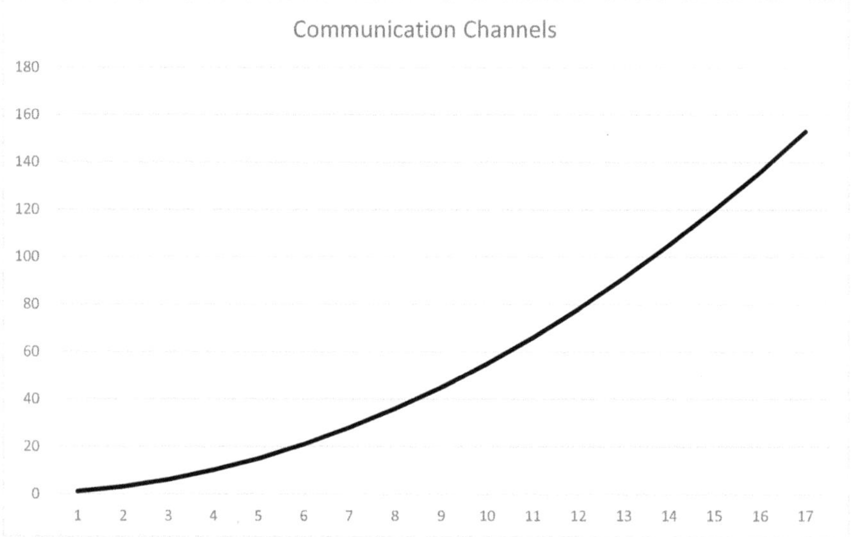

Figure 6.1 Communication channels and the number of team members.

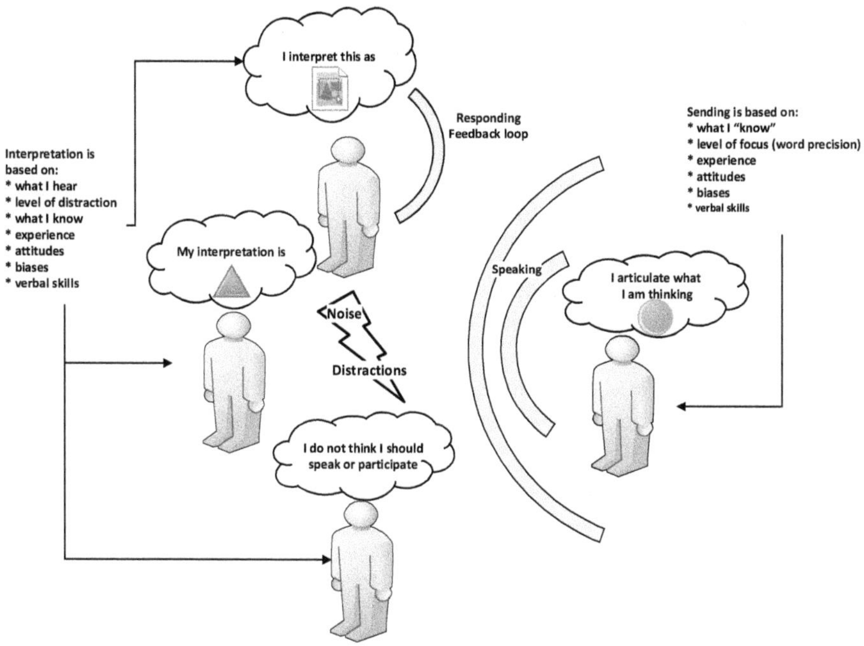

Figure 6.2 Illustration of the complexity of clear communication.

members are not communicating effectively, they may not be aware of potential risks or may not have the information they need to address risks effectively. As a result, poor communication can lead to delays, cost overruns, or other otherwise preventable adverse outcomes with better communication.

Project managers should know that communication is critical to effective organizational risk management. By promoting information sharing, collaboration, and stakeholder engagement, effective communication can help organizations identify and mitigate risks, improve decision-making, and achieve better outcomes (Figure 6.2).

6.1 Role of Communication in Risk Management

Effective communication is critical in risk management because it helps ensure that all stakeholders are aware of potential risks, understand the measures taken to manage them, and can take appropriate action to mitigate or respond to them. Here are some ways that communication plays a role in risk management:

1. **Risk identification**: Effective communication channels can help organizations to identify potential risks by allowing stakeholders to report issues or concerns before coming to fruition. Identification helps the organization anticipate and develop early action to manage and mitigate risks before becoming actuality and require escalation. The project team members bring observation of emerging events via communication.
2. **Risk assessment**: Communication can help to ensure that all stakeholders are involved in the risk assessment process, providing input and feedback on potential risks and their likelihood and impact. Assessments with diverse experiences and competencies can provide a more cohesive and accurate interpretation. Thus making better-informed decisions about which risks to prioritize and how to allocate resources to manage them.
3. **Risk management planning**: Communication is critical in developing risk management plans by ensuring that all stakeholders are engaged to create response plans, understand their roles and responsibilities in managing risks, and share an understanding of the measures taken to mitigate those risks.
4. **Risk monitoring and reporting**: Effective communication channels can help ensure stakeholders are informed about changes in the risk landscape and the status of risk management activities. This communication during the project execution means identifying emerging risks articulated through the team's appropriate action taken to manage those risks.
5. **Crisis management**: Effective communication is critical during a crisis, allowing organizations to communicate with stakeholders quickly, provide updates on the situation, and provide guidance on responding to the problem.

6. **Long-term learning**: Communication is how knowledge and experiences are shared and part of a continuous improvement approach to risk. Communication increases the probability of extending an individual's experiences and learning throughout the project and organization.
7. **Problem-solving skills** [1]: Diverse skills and perspectives can help understand the problem's nature and identify approaches that fit the constraints; this requires communication between team members as well as evoking and determining the veracity of assumption assumptions
8. **Understanding and applying multiple decision modes**: The leader makes some decisions, while the team makes others. Efficient decision-making requires the team to understand this range [1].
9. **Conflict resolution skills** [1]: Conflict within a team is not bad; creative solutions will generate conflict, and conversely, the friction causes innovative solutions. Conflict approached appropriately can yield positive results; conversely, inappropriate response to conflict can erode team cohesion. Not all conflict requires attention, but all conflict requires exploration to determine impact; a policy of ignoring is not a path to success.
10. **Continuous learning** [1]: Crafting an effective response to anticipated risk events and a prompt response to emerging events requires a constant learning approach. Constraints and assets are not consistent from project to project.

Effective communication is critical in risk management, helping to ensure that all stakeholders are informed and engaged in identifying, assessing, and managing risks. By promoting a culture of open communication and ensuring that all stakeholders are informed and engaged, organizations can reduce the likelihood of incidents and accidents and protect their reputation and bottom line (Figure 6.3).

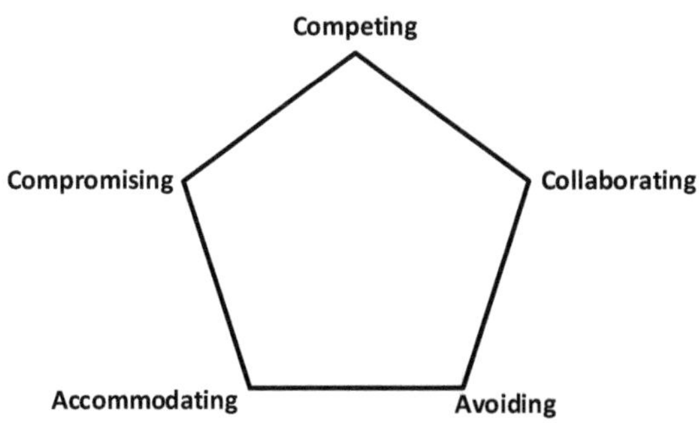

Figure 6.3 An example of conflict resolution approaches.

6.2 Organization and Structure

The organizational structure of a company can have a significant impact on communication within the organization. A well-designed organizational structure can promote effective communication, while a poorly designed system can hinder communication and lead to misunderstandings and errors (Figure 6.4).

Organizational structures provide a framework for the division of the work, how information flows between departments, and the making of decisions. Some of the critical reasons for having an organizational structure include:

1. **Clarifying roles and responsibilities**: Organizational structures define the roles and responsibilities of employees, ensuring that everyone understands what they are responsible for and how their work fits into the organization's overall objectives.
2. **Facilitating communication**: Clear lines of communication between departments and individuals help to ensure that information flows smoothly and that everyone is aware of what is happening within the organization.
3. **Enhancing efficiency**: A well-designed organizational structure helps streamline processes and reduce duplication of effort, improving overall efficiency and productivity.
4. **Supporting growth**: As an organization grows, a clear organizational structure becomes increasingly important to maintain control and manage complexity.

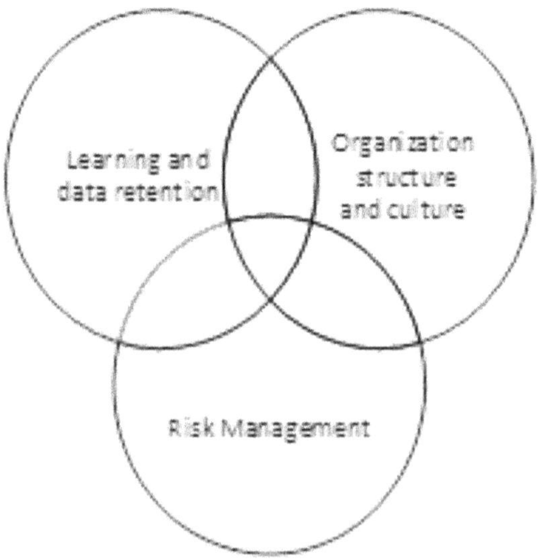

Figure 6.4 The confluence of learning, organization, and risk management.

5. **Encouraging innovation**: A well-designed organizational structure can promote creativity and innovation by allowing employees to explore new ideas and approaches within their designated areas of responsibility.

One key factor that affects communication within an organization is the level of hierarchy and the degree of centralization. In a highly centralized organization, decision-making and communication tend to be concentrated at the top of the hierarchy, leading to delays via miscommunications as information ripples throughout the chain of command. In contrast, a decentralized organization with a flatter structure can promote faster and more direct communication among employees at different levels.

Another factor that affects communication is the degree of specialization and departmentalization. In highly specialized departments, communication between departments can be more difficult, as employees may have different perspectives and technical language (for example, legal and engineering) that can be challenging to understand. On the other hand, organizations with more integrated departments can promote more effective communication and collaboration.

The physical layout of the organization can also impact communication. For example, an open office layout can promote communication and collaboration among employees, while closed offices or cubicles can hinder communication and lead to a siloed mentality.

Designing an organizational structure that promotes transparency, collaboration, and open communication channels is essential for practical project and corporate communication. This organization structure design may involve:

- Reducing hierarchy and centralization or decentralization to encourage faster and more direct communication.
- Breaking down silos and promoting cross-functional collaboration.
- Creating an open and inclusive workplace culture that encourages communication and feedback.
- Using technology to facilitate communication and collaboration, such as video conferencing, instant messaging, and project management software.

The structure of the organization will have some impact on the risk environment. For example, an organization distributed across the globe will have to contend with risks associated with this structure. There are a variety of organizational structures, a few reviewed below. Each design has benefits and comes with some downsides or risks.

6.2.1 Projectized

A projectized organizational structure has employees attached to specific products. All the necessary talents for the project are dedicated resources for projects around this product. In this structure, project managers and team members have high authority and responsibility for managing their projects.

While a projectized organization structure can provide many benefits for managing complex projects, for example, close team contact with all domains required for the project's success, it can also create challenges when managing risk. For example, one potential risk is that projects may become overly focused on achieving specific deliverables or milestones at the expense of broader organizational goals. This hyperfocus can lead to a lack of coordination and communication across projects, making managing risks at the corporate level difficult.

Another risk of a projectized organization structure is that resources may be spread thin across multiple projects, making it challenging to allocate resources effectively to manage risks. This resource limitation can also make it challenging to identify and address risks that cut across numerous projects or affect the organization.

Organizations with a projectized structure may need a proactive approach to risk management to mitigate these risks. To remediate the limitations of a projectized organization structure:

- Establishing clear risk management protocols and processes that are consistent across projects.
- Providing training and support to project managers and team members to help them identify and manage risks effectively.
- Ensuring project managers have access to the resources they need to manage risks effectively, including personnel, technology, and funding.
- Encouraging communication and collaboration across projects to identify and address risks that affect the organization.
- Develop approaches to sharing individual team knowledge and an organization's long-term goals and objectives across product lines.

6.2.2 Functional

A functional organization structure is hierarchical and based on areas of specialization or function, such as marketing, finance, verification, or operations. In this structure, employees report to a functional manager who oversees their work and sets their priorities with the project manager. This dual reporting can create challenges (Figure 6.5).

There are benefits to functional structures, especially when it comes to the development of specialization. For example, talent specialization can include processes and specific tool development to serve the domain in the context of the organization's demands. Another benefit of the functional organization is the clear lines of authority.

While a functional organizational structure can provide clear lines of authority and facilitate efficient operations within each department, it can also create challenges

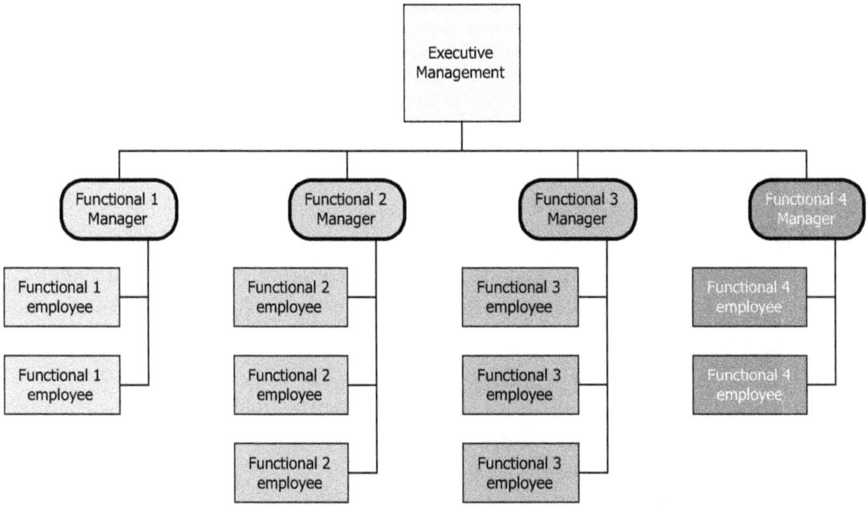

Figure 6.5 Example of a functional organization.

when managing risk. In addition, there are some downsides; in the functional organization, the manager directs the staff in ways the manager deems appropriate. As a result, the strategies and tactics taken by the manager may not be in the best interest of the project manager from their perspective. This perspective leads to potential risks in that the manager and department employees may become too focused on their specialized tasks and not have a comprehensive understanding of the broader organizational goals or the risks facing the organization. In addition, this structure can lead to a siloed mentality and a lack of collaboration across departments.

Organizations with a functional structure may need to emphasize a proactive approach to risk management to mitigate these risks. This proactive approach may involve:

- Establishing cross-functional teams to promote collaboration and communication between departments, developing an understanding of the work pipeline.
- Encouraging employees to develop a broader understanding of the organization's goals and risks
- Ensuring that decision-making processes are efficient and effective, with clear lines of responsibility and accountability
- Regularly reviewing and updating risk management plans to ensure they remain relevant and effective in changing circumstances.
- Develop a searchable central repository for sharing uncovered risks and outcomes by other departments and project teams.

6.2.3 Matrix

A matrix organization structure is a hybrid structure in which functional and project-organize employees. In this structure, employees report to the manager, who is responsible for their day-to-day work, and a project manager, who manages their work on specific projects (Figure 6.6).

While a matrix organization structure can provide many benefits, such as increased flexibility and coordination, it can also create challenges when managing risk. For example, one potential risk is that employees may become confused about their reporting lines or priorities, leading to a lack of clarity and accountability when managing risks.

Another risk of a matrix organization structure is that project and functional managers may have different goals and priorities when managing risks. For example, a project manager may prioritize delivering a project on time and within budget. In contrast, a functional manager may prioritize maintaining quality standards and minimizing organizational risk. As a result, this structure can lead to conflict and tension between different parts of the organization when identifying and managing risks.

Organizations with a matrix structure may need a proactive approach to risk management to mitigate these risks. This mitigation may involve:

- Establishing clear lines of communication and accountability between project managers and functional managers.
- Ensuring team members clearly understand their roles and responsibilities when managing risks and putting systems, processes, and structures to ensure engagement.

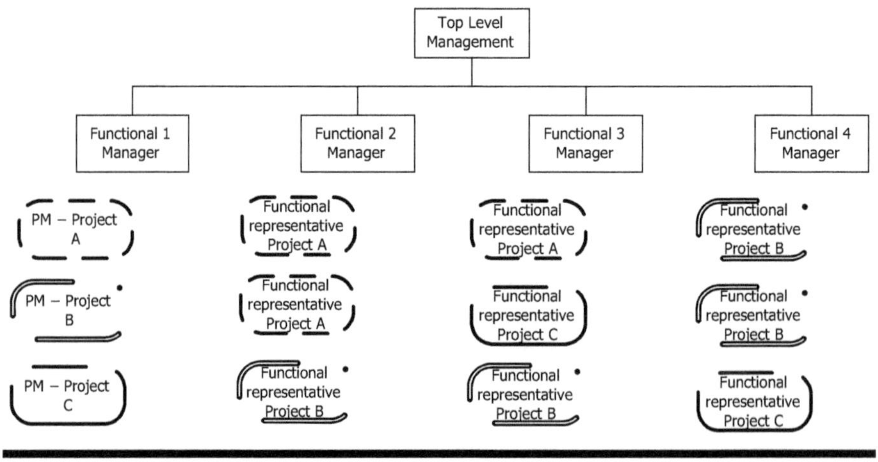

Figure 6.6 Example of a matrix organization.

- Providing training and support to project managers and functional managers to help them identify and manage risks effectively.
- Encouraging collaboration and coordination between different parts of the organization to identify and address risks that cut across projects or functions.

6.2.4 Self-Directed Work Teams (Scrum/Agile)

From experience, the self-directed work team is coming to prominence. Scrum is a framework for agile project management that emphasizes collaboration, iterative development, and constant feedback. The Scrum framework does not define a specific organizational structure but provides guidelines for how teams should work together to achieve their goals.

In a Scrum team, there are three key roles:

1. **Product Owner**: The product owner is responsible for defining the product vision and creating a product backlog, which is a prioritized list of features and functionality that the team will work on.
2. **Scrum Master**: The Scrum Master is responsible for ensuring the following of the Scrum framework, facilitating daily meetings, and helping to remove any impediments blocking the team's progress. Additionally, the Scrum Master will work with the product owner to ensure the input to the development team is clear.
3. **Development Team**: The development team is responsible for creating the product increment, a working product version that includes all the features and functionality completed during the current sprint.

Scrum teams are generally self-organizing and cross-functional, meaning that the team members have various skills and can work together to complete all aspects of the project. Therefore, the group should be small enough to work efficiently and effectively but large enough to have all the necessary skills and expertise.

The Scrum framework also includes several ceremonies or meetings that are designed to keep the team focused and on track. These ceremonies include:

1. **Sprint Planning**: A meeting where the team plans the work that will be completed during the upcoming sprint.
2. **Daily Scrum**: A daily stand-up meeting where the team members discuss their progress, any obstacles they face, and what they plan to work on next.
3. **Sprint Review**: A meeting where the team demonstrates the product increment completed during the sprint and receives stakeholder feedback.
4. **Sprint Retrospective**: A meeting where the team reflects on the previous sprint and identifies ways to improve their processes and performance.

The Scrum framework design provides a flexible and collaborative approach to project management to help teams work together more efficiently and effectively. A consistent team focused on one project provides an advantage.

6.3 Management Philosophy, Culture, and Risk

Management philosophy and organizational culture can significantly impact how organizations approach and manage risk. For example, a management philosophy prioritizes risk management is more likely to have a proactive and responsive culture. This contrasts with a management philosophy that does not prioritize risk management, which may result in a reactive and unprepared culture.

For example, a management philosophy that values risk management may prioritize identifying and assessing risks, developing response and mitigation strategies, and monitoring and controlling risks throughout the project lifecycle. In addition, improved risk management may result from a more open culture for discussing and addressing potential risks and where employees are encouraged to identify and mitigate risks proactively.

In contrast, a management philosophy that does not prioritize risk management may result in a culture that focuses on short-term goals and may not consider potential risks until they become critical issues. This lack of prioritization can lead to a culture of risk aversion, where employees are hesitant to take risks or innovate for fear of negative consequences.

Organizations should develop a management philosophy that prioritizes risk management as a core component of business strategy to promote a culture of effective risk management. Promotion can include:

- Providing resources and training to employees to help them identify and manage risks effectively.
- Encouraging open communication and collaboration between different parts of the organization to identify and address risks.
- Rewarding employees who demonstrate a proactive approach to risk management.
- Develop and implement risk management policies and procedures aligned with the organization's values and goals.
- Continuously monitor and assess risks to ensure that risk management strategies remain practical and current.

6.3.1 Command and Control, Communication, and Risk

The command-and-control management style, which emphasizes a hierarchical organizational structure and centralized decision-making, can significantly impact corporate communication and risk management.

In a command-and-control structure, communication often flows top-down, with instructions and decisions passed down from senior management to lower-level employees. Command and control approaches can create a culture where employees may be less likely to share information or raise concerns, leading to risks going unnoticed or unaddressed.

Furthermore, a command-and-control structure may discourage collaboration and information-sharing between different parts of the organization. As a result, employees may be more focused on following orders than working together to identify and address risks. This approach to management may also lead to a culture of risk aversion, where employees are hesitant to take risks or innovate for fear of negative consequences.

On the other hand, a more collaborative and participatory approach to management, where communication is more open and inclusive, can help promote effective risk management. For example, when employees are encouraged to share information and collaborate across different parts of the organization, they are more likely to identify potential risks and work together to develop mitigation strategies.

Furthermore, when communication is more open and inclusive, employees may feel more comfortable raising concerns or challenging assumptions, which can help identify and address potential risks before they become critical.

6.3.2 Egalitarian

An egalitarian management philosophy, which emphasizes shared decision-making and a flatter organizational structure, can significantly impact risk management in organizations. This approach recognizes that solutions and good ideas are not hierarchical.

In an egalitarian management structure, decision-making is more decentralized, with more input from employees at different levels of the organization. This decentralization can create a culture where employees feel empowered to share information and ideas, which can help identify potential risks and opportunities for risk mitigation.

Furthermore, an egalitarian management philosophy can encourage collaboration and information-sharing between different parts of the organization, which can help ensure that risks are identified and addressed promptly and effectively.

However, an egalitarian management philosophy can also pose some challenges to risk management. For example, ensuring that all decisions align with the organization's risk management strategy can be more challenging when decision-making is more decentralized. In addition, this philosophy can lead to inconsistencies in risk management practices across different parts of the organization, making it more challenging to identify and manage risks effectively.

Furthermore, an egalitarian management philosophy may not be well-suited to managing risks in high-pressure or time-sensitive situations, where quick decision-making and clear direction may be necessary.

An egalitarian management philosophy can be an effective approach to risk management in organizations as long as supported by clear policies and procedures and a culture that values effective risk management practices. An egalitarian approach is a practical risk management approach through establishing clear roles and responsibilities, providing adequate resources and training, and fostering open communication and collaboration.

6.3.3 Culture

Organizational culture can significantly impact how risk is perceived, managed, and addressed. For example, an organization with a robust risk management and safety culture may have policies and procedures to identify, assess, and mitigate risks while promoting a culture of transparency, accountability, and continuous improvement.

Organizational culture refers to an organization's shared values, beliefs, attitudes, behaviors, and customs. It is an organization's personality and defines how things are done within the company. It includes the company's mission, vision, goals, leadership style, communication patterns, and even the physical environment where employees work (Figure 6.7).

The organization's culture can significantly impact employee behavior, job satisfaction, and organizational performance. For example, a healthy culture can lead to better employee engagement, increased productivity, and improved customer

Figure 6.7 Example of organizational cultures.

satisfaction; a hostile culture, on the other hand, can lead to employee disengagement, high turnover rates, and decreased performance.

From experience, an overly politicized company, one where the speech can be referred to as mitigated speech or Doublespeak (check out the book by William Lutz of that same title) [2]. Mitigated speech is the language used to soften a message's impact or convey a sense of uncertainty or hesitancy. While it can be helpful in some contexts, it can also have negative implications for risk management. Here are some ways in which mitigated speech can impact risk management:

1. **It can lead to ambiguity**: The use of mitigated speech can sometimes lead to ambiguity in communication, making it difficult to understand the nature and severity of risks clearly. In addition, ambiguity does not bring the team to the point of decision-making; reducing opacity is required before determining the appropriate action.
2. **It can mask the severity of risks**: By using mitigated speech, individuals may downplay the risk severity, making it more challenging to assess and reduce those risks accurately. Projects have time constraints that require prioritization. Soft-pedaling emerging events or reporting on identified risks may result in the event being a low priority. In addition, softening language reduces the sense of urgency or the need to take action.
3. **It can create a false sense of security**: Using mitigated speech can sometimes make a false sense of security by downplaying the severity of risks. This false sense of security can lead individuals and organizations to underestimate the potential impact of risks and fail to take appropriate action to mitigate them.

There may be a few instances where mitigated speech can be helpful in some contexts; it can reduce team turbulence and have negative implications for risk management. To effectively manage risks, it is essential to communicate clearly and transparently and to avoid language that can lead to ambiguity, mask the severity of risks, or create a false sense of security. Organizations can better manage risks and protect themselves from potential harm by fostering a culture of open communication and transparency.

An organization with a weak or negative culture may be more likely to overlook risks, downplay their potential impact, or fail to take appropriate action to address them. Conversely, failure to respond aggressively can result in increased incidents, accidents, legal liabilities, and damage to the organization's reputation and stakeholder trust.

Furthermore, culture can also affect how individuals within an organization approach risk. For example, employees may feel more comfortable reporting incidents or near-misses in a culture that values open communication and encourages learning from mistakes. In contrast, a culture emphasizing blame and punishment may discourage employees from reporting risks or admitting mistakes, leading to more significant harm and long-term consequences.

A strong and positive culture can enhance an organization's ability to manage and respond to risk effectively. In contrast, a weak or negative culture can increase the likelihood of risks going unnoticed or unaddressed.

6.3.3.1 Hofstede's Cultural Dimensions [3]

Hofstede's cultural dimensions theory is a framework for cross-cultural communication that describes the effects of a society's culture on the values of its members and how these values relate to behavior. Hofstede identified six cultural dimensions (Figure 6.8).

Hofstede's cultural dimensions have been widely used and referenced in cross-cultural psychology, sociology, and management. However, like any theory or model, they are not without criticism and limitations.

One of the main criticisms of Hofstede's cultural dimensions is that they may oversimplify the complexity and diversity of cultures. Some scholars argue that cultures are not monolithic entities and that there can be significant variation within a culture and overlap between different cultures. Additionally, some researchers have noted that Hofstede's original study was limited to IBM employees, which may not represent the wider population.

Another limitation of Hofstede's cultural dimensions is that they may perpetuate cultural stereotypes and reinforce cultural essentialism. By presenting cultures as fixed, homogeneous entities, Hofstede's dimensions can support the idea that individuals from different cultures are fundamentally different and can lead to cultural biases and misunderstandings.

Despite these limitations, Hofstede's cultural dimensions have provided a helpful framework for understanding cultural differences and their impact on behavior and attitudes. They have been widely used in cross-cultural research and have helped raise awareness of cultural diversity's importance in various contexts. However, it's essential to approach these dimensions critically and recognize that they are not a definitive representation of any culture or individual.

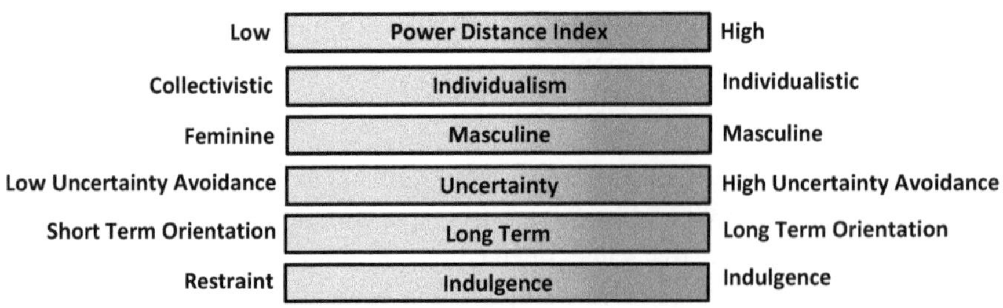

Figure 6.8 Hofstede's six cultural dimensions.

6.3.3.1.1 Power Distance Index

Power distance is a term used to describe the extent to which people in a particular culture are comfortable with unequal distributions of power and authority. It is measured on a scale from high power distance to low power distance.

In cultures with high power distance, there is a greater acceptance of unequal power distributions, and those in positions of authority are distant and unapproachable. In contrast, cultures with low power distance value equality and may have no discomfort challenging management.

Power distance curves can visually represent the differences in power distance between cultures. These curves show the distribution of responses to questions related to power distance, with cultures with a high power distance showing a steep curve and cultures with a low power distance showing a flatter curve.

For example, research has shown that Asian and Latin American cultures have higher power distance than Western cultures. In addition, in Asian cultures, respect for authority and hierarchy is often emphasized, while Latin American cultures have a greater acceptance of social inequality.

Understanding power distance and cultural differences in power distance is essential for effective cross-cultural communication and collaboration. By recognizing and respecting cultural differences, individuals and organizations can avoid misunderstandings and build stronger relationships with people from different backgrounds.

Power distance culture can have significant implications for risk management practices. In cultures with a high power distance, individuals may be less likely to question authority or raise concerns about potential risks, as they may perceive it as disrespectful or inappropriate. This reticence to challenge authority can lead to a lack of transparency and communication, increasing the likelihood of risks going unnoticed or unaddressed.

In contrast, cultures with a low power distance value open communication and collaboration, which can facilitate risk management. Individuals in these cultures may feel more comfortable speaking up and sharing concerns, which can help to identify and address potential risks more quickly and effectively.

Effective risk management in high power distance cultures may require strategies to encourage open communication and collaboration, such as anonymous reporting systems or clear channels for raising concerns. It may also be essential to provide training and support for individuals to develop the skills and confidence to speak up and challenge authority when necessary.

6.3.3.1.2 Individualism

Hofstede's cultural dimension of individualism refers to the extent to which people in a society prioritize individual freedom and autonomy over group harmony and collective goals. In individualistic cultures, people tend to focus on personal goals and achievements and may be more willing to take risks to pursue these goals. This individual pursuit can lead to a higher tolerance for uncertainty and a greater willingness to try new things and experiment, which can benefit innovation and creativity. However, it can also result in a focus on short-term gains and a disregard for potential long-term consequences or risks to the broader community.

In contrast, collectivistic cultures prioritize the group's well-being over individual needs and goals. This prioritization can lead to a more cautious approach to risk management, as considering the potential impact on the group happens before making decisions. In addition, collectivist cultures may be more likely to follow established rules and traditions, as these are important for maintaining social harmony and stability. However, this can also result in resistance to change and a reluctance to take risks that could benefit the group.

6.3.3.1.3 Masculine

Hofstede's cultural dimension of masculinity refers to the extent to which a society values traditional masculine traits, such as assertiveness, competitiveness, and ambition, versus feminine characteristics, such as cooperation, modesty, and caring for others. In cultures that score high on the masculinity dimension, such as the United States and Japan, risk-taking is a sign of strength and ambition. As a result, there may be rewards, increased status, and financial success. These end of the scale can lead to a culture of risk-taking and entrepreneurship, which can benefit innovation and economic growth.

However, it can also lead to focusing on short-term gains and disregarding potential long-term consequences or risks to the broader community. A culture that values assertiveness and competition may be more willing to take risks to gain a competitive advantage, even if this involves violating ethical or legal norms.

In cultures that score low on the masculinity dimension, such as Sweden and Norway, cooperation and consensus-building are valued over individual ambition and competition. This end of the scale can lead to a more cautious approach to risk management, considering the potential impact on the group before making decisions. However, it can also result in a reluctance to take risks that could benefit the group.

6.3.3.1.4 Uncertainty

Hofstede's cultural dimension of uncertainty avoidance refers to the degree to which a society feels threatened by uncertainty, ambiguity, and risk and how much they try to control and minimize these factors. In cultures with high uncertainty avoidance, such as Germany and Japan, people tend to be more risk-averse and prefer clear rules and structures that provide stability and predictability. This uncertainty avoidance can lead to a more cautious approach to risk management, as an evaluation of the potential consequences of a risky decision before decision-making and action. This careful decision-making can be beneficial in situations where the potential downside of a difficult decision is high, such as in the financial or healthcare industries.

However, a high level of uncertainty avoidance can also lead to resistance to change and a reluctance to take risks that could benefit the organization or society. In these cultures, new ideas and innovation may be viewed with skepticism and seen as disruptive to the established order.

In contrast, cultures with low uncertainty avoidance, such as the United States and Australia, tend to be more accepting of uncertainty and risk-taking. People in these cultures may be more willing to take risks and experiment with new ideas and approaches, even if the outcome is uncertain. This can lead to a culture of entrepreneurship and innovation, but it can also lead to a higher level of risk-taking that may not be appropriate in all contexts.

6.3.3.1.5 Long-Term

Hofstede's cultural dimension of long-term orientation refers to the extent to which a society values long-term planning and perseverance instead of short-term goals and immediate gratification. In cultures that score high on the long-term orientation dimension, such as China and Japan, people tend to focus more on long-term goals and are willing to invest time and effort to achieve them. This locus of focus can lead to a more cautious approach to risk management, considering potential long-term consequences before decision-making.

A long-term orientation can also focus on downstream effects, not just the immediate. For example, consider sustainability and environmental stewardship as the long-range impact of decisions on the natural environment. This approach can benefit organizations and societies in the long run, as it can help reduce the risk of adverse consequences and build resilience to future challenges.

In contrast, cultures that score low on the long-term orientation dimension, such as the United States and Russia, tend to focus more on short-term goals and immediate gratification. This focus can lead to higher risk-taking, prioritizing potential short-term benefits over long-term consequences.

6.3.3.1.6 Indulgence

Hofstede's cultural dimension of indulgence refers to the extent to which a society allows and encourages the enjoyment of life and personal freedom instead of suppressing gratification and adhering to strict social norms. In cultures that score high on the indulgence dimension, such as the Netherlands and Denmark, people tend to have a more relaxed attitude toward rules and regulations. As a result, they are more likely to take risks and pursue personal goals. This attitude can lead to higher risk-taking, as people may prioritize their desires and enjoyment over potential negative consequences.

However, in cultures that score low on the indulgence dimension, such as many countries in Asia and Middle Eastern countries, people tend to have a more strict and disciplined approach to life, emphasizing adhering to social norms and maintaining social harmony. This end of the scale can lead to a more cautious approach to risk management, as people may prioritize social order and stability over individual desires and goals.

6.4 Communication, Learning, and Risk

Learning and communication are critical components of effective risk management. They are closely intertwined and impact each other in several ways:

1. Learning enables individuals to understand the nature and impact of risks better. By continuously learning about the dangers they face, individuals can develop a deeper understanding of the potential consequences of those risks and how to mitigate them.
2. Effective communication is essential for sharing information about risks and risk mitigation strategies. Clear and transparent communication can help individuals understand their risks and the measures taken to address them.
3. Learning and communication can help to identify potential risks and opportunities for improvement. By encouraging open communication and a culture of continuous learning, individuals can identify potential risks and opportunities for improvement before they become significant issues.
4. Learning and communication can facilitate the development of risk management strategies. By working together to learn about the risks they face and sharing information about potential mitigation strategies, individuals can develop effective risk management strategies tailored to their specific needs.

Learning and communication are critical components of effective risk management. They enable individuals to understand their risks better, identify potential risks and opportunities for improvement, and develop effective risk management strategies. By fostering a culture of continuous learning and open communication, organizations can better manage risks and protect themselves from potential harm.

6.5 Organization and Learning

> We should be careful to get out of an experience only the wisdom that is in it – and stop there; lest we be like the cat that sits down on a hot

> stove-lid. She will never sit down on a hot stove-lid again – and that is well, but also, she will never sit down on a cold one anymore.
>
> *Mark Twain [4]*

Organizational learning can play an essential role in risk management. A learning culture can help organizations identify, assess, and manage risks more effectively while promoting a culture of transparency, accountability, and continuous improvement.

Here are some ways in which organizational learning can support risk management:

1. **Knowledge sharing**: Organizations that encourage knowledge sharing can help to spread awareness about potential risks across departments and teams. Employees with experience dealing with a particular risk can share their knowledge and best practices with others, which can help reduce the risk of incidents and accidents.
2. **Learning from incidents**: When incidents do occur, a culture of learning can help organizations to investigate the root cause of the incident, identify any gaps in their risk management processes, and implement corrective actions to prevent similar incidents from happening in the future.
3. **Continuous improvement**: Organizations prioritizing continuous improvement can use feedback from incidents, audits, and inspections to identify areas where they can improve their risk management processes. This prioritization can lead to the development of new policies, procedures, and training programs to reduce the likelihood of future incidents.
4. **Risk awareness**: A learning culture can also help raise awareness about potential risks among employees. By providing training and resources on risk management, organizations can help employees to identify potential risks and take appropriate action to mitigate them.

Organizational learning can help embed a risk management culture within an organization. By promoting a proactive approach to risk management, organizations can reduce the likelihood of incidents and accidents, protect their reputation, and create a safer work environment for their employees.

6.6 Failure Is Not Necessarily Terminal

> Good judgment comes from experience, and experience comes from bad judgment.
>
> *Rita Mae Brown*

While failure and risk are often associated with adverse outcomes, they can also provide several benefits in the context of risk management:

1. **Failure can provide valuable feedback**: When things go wrong, it offers the opportunity to learn from the experience and identify areas for improvement. In addition, feedback from previous failures refines risk management strategies and develops more effective approaches.
2. **Risk-taking can lead to innovation**: Taking calculated risks can help organizations to identify new opportunities and develop innovative solutions. By embracing risk-taking, organizations can create a culture of innovation and stay ahead of the competition.
3. **Risk management can improve decision-making**: By proactively managing risks, organizations can improve their decision-making processes. By carefully considering the potential risks and benefits of various options, decision-makers can make more informed decisions based on a thorough analysis of the situation.
4. **Effective risk management can enhance resilience**: By anticipating and preparing for potential risks, organizations can improve their strength and ability to respond to unexpected events. This improvement in stability can help reduce adverse events' impact and enable organizations to recover quickly.

Failure and risk can be daunting, but effective risk management can help organizations to embrace risk-taking while minimizing potential adverse outcomes. As a result, organizations can achieve their goals and thrive in an ever-changing environment by learning from failure, taking calculated risks, improving decision-making processes, and enhancing resilience.

6.7 Experience

> Progress, far from consisting in change, depends on retentiveness. When change is absolute there remains no being to improve and no direction is set for possible improvement: and when experience is not retained, as among savages, infancy is perpetual. Those who cannot remember the past are condemned to repeat it. In the first stage of life the mind is frivolous and easily distracted, it misses progress by failing in consecutiveness and persistence. This is the condition of children and barbarians, in which instinct has learned nothing from experience.
>
> *George Santayana [5]*

Experience, learning, and risk management are all factors to consider when managing risks in any context, whether personal or professional. Experience and learning are closely related concepts essential for personal and professional growth. Experience refers to the knowledge and skills individuals gain through interactions with the world around them. In contrast, learning refers to acquiring new knowledge and skills through education, training, and other experiences.

Experience can provide valuable insights into potential risks and how to manage them. By gaining experience in different areas, individuals can better understand the risks they may face and how to mitigate them. For example, someone who has worked in a high-risk industry, such as construction or manufacturing, may better understand the potential hazards and risks associated with those industries.

Learning can also play a role in risk management. By staying up-to-date with the latest information, regulations, and best practices, individuals can improve their ability to identify and manage risks effectively. Learning can include attending training sessions, reading industry publications, and staying informed about relevant news and developments in their field.

Regarding risk management, no plan or strategy can eliminate all risks. However, by combining experience and learning, individuals can develop a more comprehensive approach to risk management that considers a wide range of factors and potential risks.

In addition, effective risk management often involves taking calculated risks; business is about risk and reward analysis. This analysis requires projects and the organization to weigh the benefits and drawbacks of different courses of action and make informed decisions based on the available information. By taking calculated risks, individuals can maximize the potential benefits while minimizing the possible negative consequences.

Experience and learning are important factors to consider when managing risks. By combining these factors with a willingness to take calculated risks, individuals can develop effective risk management strategies to help them achieve their goals while minimizing potential adverse outcomes.

6.8 Distribution of Learning

> There is only one thing more painful than learning from experience, and that is not learning from experience.
>
> *Laurence J. Peter [6]*

The distribution of learning and risk management refers to how organizations ensure that the necessary knowledge and skills related to risk management are disseminated and shared across the organization. One way to ensure the distribution of learning and risk management is to develop a comprehensive training program covering all risk management aspects. The designed training program should meet the needs of employees at different levels and across various departments. This training can include classroom-style training, on-the-job training, online courses, workshops, and other forms of exercise.

Another way to distribute learning and risk management is to create a culture of continuous improvement that encourages employees to share their knowledge and experiences related to risk management. Knowledge-sharing is part of ongoing improvement efforts, and platforms that support communities of practice and other collaborative learning initiatives are helpful.

Organizations can also distribute learning and risk management by ensuring that all employees understand their roles and responsibilities related to risk management. For example, the organization's spreading specific, context-based job descriptions, project artifacts, performance evaluations, and other employee communications.

It is important to note that learning and risk management distribution should be an ongoing review process and updated regularly. In addition, organizations should evaluate the effectiveness of their training programs and other initiatives to ensure that they are meeting the needs of their employees and addressing any gaps in knowledge or skills related to risk management.

Learning and risk management distribution are crucial for creating an organization's safety and risk management culture. Organizations can reduce the likelihood of incidents and accidents and protect their reputation and bottom line by ensuring all employees have the necessary knowledge and skills to identify, assess, and manage risks.

6.8.1 Communities of Practice

Communities of practice (CoPs) can play a role in risk management by facilitating knowledge sharing, collaboration, and learning among individuals with shared interests and expertise. CoPs are groups of people who share knowledge and solve problems related to a specific field, profession, or domain of interest. By bringing together individuals with diverse perspectives and experiences, CoPs can help identify and address potential risks and develop strategies for managing them. The context of the CoP need not be risk management but some other key area of interest by the business. For example, for a company with critical domains related to work, verification, and testing, the organization may want to create a CoP.

One way CoPs can contribute to risk management is by fostering a culture of risk awareness and proactive risk management. Members of a CoP can share their experiences and best practices for identifying, assessing, and managing risks in their field, which can help other members develop their risk management skills and strategies. In addition, by encouraging a continuous dialogue about risk, CoPs can help members stay abreast of emerging threats and identify potential vulnerabilities in their organizations or industries.

CoPs can also facilitate collaboration and information sharing across organizational boundaries, which can be particularly valuable in managing complex or systemic risks. By bringing together individuals from different organizations, CoPs can help identify interdependencies and potential cascading effects of risks and develop coordinated strategies for managing them.

In addition to sharing knowledge and expertise, CoPs can help members build trust and relationships that can be valuable in managing risks. By working together and developing a shared understanding of risks, CoP members can build trust and confidence in each other's abilities to manage risks effectively. In addition, collaboration can facilitate effective risk communication and coordination, which is critical in responding to and recovering from unexpected events.

Communities of practice can be valuable for organizations and industries looking to improve their risk management capabilities. By facilitating knowledge sharing, collaboration, and learning, CoPs can help build a culture of risk awareness and develop effective strategies for identifying, assessing, and managing risks.

Aspect	*Communities of Practice*	*Centers of Excellence*
Definition	Groups of people come together to share knowledge and solve problems related to a specific field, profession, or interest.	A centralized unit within an organization is responsible for developing and promoting best practices in a specific area of expertise.
Purpose	To facilitate knowledge sharing, collaboration, and learning among individuals with shared interests and expertise.	To consolidate knowledge and expertise in a dedicated unit to help organizations develop and implement more effective strategies, policies, and procedures.
Focus	Sharing knowledge and best practices related to risk management.	Developing and promoting best practices in risk management.
Scope	It can be informal and include members from different organizations.	Typically focused on a specific area of expertise within a single organization.
Benefits	Can facilitate a culture of risk awareness and proactive risk management by sharing experiences and best practices. It can foster collaboration and information sharing across organizational boundaries to manage complex or systemic risks.	Provides a single point of contact for an organization's risk management expertise and resources. Ensure that risk management strategies and practices are consistent and coordinated across departments and business units. It can help identify and prioritize risks and develop targeted strategies for mitigating those risks.

Aspect	*Communities of Practice*	*Centers of Excellence*
Challenges	Measuring and quantifying the impact of knowledge sharing and collaboration can be difficult. Moreover, it may require ongoing effort to maintain engagement and participation.	It can be resource-intensive to establish and maintain. May face resistance from employees accustomed to working in silos. It may require ongoing effort to stay abreast of emerging risks and trends.

6.8.2 Centers of Excellence

Centers of Excellence (CoE) can be an effective way for organizations to improve their risk management capabilities. A CoE is a centralized unit within an organization responsible for developing and promoting best practices in a specific area of expertise, such as risk management. CoEs can help organizations develop and implement more effective risk management strategies by consolidating knowledge and expertise in a dedicated unit.

One key advantage of CoE in risk management is that they can provide a single point of contact for an organization's risk management expertise and resources. This single-point contact can help ensure that risk management strategies and practices are consistent and coordinated across different departments and business units. CoE can also help identify and prioritize risks based on their potential impact on the organization and develop targeted mitigation strategies.

CoE can also be valuable in developing and implementing risk management policies and procedures. By consolidating knowledge and expertise in risk management, CoE can help ensure that policies and procedures are based on best practices and tailored to the organization's needs. CoE can also provide training and support to help employees at all levels of the organization understand and implement risk management practices effectively.

Another advantage of CoE in risk management is that it can help organizations stay abreast of emerging risks and trends. By monitoring and analyzing new developments in risk management, CoE can help organizations adapt and adjust their risk management strategies to meet changing circumstances. This knowledge can be essential in fast-changing industries or responses to emerging risks, such as cybersecurity threats or environmental hazards.

Overall, CoE can be a valuable tool for organizations looking to improve their risk management capabilities. By consolidating knowledge and expertise in a dedicated unit, CoE can help organizations develop and implement more effective risk management strategies, policies, and procedures and stay ahead of emerging risks and trends in the field.

6.8.3 Training Internal and External

Training is critical to effective risk management for internal and external stakeholders. Effective training programs can help employees and other stakeholders understand the risks facing an organization, how to identify and assess those risks, and how to develop and implement strategies to mitigate those risks.

Internal training programs can help ensure that employees at all levels of the organization are aware of the organization's risks and understand their role in managing those risks. Such training programs can include general risk awareness training and specialized training on specific risks, such as cybersecurity, financial, or operational risks. Training delivery takes various formats, such as classroom-based training, e-learning modules, and on-the-job training.

External training programs can also be valuable in managing risk, particularly for suppliers, partners, and other external stakeholders. Such training programs can help ensure that external stakeholders understand the organization's risks and the importance of managing those risks. Training programs can include general risk awareness training and specialized training on specific risks relevant to the stakeholder's role or relationship with the organization.

One key benefit of training programs is that they can help build a culture of risk awareness and proactive risk management within an organization or across an ecosystem of partners and suppliers. By providing employees and external stakeholders with the knowledge and skills they need to identify and manage risks, training programs can help minimize the likelihood and impact of risk events.

However, developing and delivering effective training programs can also present some challenges. For example, it cannot be easy to tailor training programs to the organization's and its stakeholders' specific needs. Additionally, training programs can be resource-intensive to develop and deliver, particularly if they require specialized expertise or technology.

6.8.4 Metatag Searchable Database

A metatag searchable database is a tool that manages risk by providing a centralized repository for information related to risk management. For example, such a database can include information on threats facing the organization, risk management strategies and policies, risk assessments, and risk mitigation plans.

Organizations can use a metatag searchable database to ensure that relevant information is easily accessible to those who need it, such as risk managers, compliance officers, and other stakeholders. The database can also help ensure that information is up-to-date, accurate, easily searchable, and retrievable.

Some of the key benefits of using a metatag searchable database for risk management include:

1. **Improved data organization**: A searchable database that uses metadata can help to organize risk-related information, making it easier to find and analyze. Metadata can categorize information according to risk type, severity, likelihood, location, and other relevant factors, allowing stakeholders to find the necessary information quickly.
2. **More efficient searching**: A searchable database with metadata can enable a more efficient search for risk-related information. Stakeholders can use search terms to find specific information about potential risks rather than manually searching through large amounts of data.
3. **Better analysis**: A searchable database that uses metadata can support better analysis of risk-related data. By organizing data in a consistent and standardized manner, metadata can facilitate data analysis and help stakeholders to identify patterns and trends related to potential risks.
4. **Enhanced collaboration**: A searchable database that uses metadata can support enhanced collaboration among stakeholders involved in risk management. By providing a centralized repository for risk-related information, stakeholders can more easily share information and collaborate on risk management initiatives.
5. **Improved decision-making**: A searchable database that uses metadata can support better decision-making related to risk management. By promptly providing stakeholders access to relevant information, they can make more informed decisions about managing potential risks.

A metatag searchable database can be a valuable tool for storing and managing risk by providing a centralized repository for risk management information. In addition, by improving the accessibility and accuracy of risk management information, a searchable database can help organizations better manage risks and improve their overall risk management capabilities. This information is available for analysis (big data) over time, making predictions more competent.

6.8.5 Big Data and Risk Management

Big data can play a crucial role in risk management by allowing organizations to analyze large amounts of data in real time and identify potential risks and trends. Here are some ways in which big data and Power BI can support risk management:

1. **Identifying potential risks**: Big data can be used to analyze vast amounts of data from multiple sources, including quality, sales, performance metrics, customer feedback, and sensor data (and much more). As a result, big data can

help to identify potential risks in real time and enable organizations to take proactive measures to mitigate them.
2. **Predictive analytics**: Analytic tools can create predictive models that forecast potential risks and their impact on the organization. These tools can aid in identifying patterns and trends to predict future dangers by analyzing historical data.
3. **Real-time monitoring**: Dashboards allow the monitoring of real-time data from various sources, including product quality, project performance, product performance, and customer interactions. Analysis of this data can enable organizations to identify potential risks as they occur and respond in real time to mitigate them.
4. **Data visualization**: Tools that can create visualizations make it easier to understand complex data sets and identify potential risks. Visualization can help stakeholders to identify risks and take appropriate measures to manage them quickly.
5. **Compliance monitoring**: Big data can help monitor compliance with regulatory requirements and identify potential risks related to noncompliance. Power BI dashboards allow transparent monitoring of compliance metrics and identify areas where compliance may be at risk.

Big data and Power BI can be valuable tools in risk management, allowing organizations to analyze large amounts of data in real time, identify potential risks, and take proactive measures to mitigate them. By leveraging these tools, organizations can better understand their risk landscape and make more informed decisions about managing potential risks.

6.9 What Are Heuristics

Though typically accounting for 2% of a person's body weight, the human brain will consume an average of 20% of the daily caloric intake [7,8]. To reduce mental effort and this caloric drain, the brain finds shortcuts, reducing the complexity and clutter of the situation, making quick decisions possible.

Heuristics are mental shortcuts or rules of thumb that individuals use to make decisions or solve problems quickly and efficiently. Use heuristics in situations with uncertainty, complexity, or time pressure, and they can help individuals make reasonably good decisions based on experience.

Heuristics can take many forms and may involve simplifying complex problems, relying on previous experiences or biases, or using general rules or principles to guide decision-making. Some examples of heuristics include:

1. The availability heuristic involves making decisions based on the ease with which examples or instances come to mind. For example, if someone hears

about a plane crash on the news, they may become more afraid of flying, even though flying is statistically much safer than driving.
2. An anchoring heuristic involves using initial information as a reference point when making decisions or judgments. For example, when negotiating the price of a car, the initial asking price may influence the buyer's perception of a fair price.
3. The Representativeness heuristic involves making judgments or decisions based on how similar something is to a typical example. For example, assuming that someone quiet and introverted is also knowledgeable, simply because that is a common stereotype.

While heuristics can be helpful in many situations, they can also lead to errors and biases in decision-making. These biases require taking a moment to be aware of our heuristics and apply critical thinking and analysis to ensure the decision uses an appropriate heuristic based on reliable data.

6.10 Cognitive Bias

Cognitive biases are patterns in thinking that impact rational judgment and clear thinking. The individual will have subjective elements in assessing the circumstances that will cloud that clear thinking. It should be easy to understand that unclear thinking and biases are not ways to avoid project risks. Below are some cognitive biases that, from our experience, impact project success.

Cognitive biases can arise for several reasons, including limited information processing capacity, information overload, and the need to make quick decisions. In addition, various individual and situational factors, such as emotions, beliefs, values, and social norms, can also influence biases. Biases affect how we process and interpret information, make judgments, and respond to the environment.

6.10.1 Sunk Cost Bias

Sunk cost bias is a cognitive bias that causes individuals to make decisions based on the resources already invested in a project rather than the potential benefits or costs of continuing the project. This bias can affect project costs in several ways.

First, sunk cost bias can cause individuals to continue investing in a project that has already consumed significant resources, even if it no longer makes financial sense. For example, suppose a project has already gone over budget. In that case, individuals may feel that they have no choice but to continue investing in it, even if there is a high likelihood that the additional investment will not result in a successful outcome.

Second, sunk cost bias can lead to a failure to account for the actual cost of a project. If individuals focus on recouping the resources they have already invested, they may underestimate the cost of continuing the project. For example, they may not consider the additional resources required to address new challenges or changes in the project scope.

To mitigate the impact of sunk cost bias on project cost, it is vital to regularly assess project viability and make decisions based on the expected future benefits and costs. For example, mitigation may require a willingness to abandon a project that is not meeting its objectives, even if it has already consumed significant resources. Additionally, conducting a cost-benefit analysis that considers the resources already invested and the potential costs and benefits of continuing the project may be helpful.

6.10.2 Curse of Knowledge

The curse of knowledge is a cognitive bias that occurs when knowledgeable individuals assume that others have the same expertise and therefore do not adequately communicate information to them. This bias can lead to miscommunication, misunderstandings, and increased project risk in project management, and it runs contrary to spreading learning through the project team. In addition, this bias can lead to unclear communication about project goals, risks, and strategies, resulting in misunderstandings and mistakes. For example, if a project team member assumes that everyone understands a technical term or concept, they may not explain it adequately, leading to confusion and errors in decision-making.

The curse of knowledge can also lead to overconfidence in project risk assessments. When project team members have specialized knowledge or expertise, they may overestimate their ability to assess project risks and make decisions accurately. As a result, the curse of knowledge bias can fail to identify and mitigate potential risks, leading to project failure or delays.

To mitigate the impact of the curse of knowledge on project risk, project managers and team members need to recognize the bias and work to overcome it. Recognition of the bias involves using clear and straightforward language to communicate information to team members and stakeholders and seeking feedback to ensure that information is understood. Additionally, it may be helpful to engage external experts or consultants to objectively assess project risks and strategies and challenge assumptions and biases. By addressing the curse of knowledge, project managers can improve communication, reduce misunderstandings, and minimize the risk of project failure.

6.10.3 Optimism and Pessimism Bias

Optimism and pessimism biases are cognitive biases that can impact project risk by influencing how project team members perceive and respond to risks and uncertainties. Optimism bias is the tendency for individuals to be overly optimistic about the likelihood of positive outcomes and underestimate the possibility of adverse effects. In project management, this bias can lead to a lack of consideration of potential risks and uncertainties, resulting in unrealistic project plans, schedules, and budgets. Optimism bias can also lead to underestimation of the severity of threats, resulting in inadequate risk mitigation measures and a higher likelihood of project failure.

Pessimism bias is the tendency for individuals to be overly pessimistic about the likelihood of positive outcomes and overestimate the possibility of adverse effects. This bias can lead to excessive risk aversion in project management, resulting in overly conservative project plans, schedules, and budgets. Pessimism bias can also lead to overestimating the severity of risks, resulting in overinvestment in risk mitigation measures and unnecessary delays and costs.

To mitigate the impact of optimism and pessimism biases on project risk, project managers and team members need to recognize and address these biases. Mitigation may involve:

- **Conducting realistic risk assessments**: Project teams should take a systematic approach to risk assessment, considering all potential risks and uncertainties and objectively evaluating the likelihood and impact of each risk.
- **Considering alternative scenarios**: Project teams should consider alternative scenarios and outcomes, including best-case, worst-case, and most likely scenarios, and develop contingency plans for each.
- **Regularly reassessing risks**: Project teams should regularly reassess risks throughout the project lifecycle and adjust risk management strategies as necessary.
- **Encouraging diverse perspectives**: Project teams should seek input from various stakeholders, including subject matter experts, to challenge assumptions and biases and ensure a balanced assessment of risks.

6.10.4 Confirmation Bias

Confirmation bias is a cognitive bias that can impact project risk by leading project team members to selectively seek, interpret, and remember information that confirms their pre-existing beliefs or hypotheses while ignoring or discounting information that contradicts them.

In project management, confirmation bias can lead to a failure to identify and adequately assess potential risks and uncertainties, resulting in incomplete risk management strategies and increased project risk. For example, suppose project team members have preconceived notions about the feasibility or success of a particular project approach or technology. In that case, they may selectively seek information that confirms their beliefs while ignoring information that suggests otherwise. Narrow focus data selection can result in an incomplete assessment of project risks and a failure to develop effective risk management strategies.

To mitigate the impact of confirmation bias on project risk, project managers and team members need to recognize and address this bias. Mitigation may involve:

- **Encouraging diverse perspectives**: Project teams should seek input from various stakeholders, including those with different views or opinions. Encouraging open discourse helps challenge assumptions and biases and ensure a balanced assessment of risks.
- **Actively seeking contrary evidence**: Project teams should actively seek out information that challenges their preconceived notions and hypotheses and objectively evaluate the strengths and weaknesses of each perspective.
- **Regularly reassessing risks**: Project teams should regularly reassess risks throughout the project lifecycle and adjust risk management strategies based on new information and insights.
- **Conducting objective analyses**: Project teams should use accurate data and analyses, rather than relying solely on subjective opinions or assumptions, to assess project risks and evaluate potential solutions.

6.10.5 Anchoring Bias

Anchoring bias is a cognitive bias that can impact project risk by leading project team members to rely too heavily on the first piece of information they receive when making decisions, even if it is not necessarily relevant or accurate. In project management, anchoring bias can lead to an inaccurate assessment of project risks, resulting in inadequate or ineffective risk management strategies. For example, suppose the project team gives an initial estimate for the cost or duration of a project. In that case, they may be anchored to this estimate and fail to consider other factors that could impact the project, such as changes in scope or unforeseen risks.

To mitigate the impact of anchoring bias on project risk, project managers and team members must recognize and address this bias. Mitigation may involve:

- **Gathering multiple sources of information**: Project teams should consider various sources of information when making decisions rather than relying solely on the first piece of information they receive.
- **Challenging initial assumptions**: Project teams should challenge initial assumptions and estimates and actively seek information that may contradict or challenge them.
- **Regularly reassessing risks**: Project teams should regularly reassess risks throughout the project lifecycle and adjust risk management strategies based on new information and insights.
- **Using objective data**: Project teams should use accurate data and analyses to assess project risks and evaluate potential solutions rather than relying solely on subjective opinions or assumptions.

6.10.6 Clustering Illusion

The clustering illusion is a cognitive bias that can impact project risk by leading project team members to see patterns or clusters in data that are nonexistent or overestimates the significance of existing practices. In project management, the clustering illusion can lead to an inaccurate assessment of project trends or risks, resulting in inadequate or ineffective risk management strategies. For example, if the project team notices that several risks have occurred within a short period, they may believe that they are more likely to happen in the future or are related, even if they are not.

To mitigate the impact of the clustering illusion on project risk, project managers and team members need to recognize and address this bias. Mitigation may involve:

- **Gathering and analyzing data objectively**: Project teams should collect and analyze data objectively and systematically, avoiding subjective interpretations or assumptions. See the chapter on metrics for how to
- **Testing hypotheses**: Project teams should test ideas and assumptions using objective data and avoid jumping to conclusions based on patterns or clusters that may not be statistically significant.
- **Seeking alternative explanations**: Project teams should consider alternative explanations for patterns or clusters in data and evaluate the strength of the evidence supporting each resolution. Following up with experimentation to determine the dynamic.
- **Regularly reassessing risks**: Project teams should regularly reassess risks throughout the project lifecycle and adjust risk management strategies based on new information and insights.

6.10.7 Group Think

Groupthink is a phenomenon that can impact project risk by leading project teams to make flawed decisions or overlook significant risks due to a desire for conformity and consensus. In project management, groupthink can occur when team members prioritize agreement and harmony over critical thinking and independent analysis. Prioritizing conformity over critical thinking can lead to an incomplete assessment of project risks and a failure to develop effective risk management strategies.

To mitigate the impact of groupthink on project risk, project managers must encourage open communication, diverse perspectives, and independent analysis. Mitigation may involve:

- **Encouraging diverse perspectives**: Project teams should seek input from various stakeholders, including those with different views or opinions. Evoke the background assumptions of the team members. Diverse perspectives can help challenge assumptions and biases and ensure a balanced assessment of risks.

- **Fostering a culture of open communication**: Project managers should create a culture where team members feel comfortable expressing their views and opinions, even if they differ from the group. A mature team has productive ways of managing divergent ideas. A critique of these ideas, especially those contrary to the group, is a psychologically safe environment [9].
- **Encouraging critical thinking**: Project managers should encourage critical thinking and independent analysis among team members and avoid pressuring team members to conform to a particular viewpoint.
- **Assigning a devil's advocate**: Assigning a team member to play the devil's advocate can help challenge assumptions, highlight potential risks, and ensure consideration of all relevant perspectives. It is only possible to know the relevance upon exploration.
- **Regularly reassessing risks**: Project teams should regularly reassess risks throughout the project lifecycle and adjust risk management strategies based on new information and insights.

6.10.8 Halo and Horns Effect

The halo and horns effect is a cognitive bias that can impact project risk by leading project team members to make biased judgments based on their overall impression of a person, organization, or idea. For example, in project management, the halo effect can occur when team members have a positive image of another team member, stakeholder, organization, or idea and overestimate the potential benefits while overlooking potential risks and drawbacks or considering other inputs. Conversely, the horns effect can occur when team members have a negative impression of a stakeholder, organization, or idea and underestimate its potential benefits while overestimating potential risks or drawbacks. The perceived value of an idea links to the perceived value of the person delivering it. Jim is always on time; we like Jim. Jim brings an idea to the team; there is a tendency to accept Jim's idea without questioning our thoughts about Jim taint an honest review.

To mitigate the impact of the halo and horns effect on project risk, project managers and team members need to recognize and address these biases. Mitigation or remediation may involve:

- **Gathering objective data**: Project teams should collect accurate data on stakeholders, organizations, or ideas and avoid relying solely on subjective impressions or opinions.
- **Challenging assumptions**: Project teams should challenge assumptions and biases and seek alternative viewpoints or perspectives.

- **Conducting a thorough risk analysis**: Project teams should conduct a comprehensive risk analysis to identify potential risks and benefits associated with stakeholders, organizations, or ideas and evaluate them objectively.
- **Using multiple sources of information**: Project teams should use various sources, including data from stakeholders, organizations, or ideas, to develop a more comprehensive understanding of potential risks and benefits.

6.10.9 Dunning–Kruger Effect

The Dunning–Kruger effect is a cognitive bias that can impact project risk by leading individuals to overestimate their knowledge, skills, or abilities in a particular domain and underestimate the complexity or difficulty of a task.

In project management, the Dunning–Kruger effect can occur when team members have a limited understanding of a particular domain or task but overestimate their ability to manage related risks. This belief can lead to incomplete or inaccurate risk assessments and a failure to develop effective risk management strategies.

To mitigate the impact of the Dunning–Kruger effect on project risk, it is vital for project managers to:

- **Encourage self-awareness**: Project managers should encourage team members to reflect on their knowledge, skills, and abilities and be aware of the limits of their expertise.
- **Training and support**: Project managers should provide training and support to team members to help them better understand the project domain and associated risks.
- **Seek external expertise**: Projects do not always have required internal expertise for the scope. In these cases, seek knowledge from domain experts or consultants to assess risks comprehensively.
- **Conduct independent reviews**: Project teams should conduct independent reviews of risk assessments and risk management strategies to identify potential gaps or oversights.

6.10.10 Survivor Bias

Survivor bias is a cognitive bias that can impact project risk by leading project managers to overestimate the success rate of projects, based only on the outcomes of successful projects, while ignoring the failure rate of other projects that did not survive.

In project management, survivor bias can occur when project managers evaluate the success of a project based solely on the outcomes of successful projects that have survived and ignore the potential risks and challenges faced by projects that did not survive. This bias can lead to an overestimation of the success rate of projects and a failure to identify and manage potential risks. To mitigate the impact of survivor bias on project risk, it is for project managers to:

- **Conduct a comprehensive risk assessment**: Project teams should conduct a thorough risk assessment that considers potential risks and challenges faced by all projects, including those that did not survive.
- **Analyze successful and failed projects**: Project teams should analyze successful and failed projects to identify common factors contributing to their success or failure.
- **Learn from past failures**: Project teams should learn from past failures to avoid repeating the same mistakes in future projects.
- **Consider alternative scenarios**: Project teams should consider alternative strategies to evaluate potential risks and outcomes under different circumstances.

6.11 Not So Fast

From the previous text, one probably would believe that all that is required is to capture the things that go poorly and well throughout the organization, especially the events with poor outcomes. The problem is that there are subtle interactions we may be unaware of that may impact the result of our endeavors. This interaction of variables and parameters may not be known. Even if the variables are known, interactions or influences may not be known or considered. Communication, learning, and a record of past risk events can help make good decisions. However, decisions made under one set of circumstances that fail do not mean that making those same decisions in what seems to be a similar set of events does not necessarily lead to a similar failure. However, it is good to consider those past results and make some decisions based on analysis to make this strategic decision.

References

1. E. Verzuh, *The Fast Forward MBA in Project Management*, 6th ed., John Wiley & Sons, Inc, 2021.
2. W. D. Lutz, *Doublespeak*, Harper & Row, 1989.
3. G. Hofstede, *Culture's Consequences: International Differences in Work-Related Values,* ,Sage Publications, 1984.
4. M. Twain, *Following the Equator: A Journey Around The World*, American Publishing Company, 1897.
5. G. Santayana, *The Life of Reason or The Phases of Human Progress*, C. Scribner's Sons, 1905.
6. L. J. Peter, *Peter's Almanac*, William Morrow and Company, 1982.

7. M. Heid, "Does Thinking Burn Calories? Here's What the Science Says," *Time.com*, 19 September 2018. [Online]. Available: https://time.com/5400025/does-thinking-burn-calories/#:~:text=While%20the%20brain%20represents%20just%202%25%20of%20a,subtly%20affect%20the%20way%20the%20brain%20consumes%20energy. [Accessed 26 March 2023].
8. D. D. Clark and L. Sokoloff, "Circulation and Energy Metabolism of the Brain," in *Basic Neurochemistry: Molecular, Cellular and Medical Aspectsi*, eds. Siegle, G. J., Agranoff, B. W., Albers, R. W., Fisher, S. K., & Uhler, M. D., Lippincott, 1999, pp. 637–670.
9. M. E. Raichle and D. A. Gusnard, "*Appraising the Brain's Energy Budget*," National Library of Medicine, 6 August 2002. [Online]. Available: www.ncbi.nlm.nih.gov/pmc/articles/PMC124895/. [Accessed 26 March 2023].

Chapter 7

Advanced Topics in Risk Management

> Risk? Risk is our business – nothing great can be accomplished without being willing to take risks.
>
> *Captain James T. Kirk, Starship Enterprise [51]*

The previous chapters describe practices, processes, and procedures to identify, analyze, plan, track, and handle risk created by uncertainty, with defined approaches that increase the probability of project success (PoPS).[1] In this chapter, advanced risk management topics are presented and applied to projects once the straightforward approaches have been put in place.

> Risk is Uncertainty That Matters [69].

Guided by the materials in the previous chapters, effective risk management means:

- **Continuously managing** risk produced by uncertainty to create a positive correlation between risk management and increased probability of project success [52].
- **Determining which risks are important** to handle in a prioritized model, the risk interactions, statistical dependencies, interdependencies, propagation, and evolution.
- **Implementing strategies to handle risk** with mitigation, correction, prevention, and avoidance, starting with RCA of the uncertainties, the corrective or preventive actions needed to remove or prevent the conditions, and actions creating risks.

DOI: 10.1201/9781003425465-7

Continuous Risk Management (CRM) is a set of principles, concepts, and functions providing solutions to project failures by applying continuously assessing what can go wrong, why it can go wrong, determining which risks are most important, and implementing strategies to *handle* these risks,[2] by [2]:

- **Preventing problems before they occur** with *pre*-mortems using Root Cause Analysis (RCA) of sources of uncertainty identifies the conditions and actions and takes corrective and preventive actions to remove the condition or protect from the natural variance before the risk becomes an issue.
- **Enabling effective use of resources** through early identification of problems and providing input to management decisions regarding resource allocation.
- **Promoting teamwork** by involving all personnel at all levels of the project and focusing their attention on the shared vision of the mission or strategy to provide the mechanism to achieving the needed Measures of Effectiveness and Measures of Performance as planned, for the needed cost on the needed date, in the presence of uncertainty creating risk.

CRM provides a discipline environment for proactive decision-making to [106]:

- Continually assess what can go wrong and determine the impact on the project.
- Determine which risks are important to handle with their corrective and preventive handling strategies.
- Implement the handling strategies with to reduce risk action or consume margin.
- Assure corrective and preventive actions working measure effectives of the handling strategies.

A Critical Reminder Before Proceeding.

All Risk Comes From Uncertainty

The uncertainty that creates project risk comes in two ways to managing projects [1]:[3]

- **Aleatory Uncertainty**: Comes from *frequentist* or *statistical* probability – *alea* is a single die in Latin. This uncertainty comes from random or naturally occurring stochastic processes that can be estimated from historic data or probabilistic models of a naturally occurring process. When events and variables are inherently random and treated as nondeterministic in nature, the uncertainty is attributed to a physical process. It cannot be reduced or eliminated by enhancing the underlying knowledge base [111].
- **Epistemic Uncertainty**: Comes from *subjective* probability, which measures the probabilistic belief in a proposition. This uncertainty is from the lack of

knowledge. *Epistemology* is the study of knowledge. This uncertainty is created by *missing knowledge*. Just because some value is uncertain does not mean it is random in the way an *aleatory* uncertainty is random.

7.1 Root Cause Analysis – The Foundation of All Successful Risk Managements

> Risk Management is the foundation of effective problem-solving [10].
>
> Root Cause Analysis is the foundation of effective Risk Management [48].

The missing link in Risk Management is closed by asking a simple question – *why is this uncertainty (reducible or irreducible) that creates risk present on our project?*

To be effective, Risk Management must identify potential failure modes (issues) before they occur, not just after – the traditional RCA paradigm. To do this, we start with RCA to discover the conditions and actions that create the risk BEFORE they become issues. RCA is a critical success factor for risk management, starting with risk identification, then assessing what went wrong and why, and developing corrective and preventative action plans to eliminate uncertainties or provide margin and reserves to protect from the uncertainties.

7.1.1 Origins of Root Cause Analysis

> Probability is the Guide to Life – Cicero (107 BC).

RCA is the process to identifying the *reason(s)* for a problem, when prevented or corrected will prevent the problem from occurring or reoccurring. There are five origins of RCA and its connection to increasing the probability of project success:

- **Safety-Based**: Developed from accident analysis and occupational health and safety.
- **Production-Based**: With origins in quality control for manufacturing, product usage, and operations.
- **Process-Based**: Following production-based applied to business processes.
- **Failure-Based**: Failure analysis applied to engineering, operations, and maintenance processes.
- **Systems-Based**: The integration of the first four domains, along with change management, risk management, and systems analysis.

RCA is a research-based process to identify the *reason(s)* the uncertainties that create risk exist – both reducible and irreducible uncertainties. There are many methods for RCA [66]. In this book, we describe the Apollo Method [12].

RCA can be applied in a systematic process to identifying the sources of uncertainty that create a risk to project success and the handling strategies for responding to them. RCA is based on the principle that effective management requires more than *putting out fires* for problems that develop but finding the corrective or preventive actions to remove, eliminate, or prevent their impacts [50].

RCA is the use of methods and tools that create a confident understanding of the causes leading to particular effects impacting the project's probability of success. The depth of the RCA is sufficient when the underlying cause(s) are sufficiently understood to allow the prevention of recurrence of the effects. This includes complete resolution of all of the possible causes (conditions and actions) that can or have contributed to the effect, that the sources of uncertainty are clearly understood, and corrective or preventive actions that will conclusively prevent the recurrence of the effect [66].

RCA is the foundation of Risk Management through four elements [12]:

1. Cause and Effect are the same thing.	2. Causes and Effects are part of an infinite continuum.
3. Every Effect has at least two causes in the form of Actions and Conditions.	4. An Effect (a risk that has become an issue) exists only of its Cause(s) exist at the same point in time and space (location).

> Ignorance is a most wonderful thing.
> It facilitates magic.
> It allows the masses to be led.
> It provides answers when there are none.
> It allows happiness in the presence of danger [12].

All project success starts with *managing in the presence of uncertainty* that creates risk. The better the underlying causes of these uncertainties are understood, the better they can be *handled.*[4] The more causal relationships are understood, the better the forecasting of future performance can be made, and the probability of success increased [12].

RCA identifies not just the *proximate* cause but the *root cause* of problems or events that have occurred or possibly may occur and an approach for responding to them.[5] RCA is based on the principle that effective management, in the presence of uncertainty, requires more than just "putting out fires" for problems that develop but finding a way to prevent them.

This approach starts by analyzing adverse events and their impact on the probability of project success. Initially developed to analyze industrial accidents, RCA is now deployed as an error analysis tool in many domains. A central tenet of RCA is to identify underlying uncertainties that increase the likelihood of risk while avoiding focusing on individual mistakes.

RCA uses a systems approach to identify both active errors (errors occurring at the point of interface between elements of a complex system) and latent errors (the hidden problems within the system that contribute to adverse events).

There are three core causes of project risk which RCA can reveal:

- Physical
  - A tangible object, system, process, or outcome fails in some way.
  - Some work processes are delayed.
  - The labor, material, equipment, or services cost increased without margin or reserve.
- Human
  - A person did something wrong or did not do something right.
  - Human causes usually lead to a physical cause.
- Organizational
  - A system, process, or policy that is faulty and creates undesirable effects.

RCA asks and answers basic questions:

- What happened? – An outcome of an action or condition of the root cause.
- When did it happen? – The period of time the Effect of the condition or action occurred.
- How did it happen? – The enabling mechanisms of the condition or action.
- Why did it happen? – The triggering condition or action.
- What can be done to correct or prevent the condition or action-creating Effect from happening again? – The corrective or preventive actions to handle the conditions or actions.

These questions are typically asked after an incident in Figure 7.1. Risk Management defines the process of planning, organizing, leading, and controlling activities of an organization to minimize the risks, created by uncertainty.

The diagram in Figure 7.1. is from the Apollo Method, where the *Effect* (the undesirable outcome) requires both an *Action* to be performed and a *Condition* to be in place that allows the *Action* to occur in the same period of time. As well, how the Action or Condition was recognized is needed, in the example, this can be an *Observation*, a sound that was heard, a verbal statement.

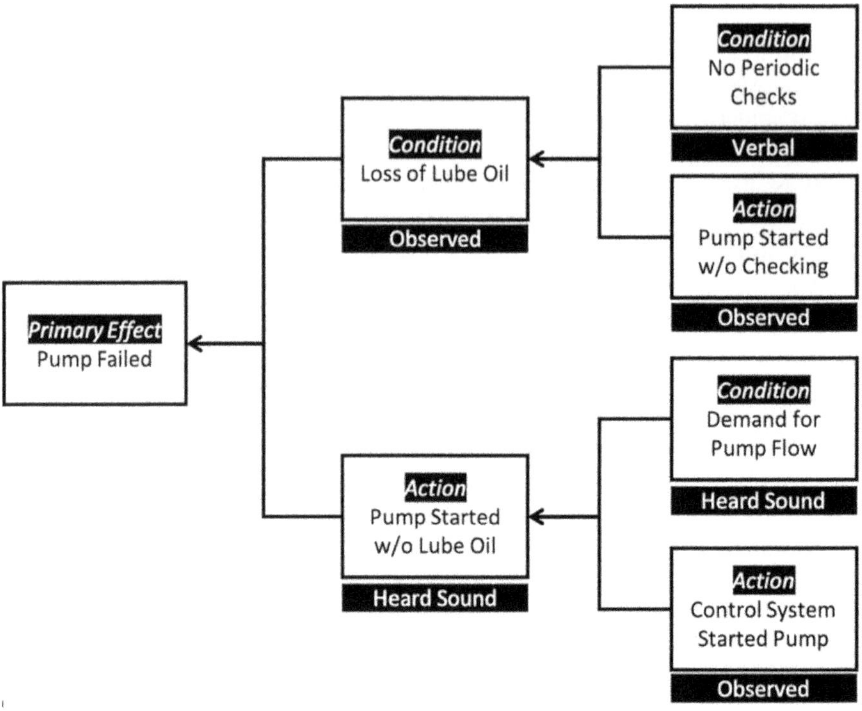

Figure 7.1 A simple cause and effect diagram. When called upon to start the pump, it failed to start.

The traditional understanding of RCA is it is performed *after* a problem has occurred. This is the *postmortem* paradigm of RCA. In the Risk Management paradigm, RCA is used in its *premortem* form [9].

Project premortems are about discovering what can go wrong *before* it goes wrong. RCA using premortems can convert assessment of what the *cause* of a problem, into what *might* be causes of problems in the future. For any *causal* or *permitting* factors that create a future risk, there is an opportunity to create corrective or preventive actions to *handle* the risk.

This is a *root cause projection* (RCP) approach to risk management [11]. In RCA, causes of risk are anticipated – projecting the future.

7.1.1.1 The Difference Between Risk and Uncertainty

Throughout this book, we have stated that risk comes from uncertainty. It is important to distinguish between *risk* and *uncertainty* [43]. This separation is not made in traditional risk management processes found at PMI and other project management sources.

- **Uncertainty** is an indefiniteness about the outcome of a situation. For projects, uncertainty is assessed in cost-estimating models of the risk (or probability) that a specific funding level will be exceeded. In schedule estimating models of the risk, the project and its deliverables will exceed the planned delivery date.
- Uncertainty is the indefiniteness of a project's plans. It represents a fundamental inability to predict the outcome of a future event perfectly. Uncertainty is characterized by a probability distribution, which is based on a combination of the prior experience of the assessor and historical data.
- **Risk** is the chance of loss or injury. In a situation that includes favorable and unfavorable events, risk is the probability that an unfavorable event will occur. A risk is an event not in the projects baseline plan that is an undesirable outcome (discrete risk).
- This definition is one seen in a risk matrix. The event is characterized by a probability of occurrence and an expected impact if the event did occur.

7.1.2 Quantification of Uncertainties That Create Risk

> **Uncertainty** has been called *An Unintelligible Expression Without A Straightforward Description.*[6]

Quantification of uncertainty is a decision-support methodology for complex technical decisions. This process focuses on the identification, characterization, and analysis of uncertainty that creates risk to performance thresholds (cost, schedule, and technical performance) and their associated handling strategies for projects and programs evaluated with modeling and simulation.

For any risk management process to be successful, and especially the advanced approaches described in this chapter, we need to start with *quantifiable* assessments of the reducible (Epistemic) and irreducible (Aleatory) uncertainties that create risk.

In the presence of these two uncertainties Uncertainty Quantification (UQ) is the basis of increasing the probability of project success. UQ is the quantitative characterization and reduction of uncertainties as part of a decision-support method for complex technical decision processes. UQ attempts to determine how likely certain outcomes will be if some aspect of the system is not exactly known. Risk Management is well developed in several domains but [31–34].

Capturing risks that result from reducible and irreducible uncertainties is the first step in increasing the probability of project success. For this approach to be successful, the uncertainties must be properly modeled to quantify the resulting risk and create robust and reliable handling strategies from both the technical performance and programmatic performance point of view.

7.1.2.1 Quantification of Handling Strategies to Protect Project from Uncertainties

It is better to be approximately right than to be precisely wrong.

Warren Buffet

Cost, Schedule, and Technical Margin protects the project from naturally occurring Aleatory uncertainties. Risk *Buydown* strategies for these three classes of risk, protect the project from Epistemic uncertainty by assessing the probability of occurrence, probability of impact, and probability of residual uncertainty impacting the probability of project success.

Quantification of Margin and Uncertainty (QMU) is focused on characterizing the detail of the sources of uncertainty in a model, quantifying the uncertainty in the system response output variables. These sources are described as probability distributions to account for the stochastic nature of the uncertainty. The characterization of uncertainty provides for the comparisons of margins for to protect from aleatory uncertainty and probability of occurrence for epistemic uncertainty.

QMU provides risk-informed decision-making processes where simulation (Monte Carlo Simulations, Method of Moments) provides inputs to the decision-making authority, as shown in Figure 7.2.

In this book, we don't recommend *qualitative* assessments of the uncertainties, the risks they create, and the impacts on the probability of project success [72,73]. The qualitative risk matrix presents the probability of risk occurrence – the frequency of occurrence, and the severity of the outcome should the risk be realized.

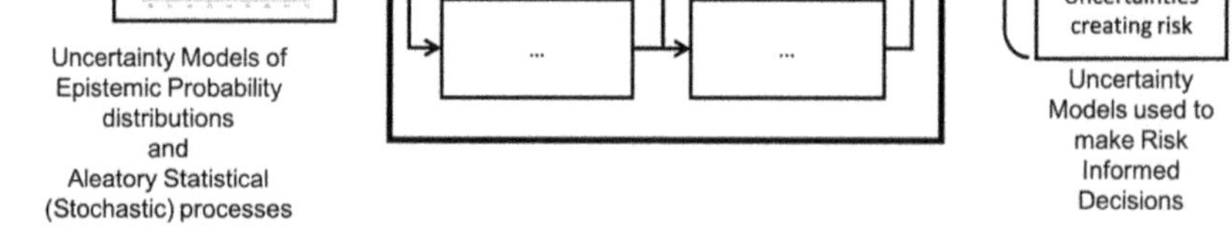

Figure 7.2 Quantifying margins and uncertainties provide decision making information for how risk impacts the probability of project success based in aleatory (irreducible) and epistemic (reducible) uncertainties, with each subsystem element driven by uncertainties and its interactions and interdependencies with the other subsystems.

Modeling risk with qualitative matrices is inherently ambiguous and have limited ability to rank qualitative risks with any confidence [74].

QMU focuses on quantification of the ratio of planned cost, schedule, and technical performance margin to model uncertainty's impact on the probability of project success. The process begins with the identification of the key performance thresholds of the project, which are found in the schedule and related costs, and the technical performance measures of the deliverables. These thresholds (also referred to as performance gates) can specify an upper bound of performance, a lower bound of performance, or both in the case where the metric must remain within the specified range. For each of these performance thresholds, the associated performance margin must be identified [40,42].

QMU supports risk-informed decision-making processes where computational simulation results provide one of several inputs to the decision-making authority.

7.1.2.2 Approaches to Uncertainty Quantification

> Model-based Uncertainty Quantification is the next step in applying risk management to increase the probability of project success [113].

Quantifying the uncertainty-creating risk is required before uncertainty reduction can take place. The two types of uncertainty creating risk:

- **Aleatory Uncertainty**: Statistical uncertainty created by a stochastic process representing the unknowns that differ as a function of time.
- **Epistemic Uncertainty**: Systematic uncertainty due to the lack of knowledge due to random variations of the process.

These two uncertainties can be quantified in a forward propagation where the uncertainties are propagated through the system to create an overall uncertainty. The inverse uncertainty quantification represents the estimated behavior (in this case, the risk) from the actual behavior for an unknown risk parameter.

- **Forward Uncertainty Quantification**: The quantification of uncertainties in system output(s) propagated from uncertain inputs. This assessment focuses on the influence on the outputs from the parametric variability listed in the sources of uncertainty, the processes of handling these uncertainties and the output of this process to be used for Risk Management, as shown in Figures 7.2 and 7.3. The targets of forward uncertainty propagation analysis include:
  - To evaluate low-order moments of the outputs, the mean, and variance of the uncertainty and resulting risk.
  - To evaluate the reliability of the outputs. This is especially useful in reliability engineering, where outputs of a system are usually closely related to the performance of the system.

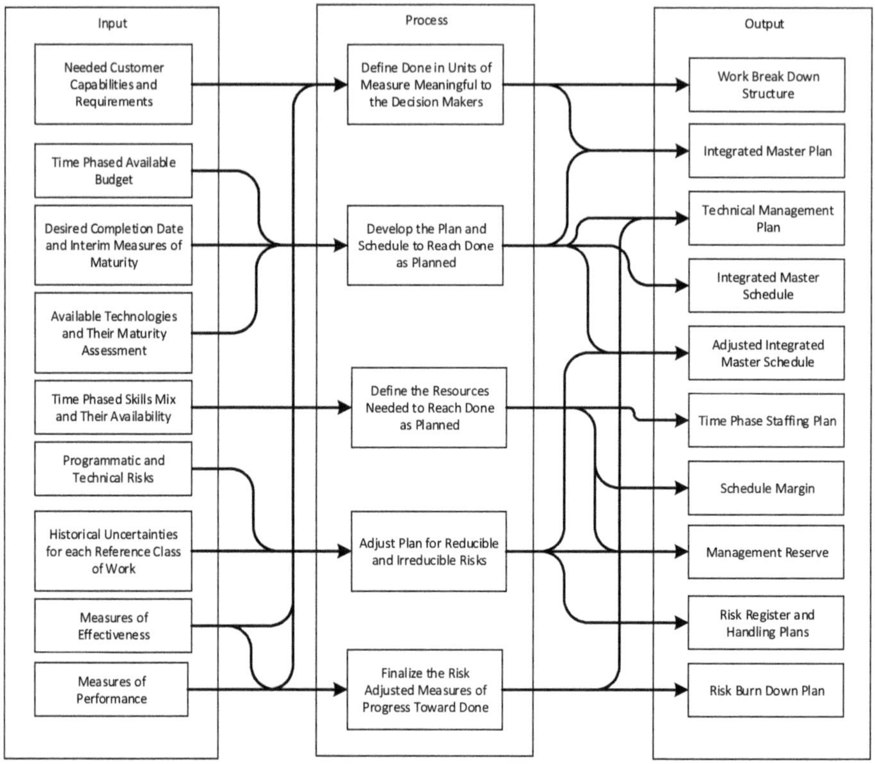

Figure 7.3 Data and processes needed to increase the probability of project success. For each data and process item in Figure 7.3 there is a risk created by Aleatory and Epistemic uncertainties shown in Tables 7.1, 7.2, and 7.3.

- To assess the complete probability distribution of the outputs. This is useful in the scenario of utility optimization, where the complete distribution is used to calculate the utility.
- **Inverse Uncertainty Quantification**: Estimates the variance between the actual outcomes and the estimated model of the risk (bias correction) and estimates the values of unknown parameters in the model if there are any (parameter calibration or simply calibration).

The scenarios of inverse quantification include:

- Bias correction quantifies the model inadequacy.
- Parameter calibration estimates the values of one or more unknown parameters in the risk model.
- Bias correction AND parameter calibration – assesses an inaccurate model with one of more unknown parameters, and the model updating processes combined (Tables 7.1–7.3).

Table 7.1 The Risk Associated with the Inputs Needed to Increase the Probability of Success. Each Risk Can Be Created by Aleatory and/or Epistemic Uncertainty. Corrective or Preventive Actions Are Required to *Handle* the Resulting Risk

Input Data Needed to Increase Probability of Program Success		
Inputs	*Aleatory Risk*	*Epistemic Risk*
Needed Customer Capabilities and Requirements	Aleatory uncertainties derived from Reference Classes and other models applied to Capabilities.	Epistemic uncertainties derived from system engineering model of needed Capabilities.
Time Phased Available Budget	Variance in spend plan and variances in efficacy of that spend to produce value must have margin to assure sufficient budget is allocated to produce the planned product value for the planned cost.	Probabilistic risks require planned work effort to reduce the uncertainty and buy down the risk at the planned point in the schedule.
Desired Completion Date with Interim Measures of Maturity	Confidence intervals around the delivery dates in the IMS and other planning documents must be produced with modeling processes using both reducible and irreducible uncertainties. But epistemic and aleatory uncertainties create risk to completing on or before the needed dates.	
Available technologies and their maturity assessment	Unaddressed Variances in the maturity of the technologies.	Unmitigated risks in the technology.
Time phased skills mix and their availability	Variances in the availability of the skills and the efficacy of those skills to produce the needed value.	Unaddressed efficacy of staff.
Historical Uncertainties for each Reference Class of Work	Past performance of efficacy of labor absorption.	Past technical performance of products, services, components, or systems.

Table 7.2 The Risk Associated with the Processes Needed to Increase the Probability of Program Success

Processes Needed to Increase Probability of Program Success		
Source	*Aleatory Risk*	*Epistemic Risk*
Define Done in Units of Measure Meaningful to the Decision Makers.	Naturally occurring variances in each of the measures – MOE, MOP, TPM, KPP.	Event based uncertainties in each of the measures – MOE, MOP, TPM, KPP.
Develop the Plan and Schedule to reach Done as planned.	For both reducible and irreducible uncertainties, the Plan and Schedule must include the margin and risk reduction work activities. These processes must be captured in the Risk Register, but work needed to deal with them must be shown the IMP/IMS.	
Define the Resources needed to reach Done as planned.	For both reducible and irreducible uncertainties, the resource management processes must assure the margin and risk reduction work activities are properly staffed. These processes must be captured in the Risk Register, but work needed to deal with them must be shown the IMP/IMS.	
Adjust Plan for reducible and Irreducible risks.	With the identified reducible and irreducible uncertainties, vertical and horizontal traceability must be visible in the IMP/IMS.	
Finalize the Risk adjusted measures of progress toward Done.	For each identified uncertainty and resulting risk, assess impact on the MOE, MOP, TPM, and KPP in the IMP/IMS and provide reduction plan or margin to assure risk is reduced as needed to increase the probability of program success.	

Table 7.3 The Risks Associated with the Outputs of the Processes Needed to Increase the Probability of Project Success

Output Data Needed to Increase Probability of Program Success		
Output	*Aleatory Risk*	*Epistemic Risk*
Work Breakdown Structure	Identify aleatory risks by WBS element.	Identify Epistemic risk by WBS element.
Integrated Master Plan	Identify aleatory risks by IMP element.	Identify Epistemic risk by IMP element.
Technical Performance Plan with TPM's	Define Technical Performance Plan assurance in the presence of aleatory uncertainties.	Define epistemic risk buy down plan for each Technical Performance Measure.

Table 7.3 (Continued) The Risks Associated with the Outputs of the Processes Needed to Increase the Probability of Project Success

Output Data Needed to Increase Probability of Program Success		
Output	*Aleatory Risk*	*Epistemic Risk*
Initial Integrated Master Schedule	The IMS at Authorization to Proceed (ATP) and possibly Integrated Baseline Review (IBR) will not have sufficient *reference class* data to a credible assessment of Aleatory uncertainty.	Event based uncertainty are likely in the future, so credible modeling of Epistemic uncertainty requires more maturity.
Adjusted Integrated Master Schedule	As the program proceeds the fidelity of the Reference Class Forecasting data improves.	As knowledge is acquired reduction in the Epistemic takes place – this is the *Cone of Uncertainty* paradigm.
Time Phased Staffing Plan	Natural variances in the productivity of the staff creates uncertainty and resulting risk.	Event based uncertainty, turnover, reassignment, and other disruption impact productivity.
Schedule Reserve	Naturally occurring variances in the work productivity creates risk to completing work as planned.	Event based uncertainties associated with the work processes.
Management Reserve	Management Reserve early in the program is usually based on models built during the proposal. As the program proceeds better models of aleatory uncertainty emerged.	Management Reserve models of epistemic uncertainty mature as the program proceeds.
Risk Register with Mitigation Plans	The Risk Register must contain the range of uncertainties for work in the IMS.	Risk Register must contain the event-based risks, their mitigations, and residual risks contained in the IMS.
Risk Burn Down Plan with Quantified Measures of Risk	Reduction in the aleatory uncertainties modeled as the *Cone of Uncertainty*, showing the planned risk reduction as the program proceeds.	Measurement of the risk burn down is subject to epistemic uncertainty in the measurement process. As well subject to calibration of the risk ranking in the burn down process.

7.1.2.3 Methods of Uncertainty Quantification

For several decades, research shows how to solve uncertainty quantification problems [45]. The focus has been on uncertainty propagation [46]. Recently, several approaches for inverse uncertainty quantification problems have been developed and been shown to be useful for most small to medium-scale risk management problems.

Uncertainty implies a lack of information. This can be a lack of understanding about a probabilistic event (Epistemic) or about the range of outcomes of a process (Aleatory). There are several methods modeling forward uncertainty propagation:

- **Monte Carlo Simulation**: Schedule network of work with aleatory uncertainties assigned to task duration and epistemic uncertainties assign technical performance measures and cost models.
- **Adaptive sampling**: A general technique for estimating properties of a distribution – in this case, the behaviors of the underlying risk process – while only having samples generated from a different distribution from the distribution of interest.
- **Fuzzy theory risk estimates**: A form of many-valued logic in which the truth values of variables may be any real number between 0 and 1. It is employed to handle the concept of partial truth, where the truth value may range between completely true and false.

Methods for Inverse uncertainty quantification:

- **Frequentist**: Using regression analysis, least square assessment to produce standard error parameter estimates of the risk and its reduction as a function of time.
- **Bayesian**: Using a modular Bayesian approach to solve the bias correction and parameter calibration.

7.1.2.4 Identifying Risk Sources with Premortem

> In health care, a post-mortem can be required after a patient has died to establish why, and sometimes when and how, the patient died. Many projects are likely to fail, with reasons including the need for more tools to facilitate change and failure to consider the organizational and environmental situation a change project faces. When projects or initiatives fail, clinicians often carry out a 'post-mortem', trying to understand the factors that contributed to the failure, aiming to learn lessons and not repeat the same mistakes [82].

A premortem is the opposite of a postmortem. A project postmortem is similar to a medical postmortem, where an assessment is made of what caused the patient's death. In the project domain, the postmortem is the death of the project that showed up late, was over budget, and didn't deliver the needed capabilities [9,75].

Projects fail for things that could have been known if we had only asked *how can this project fail?* When knowledgeable dissenters speak up, the project's chances of success are increased. A PreMortem – the opposite of a Postmortem – is an exercise conducted with assumption that the project has failed and looking back to the causes of the failure [77].

The Premortem is performed at the beginning of the project so the project can be improved rather than autopsying the project after it's failed – the RCA of a failed project. The premortem process uses retrospective hindsight to identify risks. This insight has the project team assume the project has failed and they then postulate the risk events that occurred that contributed to the project's failure [76,77,81].

The team generates plausible reasons for this failure, and these reasons become the critique of the plan, processes, design, and all other activities around the project.

The typical risk assessment asks – What or the risks to the project's success? The premortem asks what are the risks that cause the project to fail?

Premortems produce insight not found in other risk analysis methods:

1. Pretend the project has failed.
2. Discover the reasons for this failure.
3. Gather and prioritize the reasons for project failure.
4. Take corrective or preventive actions to address these reasons.

Predicting incidents, risks, disruption, and other undesirable outcomes is a critical success factor for all project risk management. The premortem process uses retrospective hindsight to identify risks. Retrospective hindsight is a technique that has the project team assume the project has failed and then postulate the risk events that have occurred and contributed to the project failure. The process uses isolation techniques during risk brainstorming and team synergy to elicit risks and handling strategies such that all identified risks are handled to the best ability of the team.

The outcomes of the premortem are *precursors*, which are previous similar situations with severe consequences and/or an event or situation that, if it had included (or not included) some other behavior or condition, an adverse event would have occurred. With the outcomes of premortem, a risk estimate can be informed by intuitive or expert information developed in the premortem and conduct an analysis of predictability of cost, schedule, and technical performance risks, and make adjustments to correct expert or intuitive assessments.

While we start risk Analysis with the risks identified in the Risk Register the premortem may reveal risks not in the risk register, but still possible for occurring. The premortem can identify risks not revealed through the standard risk management process. One of the beneficial outcomes of premortems is the analysis of *near misses*. When the necessary exacerbating risk factors are highly likely, the precursor is often called a *near miss*. One example is running a red light in a busy intersection without a collision. The exacerbating factor would have been a crossing vehicle in the intersection. Another example would be a high voltage powerline break with no injury to the workers because they were at lunch.

7.1.3 Monte Carlo Risk Analysis

The first step in Risk Quantification is define the likelihood the risk will occur and the likelihood of the impact on the project if the risk does occur. These are two discrete probability values for Epistemic uncertainties. The same is the case of Aleatory uncertainties. The likelihood a duration, cost, or technical performance will be of a specific value and the likelihood of the impact on the budget, delivery date, or capability produced by the project.

In frequentist statistics, a parameter is considered a fixed, but unknown. A particular statistical estimator for the parameter cannot be judged from the value it gives. The parameter is unknown, so we cannot know the value the estimator should be giving. If we know the value of the parameter, we would not be using an estimator.

Monte Carlo methods are a class of computational algorithms that rely on repeated random sampling to compute their results. Monte Carlo methods are often used in simulating physical and mathematical systems. These methods are most suited to calculation by a computer and tend to be used when it is infeasible to compute an exact result with a deterministic algorithm [55].

The MCS method is named after the city of Monte Carlo in the principality of Monaco. In the Monet Carlo casinos, a roulette wheel is a simple random number generator. The name and the systematic development of Monte Carlo methods dates from 1944 and the Manhattan project. Before MCS, simulations of statistical sampling were used to estimate the uncertainties in simulation [54,55].

The MCS method inverts the approach of the frequentist, by solving deterministic problem through the generation of random numbers used to model project duration, cost, and other parameters. The MCS method provides approximate solutions to a variety of mathematical problems by performing statistical sampling from a population of samples matching the range of samples of the possible values found on a project parameter. Typically, these samples are *drawn* from *under* a probability distribution function, representing a statistical or probabilistic process. With the statistical distribution of the possible samples of a parameter – a cost, schedule duration, or technical performance parameter – the MCS draws samples from the distribution and places them in the schedule, cost, or technical perform model, and determines the resulting outcomes.

MCS works to:

1. Produce values of a parameter from a statistical distribution representing the possible values for that parameter. Use this number in a mathematical model associated with the distribution.
2. Use the values drawn from the distribution to run a model of the project – for example a duration in a schedule. With this value used on a task duration, cost, or other parameters an outcome is produced.
3. The results of each single trial are saved for analysis (project duration, cost, and other parameters). Repeat this process hundreds to thousands of times, each time using a new value drawn from the statistical distribution. After these trials have been saved, there will be a distribution of project output parameters, representing the value of interest on a chart.

The probability distributions used by MCS include:

- **Normal**: Sometimes called a "bell curve" defines mean and a standard deviation of the sample values. Values near the mean are most likely to occur. The normal distribution is symmetric and describes natural phenomena like people's heights, cost inflation rates, and energy prices.
- **Lognormal**: Unlike the Normal distribution, the lognormal distribution is positively skewed, and represents values whose logarithm is Normally distributed. Lognormal distributions include real estate property values, stock prices, and oil reserves.
- **Triangle**: Defines the minimum, most likely, and maximum values. Values around the most likely are more likely to occur. Variables that could be described by a triangular distribution include past sales history per unit of time and inventory levels.

- **PERT (Program Evaluation Review Technique)**: Defines minimum, most likely, and maximum values, like the triangular distribution. PERT distribution can describe the duration of a task in a project management model. PERT = ((Optimistic + (4 × Most Likely) + Pessimistic)/6)[7] [67].
- **Discrete**: The user defines specific values that may occur and the likelihood of each. An example might be the results of a lawsuit: 20% chance of positive verdict, 30% change of negative verdict, 40% chance of settlement, and 10% chance of mistrial.

With a model of the project, the interconnections of the components – tasks, risks, deliverables, technical architecture – MCS can produce a risk-adjusted model of those outcomes by:

- Examining all possible states of a variable, not just the Mean and Variance.
- Providing an accurate estimate of completion within the variance's ranges of the upper and lower ranges of the Most Likely values used in the MCS.
- Overall duration distribution.
- Confidence interval (accuracy range).

With this information, the MCS produces:

- A confidence level of the variables of the project.
- The "on or before" confidence of a delivery date.
- The "at or below" confidence of a cost.
- The "inside the margin" for a technical performance measure.
- The probability of occurrence of a risk, the probability that the corrective or preventive actions will be effective to a needed level.

The key advantage of MCS is the lack of need for past empirical data. MCS can be used to advantage if we do, but we don't need it for the MCS algorithm to work [56].

7.1.4 Reference Class Forecasting

Reference Class Forecasting (RCF) is a method to remove optimism bias and strategic misrepresentation in cost and time to complete forecasting of projects and programs [79]. RCF provides an estimating technique that compares past information – in this case, risk assessments – that can eliminate optimism bias resulting from poor estimates risk starting with the probability of occurrence of a risk and probability of impact from those risks.

RCF can remove optimism bias and strategic misrepresentation in cost and time-to-completion forecasting of projects by examining data from past projects [35,62,63]. RCF starts by identifying a *class* of projects, with their risks that are similar to the current project.

The theories behind RCF were developed by Daniel Kahneman and Amos Tversky, who found that judgment by *humans* is generally optimistic from their overconfidence and biases due to insufficient consideration of distributional information about outcomes. Therefore, people tend to underestimate the costs, completion times, and risks of planned actions, whereas they tend to overestimate the benefits of those same actions. Such error is caused by actors taking an "inside view," where focus is on the constituents of the specific planned action instead of on the actual outcomes of similar ventures that have already been completed [79].

Kahneman and Tversky [80] suggest disregarding the statistical distributional information and focusing on single-point estimates is a major source of error in estimating – in this case, risk. They recommend that estimators "should therefore make every effort to frame the forecasting problem so as to facilitate using all the distributional information that is available." Estimates should not be confined to the most likely value but present the full range of estimates. Newer methods like MCS presents a range of outcomes, MCS still results in an insider's view that is prone to underestimation. Kahneman and Tversky argue that using distributional information from previous ventures similar to the one being estimated is taking an "outside view."

RCF requires three steps [64]:

1. Identify relevant reference classes of risk on past projects that are broad enough to be statistically meaningful but narrow enough to be comparable with the specific project.
2. Establish a probability distribution for the selected reference class. For success, this requires access to credible, empirical data for a sufficient number of projects within the reference class to make statistically meaningful conclusions.
3. Compare the assessed project distributions with the reference class distributions, to establish the most likely outcome for the specific project.

7.1.5 Dependencies, Structures, and Correlations of Risk

> When risk is modeled as a collection of non-stationary or stationary stochastic processes[8] interacting with each other and other elements of the project modeled in the Integrated Master Schedule, the risk that impacts the probability of project success is no longer static. The risks and the relationships are dynamic [24].

Managing complex interrelated risks, requires integrating multiple dimensions of the risks, using the classical characteristics of probability and impact. Risk interactions are analyzed to make decisions based on project complexities through a Design

Structure Matrix (DSM), simulating the interactions and taking corrective and preventive actions to reduce the impact of risk in the following five steps:

1. Identify the interactions between risks. This is a binary identification of a potential cause-and-effect relationship between two events. This is done using a risk matrix based on the DSM.
2. Assess the strength of each interaction of the risks identified in Step 1.
3. Model the network based on risk interactions in the simulation context.
4. Design simulation experiments that will be run in order to test different parameters and to anticipate different propagation scenarios.
5. Analyze the simulation results of the mitigation plan (or response plan) and determine where are the changes in terms of risk assessment or risk ranking, and where are the mitigation possibilities in terms of actions.

This approach extends the traditional Risk Management Process by simulating risk-on-risk effects. These effects may be different than the initial values captured in traditional risk management processes. This approach then takes nontraditional mitigation actions, by modeling the mitigation of the propagation links, instead of mitigating risk occurrence as a standalone process [92].

The DSM provides a common perspective of a system, increases designers' understanding of the cause-and-effect relationship occurring within the system, helps organize this knowledge, and channels creativity and innovation toward beneficial improvements – DSM helps people better manage complexity.

The relationships between work activities in the Integrated Master Schedule (IMS) and the WBS are dynamic and change over time. This means Risk Management must be a continuous process [22]. The first step in addressing the management of risk created by aleatory, epistemic, and ontological[9] uncertainty – modeled by their distribution and density functions – is to develop a model of the structure of the risks, their interrelationships, correlations, propagation to the future, and the impact on the elements of the project [25].

The categorization of risk starts with the categorization of the uncertainties that create the risk. These risks are usually started in the requirements stage of the project, covering technical, cost, and schedule requirements [23]. Most important are the dynamic correlations between risks. Since risk is created by uncertainty, these correlations are not static, they are dynamic. They drive risk but also drive the schedule of work [25].

Modeling risks as *trees* in the Risk Breakdown Structure (RBS) fails to identify interactions between these risks. The same is true for Failure Modes and Effects Analysis (FMEA) and Bayesian Belief Networks, which model risk interactions, from multiple inputs through the risk-generating processes, to multiple outputs as static relationships. The growing complexity of projects requires models of complex interacting risks, creating *loops* of propagating risks that amplify the original risk [16,25–27].

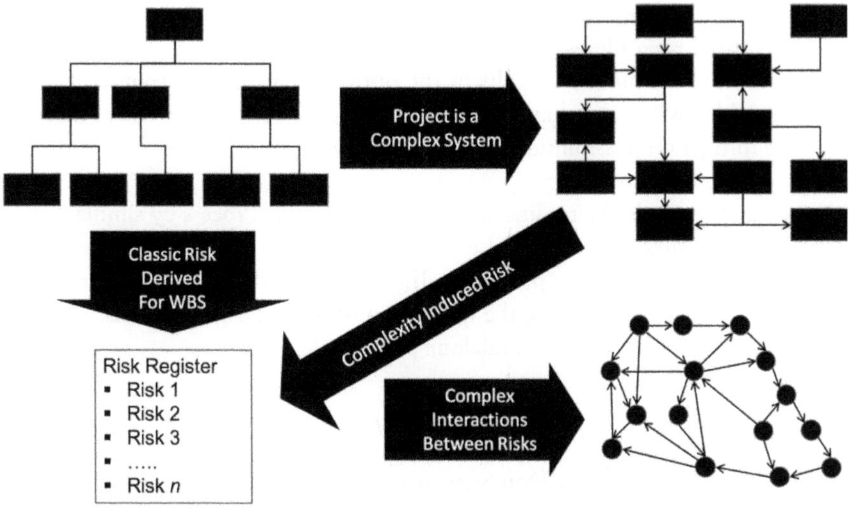

Figure 7.4 Modeling the complexity of risks and their impacts on the probability of project success starts with the interactions between the risks not normally modeled in the traditional hierarchical risk management processes, based on the work breakdown structure or a traditional risk register.

In traditional risk management, a list of *reducible* uncertainties and the risks they create are captured in a Risk Register, analyzed for the probability of occurrence, probability of impact, probability of residual risk once handling has been applied. The *irreducible* uncertainties and the risks they create are modeled with statistical processes.

These approaches are based on identifying the risks and sometimes the *drivers* of the risks and the outcomes to the project when the risk turns into an issue. But there is more going on in the project than this paradigm captures (Figure 7.4).

Managing complex interrelated risks, requires integrating multiple dimensions of the risks, using the classical characteristics of probability and impact. Risk interactions need to be analyzed to make decisions based on project complexities. An effective method for doing this is through a DSM, simulating the interactions and taking corrective and preventive actions to reduce the impact of risk in the following five steps:

1. Identify potential interactions between risks. This is a binary identification of a potential cause-and-effect relationship between two events. This is done using a risk matrix based on the DSM.
2. Assess the strength of each interaction of the risks identified in Step 1.
3. Model the network based on risk interactions in the simulation context with software such as Arena.

4. Design simulation experiments that will be run to test different parameters and anticipate different propagation scenarios.
5. Analyze the simulation results of the mitigation plan (or response plan) and determine where the changes are regarding risk assessment or risk ranking and the mitigation possibilities in terms of actions.

This approach extends the traditional Risk Management Process by simulating risk on risk effects. These effects may be different than the initial values captured in traditional risk management processes. This approach then takes non-traditional mitigation actions, by modeling the mitigation of the propagation links, instead of mitigating risk occurrence as a standalone process.

7.1.5.1 Design Structure Matrix Topology

The DSM was introduced by Don Stewart in 1981 for task-based system modeling and initially used for planning issues. It has been widely used for modeling the relationship between product components, projects, people, and work activities. DSM relates entities with each other in ways schedules cannot. It can be used to identify appropriate teams, work groups, and a sequence of how the tasks can be arranged. Risk interaction within systems and sub-systems, between functional and physical elements can also be modeled with DSM.

A DSM is a square matrix, with labels on rows and columns corresponding to the number of elements in the system. Each cell in the matrix represents the directed dependency between the related elements of the system. The DSM allows self-loops (an element is directly linked to itself). These self-linked relationships appear in diagonal cells.

Figure 7.5 shows the structure of a DSM relating entities of one kind to each other. The tasks that constitute a complete project can be used to identify appropriate teams, work groups, and the sequence of how tasks can be arranged. In the

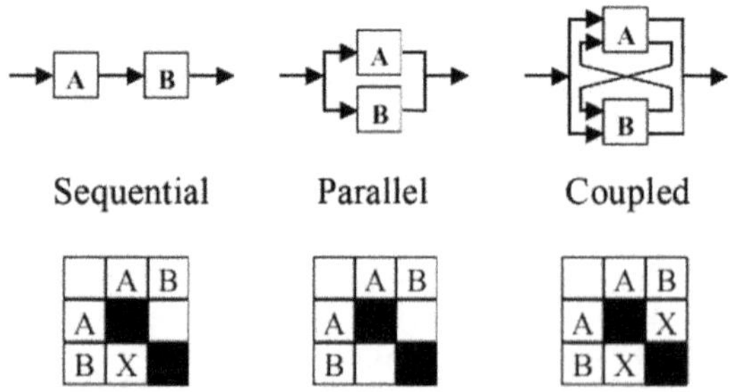

Figure 7.5 Representations of three interactions between risk elements in a directed graph.

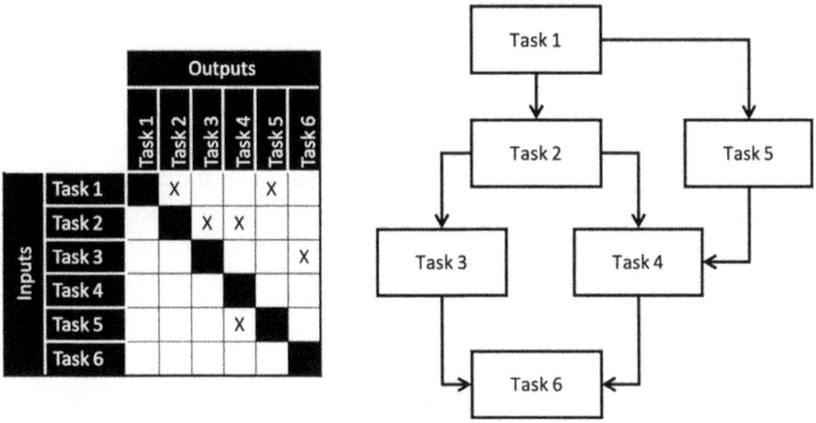

Figure 7.6 The task dependencies of the risk dependencies and interactions are represented in a DSM in the left. The DSM can be used to represent the interdependencies of risk drivers for the project and the propagation of risk of the tasks on the right.

same way, the DSM and the multiple-domain matrix (MDM) can be used to identify risk interactions across different domains of project, where a standard DSM can model a single domain.

The DSM can model:

- Development processes where activities produce deliverables and design iterations can be modeled showing the flow of dependencies between the work elements.
- Organizational processes showing the dependencies between people, teams, departments and the information flow between them.
- System design with maps of the components of the system, their interdependencies.

For risk management, the DSM process.

Uncertainties between element relationships can be modeled to represent technical performance or uncertainties related with the risk of the element's reducible or irreducible risk (Figure 7.6).

7.1.5.2 DSM and Risk Management

Managing in the presence of uncertainty requires the coordination of potentially hundreds of *moving parts* at any one time, the deliverables from these activities and the risks associated with the work. Dependencies between project elements which increase risks are part of any complex project. Problems in one element can propagate to other elements directly or indirectly through intermediate elements – risk propagation. This complexity creates a number of phenomena, positive or negative, isolated or in chains, local or global, that will impact the success of the project if not properly handled.

Risks associated with project complexities, from design changes, to technical shortfalls, to the mismatch of available resources with the plan, can be reduced by increasing the visibility of this complexity and its propagation associated with each system element [19]. This starts with analyses of complexity-related interactions, measurement, and prioritization of the *handling* of these risks. DSM can be used to model the risk structure between each element and across the project.

7.1.5.3 Modeling Risk Drivers and Risk Propagation with DSM

Risk is directly related to complexity of the underlying system [28]. For engineered systems, risk is defined as [29]:

- A measure of future uncertainties in achieving project performance within defined cost, schedule, and performance constraints.
- Measures associated with all aspects of a project (threat, technology maturity, supplier capability, design maturation, performance against plan).
- Potential variation in the planned approach and its expected outcome.

The DSM method is an information exchange model of the representation of complex task (or team) relationships to determine a sensible sequence (or grouping) for the tasks (or teams) being modeled [30].

No matter how the project is organized, there are always intersections between the components needed to share information on risk impacts on other components. DSM provides visibility and insight to risks created by complexity found in engineered systems where these unavoidable interdependencies exist.

The risk DSM (RSM) paradigm has three components.

- The undesirable effect that creates risk has two components. (1) the condition allowing the root cause and activity to occur. (2) Root Cause for risk occurrence by determining the known causal relationships to include the actions and conditions for the effect [12].
- A probability of occurrence or naturally occurring statistical process that is the source of risk to the project.
- A consequence from this occurrence – an event or naturally occurring process – is modeled in a similar way, along with the residual risk from the handling processes.

Beyond the probability of occurrence and its impact of a risk, it is critical to model the connectivity of the evolving risk processes [105]. Risks are typically modeled as

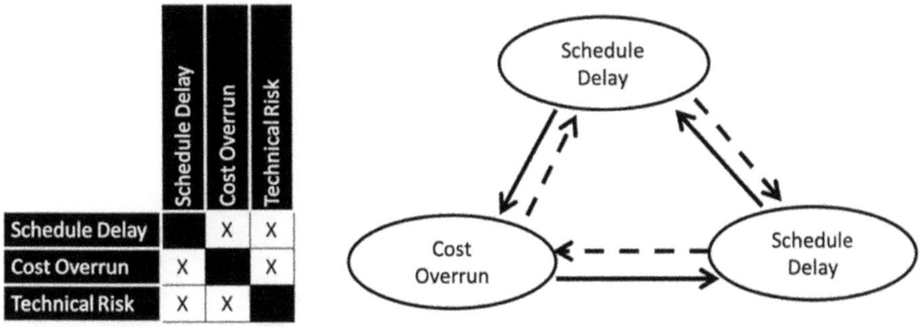

Figure 7.7 Traditional risk models cannot model loops. Actual project risk models do contain loops.

independent activities. When the propagation of a *risk chain* and its interactions is not properly modeled, the consequences of this propagation cannot be clearly identified or managed [30]. The design and development of complex systems require the efforts of hundreds of systems and subsystems. The interactions between the elements and the risks associated with each of those interaction is modeled with DSM. The probabilistic (reducible) correlations between the risks and the irreducible risks due to propagation of uncertainty is represented by DSM and the details of those interactions. This matrix-based (DSM) risk propagation is used to calculate risk propagation and reevaluate risk characteristics such as probability and criticality as the project proceeds.

DSM and the resulting Risk Structure Matrix (RSM) can model the loops and risk propagation needed to assess the actual impacts of risk on the Probability of Project Success on actual projects, as shown in Figure 7.7.

The DSM for an example project, the SAMPEX satellite in Figure 7.8, can be used to construct RSM and define the probability of occurrence outcomes of the risk handling for a complex project using the Arena tool [5].

This starts with building the DSM of the system components listed in the left-hand column. The loops can then be modeled from this DSM into a RSM, directly derived from the DSM.

7.1.5.4 Representing Risk Interactions with DSM

There are three types of risk interactions between risks in the DSM:

- **Dependent risks**: That are engaged in precedence relationships.
- **Interdependent risks**: That are engaged in mutually dependent relations, or within a large loop.
- **Independent risks**: That are not related to other risks but impact the project independently.

		1	2	3	4	5	6	7	8	9	10	11	12	13	14	15	16	17	18	19	20
Antenna	1	■	X	X	X				X					X			X	X			
Coupler	2		■	X	X						X							X			
Diplexer	3			■				X			X					X		X			
Transponder	4				■				X		X			X				X			
1773 Data Bus	5					■					X					X		X			
Data Processing Unit	6						■				X					X					
Low Energy Ion Analyzer	7							■			X										
Heavy Ion Large Telescope	8			X			X		■		X					X		X			
Proton/Electron Telescope	9									■				X							
Mass Spectrometer Telescope	10							X			■					X					
Attitude Control Electronics	11							X				■				X		X			
Attitude Control Sensors	12							X					■			X		X			
Attitude Control Actuators	13										X			■		X		X			
Mechanisms and Pyros	14													X	■	X					
Solar Arrays	15							X								■					
Battery	16							X	X							X	■	X			
Power Supply Electronics	17							X								X		■			
Passive Thermal Controls	18															X			■		
Scout Launch Vehicle	19						X		X		X			X						■	
Space Craft Structure	20						X	X	X		X				X			X	X		■

Figure 7.8 Risk modeling using a DSM of NASA SAMPEX (Solar Anomalous and Magnetosphere Particle Explorer) space craft. The network of connections is shown in Figure 7.9, showing the loops in the propagation of risk between individual elements of the spacecraft.

These interactions can be classified into categories using a model to identify different kinds of relationship links between risks.

- **Hierarchical link:** Divides the system into subsystems or modules divided into components.
- **Contribution link:** A modeling element can influence a soft goal positively or negatively.
- **Sequential link:** Link between risks that are dependent on each other.
- **Influence link:** Links that influence other elements of the matrix but are not directly connected.
- **Exchange link:** Links in which an exchange in state takes place, either bidirectional or unidirectional.

Links with different natures can exist between two risks. These can be expressed as causal relationships.

With existing methodologies, individual risks are identified and analyzed independently. The relationships between risks in actual projects are more complex in both structure and context. Organizational and technical complexity must also be included in the model. This introduces complexity in an interacting risk network [16]. In a complex project there can be propagation from one *upstream* risk to several *downstream* risks. The resulting *Downstream* impacted risk may create additional *upstream* risks. This result is a *domino effect, chain reaction* or *looping* risk structures [17].

The tradition Risk Register, and sequential risk driver paradigm cannot model these risk conditions, which occur very often on complex projects [16].

Using DSM as the basis of risk modeling in an RSM provides a technique to model these looping structures.

7.1.5.5 Simulating Risk Networks in Arena

Calculating the risk resulting from these interactions in Figure 7.9 is difficult with a modeling tool, since the model is complex and contains loops. Static risk registers, MCS, or Method of Moments [47] modeling in the IMS [18], will show the impact

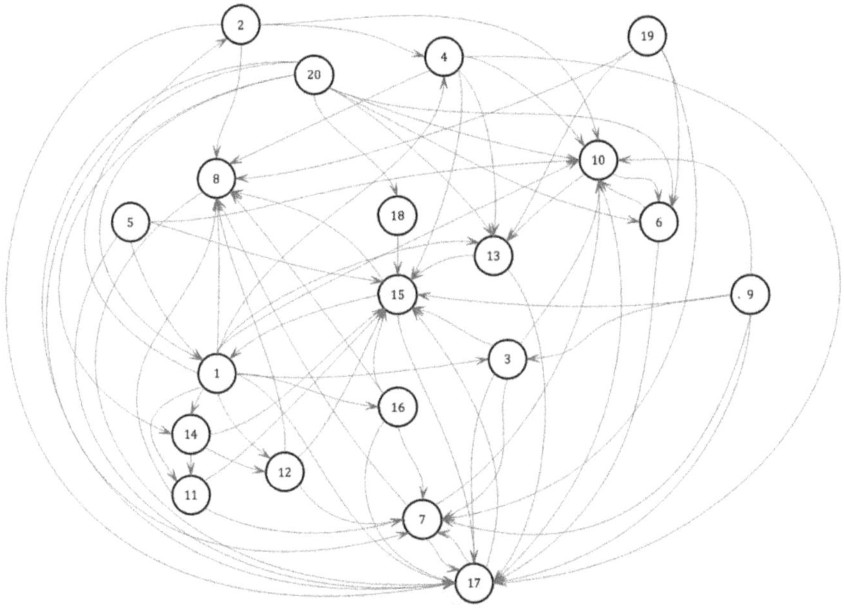

Figure 7.9 Risk interactions modeled as a network from the risk structure matrix for SAMPEX in Figure 7.8, including *loops* that create a *domino* effect from one risk to another, that propagate from one portion of the project to another impacting cost, schedule, and technical risks and finally impacting the probability of project success. Each node has a *probability of occurrence* and each arch has a *probability of impact.*

Note: Arena is a discrete event simulation tool that can be used to model the interaction and propagation of risk using a network model of how these risks are structured in a project. www.arenasimulation.com/ is the Rockwell Automation site for the Arena application.

of risk on cost and schedule. But these processes don't show impact of one risk on other risks, through their interactions with each other.

These risk interactions can be modeled with the Arena tool for the network of risks, the risk probability parameters, and the transition (propagation) probabilities to each interaction link.

- **Transition probability**: In the simulation model, evaluated causal conditional probability can also be interpreted as transition probability between two risks. In the network with n risk nodes, transition probabilities are in a square matrix with n × n elements of probability.
- **Spontaneous probability**: In project risk networks, risks may be caused by an external event or a risk that has not been identified. These risks may also occur spontaneously due to some unknown or undefined reason outside the system. Spontaneous probability can be interpreted as the evaluated likelihood of a risk, which is not the effect from other activated risks.

Spontaneous risks and their probabilities are the starting point for modeling of the network of risks. In the traditional Risk Register or Static Risk Driver paradigms, this *spontaneous* risk model represents the Probability of Occurrence for an Epistemic uncertainty or the statistical behavior of an Aleatory uncertainty, both creating a risk. While these traditional approaches are useful, they cannot model the propagation of risk through the system in a statistically sound manner needed to not only correct the impact of risk but prevent risk from occurring in advance.

7.1.6 Effectiveness of Risk Assessment

Several risk analysis tools and risk modeling methods are available in the complex project domain, including fault tree analysis, failure mode and effects analysis, and modeling and simulation. Risk analysis results are used in risk assessments where the goal is to assess the confidence in the analysis results and determine if the level of risk is acceptable, tolerable (operationally manageable), or unacceptable. These assessments directly contribute to the Probability of Project Success.

The effectiveness of risk assessments is impacted by three major factors limiting the accuracy of the outcomes. These include the evolving understanding of the cost, schedule, and technical domain and its uncertainties, the inherent random nature of cost, schedule, and technical phenomena, and learning from experience involving untestable assumptions in rational processes of inductive reasoning about this world.

Considerations of ontological uncertainties (what exists and its nature) and epistemological uncertainties (acquisition and thoroughness of knowledge about what exists) complicate the assessment of risk since any truly objective and accurate assessment of risk is not possible, except for the simplest of situations. Situations involving complexity, uncertainty, and ambiguity require subjective judgments and considerations of stakeholder values and preferences to arrive at a decision.

> The approach is to model these uncertainties, the connections between them, the propagation of these connections, the resulting risks, the impacts of each risk, the propagation of those risks, and that risk's impact in the Probability of Project Success.

7.1.6.1 Qualitative Risk Analysis

Qualitative risk analysis is the process of prioritizing individual project risks for further analysis or action by assessing their probability and impact as well as other characteristics. This approach prioritizes risk using a pre-defined risk rating scale, usually High, Medium, or Low. Or a Five-point scale that can be assigned these High, Medium, and Low scales, with two intermediate ranges. The probability is defined on a scale between one and five, with five being the highest probability of occurrence and highest impact [65].

7.1.6.2 Quantitative Risk Analysis

Quantitative risk analysis is process of numerically analyzing the combined effect of identified individual project risks and other sources of uncertainty on overall project objectives [65].

Qualitative Risk Analysis	*Quantitative Risk Analysis*
• Quick, easy, simple ranking • Subjective scale • Used to evaluate individual risks	• Requires model data • Objective numeric scale • Used to evaluate numerical assessment of overall project risk

7.1.7 Estimating Methods

Selection of an appropriate estimating method (Analogy, Cost Estimating Relationship (CER), Cost Models, Level of Effort, Engineering Judgment, or Task Based) begins with the type and availability of data to support the estimate.

Consider that a well-supported data-driven estimate utilizes verifiable information traceable to approved Business Systems (e.g., Accounting System, Procurement System, Time Keeping System, etc.) and applies adjustments as warranted with appropriate, concise, and complete justification and rationale. Table 4 defines the estimating methods and the minimum information required for each one.

Table 7.4 Estimating Methods Using to Increase the Probability of Project Success

Method	*Description*
Analogy	• Analogy is an estimate derived from the historical actual cost/ hours of a similar system/subsystem/end item. Factors may be applied for scope, technical and programmatic differences. • Identify the analogous project that has already been completed and why it is relevant to the same or similar task estimate. Include the relevant project name, project/contract number, period of performance, and task definition • Describe the CWBS element from which the analogous historical data is derived and make a subjective evaluation and identification of the differences between the new system and historical system(s). The hours and cost impact of the technical differences must be identified. • Describe a clear trace to how the analogous data was used to derive the current estimate. • This method is appropriate very early in the project life cycle when the system is not yet fully defined.
Cost Estimating Relationships (CER)	• A CER estimate is based on relevant historical, statistically correlated relationships. The mathematical equation represents the statistical relationship between independent and dependent variables of historical data. An assessment defines the degree of similarity, enabling the estimator to develop comparative values (e.g., hours per drawing design). Percentage relationships, which are also a form of a CER, are based on cost history, the results crosschecked with similar projects, and a graph or a table backs up the percent relationship in the BOE to show the proportion of the relationship. • Identify the base (i.e., independent variables) to which the CER is applied. Describe the database used to create the CER and provide the relevant statistics, such as mean and standard deviation of independent variables, number of data points, data range, standard error of the CER, R2, *t*-statistics, *F*-statistic, and prediction intervals. • List the equation, input variables used for the estimate, and the output value calculated. • If any discrete adjustments are made to the output value, describe and provide rationale for the adjustment and the resultant estimate. • Annotate if the CER is reviewed and approved by DCMA or another government agency. • If the CER is published or provided by another organization, identify the source. Contractor in-house CERs will be documented and provided as part of the proposal.

Table 7.4 (Continued) Estimating Methods Using to Increase the Probability of Project Success

Method	*Description*
Cost Model	• A Cost Model is a mathematical compilation of one or many estimating techniques that derives project cost or effort from attributes/metrics of the subject project. Examples of project metrics include weight, power, complexity, quantity, source lines of code (SLOC), and COTS product characteristics. The measurement is based on the technical, physical, or other end item characteristics. Cost Models may be internally developed or commercially available. • State the cost model used and describe the appropriateness of the model. • Include the name of the model and version number. • List the types and values of primary model input parameters used for the estimate. • Describe the method in which the model was calibrated and validated using historical company data. • Provide the model output and relate it to the proposed resource estimate. • Cost estimates using models shall be broken into labor, materials, subcontract and other direct cost elements using reasonable and supportable allocation techniques, if applicable. Labor costs shall be further broken out into equivalent labor hours using reasonable and supportable labor rates. • This method is appropriate early in the project life cycle when detailed specifications are not available, but a database of like systems, performance specifications and costs is available. This method often serves as a useful check of an estimate made using another method.
Level of Effort	• Level of Effort is an estimate based on identifying resource requirements to support specific identified tasks that are often based on a predetermined level of support for a given period of time. This estimate type is minimally affected by product scope and/or quantity changes. • Include allocation of personnel by account to cover specific tasks for a predetermined length of time. • Provide rationale for period of performance. • Use appropriate Manpower Conversion Factor (MCF) such as hours per month, hours per day, hours per shift.

(Continued)

Table 7.4 (Continued) Estimating Methods Using to Increase the Probability of Project Success

Method	*Description*
Engineering Judgement	• Engineering Judgment is an estimate based on subject matter expert experience with no specific relevant historical actual cost/hours identified. The subject matter expert develops the estimate based on the product description and tasks and operations required to be performed by the responsible department to manufacture/produce the product. • Provide a detailed explanation of the basis of the engineering judgment. • Include the qualifications of the individual making the judgment.
Task Based	• Task Based is an estimate developed at the lowest level of the WBS (at the detail, sub-assembly and assembly levels) based on a standard and/or historical performance of accomplishing comparable tasks. • The direct labor hours required to complete the work are estimated from engineering drawings and specifications, usually by an industrial engineer using company or general industry standards. The engineers may also estimate raw materials and purchase parts requirements. The remaining cost elements, such as tooling, quality control, other direct costs, and various overhead charges including systems engineering and project management must also be factored in. • Provide the basis and applicability of any labor standard proposed. Ensure standards account for all paid time to perform the required tasks (e.g., personal, fatigue, and delay) and other non-work time. • Provide historical basis or other methods used to estimate the costs of raw materials and purchased parts by WBS element.

7.2 Risk Management Tools

Risk analysis and management tools serve multiple purposes and come in many shapes and sizes. Some risk analysis and management tools include those used for [14]:

- **Strategic and Capability Risk Analysis**: Focuses on identifying, analyzing, and prioritizing risks to achieve strategic goals, objectives, and capabilities.
- **Threat Analysis**: Focuses on identifying, analyzing, and prioritizing threats to minimize their impact on national security.
- **Investment and Portfolio Risk Analysis**: Focuses on identifying, analyzing, and prioritizing investments and possible alternatives based on risk.

- **Project Risk Management**: Focuses on identifying, analyzing, prioritizing, and managing risks to eliminate or minimize their impact on a project's objectives and probability of success.
- **Cost Risk Analysis**: Focuses on quantifying how technological and economic risks may affect a system's cost. Applies probability methods to model, measure, and manage risk in the cost of engineering advanced systems.

7.2.1 The Risk Register Is the Starting Point for All Risk Managements

Making decisions about activities to increase the probability of project success uses the Risk Register as the document to capture information to be used as input to the "risk informed decision making" processes.

Here's one example of many in our domain of product and services inside business governance processes [57].

The RR is the capture document, used by all other processes in "risk informed decision making"

- Investment decisions
- Cost and schedule forecasting
- Customer strategy plans
- ROI for any expenditures – internal or external funding

and the biggest one of all, that is asked every week at the status standup.

> What the probability of success for the work we're paying you to deliver in exchange for the money we're paying you?

Every risk (reducible and irreducible) impacting the Probability of Business, Technical, Customer, Operation, or Compliance Success is held in the Risk Register. The RR is the single source of truth for all we do. All our suppliers and our customer partners impact that probability of success.

If it's not in the Risk Register, it's not a risk.

As stated in our regulations, the Risk Register is the "document of record" for capturing risks to your success.

- "… the risk register is a document used as a risk management tool to guide the project team in their risk management endeavors including fulfill regulatory compliance and acting as a repository for all risks identified."
- "The risk register includes all information about each identified risk, such as the nature of that risk, level of risk, who owns it and what are the mitigation measures in place to respond to it."

7.2.1.1 A List of Risk Register Elements

The risk register or risk log is a *database* captured in a risk management tool. The Risk Register format is dictated by the size of the project and the ease of compiling the necessary reports. Following fields should appear in the risk register and a description of those fields. The *database* should be capable of generating reports based upon querying various fields and dates for open risks and trigger dates and handling currently operable responses [57].

- **Risk**: As identified and should include the cause, the risk likelihood, and the effect (consider separate sub-fields for each to allow search capabilities on common causes of risks). The preferred statement should be in the affirmative to gain the most effective risk-handling responses or strategies.
- **Risk Identification Number**: A unique identification number for the risk.
- **WBS**: The Work Breakdown Structure identification number.
- **Risk Owner**: Person responsible for tracking, monitoring, documenting, and ensuring the handling response or strategy is implemented and reported upon.
- **Risk Category**: Assigned for grouping or from RBS analysis.
- **Risk Status**: Open or closed.
- **Risk Assumptions**: Any assumptions pertaining to the risk itself. The identification of assumptions may be clues to other risks.
- **Risk Probability and Basis**: The likelihood of this event occurring. Use the appropriate qualitative risk analysis matrix.
- **Risk Consequence and Basis**: The outcome of this event. Use the appropriate qualitative risk analysis matrix.
- **Risk Level**: The intersection of the probability and consequence on the appropriate qualitative risk analysis matrix, which determines the overall potential risk impact to the project.
- **Risk Monitoring Trigger**: An early warning signs that this risk is about to occur.
- **Success Metric**: Measure by which the Federal Project Director or Contractor Project Manager will know that the avoidance strategy or handling response or strategy has been successful.
- **Avoidance Strategy**: If there is an avoidance strategy to eliminate risk completely it should go in this field. Avoidance is a type of risk handling strategy.
- **Risk Handling Strategy**: The step-by-step (similar to a project plan) approach to eliminating or reducing the risk if no avoidance strategy is immediately available; includes the dates for completion. Include the probability of success for the risk handling strategy and consider probabilistic branching to account for the handling strategy failing.
- **Cost (for risk handling strategy)**: The necessary cost for implementing the handling strategy.

- **Cost Assumptions**: Any assumptions that relate to the cost contingency values.
- **Schedule (for Handling Strategy)**: Necessary schedule for implementing the risk handling strategy.
- **Schedule Assumptions**: That relate to the schedule contingency values.
- **Residual Risk**: Any remaining risk once the risk handling strategy is completed.
- **Risk Handling Strategy for Residual Risk**: That may be filled in depending upon the level of risk perceived by the Federal Project Director or the Contractor Project Manager.
- **Residual Risk Probability and Basis**: The likelihood of this event occurring. Use the appropriate qualitative risk analysis matrix.
- **Residual Risk Consequence and Basis**: The outcome of this event. Use the appropriate qualitative risk analysis matrix.
- **Residual Risk Level**: The intersection of the probability and consequence on the appropriate qualitative risk analysis matrix, which determines the overall potential risk impact to the project.
- **Secondary Risk**: The risk arising as a direct result of the implementation of a risk handling strategy.
- **Secondary Risk Probability and Basis**: The likelihood of an event occurring. Use the appropriate qualitative risk analysis matrix.
- **Secondary Risk Consequence and Basis**: The outcome of an event. Use the appropriate qualitative risk analysis matrix.
- **Secondary Risk Level**: The intersection of the probability and consequence on the appropriate qualitative risk analysis matrix, which determines the overall potential risk impact to the project. Trigger Date: Early warning sign of the date that this risk is about to occur.
- **Trigger Metric**: The event, occurrence or sequence of events that indicates the risk may be about to occur, or the pre-step for the risk indicating that the risk will be initiated.

7.2.2 Sample of Risk Management Tools

Here is a list of risk management tools. We are not endorsing any tool but providing a sample of the varied tools used to manage projects in the presence of uncertainty.

- **Arena Simulation**: www.arenasimulation.com/
- **Arena Risk**: https://arenariskmanagement.com/risk-management
- **Agena Risk**: www.agenarisk.com/
- **Bayesia Expert Knowledge Elicitation Environment (BEKEE)**: https://library.bayesia.com/articles/#!bayesialab-knowledge-hub/2850917

- **Risky Project**: http://intaver.com/products/riskyproject-professional/
- **Palisades**: www.palisade.com/
- **RiskNav®**: www.thegibsonedge.com/risknav
- **Risk Radar**: www2.mitre.org/work/sepo/toolkits/risk/ToolsTechniques/RiskRadar.html
- **Active Risk Manager**: https://sword-grc.com/sword-active-risk-manager/
- **Acumen Risk**: www.deltek.com/en/products/project-and-portfolio-management/acumen/modules/acumen-risk
- **@RISK for Microsoft Project**: www.palisade.com
- **Active Risk Manager**: www.sword-grc.com
- **Analytica**: www.lumina.com
- **CRIMS**: www.expertchoice.com
- **CRYSTAL BALL**: www.oracle.com/applications/crystalball/
- **Designsafe**: www.designsafe.com
- **DMT**: www.dependency.com
- **DPL**: www.adainc.com
- **Goldsim**: www.goldsim.com
- **Monte Carlo**: www.primavera.com
- **Moovila**: www.moovila.com/
- **OpenPlan Professional**: www.deltek.com/en/products/project-and-portfolio-management/open-plan
- **PANDORA**: www.bmtrcl.com
- **Panorama PSA**: www.panorama.com
- **Pertmaster Professional + Risk**: www.prcsoftware.com/category/knowledge-base/pertmaster
- **PHA-Pro 5**: www.sphera.com/pha-pro-software/
- **Powersim Solver**: www.powersim.com
- **Precision Tree**: www.palisade.com/precisiontree/
- **Predict Risk Analyser**: www.riskdecisions.com
- **Predict Risk Controller**: www.riskdecision.com
- **ProAct**: www.protectbenefitrisk.eu/PrOACT-URL.html
- **Risk in Action**: www.adacel.co.uk
- **Risk Matrix**: www.mitre.org
- **Risk Maturity Model**: www.hvr-csl.co.uk
- **Risk Radar**: www.spmn.com
- **Risk Com**: www.ciria.org.uk
- **RiskEZ**: www.pinyonsoftware.com
- **RiskFolio**: www.pypi.org/project/Riskfolio-Lib/
- **Risk Tools**: www.risk-reward.com
- **Risk Trak**: www.risktrak.com
- **SCRAM**: www.redbay.com.au/products/scram
- **STRAD**: www.stradspan.com/products.htm

Notes

1 The concept of Probability of Project Success is designed to improve the ability of project and program managers to accurately assess a project's ability to succeed and to clearly and concisely represent that success as a statistical probability number.

2 In this book we use *handling* as the general term for responding to the risk. *Mitigation* is one of several *handling strategies*.

3 There is a third type of uncertainty – Ontological uncertainty is a state of complete ignorance. Not only don't we not know, but we also don't even know what we don't know. This is the basis of the Unknown Unknowns.

4 Again, in this book we use the term *risk handling* rather than the more common *risk mitigation*. Mitigation is one of four *handling strategies*.

5 A proximate cause is immediately responsible for a problem. The root causes are the underlying reason for the proximate cause. This is the difference between a symptom and the actual causes.

6 Uncertainty must be taken in a sense distinct from the familiar notion of risk, from which it has never been properly separated … . The essential fact is that "risk" means in some cases a quantity susceptible of measurement, while at other times it is something distinctly not of this character; and there are far-reaching and crucial differences in the bearings of the phenomena depending on which of the two are present and operating. It will appear that a measurable uncertainty, or "risk" proper, as we shall use the term, is so far different from an unmeasurable one that it is not in effect an uncertainty at all. – *Risk, Uncertainty, and Profit*, Frank Knight (1885–1972), University of Chicago Press, 1921. Available from Martini Fine Book, 2014.

7 The PERT charts were first used by the U. S. Navy on the Polaris submarine program, in 1957. The standard deviation of "6" was fixed to meet the target goals of the program and *assumes* the optimistic and pessimistic values are separated by one standard deviation – a naïve assumption at best [68].

8 A stochastic process is stationary if its statistical properties do not change over time. This means the underlying processes are identically distributed and independent of each other. A non-stationary stochastic process has a time-varying mean and variance or both.

9 Ontological uncertainty represents a state of complete ignorance. Not only do we not know, but we do also not know what we do not know.

References

1. "Dicing with the unknown," *Significance*, September 2004.
2. "*Continuous Risk Management Guidebook*," Christopher J. Alberts, Audrey J. Dorofee, Ron Higuera, Richard L. Murphy, Julie A. Walker, and Ray C. Williams, Software Engineering Institute, January 1996.
3. "1.0 Basis of Estimate (BOE) 'How To' ", JSCC BOE Guidebook.
4. "NASA's Risk Management System," Jeevan S. Perera, NASA, Lyndon B. Johnson Space Centre, 22 March 2011.

5. "Utilization of Dependency Structure Matrix Analysis to Assess Implementation of NASA's Complex Technical Projects," Timothy K. Brady, Masters of Science in Engineering and Management, MIT, February, 2002.
6. "The Background and Theory of Integrated Risk Management," Final Report, NASA/ASEE Summer Faculty Fellowship Program 1994, Johnson Space Center.
7. "*Advanced Risk Analysis for High-Performing Organizations*," Christopher Alberts and Audrey Dorofee, Carnegie Mello Software Engineering Institute, 2006.
8. "*What Is Advanced Project Risk Management?*" Rubin Jen, Beyond Execution, 3 March 2011, www.slideshare.net/rubinjen/what-is-advanced-project-risk-management
9. "Performing a Project Premortem," Gary Klein, *Harvard Business Review*, Volume 9, September 2007. https://hbr.org/2007/09/performing-a-project-premortem
10. "*Root Cause Analysis as Part of Enterprise Risk Management*," Wendell Bosen and Kristina Narvaez, RIMS, Utah Chapter. http://utah.rims.org/home
11. "The Root Cause Project Technique – Create Useful Strategies to Mitigate Risks," B. C. Chadbourne, *PMI Annual Seminars and Symposium*, Nashville, TN, 1 November 2001.
12. *Apollo Root Cause Analysis: Effective Solutions to Everyday Problems Every Time*, 3rd ed., Dean L. Gano, Apollonian Publications, Richland, WA, 2007.
13. *Bow Ties in Risk Management: A Concept Book for Process Safety*, Center for Chemical Process Safety of the American Institute of Chemical Engineers, Wiley, 2018.
14. "Risk Management Tools," *MITRE Systems Engineering Guide*, www.mitre.org/publications/systems-engineering-guide/acquisition-systems-engineering/risk-management/risk-management-tools
15. "*Quantitative Approach to Technical Performance Measurement and Technical Risk Analysis Utilizing Bayesian Methods and Monte Carlo Simulation*," Lewis, T. L., Ph. D. Thesis, The George Washington University, 16 May 2010.
16. "*Analysis of Current Project Risk Management Methodologies and Required Improvements (Working Paper)*," F. Marle, École Centrale, Paris.
17. "*Project Risk Propagation Modeling of Engineering, Procurement and Construction*," A. Atin, Ph.D. Thesis, Wayne State University, 2016.
18. DOD, "Integrated Program Management Report (IPMR), DI-MGMT-81861, 20 June 2012.
19. "Evaluating the Risk of Change Propagation," Oduncuoglu, A. and Thomson, V., *International Conference on Engineering Design*, 15–18 August 2011.
20. "Dealing with project complexity by matrix-based propagation modelling for project risk analysis," Chao Fang and Franck Marle, *Journal of Engineering Design*, Volume 24, Issue 4, 2012. DOI:10.1080/09544828.2012.720014
21. "Modelling Risk Interactions To Reevaluate Risks In Project Management," Chao Fang, Franck Marle, and Ludovic-Alexandre Vidal, *12th International Dependency And Structure Modelling Conference*, DSM'10, 22–23 July 2010, Cambridge, UK
22. "The Risk of Using Risk Matrix in the Assessing of Safety," V. Ho, HAKRMS, Safety Engineering Lecture Series 2.2, 16 November 2010.
23. *Systems Requirements Analysis*, J. O. Grady, Academic Press, 2006.
24. "*Modeling and Analysis of Propagation Risk in Complex Projects: Application to the Development of New Vehicles*," H. Jaber, Chemical and Process Engineering, Université Paris-Saclay, 2016.

25. "Interactions-Based Risk Network Simulation for Project Risk Prioritization." F. Marle, PMI *Research Conference: Defining the Future of Project Management*, Washington, DC, 2010.
26. "Potential Applications of DSM Principles in Project Risk Management," F. Marle and L.-A, Vidal, *10th International Design Structure Matrix Conference*, 11–12 November 2008.
27. "Schedule Best Practices including Schedule Margin and Schedule Risk Analysis," J. Owen, 2017 EVMP Forum, August 24th and 25th, 2017.
28. *Quantitative risk – Phase 1*. R. R. Nilchiani, A. Mostashari, S. Rifkin, W. Bryzik, and G. Witus, Systems Engineering Research Center – University Affiliated Research Center, Stevens Institute of Technology, 29 May 2013.
29. "Complexity in an Unexpected Place: Quantities in Selected Acquisition Reports," G. A., Davis, M. L. Giles, and D. M. Tate, *Institute for Defense Analyses*, IDA Paper P-8490, December 2017.
30. "An Introduction to Modeling and Analyzing Complex Product Development Processes Using the Design Structure Matrix (DSM) Method," A. A. Yassine, *Urbana*, January 2004.
31. "Management Disciplines: Harbingers of Successful Programs," D. D. Acker, *Defense Systems Management Review*, Summer 1979, Volume 2, Number 3, pp. 7–20.
32. "Quantification of Margins and Uncertainties," D. Eardley, et. al., The Mitre Corporation, JASON report JSR-04-330, 23 March 2005.
33. "Treatment of aleatory and epistemic uncertainty in performance assessments for complex systems," J. C. Helton and D. E. Burmaster, *Reliability Engineering and System Safety*, Volume 54, Issues 2–3, 1996, pp. 91–94.
34. "*Risk Management using Dependency Structure Matrix*," I. Petković, Workshop in Opatija, 2–8 September 2012, Academic Exchange Service, German.
35. "From Nobel Prize to Project Management: Getting Risks Right," Bent Flyvbjerg, *Project Management Journal*, Volume 37, Issue 3, August 2006, pp. 5–15.
36. "Project Scheduling: Improved Approach to Incorporate Uncertainty Using Bayesian Networks," Vahid Khodakarami, Norman Fenton, and Matin Neil, *Project Management Journal*, June 2007.
37. "*Applying Bayesian Networks to Model Uncertainty in Project Scheduling*," Vahid Khodakarami, Queen Mary Research Online, 2009.
38. *Bayesian Methods for Hackers: Probabilistic Programming and Bayesian Inference*, Cameron Davidson-Pilon, Addison Wesley Data & Analytics Series, 2016.
39. "Bayesian Inference for NASA Probabilistic Risk and Reliability Analysis," NASA/SP-2009-569.
40. "*Ideas Underlying Quantification of Margins and Uncertainties (QMU): A White Paper*," Martin Pilch, Timothy G. Trucano, and Jon C. Helton, Sandia Report, SAND 2006-5001, September 2006.
41. "*Quantification of Margins and Uncertainties (QMU)*," D. Eardley (Study Leader), The Mitre Corporation, 23 March 2005.
42. "*Conceptual and Computational Basis for the Quantification of Margins and Uncertainty*," Jon C. Helton, SAND2009-3055, Sandia National Laboratories, June 2009.
43. "Appendix G: Cost Risk and Uncertainty Methodologies," *NASA Cost Estimating Handbook*, Version 4.0.

44. "*Establishing System Measures of Effectiveness*," John M. Green, Raytheon Naval & Maritime Integrated Systems.
45. "Defining Uncertainty: A Conceptual Basis for Uncertainty Management in Model-Based Decision Support," Walker, W.E., Harremoës, P., Rotmans, J. van der Sluijs, J.P., van Asselt, M.B.A., Janssen P., and Krayer von Krauss, M.P., *Integrated Assessment*, Volume 4, Issue 1, 2003.
46. "Approximate Propagation of both Epistemic and Aleatory Uncertainty through Dynamic Systems," Terejanu, G., Singla, P., Singh, T., and Scott, P. D., *The 13th International Conference on Information Fusion*, Edinburgh, UK, July 2010.
47. "Topic 13 – Methods of Moments," in *Introduction to the Science of Statistics*, Joseph C. Watkins, University of Arizona.
48. *Tame, Messy and Wicked Risk Leadership*, David Hancock, Taylor & Francis, 2010.
49. "An essay towards solving a problem in the doctrine of chances." T. Bayes. *Philosophical Transactions of the Royal Society*, Volume 53, 1763, pp. 370–418.
50. "*Root Cause Analysis*," Washington State Department of Enterprise Services.
51. "Return to Tomorrow," *The Original Series*, first aired, 9 February 1968.
52. "Continuous Risk Management at NASA," Ted Hammer and Dr. Linda Rosenberg
53. "*Risk Analysis: Literature Review of Methods of Representing Uncertainty*," Enrico Zia and Nicola Pedroni, FONCSI, 2013-03.
54. "*The Beginning of the Monte Carlo Method*," N. Metropolis, *Los Alamos Science*, Special Issue, 1987.
55. "Stan Ulam, John Von Neumann, and the Monte Carlo Method," Roger Eckhardt, *Los Alamos Science*, Special Issue, 1987.
56. "Combining Monte Carlo Simulation and Bayesian Networks Methods for Assessing Completion Time for Projects Under Risk," Ali Namazian, Siamak Haji Yakhchali, Vahidreza Yousefi, and Jolanta Tamošaitienė, *International Journal of Environmental Research and Public Health*, Volume 16, 2019, pp. 5024.
57. "*Risk Management Guide*," DOE G 413.3-7A, CHG 1, 10-22-2015, U. S. Department of Energy, Washington, DC, 20585.
58. Fundamentals of Risk Management, Understanding, Evaluating and Implementing Risk Management, Paul Hopkin, IRM, 2010.
59. "Automated Risk Identification of CMMI Project Planning Using Ontology," Chanapan Rojrattanakorn and Wiwat Vatanawood, *5th International Conference on Applied Computing and Information Technology*,
60. "NASA Risk-Informed Decision-Making Handbook," NASA/SP-2010-576, Version 1.0, April 2010.
61. "Pitfalls in Risk Calculations," G. Apostolakis and S. Kaplan, *Reliability Engineering*, Volume 2, pp. 135–145, 1981.
62. "Why Your IT Project May Be Riskier Than You Think," Bent Flyvbjerg and Alexander Budzier, *Harvard Business Review*, September 2011.
63. "*Eliminating Bias Through Reference Class Forecasting and Good Governance*," Bent Flyvbjerg, *Concept Report, No. 17, Chapter 6, NTNU*, 1 April 2007.
64. "Optimism and Misrepresentation in Early Project Development," Bent Flyvbjerg, in *Making Essential Choices with Scant Information: Front-End Decision Making in Major Projects*, edited by Terry Williams, Kjell Sunnevag, and Knut Samset, Palgrave Macmillan, 2009.

65. "PMBOK, 6th ed.," Project Management Institute.
66. "Root Cause Investigation Best Practices Guide," Roland J. Duphily, Aerospace Corporation, 30 May 2014.
67. "Application of a Technique for Research and Development Program Evaluation," D. G. Malcolm, J. H. Roseboom, and C. E. Clark, *Operations Research*, Volume 7, Issue 5, 27 April 1959.
68. "Understanding PERT, Programme Evaluation Review Technique," Pat Weaver, Mosaic Projects, https://mosaicprojects.wordpress.com/
69. "The Project Business Glossary," Version 1, *Project Business Foundation*, 26 November 2020, https://my.project-business.org/resources/Documents/PBF_Downloads/Project_Business_Management_Glossary.pdf
70. "NASA Systems Engineering Handbook," Rev 2, 2017.
71. "Basis of Estimate," AACE 34R-05.
72. "What's Wrong with Risk Matrices?" Louis Anthony (Tony) Cox Jr., *Risk Analysis*, Volume 16, April 2008.
73. "Risk Matrices: Implied Accuracy and False Assumptions," Alexander Pickering and Stephen P. Cowley, *Journal of Health & Safety Research & Practice*, Volume 2, Issue 1, October 2010.
74. "Optimal Design of Qualitative Risk Matrices to Classify Quantitative Risks," Bill Huber and Tony Cox, *SRA 2008 Annual Meeting*.
75. "Mitigating Cognitive Biases in Risk Identification: Practitioner Checklist for the Aerospace Sector," Debra L. Emmons, Thomas A. Mazzuchi, Shahram Sarkani, and Curtis E. Larsen, *Defense ARJ*, January 2018, Volume 25, Issue 1, pp. 52–93.
76. "The Use of PreMortem techniques in Risk Identification," EFCOG Position Paper, May 2017.
77. "Evaluating the Effectiveness of the PreMortem Technique on Plan Confidence," Beth Veinott, Gary A. Klein, and Sterling Wiggins, *Proceedings of the 7th International ISCRAM Conference*, Seattle, WA, May 2010.
78. *Bayesian Networks An Introduction*, Timo Koski and John M. Noble, John Wiley & Sons, 2009.
79. "Reference Class Forecasting for Hong Kong's Major Roadworks Projects," Bent Flyvbjerg, Chi-keung, and Wing Huen Fok, *Proceedings of the Institution of Civil Engineers* 169, November, Issue CE6, pp. 17–24.
80. "On the interpretation of intuitive probability: A reply to Jonathan Cohen," Daniel Kahneman and Amos Tversky, *Cognition*, Volume 7, Issues 4, pp. 409–411, 1979.
81. "Accident Precursor Analysis and Management-Reducing Technological Risk Through Diligence," James R. Phimister, Vicki M. Bier, Howard C. Kunreuther editors, National Academy of Engineering, 2004.
82. "Pre-empting project failure by using pre-mortem," Judy Mckimm, *British Journal of Hospital Medicine*, October 2017.
83. "A Combined Monte Carlo and Probabilistic Approach to Uncertainty Propagation in Event Tree Analysis," Piero Baraldi and Enrico Zio, *Risk Analysis*, Volume 28, Issue 5, 2008.
84. "Probabilistic Risk Assessment Procedure Guide for NASA Managers and Practitioners," Version 1.1, NASA/SP-2011-3421, 2nd ed., December 2011.

85. "Fault Tree Handbook with Aerospace Applications," *NASA Office of Safety and Mission Assurance*, NASA Headquarters, Washington, DC, August 2002.
86. "IEC 61025, Fault Tree Analysis (FTA)," Second Edition 2006-12.
87. "Fault Tree Handbook, NUREG-0492," Nuclear Regulatory Commission, January 1981.
88. "15. Fault Tree Analysis (TFA)," Quality Management in the Bosch Group, 2015.
89. "*Cost-Benefit Analysis: Proposed Safety Upgrades to Currently Operating Nuclear Power Plants*," MS Thesis, Jonathan T. Jordahl, Oregon State University, 13 September 2016.
90. "Dynamic Fault Tree Analysis: State of the Art in Modelling, Analysis and Tools," Koorosh Aslansefat, Sohag Kabir, and Gheraibia Youcef, *Reliability Management and Engineering*, 2020.
91. "Essential Views of the Integrated Program Management Reports," Thomas J. Coonce, *Institute for Defense Analyses*, IDA D-5593, September 2015.
92. "Interactions-based risk network simulation for project risk prioritization," Franck Marle, *PMI Research Conference*, 2010.
93. "A Hybrid Modular Approach for Dynamic Fault Tree Analysis," Sohag Kabir, Koorosh Aslansefat, Ioannis Sorokos Yiannis Papadopoulos, and Savas Konur, *IEEE Reliability Society*, Volume 8, 2020.
94. "Advancing Dynamic Fault Tree Analysis, Get Succinct State Spaces Fast and Synthesis Failure Rates," Matthias Volk, Sebastian Junges, and Joost-Pieter Katoen, *Software Modeling and Verification*, RWTH Aachen University Germany, 25 April 2016.
95. "Dynamic Fault Tree Analysis Based on Petri Nets," Xiaojie Zhang, Qiang Miao, Xianfeng Fan, and Dong Wang, *IEEE International Conference of Reliability, Maintainability and Safety, ICRMS* 2009.
96. "Dynamic Fault Tree Analysis Using Input/Output Interactive Markov Chains," Hichem Boudali, Pepijn Crouzen, and Mariëlle Stoelinga, *37th Annual IEEE/IFIP International Conference on Dependable Systems and Networks*, 2007.
97. "Dynamic Fault Tree Analysis using Monte Carlo Simulation in Probabilistic Safety Assessment," K. Durga Rao, V. Gopika, V.V.S. Sanyasi Rao, H.S. Kushwaha, A.K. Verma, A. Srividya, *Reliability Engineering and System Safety*, Volume 94, 2009, , pp. 972–883.
98. "Fault tree analysis: A survey of the state-of-the-art in modeling analysis and tools," Enno Ruijters and Mariëlle Stoelinga, *Computer Science Review*, Volumes 15–16, February–May 2015, pp. 29–62.
99. "An Overview of Fault Tree Analysis and Its Application in Model Based Dependability Analysis," Sohag Kabir, *Expert Systems with* Applications, Volume 77, 1 July 2017, pp. 114–135.
100. "Project Risk Management Using the Project Risk FMEA," Thomas A. Carbone and Donald D. Tippett, *Engineering Management Journal*, Volume 16, Issue 4, December 2004.
101. "FMEA and PMBOK Applied to Project Risk Management," Flavio Roberto Souza dos Santos and Sando Cabral, *Journal of Information Systems and Technology Management*, Volume 5, Issue 2, pp. 347–364, 2008.

102. "NASA Risk Management Handbook," NASA/SP-2011-3422, Version 1.0, November 2011.
103. "Learning from Risk Management – Applying Root Cause Analysis and Failure Mode and Effects Analysis to our Compliance Programs," Margaret Hambleton, Systems Compliance Director, Catholic Health West.
104. *Element of Probability and Statistics: An Introduction to Probability with de Finetti's Approach and to Bayesian Statistics*, Francesca Biagini and Massimo Campanino, Springer, 2016.
105. "Modeling Risk Interactions to Re-Evaluate Risks in Project Management," Chao Fang, Franck Marle, and Ludovic-Alexandre Vidal, "12th *International Dependency and Structure Modeling Conference*, DSM '10, 22–23 July 2010.
106. "Continuous Risk Management at NASA," Ted Hammer and D.R. Linda Rosenberg, *Software Assurance Technology Center*, 5/99.
107. "A Methodology for Project Risk Analysis Using Bayesian Belief Networks Within a Monte Carlo Simulation Environment," Javier F. Ordóñez, University of Maryland, 2007.
108. "Foundation of Risk Concept," Norikazi Hara, *Proceedings of Joint ESA-NASA Space-Flight Safety Conference, ESTEC*, Noordwijk, Netherlands, 11–14 June 2002.
109. "MatCarloRe: An Integrated FT and Monte Carlo Simulink Tool for the Reliability Assessment of Dynamic Fault Tree," Gabriele Manno, Ferdinando Chiacchio, Lucio Compagno, Diego D'Urso, and Natalia Trapani, *Expert Systems with Applications*, Volume 39, 2012, pp. 10344–10342.
110. "What's Right with Risk Matrices?" 31000risk, 9 April 2011.
111. *Probability, Statistics, and Reliability for Engineers and Scientist*, 3rd ed., Bilal M. Ayyub and Richard H. McCuen, CRC Press, 2011.
112. "Representation of Analysis Results Involving Aleatory and Epistemic Uncertainty," J. C. Helton, J. D. Johnson, W. L. Oberkampf, and C. J. Sallaberry, *SAND2008-4379*, 2008.
113. "Basic Framework and Main Methods of Uncertainty Quantification," Juan Zhang, Junping Yin, and Rull Wang, *Mathematical Problems in Engineering*, Volume 2020, Issue 1, pp. 1–18.

Chapter 8

The Practices of Risk Management

8.1 Department of Energy Risk Management

Risk Management in DOE starts with DOE Enterprise Risk Management (ERM) Guidance, which provides DOE's framework for ERM as required by the Office of Management and Budget (OMB) Circular A-123, Management's Responsibility for ERM and Internal Control. The ERM guidance includes risk management, internal controls, and a fraud risk framework that meets the Government Accountability Office (GAO) requirements, A Framework for Managing Fraud Risks in Federal Programs.

An agency's ERM framework includes the following elements:

- Risk appetite is the amount of risk an organization is willing to accept to pursue its mission and vision. The organization's senior-level leadership establishes it and serves as the guidepost to set strategy and select objectives.
- Risk tolerance – acceptable level of variance in performance relative to achieving objectives. It is generally established at the program, purpose, or component level. In setting risk tolerance levels, management considers the relative importance of the related objectives and aligns risk tolerance with risk appetite.
- A portfolio view of risk provides insight into all areas of organizational exposure to risk (such as reputational, programmatic performance, financial,

 DOI: 10.1201/9781003425465-8

information technology, acquisitions, human capital, etc.), thus increasing the chances of experiencing fewer unanticipated outcomes and executing a better assessment of risk associated with changes in the environment.

The ERM model defines how to apply risk management by including:

1. Establishing the context by understanding the internal and external environments of the organization.
2. Initial risk identification uses a systematic approach to recognizing the potential for undesired outcomes.
3. Analyzing and evaluating the risks to include the probability and impact.
4. Developing alternative risk responses that are guided by the organization's risk appetite.
5. Responding to risks by deciding and executing the best course of action for the appropriate response strategy.
6. Monitoring the performance to determine whether the executed response strategy achieved the goals and objectives.
7. Conducting continuous risk identification, which is an ongoing process.

Each organization in the DOE develops a Risk Management Plan (RMP) that follows DOE Order 413.3-7A Chg 2, Risk Management Guide, provides nonmandatory risk management approaches for implementing the requirements of DOE O 413.3B, Program and Project Management for the Acquisition of Capital Assets. This guide takes a continuous and iterative process, including updating project risk documents and the risk management plan emphasizing implementation communication of the risks and actions taken. These guidelines are tailored to the specific program approaches and the project's needs.

The 413 guide provides the framework for identifying and managing critical technical, schedule, and cost risks and how it integrates with the development and consistent use of government contingency and contractor management reserve. This guide states that risk management is an essential element of every project, with practices based on the following:

- The project complexity.
- The size and duration of the project.
- The initial overall risk determination of the project.
- The organizational risk procedures.
- The available personnel and their skill levels for performing risk management.
- The available relevant data and its validation.

Tailoring of the risk management process generally includes selecting what risks to manage based on risk level actively, determining whether to perform a quantitative analysis, types of analysis to be performed, communication plan requirements, and classes and Frequency of reporting and monitoring. This guidance and advice are focused on the following objectives:

- Identify the risk management processes.
- Identify the steps necessary to facilitate the implementation of those processes.
- Provide lifecycle risk management guidance.
- Provide risk management documentation guidance.
- Provide risk management monitoring and reporting guidance.

While this approach applies to the management of DOE projects, they are not intended to replace assessment processes developed for nuclear safety, climate change, and environmental safety, health, and quality (ESH&Q). It should also not be intended to replace assessment processes developed for safeguards and security. This guidance also recognizes the benefit and necessity of early consideration and integration of climate change, safety, and security-related project risk into the project risk management process.

While the DOE risk management guide provides straightforward processes, its best contribution is the content of the risk register, Attachment 5, where the following items are in the risk register:

- **Risk**: Risk as identified should include the cause, the risk likelihood, and the effect (consider separate sub-fields for each to allow search capabilities on common causes of risks). The preferred statement should be in the affirmative to gain the most effective risk-handling responses or strategies.
- **Risk Identification Number**: Unique identification number for the risk.
- **WBS**: Work Breakdown Structure identification number.
- **Risk Owner**: Person responsible for tracking, monitoring, documenting, and ensuring the handling response or strategy is implemented and reported upon.
- **Risk Category**: Category assigned for grouping or from Risk Breakdown Structure analysis.
- **Risk Status**: Open or closed.
- **Risk Assumptions**: Any assumptions pertaining to the risk itself. The identification of assumptions may be clues to other risks.
- **Risk Probability and Basis**: Likelihood of this event occurring. Use the appropriate qualitative risk analysis matrix.
- **Risk Consequence and Basis**: Outcome of this event. Use the appropriate qualitative risk analysis matrix.
- **Risk Level**: The intersection of the probability and consequence on the appropriate qualitative risk analysis matrix, which determines the overall potential risk impact on the project.
- **Risk Monitoring Trigger**: Early warning signs that this risk is about to occur.

- **Success Metric**: Measure by which the Federal Project Director or Contractor Project Manager will know that the avoidance strategy or handling response has succeeded.
- **Avoidance Strategy**: If there is an avoidance strategy to eliminate risk completely, it should go in this field. Avoidance is a type of risk-handling strategy.
- **Risk Handling Strategy**: Step-by-step (similar to a project plan) approach to eliminating or reducing the risk if no avoidance strategy is immediately available; includes the dates for completion. Include the probability of success for the risk-handling strategy and consider probabilistic branching to account for the handling strategy failing.
- **Cost (for risk handling strategy)**: Necessary cost for implementing the handling strategy.
- **Cost Assumptions**: Assumptions that relate to the cost contingency values.
- **Schedule (for handling strategy)**: Necessary schedule for implementing the risk handling strategy.
- **Schedule Assumptions**: Assumptions that relate to the schedule contingency values.
- **Residual Risk**: Remaining risk once the risk handling strategy is completed.
- **Risk Handling Strategy for Residual Risk**: May be filled in depending upon the level of risk perceived by the Federal Project Director or the Contractor Project Manager.
- **Residual Risk Probability and Basis**: Likelihood of this event occurring. Use the appropriate qualitative risk analysis matrix.
- **Residual Risk Consequence and Basis**: Outcome of this event. Use the appropriate qualitative risk analysis matrix.
- **Residual Risk Level**: The intersection of the probability and consequence on the appropriate qualitative risk analysis matrix, which determines the overall potential risk impact on the project.
- **Secondary Risk**: Risk arising as a direct result of the implementation of a risk-handling strategy.
- **Secondary Risk Probability and Basis**: Likelihood of an event occurring. Use the appropriate qualitative risk analysis matrix.
- **Secondary Risk Consequence and Basis**: Outcome of an event. Use the appropriate qualitative risk analysis matrix.
- **Secondary Risk Level**: The intersection of the probability and consequence on the appropriate qualitative risk analysis matrix determines the project's overall potential risk impact.
- **Trigger Date**: Early warning sign of the date that this risk is about to occur.
- **Trigger Metric**: Event, occurrence, or sequence of events that indicate the risk may be about to occur, or the pre-step for the risk indicating that the risk will be initiated.

No other risk guidance has this level of detail. So, when you start your risk register, start with the DOE content.

8.2 Aerospace and Defense Risk Management

Like all industries, aerospace and defense have risks created by reducible and irreducible uncertainties, where risk management is an integral part of program management and systems engineering. In the presence of the complexity of aviation, space, and defense processes, products, and services and the severity of the potential consequences of failures, a formal process to manage operational risks is required.

In aerospace and defense, risk measures the potential inability to achieve overall program objectives within defined cost, schedule, and technical constraints. The A&D risk framework starts with ISO/IEC/IEEE 16085 and its detailed risk management activities and tasks aligned with ISO 31000.

The formality of this approach includes the standard approaches:

- Risk planning.
- Risk identification.
- Risk analysis.
- Risk handling.
- Risk monitoring.

In the A&D domain, risk and hazard are usually separated.

- **Hazard**: A state or a set of conditions, internal or external to a system, that has the potential to cause harm. Examples of hazards include materials, energy sources, or operational practices that, in uncontrolled situations, can lead to scenarios that could produce death, injury, illness, equipment loss or damage, or damage to a protected environment.
- **Risk**: The potential for shortfalls, which may be realized in the future, with respect to achieving explicitly stated performance requirements. A set of triplets characterizes risk: (1) the scenario(s) leading to degraded performance in one or more performance measures, (2) the likelihood(s) of those scenarios, and (3) the consequence(s) of the impact on performance that would result if those scenarios were to occur.

In the aerospace and defense domain, three definitions are used when discussing risk.

- **Risk**: Risks are future uncertainties relating to achieving program technical performance goals within defined cost and schedule constraints. Defined by (1) the probability of an undesired event or condition and (2) the consequences, impact, or severity of the undesired event, were it to occur.
- **Issue**: Current problems (realized risks) should be addressed with action plans, resourced, and resolved.
- **Opportunity**: Opportunities are events that may or may not occur that have the potential to improve the program in terms of cost, schedule, and

performance. PMs should use opportunity management to identify, analyze, plan, implement, and track initiatives that can improve the program's cost, schedule, and/or performance baseline by reallocating program resources. Defined by (1) a likelihood of the future event occurring and (2) a benefit associated with the future event.

The DoD Risk Management process is fundamental to the acquisition process, guided by DoDI 5000.02 (Operations of the Defense Acquisition System).

8.2.1 References of A&D Risk Management

- NASA/SP-2011-3422 NASA Risk Management Handbook.
- NASA/SP-2010-576 NASA Risk Informed Decision Making Handbook.
- Department of Defense Risk Management Guide for Defense Acquisition Programs.
- Department of Defense Risk, Issue, and Opportunity Management Guide for Defense Acquisition Programs, January 2017.
- Air Force Instruction 90-802: Risk Management.
- **FAA-H-8083-2A**: Risk Management Handbook, US Department of Transportation.

8.3 Information Technology Risk Management

In the rapidly evolving world of technology, risk management plays a critical role in ensuring that businesses can operate in a secure and sustainable manner. The IT sector, in particular, is heavily dependent on risk management to mitigate the risks associated with data breaches, system failures, and cyber-attacks.

In the IT sector, risk management is the process of identifying, assessing, and mitigating risks that can negatively impact an organization's operations, assets, or reputation. The goal of risk management is to minimize the likelihood of a risk occurring, or reduce its impact if it does happen. In the IT sector, risks can take many forms, such as cyber-attacks, data breaches, software failures, and system outages.

Risk management allows IT managers to balance the operational and economic costs of protective measures and achieve gains in mission capability by protecting the IT systems and data that support their organizations' missions.

The primary risk to Information technology Systems is cybersecurity threats. Integrating risk management into the Software Development Lifecycle (SDLC) is the foundation for increasing the system's reliability. This starts with a risk assessment:

- System characterization
- Threat identification

- Vulnerability
- Control analysis
- Likelihood determination
- Impact analysis
- Risk determination
- Control recommendations
- Results documentation

8.3.1 Standards and Regulations for IT Risk Management

There are various standards and regulations that guide the process of risk management in the IT sector. Here are some of the most important ones:

- **ISO 27001**: This is an international standard that provides a framework for establishing, implementing, maintaining, and continually improving an information security management system (ISMS). It outlines a systematic approach to managing sensitive information, including risk management, and is widely recognized as the gold standard for information security management.
- **NIST cybersecurity framework**: The National Institute of Standards and Technology (NIST) developed this framework to help organizations manage and reduce cybersecurity risk. It provides a flexible, voluntary, and risk-based approach to managing cybersecurity risk, and is widely adopted by organizations in the public and private sectors.
- **PCI DSS**: The Payment Card Industry Data Security Standard (PCI DSS) is a set of security standards designed to ensure that all companies that accept, process, store, or transmit credit card information maintain a secure environment. It includes a comprehensive set of requirements for managing cardholder data, including risk management.
- **GDPR**: The General Data Protection Regulation (GDPR) is a comprehensive data protection regulation that applies to all companies that process the personal data of EU residents. It requires organizations to implement appropriate technical and organizational measures to ensure the security of personal data, including risk management.
- **HIPAA**: The Health Insurance Portability and Accountability Act (HIPAA) is a US law that sets national standards for protecting the privacy and security of personal health information. It requires healthcare organizations to implement appropriate administrative, physical, and technical safeguards to protect electronic protected health information (ePHI), including risk management.

These standards and regulations provide a framework for IT risk management, but they are not exhaustive. Many organizations develop their own internal policies and procedures for managing risk, which may go beyond the requirements of these standards and regulations.

8.3.2 Risk Management Process in IT Sector

The process of risk management in the IT sector typically involves the following steps:

1. **Risk identification**: The first step in the risk management process is to identify potential risks that could impact the IT system. This could involve reviewing the system architecture, software and hardware components, and processes to identify potential vulnerabilities.
2. **Risk analysis**: After identifying the potential risks, the next step is to analyze each risk to determine its likelihood and potential impact on the IT system. This analysis could be based on historical data, industry trends, or expert judgment.
3. **Risk evaluation**: Once the risks have been analyzed, they are then evaluated to determine which ones require immediate attention and which ones can be monitored over time. This evaluation typically involves assessing the potential consequences of each risk and weighing them against the cost and effort required to mitigate them.
4. **Risk treatment:** The fourth step in the risk management process involves treating the identified risks. This could involve taking steps to mitigate the risk, such as implementing security controls or improving processes, or accepting the risk and developing a plan to manage it.
5. **Risk monitoring**: After the risks have been treated, they must be monitored to ensure that the mitigation measures are effective and that new risks do not emerge. This could involve regular system scans, vulnerability assessments, and other monitoring activities to detect any new or emerging risks.
6. **Risk communication**: Throughout the risk management process, it is important to communicate with stakeholders about the risks and the steps being taken to manage them. This could involve reporting on risk assessments, providing training and awareness programs, and engaging with stakeholders to address any concerns they may have.

8.3.2.1 IT Risk Management Characteristics

- Focus on system failure
- Business continuity/Redundancy
- Continuous development and deployment
- Change is a significant source of risk

8.3.2.2 References for IT Risk Management

- Risk Management Guide for Information Technology Systems, NIST SP 800-30.
- ISO 27001: "ISO/IEC 27001:2013 – Information security management systems – Requirements." ISO, 2013, www.iso.org/standard/54534.html

- NIST Cybersecurity Framework: "NIST Cybersecurity Framework." National Institute of Standards and Technology, 16 April 2018, www.nist.gov/cyberframework
- PCI DSS: "Payment Card Industry (PCI) Data Security Standard." PCI Security Standards Council, 2021, www.pcisecuritystandards.org/pci-security-standards/pci-dss
- GDPR: "General Data Protection Regulation (GDPR)." European Union, 2016, eur-lex.europa.eu/legal-content/EN/TXT/?uri=CELEX%3A32016R0679
- HIPAA: "Summary of the HIPAA Privacy Rule." US Department of Health & Human Services, 24 February 2020, www.hhs.gov/hipaa/for-professionals/privacy/index.html
- "Risk Management in Information Technology." Techopedia, 10 February 2022, www.techopedia.com/definition/24599/risk-management-in-information-technology-it
- "Risk Management Process." SANS Institute, 2022, www.sans.org/cyber-security-resources/risk-management-process/
- ISO (International Organization for Standardization). (2018). ISO 31000:2018 Risk management–Guidelines. ISO.

8.4 Process Industries[1]

The process industry is a sector of the economy that includes the production of goods by transforming raw materials through physical and/or chemical processes. Unlike the discrete manufacturing industry, which produces individual items or parts, the process industry produces products in bulk, such as chemicals, pharmaceuticals, food and beverages, paper, and plastics.

Process industries are characterized by continuous or semi-continuous operations that involve a series of interconnected processes or stages. These processes often involve the use of specialized equipment and technologies, such as distillation columns, reactors, and centrifuges, to produce the desired product.

The process industry typically involves large-scale production facilities and requires significant capital investment in equipment, infrastructure, and research and development. Due to the nature of their operations, process industries are subject to strict safety and environmental regulations to prevent accidents and minimize the impact of their activities on the environment.

Similar to other highly regulated, high-risk sectors the process industry must contend with risk associated with the use of hazardous materials. What sets this industry apart is that the production process itself is considered as hazardous. Loss of control of this process may result in significant harm to the environment, people, assets, and harm to communities that the plant operates within.

For this reason, an entire discipline called, "Process Safety Management" is the primary (but not the only) focus of risk management (Figure 8.1).

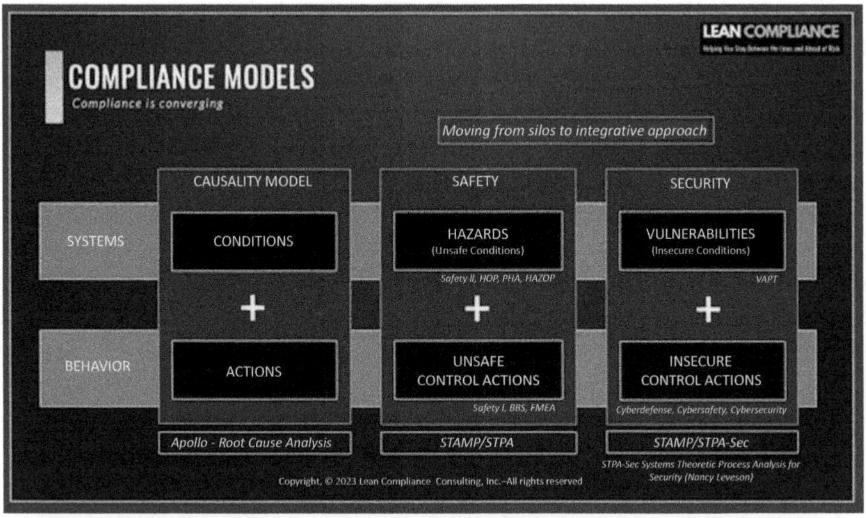

Figure 8.1 Convergence of causality and compliance systems models.

8.4.1 Process Safety Management

Process safety management (PSM) is a comprehensive approach to managing the hazards associated with processes involving highly hazardous chemicals. It involves identifying potential hazards, implementing controls to prevent or mitigate them, and continuously monitoring and improving the overall safety performance of the process. Effective process safety management (PSM) can help organizations to prevent catastrophic incidents, protect the health and safety of workers, and safeguard the environment.

The United States Occupational Safety and Health Administration (OSHA) defines PSM as "the proactive identification, evaluation, and mitigation or prevention of chemical releases that could occur as a result of failures in process, procedures, or equipment" (source: OSHA, "Process Safety Management").

The Center for Chemical Process Safety (CCPS) defines PSM as "a disciplined framework for managing the integrity of operating systems and processes that handle hazardous substances" (source: CCPS, "Guidelines for Process Safety Management").

In all cases, PSM is focused on risk.

8.4.2 How PSM Is Used to Contend with Risk

To ensure process safety, formal risk management is mandated in the process industries. Controlling risks in high-hazard industries requires a robust PSM system and the experienced application of Process Hazard and Risk Analysis (PH&RA) techniques.

High-hazard industries are mandated to have PSM systems, informed by OSHA 1910.119. Conventional Process Safety Management (PSM), which is compliance-oriented and dictated by regulatory bodies worldwide, has not prevented accidents and disasters. While appropriate for evaluating a program against a given standard, traditional audits fail to address organizations' capability and culture, which are critical in determining process safety outcomes.

OSHA 1910.119 states that PSM standard requirements are intended to eliminate or mitigate the consequences of such releases – a risk-handling *strategy*. The standard emphasizes the application of management controls when addressing the risks associated with handling or working near hazardous chemicals. These include:

- **Process safety information**: Identifies the hazards presented by chemicals processed onsite, the equipment used, and any technologies incorporated.
- **Process hazard analysis (PHA)**: Evaluates human factors, engineering and administrative controls, and consequences of accidental chemical releases from processes.
- **Operating procedures**: Develop clear, accurate instructions for startup, normal operations, emergency shutdowns, etc., which can be followed by employees operating processes.
- **Nonroutine work authorization**: Development of plans, procedures, and training for nonroutine work, such as hot work, confined space entry, etc.
- **Employee participation**: Involving employees in the development of PHAs and providing access to plans.
- **Pre-startup safety review**: Establishes processes for confirming that new or changed equipment or procedures will not affect current processes or create new hazards.
- **Mechanical integrity of equipment**: Establishes schedules for inspecting, testing, and maintaining processing equipment.
- **Training**: Teaches employees to recognize hazards, follow established procedures and know what to do when emergencies arise.
- **Contractors**: Coordinate training, plans, and processes with outside workforces to ensure the safety of both employees and the outside workforce.
- **Management of change**: Evaluates changes to process chemicals, technology, equipment, and procedures.
- **Incident investigation**: Reviews incidents and near misses to determine root causes so that plans can be amended to avoid the event in the future.
- **Emergency preparedness, planning, and response**: Creates and implements an Emergency Action Plan (EAP) that outlines specific actions that employees will take when there is a chemical release.
- **Auditing and continuous improvement**: Regularly audit the process to ensure that it is being operated safely and that all control measures are

effective. Identify areas for improvement and implement corrective actions as necessary.

This approach is commonly used in various industries that handle hazardous chemicals, such as chemical manufacturing, oil and gas production, and pharmaceuticals.

8.4.3 Other Risk Disciplines within Process Safety

- Functional Safety
- Cybersecurity
- Occupational health and safety
- Environmental Risk

8.4.4 Process Safety Risk Management Characteristics

- Hazard-Centric Risk Model.
- Eliminate the hazard – eliminate the risk.
- Precautionary principle is the primary risk strategy.
- Safety is a controls problem (Nancy Leveson).
- Risk management practices are mandated and supported by industry associations.
- Moving toward risk-based safety management – proactive rather than reactive.
- Moving away from the event horizon.
- Reliability over resilience.
- Change is a significant source of risk.

8.4.5 Risk Attitude

In the process industry, the precautionary principle is an important concept in risk management. It suggests that when making decisions, it is essential to take a cautious approach.

This means that if there is uncertainty about the potential risks associated with a particular action, decision-makers should take preventive measures, even in the absence of conclusive scientific evidence of harm. The burden of proof falls on those advocating for the new technology, chemical, or otherwise to demonstrate that it is not harmful.

By taking a precautionary approach, process industry professionals can protect the health and safety of workers and the public, as well as safeguard the environment. It is crucial to identify potential hazards and take steps to mitigate them before introducing new processes or substances into the production system. Ultimately, the precautionary principle is about prioritizing safety and minimizing risk, even when the evidence is uncertain.

8.4.6 Future of Risk Management

The future direction of PSM is likely to focus on several key areas:

- **Integration of technology**: Advancements in technology will play a critical role in the future of PSM, with a focus on the use of automation, machine learning, and artificial intelligence to improve risk assessment, incident prediction, and decision-making.
- **Holistic approach**: The future of PSM will involve a more comprehensive, systems-based approach to risk management. This means that companies will need to take an integrated approach, considering the impact of process safety on both their operations **and their broader communities**.
- **Risk-based approach**: PSM will continue to evolve toward a more proactive and risk-based approach. Companies will need to identify and prioritize the most significant risks to their operations and take appropriate measures to mitigate these risks.
- **Focus on human factors**: While technology and risk management systems are important, the human element remains critical in PSM. The future of PSM will likely involve a greater focus on human factors, including training, communication, and organizational culture, to improve safety performance.
- **Regulatory risk**: Changes in regulations and standards related to PSM will continue to shape the future of the discipline. Companies will need to stay up-to-date on these changes and adjust their practices accordingly to remain compliant and improve safety performance.
- **Functional safety**: Ensuring the safety of safety-critical equipment, such as control systems, alarms, and interlocks, will remain a critical aspect of PSM.
- **Cybersecurity**: This refers to the protection of industrial control systems and sensitive data from unauthorized access, use, disclosure, disruption, modification, or destruction, to ensure the safe and reliable operation of critical infrastructure.
- **AI safety**: As AI becomes more prevalent in industrial processes, ensuring that AI systems are designed and implemented in a way that is safe, ethical, and aligns with the values and objectives of the organization will be essential.

Although risk management in the process industry may be viewed as a mature and possibly solved problem, it also presents the greatest potential for risk. Failure to maintain diligence and ongoing learning can cause plants to become complacent and less prepared, ultimately increasing the likelihood of loss of process control.

It is important to recognize that risks and hazards can evolve over time, and new technologies and processes can introduce new types of risk. Therefore, it is crucial for process industry professionals to remain vigilant and continuously update their risk management strategies to ensure that they are prepared for any potential threats.

Failure to do so can result in an increased likelihood of incidents or accidents, potentially causing harm to workers, the environment, and the public.

8.4.7 References for Process Industry Risk Management

- Risk Management Practices in the Process Industries, Report Number 18, European Process Safety Centre, 2012.
- Nancy Leveson systemic risk management – social technical hazardous materials
  - Layer of protections
- Leveson, Nancy. "A New Era for Process Safety?" Process Safety Progress, vol. 37, no. 3, September 2018, pp. 163–165.
- Lees, F. P. (2012). *Loss Prevention in the Process Industries: Hazard Identification, Assessment and Control*. Elsevier.
- Vinnem, J. E. (2014). *Risk Management and Governance: Concepts, Guidelines and Applications*. CRC Press.
- HSE (Health and Safety Executive). (2013). *Process Safety Leadership – A Guide for Senior Leaders*. Retrieved from www.hse.gov.uk/pubns/books/hsg65.htm
- CCPS (Center for Chemical Process Safety). (2019). *Guidelines for Risk Based Process Safety*. Wiley.
- Plant, A. (2015). *Process Risk and Reliability Management: Operational Integrity Management*. Elsevier.
- Fraser, B. (2015). *Process Safety Management: Leveraging Networks and Communities of Practice for Continuous Improvement*. Wiley.
- Safety and Reliability Society. (2013). *Guidelines for Risk Assessment and Management in the Petroleum Industry*. Wiley.
- API (American Petroleum Institute). (2016). *Recommended Practice 580, Risk-Based Inspection*. API.
- ISO (International Organization for Standardization). (2018). *ISO 31000: 2018 Risk management – Guidelines*. ISO.
- OSHA (Occupational Safety and Health Administration). (1992). *Process Safety Management of Highly Hazardous Chemicals*. OSHA Standard 1910.119.
- ASME (American Society of Mechanical Engineers). (2018). *Pipeline Risk Management Manual*. ASME.
- PHMSA (Pipeline and Hazardous Materials Safety Administration). (2021). *Pipeline Safety Regulations*. Retrieved from www.phmsa.dot.gov/pipeline-regulations
- API (American Petroleum Institute). (2021). *Recommended Practice 1173, Pipeline Safety Management Systems*. API.
- NACE (National Association of Corrosion Engineers). (2018). *Integrity Management of Pipelines*. NACE.
- EPA (Environmental Protection Agency). (2021). *Risk Management Plan Rule*. Retrieved from www.epa.gov/rmp/risk-management-plan-rmp-rule

- NFPA (National Fire Protection Association). (2021). *NFPA 652: Standard on the Fundamentals of Combustible Dust*. NFPA.
- CSB (Chemical Safety and Hazard Investigation Board). (2019). *Investigation Reports*. Retrieved from www.csb.gov/investigations/reports/
- IChemE (Institution of Chemical Engineers). (2020). *Process Safety Handbook*. IChemE.
- API (American Petroleum Institute). (2018). *Recommended Practice 2350, Overfill Protection for Storage Tanks in Petroleum Facilities*. API.

8.5 Cyber Security (Critical Infrastructure)

The world is becoming increasingly interconnected, and as a result, the threat landscape for critical infrastructure is expanding. Cyberattacks on critical infrastructure, such as power grids, water treatment facilities, and transportation systems, can have devastating consequences on public safety, national security, and the economy. Therefore, it is crucial for organizations responsible for critical infrastructure to prioritize cybersecurity and risk management.

Risk management is the process of identifying, assessing, and mitigating risks that may affect an organization's ability to achieve its objectives. In the context of critical infrastructure cybersecurity involves identifying and prioritizing the most significant threats, vulnerabilities, and potential impacts, and taking proactive measures to prevent, detect, and respond to cyber incidents.

The following are essential considerations for effective cybersecurity risk management:

1. **Conduct a comprehensive risk assessment:** A risk assessment is the foundation for any effective cybersecurity strategy. Critical infrastructure organizations should conduct a comprehensive risk assessment to identify potential threats, vulnerabilities, and impacts to their operations. The risk assessment should be updated regularly to reflect changes in the threat landscape and the organization's operations.
2. **Implement a multi-layered defense strategy**: A multi-layered defense strategy involves implementing multiple security measures, such as firewalls, intrusion detection and prevention systems, access controls, and encryption, to protect critical assets and systems. This strategy should be designed to detect and prevent cyber threats at different stages, from the perimeter to the endpoint.
3. **Implement strong access controls**: Access controls are critical for preventing unauthorized access to critical infrastructure systems and data. Organizations should implement strong access controls, such as two-factor authentication, password policies, and least privilege, to ensure that only authorized personnel can access critical systems and data.

4. **Regularly patch and update systems**: Cyber attackers often exploit known vulnerabilities in systems and software to gain unauthorized access. Critical infrastructure organizations should regularly patch and update their systems and software to address known vulnerabilities and stay ahead of emerging threats.
5. **Conduct regular security awareness training:** Employees are often the weakest link in an organization's cybersecurity defenses. Critical infrastructure organizations should conduct regular security awareness training to educate employees on cybersecurity best practices, such as phishing prevention, password management, and incident reporting.
6. **Develop and test incident response plans**: Incident response plans are critical for minimizing the impact of a cyber incident on critical infrastructure. Organizations should develop and regularly test incident response plans that include procedures for detecting, reporting, containing, and recovering from cyber incidents.
7. **Collaborate with industry peers and government agencies**: Cyber threats to critical infrastructure are often cross-sector and require collaboration between industry peers and government agencies. Critical infrastructure organizations should participate in information sharing and collaborate with industry peers and government agencies to stay abreast of emerging threats and best practices.

8.5.1 Cybersecurity Risk Management Characteristics

- Vulnerabilities are considered as hazards.
- Eliminate the vulnerability – eliminate the risk.
- The landscape of vulnerabilities is the attack surface.
- Threats are attempts to exploit vulnerabilities by bad actors.
- hreat propagation (cascading of consequences) is a real concern as it is in the process industry.
- Similarities with risk management in the process industry, different terminology, and not as mature.
- Resilience is the goal; reliability is the ideal.
- Cybersecurity is in its infancy compared with other risk disciplines.
- Risk assessment is mostly qualitative (FAIR Institute).

8.5.2 References for Cyber Security (Critical Infrastructure)

- Department of Homeland Security. (2018). *National Critical Infrastructure Security and Resilience Research and Development Plan.*
- National Institute of Standards and Technology. (2018). *Framework for Improving Critical Infrastructure Cybersecurity.*
- World Economic Forum. (2020). *Cybersecurity Leadership Principles: Lessons Learned During the COVID-19 Pandemic to Prepare for the New Normal.*

- Industrial Control Systems Cyber Emergency Response Team. (2021). *Risk Management for Industrial Control Systems.*
- National Cybersecurity and Communications Integration Center. (2016). *Best Practices for Industrial Control System Cybersecurity.*

8.6 Automotive

Vehicles are costly and consume time to produce (Figure 8.2). The consequences of error in design or manufacturing can result in significant loss to the company and, worse yet, an adverse impact on the customer or society. Some industry groups promote industry processes: SAE International and The Automotive Industry Action Group (AIAG).

8.6.1 SAE International

SAE International (formerly the Society of Automotive Engineers) was a global professional organization founded in 1905. SAE International is headquartered in Warrendale, Pennsylvania, and has offices in several countries worldwide.

SAE International's mission is to advance mobility knowledge and solutions for the benefit of humanity. SAE International provides a forum for industry, academia, and government to collaborate and develop technical standards, best practices, and educational resources related to aerospace, automotive, and commercial vehicles. J-standards are technical descriptions of requirements a vehicle must adhere to or conditions to which a vehicle is subjected. Those in the industry often write these standards in these specific domains. These standards are written by groups of engineers in the industry, ensuring the J-standards are multi-perspective.

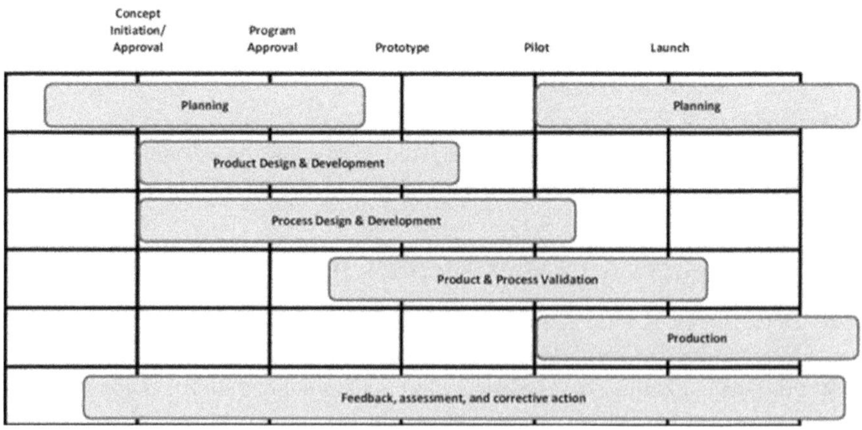

Figure 8.2 Vehicles have a wide range of applications.

SAE International also provides professional development and training opportunities and hosts events and conferences to bring together experts in the mobility industry to share knowledge and ideas. Additionally, SAE International sponsors student design competitions, scholarships, and other initiatives to support the next generation of mobility professionals.

8.6.2 Automotive Industry Action Group

The AIAG is a nonprofit organization founded in 1982 by a group of automotive industry executives to improve the competitiveness of the North American automotive industry. The AIAG is headquartered in Southfield, Michigan, and has offices in Mexico and China.

The AIAG develops and publishes industry standards and best practices for supply chain management, quality, and corporate responsibility. Some of the most well-known AIAG standards include:

1. **Advanced Product Quality Planning (APQP)**: A framework for managing product/process development and ensuring product quality.
2. **Production Part Approval Process (PPAP)**: A set of documents and procedures to ensure that components and parts meet the required quality standards before being approved for use in production.
3. **Measurement Systems Analysis (MSA)**: A set of procedures for evaluating the accuracy and reliability of measurement systems.
4. **Failure Mode and Effects Analysis (FMEA)**: A systematic approach for identifying and preventing potential failure modes in products and processes.
5. **Materials Management Operations Guideline/Logistics Evaluation (MMOG/LE)**: A set of best practices for managing materials and logistics in the automotive industry.
6. **Supply Chain Risk Management (SCRM)**: A set of practices for identifying and managing risks in the automotive supply chain.

8.6.2.1 IATF 16949/ISO 9001:2015

International Automotive Task Force, IATF 16949/ISO 9001 are process specification documents describing an automotive company's quality management system. These systems ensure a repeatable and low-risk outcome for new products developed by the OEM (original equipment manufacturer).

The level of risk in terms of the organization's ability to meet its objectives and customer expectations will vary considerably from organization to organization and within organizations from process to process. Consequently, the robustness of the process for determination of risk and the product, service, or system controls applied will vary.

"Risk-based thinking" means considering risk qualitatively (and quantitatively, depending on the organization's context). Defining the degree of formality needed to plan and control the quality management systems and its component processes activities.

8.6.3 Rules Related to Risk-Based Thinking[1]

1. Risk recognition, evaluation, and mitigation must be a priority and responsibility of the organization's leadership, not delegated.
2. Don't shoot the messenger; Employees will not identify risks if they do not receive an open environment to share risk information – a reward for identifying risks would be good).
3. Have a formal and repeatable set of risk management processes (such as FMEA).
4. Participants must be trained and competent in risk assessment practices.
5. Risks must be determined, assessed, reviewed, and acted upon regularly.
6. Risk consideration must be a central focus of management reviews.
7. Assess working groups and review activities promptly scheduled when there is evidence of adverse effects from known or unexpected risks.
8. Assign risk mitigation activities only to staff with the authority to implement and maintain mitigation action.
9. Risk-based approaches must never be outsourced.
10. The organization must consider risks beyond cost schedule and technical performance (Cross-program, social, political, and economic impacts).
11. Identified risks must be clearly defined. Use the "Condition-If-Then" protocol.
12. Approaches to proper risk management (SARA for Share Avoid Reduce Accept | A-CAT for "Avoid, Control, Accept Transfer").
13. IATF aligns "Risk Analysis" with FMEA (Failure Mode Effects Analysis). (Note: that form "Risk Management" is not required by ISO 9001 while "Risk Analysis" and by extension, "Risk Management" is a requirement of IATF 16949).

8.6.4 Advanced Product Quality Planning

The automotive industry employs an approach to new product development called Advanced Product Quality Planning (APQP). This approach provides a logical course for product development with a rationale sequence for the effort while remaining flexible enough to adapt to meet the specific requirements of a particular project, including embedded software development and other industries. APQP was born out of a collaboration of various automobile manufacturers through the AIAG.

8.6.5 Generalized Approach

The APQP philosophy is one of concurrency of the multiple discipline effort required to define, develop, and effectively manufacture an automotive product. To ensure timely delivery, as the product is designed, so too is the manufacturing line. This process can only begin once the technology is stable and known by those applying the technology. In this way APQP is only connected to harnessing the known technology.

It is composed of a logical sequence of events (not just product development or manufacturing) which, in turn, are supported by a well-defined collection of tools. A substantial constituent of APQP is the focus on feedback from within the enterprise, the supply base, and customers. The input required by APQP provides a mechanism for true control in the control system sense. The approach is also congruent with Shewhart Plan-Do-Check-Act (PDCA) cycle popularized by W. Edwards Deming and often called the Deming loop.

8.6.6 APQP Phases

APQP supports a minimum of five phases [2] (Figure 8.3):

1. Plan and define the program.
2. Product design and development.

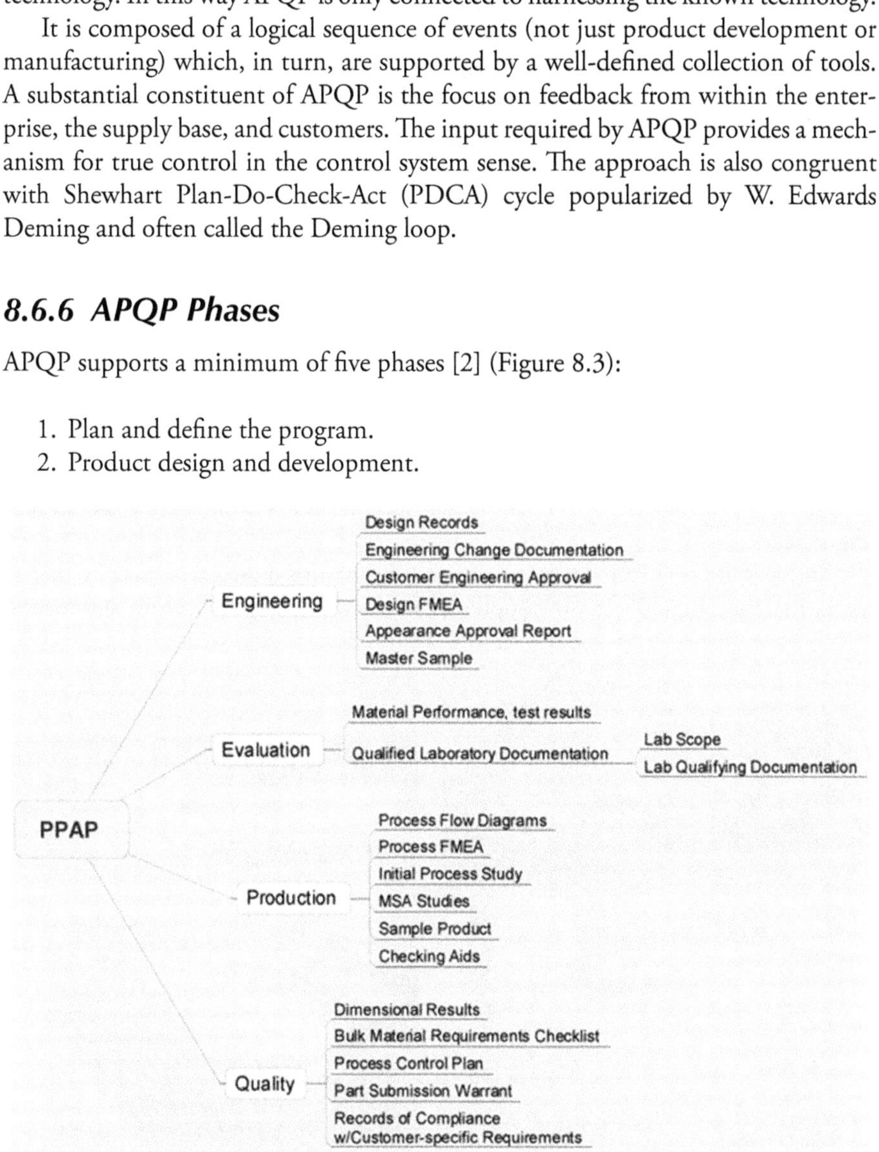

Figure 8.3 AIAG development process [3].

3. Process design and development.
4. Product and process verification and validation.
5. Feedback, assessment, and corrective action.

The first four phases often occur as a staggered or overlapping concurrent engineering approach. The last bullet should occur throughout the process.

The APQP phases can be used directly as project phases. However, since the phases are by discipline or domain, and success requires domain interactions, it is prudent to set up more by objective or point in the processes. Additionally, since this is a high-level breakdown, we recommend increasing details beyond that provided by the AIAG document specific to your effort. The phases can provide a basis for gate reviews or kill points through the project lifecycle. This approach makes detailed project planning possible by decomposing the project scope into the actions required per the organization and customer needs. As such, we can use APQP to help us plan and define the entire development program, from customer input to manufacturing and launch.

8.6.7 Production Part Approval Process (PPAP)

The supplier management portion of the APQP approach is formal. A PPAP submission has 18 required documents, which include all design-oriented documents, all primary process-oriented documents, appearance, and materials assessment (Figure 8.4).

The benefits of PPAP are various, but one of the most important is that it represents the last chance for suppliers to review themselves before submitting

Figure 8.4 PPAP structure [2,4].

results to the customer – ultimately, being more critical to the supplier than the customer. In addition, it decidedly formalizes the release relationship from supplier to customer and standardizes the documentation required for the complete submission.

The defects of PPAP are the following:

- It can become a mere formality.
- Slipshod work on component documents misses the point for both supplier and customer.
- Often, customers don't review very well.
- May stay in a condition called 'interim PPAP' for years.

8.6.8 Design for Six Sigma

Design for Six Sigma (DFSS) is a systematic approach to product and process development that employs statistical tools and techniques to create products that match the needs and expectations of customers while decreasing variation and errors. DFSS is a data-driven method to optimize product design and development processes to provide high-quality products that match the needs and expectations of customers.

The essential principles and concepts that drive the DFSS approach to product and process development are called DFSS fundamentals. These basics include customer focus, a data-driven approach, resilient design, risk management, cross-functional cooperation, and continuous improvement. Understanding the needs and expectations of the client is the starting point for DFSS. This process involves gathering data and input from consumers and other stakeholders to determine essential requirements and expectations.

A data-driven strategy entails optimizing product and manufacturing line design and development processes using statistical tools and methodologies and gathering and evaluating data to uncover trends, patterns, and areas for improvement.

Another crucial DFSS element is a robust design. It entails creating goods and systems that can consistently work under various scenarios and identifying and reducing sources of variance that can influence product performance.

Risk management is also an essential component of DFSS. It entails evaluating possible risks and hazards linked with the product and developing it to reduce these risks. Another important DFSS element is cross-functional cooperation. It involves assembling teams of engineers, designers, quality control professionals, and other stakeholders to optimize product design and development processes.

Lastly, a critical DFSS basic is an ongoing improvement. It entails constantly assessing product performance and identifying areas for improvement; this involves gathering consumer and stakeholder input, evaluating data, and applying changes to improve product design and development processes.

Ultimately, the DFSS foundations provide a disciplined approach to product and process development focused on satisfying customers' requirements and expectations while minimizing variance and faults. Organizations may build high-quality products that match consumer requirements and expectations while cutting costs and boosting efficiency by implementing these elements into product development procedures [5].

8.6.9 Functional Safety

Functional safety is an integral part of automotive risk management. It entails designing systems and products to ensure they work safely despite failures or defects. It involves creating plans that recognize and respond to possible dangers, reducing the likelihood of accidents, injuries, or equipment damage. Functional safety is especially critical in automotive, aerospace, and medical equipment industries, where even minor failures can have catastrophic implications. ISO 26262 (for automotive) and IEC 61508 (for general applications) functional safety standards give guidelines on designing and building safety-critical systems to guarantee that they fulfill the needed safety criteria.

The capacity of a system to fulfill its intended function correctly and safely amid dangers or flaws is functional safety. Functional safety aims to prevent or limit the consequences of failures, such as injury, equipment damage, or environmental harm. The practice of detecting, analyzing, and minimizing risks connected with a product or process is known as risk management. Risk management aims to reduce the possibility and effect of possible risks, including functional safety hazards [6]. Functional safety and risk management are inextricably linked because functional safety is a crucial component of risk management.

8.6.10 SIL

Achieving functional safety requires starting with a risk assessment, which is a crucial step. Assessment entails identifying potential risks and evaluating the likelihood and probable severity of harm caused by each risk. The safety-related system's appropriate safety integrity level (SIL) is chosen based on the risk assessment findings. The safety integrity scale has four levels, with level 1 (SIL1) being the lowest and level 4 (SIL4) being the highest. The requirements are necessary to achieve each SIL specified in the standard. To achieve the target decreased likelihood of harmful failure, standards grow stricter at increasing SILs. The system is designed to achieve the required SIL while functioning well in all foreseen scenarios [7].

A safety-related system must pass verification and validation to fulfill the necessary SIL. While *validation* entails testing the system to ensure it runs properly and performs the necessary SIL, *verification* requires confirming that the system's design complies with the established safety requirements. Also included in the report is how safety-related software contributes to functional safety. A safety-related system's overall safety performance may be significantly influenced by its software. The notion of software safety integrity levels (SW-SILs) is introduced in the study, which also offers instructions on choosing the right SW-SIL for safety-related software.

8.6.11 ISO 26262

An international standard for functional safety in motor vehicles, ISO 26262, was initially released in 2011. The standard outlines the requirements for designing, installing, and testing vehicle safety-related systems and offers a framework for their development.

The goal of ISO 26262 is to guarantee road safety for cars equipped with sophisticated electronic systems. It is especially crucial for brakes, steering, and accelerator systems, which are essential for the vehicle's safe operation. The standard addresses every stage of the lifecycle of safety-related systems, including concept and design, manufacturing, use, and decommissioning.

The ten parts comprising ISO 26262 each cover a different topic within the standard. The components are the management of functional safety, the creation of hardware and safety standards, the creation of software, and testing and verification. The standard also specifies four Automotive Safety Integrity Levels (ASILs), which assess the risk level of a system and establish the necessary conditions for its design and testing. It is impossible to emphasize the significance of functional safety. Several sectors use safety-related systems, including transportation, industry, energy, and healthcare. Any malfunction in these systems intended to safeguard humans and the environment could have detrimental effects. Minor injuries to fatalities and severe environmental harm are possible outcomes of a safety-related system failure. For the organizations in charge of these systems, there may be severe financial and reputational implications in addition to the human cost.

Functional safety offers a methodical way to ensure safety-related systems function properly and dependably. Functional safety can help prevent failures and ensure that safety-related systems provide the necessary level of safety performance by detecting potential hazards, evaluating the associated risks, and putting mitigation measures in place.

Functional safety offers a framework to ensure that safety-related systems are planned and developed consistently and methodically, which is one of its main advantages. This can aid in ensuring that safety-related systems remain dependable and maintain the necessary levels of safety performance during their operational lifetime. In addition, systems related to safety can function more effectively and efficiently with functional safety. Safety-related systems can be built to function more effectively, lowering the risk of downtime or inefficiency by recognizing and minimizing potential hazards.

The ability of functional safety to assure regulatory compliance is another significant advantage. Functional safety offers a way to prove compliance with the stringent safety rules that apply to many businesses. Functional safety can also contribute to greater customer trust in safety-related systems. Organizations can show their dedication to safety and earn their consumers' trust by ensuring safety-related systems satisfy the necessary safety performance.

Ultimately, it is impossible to overestimate the significance of functional safety. Systems that deal with safety are essential for safeguarding both people and the environment, and any malfunction can have negative effects. Functional safety can help prevent failures, improve efficiency and effectiveness, maintain regulatory compliance, and foster customer confidence by offering a systematic way to ensure these systems' safety performance. The Technical Report TR 61508-0 is a valuable tool for designers and developers of safety-related systems because it gives them the information and resources they need to achieve functional safety and guarantee the security of the systems they create.

8.6.12 Vehicle Platform Management

There are a few benefits and risk reduction via vehicle platform management, starting with reduced development time and cost. A well-managed platform can help streamline the material selection, systems interfaces, and manufacturing processes, making developing new automotive systems faster and more cost-effective. A platform approach makes it possible to use the same components on various vehicles produced by the OEM (original equipment manufacturer).

Next, vehicle platform management, done well, will show improved quality and reliability. Effective platform management involves rigorous testing and validation of the system over wide-ranging applications, which helps improve the quality and reliability of the final product. In addition, shared material and manufacturing processes reduce variability and associated risk.

A well-designed platform is flexible and scalability. Platform management means the design fits can be easily adapted and scaled to meet the needs of different applications, reducing the need for separate platforms for each use case.

Platform management produces standardized interfaces and protocols, which help simplify the system and reduce potential errors. In addition, standardization can help reduce costs through the volume purchase of components and aftermarket inventory and support.

Projects introducing standardized components have lower technology risks, as the element introduced by the project is on one or more vehicle platforms. The technology's stability, standard interfaces, and team experience with the component before the project presents a new element or subsystem into another platform.

8.7 Construction[2]

> The first step in the risk management process is to acknowledge the reality of risk. Denial is a common tactic that substitutes deliberate ignorance for thoughtful planning.
>
> *Charles Tremper*

8.7.1 Steven G. Lauck Writes This Section

Construction is complex, from idea to turnover, massive investments, and various knowledge domains. Identifying what can go wrong from the beginning is critical to achieving success. Understanding that identifying risks early in the process allows for establishing triggers and plans to handle any trouble when it occurs.

The purpose of this chapter is to present information about the areas of the most significant potential risk for Construction projects. Under each domain are listed potential risks; some have a case example to explain the impact of the threat or lack of identifying one. Each area will end with questions to consider when conducting Risk Interviews and Risk meetings for Risk Identification.

We undertake due diligence and a comprehensive investigation during the Risk Identification phase. Some areas presented for risk consideration may be perceived as farfetched but should still be considered and recorded. The Risk Assessment phase can weed out the most unlikely risks on each project. Also, the lists are not all-inclusive or a one-shot event; the information presented is to inspire more in-depth Risk Identification and ongoing review of emerging risks.

As part of the risk identification process in construction, one needs to think about the consequences if the risk happens and document the assumptions, including the best information available at that time that provides the basis for the belief.

> We have, perhaps too often, taken a best-case scenario and then committed to delivering on it, when in order to deliver on it, we have to have seven or eight miracles occur.
>
> *U.S. Deputy Energy Secretary Bruce Carnes in 2005 (Gabel 2006)*

8.7.2 Contractor/Subcontractors

From experience, most of the risks pertain to the Bidder Selection process. First, the project manager should work closely with procurement to review potential bidders. Selecting the right contractor and subcontractors is crucial for the best chance at project success.

Business form: The business form of a contractor organization can be a risk to a project, identification of the best solution for these circumstances. Types of forms:

- Sole proprietorship.
- General partnership.
- Limited liability partnership.
- Limited partnership.
- Limited liability company.
- Business corporation.

Each form has its associated possible risks.

Potential risks:

1. Union Contract ending.
2. Contractors using underqualified workers.
3. Contractors employing too few or too many sub-contractors.
4. Contractors and sub-contractors with pending litigation.
5. Contractors requesting large down payments with signed contract/purchase order.
6. Contractors without backup plans for resource shortages.
7. The contractor requesting more time to bid.
8. Contractor default.

Questions to consider:

1. If the contractor is a union shop, What is the current status of the union contract?
2. Are there any outstanding legal issues the contractor is facing?
3. What is the financial health of the contractor?
4. What is the current workload of the contractor?
5. Any experiences with human resource shortages?
6. Is there a process to pay a large down payment?

8.7.3 Contract/Procurement

The procurement department in itself has possible risks. This heading focuses on the procurement of products and services for executing the construction project.

Potential risks:

1. Not enough qualified bidders.
2. Single bidders for specialty products and special services.
3. Lack of diversity among bidders.
4. The slow response by bidders.
5. Special Terms and Conditions request.
6. Not using a formal contract – just issuing a purchase agreement or purchase order.
7. Contract not signed by start date.
8. Supply Chain breakdowns – due to Labor issues, fees, customs for international shipments, politics in this country or the shipping from the government, or weather systems.
9. Low bidder – contractor did not understand the full scope and obligation (always qualify the bid)
   - Accepting a low bid is a considerable risk. In a few cases, the low bidder is basing his request on the request being taken and then using Change

Requests to up the final payment. Base strategy on documents, a risk area later in this chapter. The bidder identifies areas of weak descriptions or incomplete information, knowing there is little or no challenge to a possible Change Request. At any rate, a formal articulation of the scope and an articulated change process with the customer and supplier.

Questions to consider:

1. Does procurement have a standard Terms and Conditions (T&Cs) Document?
2. If so, can the T&Cs document be altered per a particular contractor's request to align with the contractor's T&Cs or expectations? Again, this usually has to do with the timing of payments.
3. Is there a standard contract used by procurement? Is it alterable? Some 'basic' procurement contracts do not fit all construction situations. Any proposed alteration will need the legal department's review and approval, so ensure the schedule includes this time. The legal department could take a few weeks, depending on the alterations.
4. What if something goes wrong, Is Arbitration and legal action plainly explained?
5. Can the project manager review (and sign off) every purchase order/contract before issuing it? These reviews keep purchase orders from being given without the project manager's knowledge, which can lead to confusion and cost overruns.

8.7.4 Contractor Performance

Regarding performance, when considering the bidders, this is at all levels of the project; include a review of any historical data Procurement has from previous contractors under consideration in the RFQ/P process.

Potential risks:

1. Does not perform to contract.
2. Default of some work or contract.

Questions to consider:

1. Can the bidding contractor provide references? Beware of Contractors that say, "Let me know which ones you plan to call" or "I can provide references but let me know before you call them." The reasoning could be that he wants to notify the individual that your firm will be calling, just as a heads-up to the individual. But it could also be that the contractor wants to direct you to contact specific individuals.

8.7.5 Documents

Construction projects are a pile of documents, even in this paperless business society we are supposed to be in. Documents are created, filed, and transmitted electronically; eventually, someone hits the print button.

Potential risks:

1. Poorly written documents.
2. Everyone is not on the same version of an app or software.
3. No version control.
4. Lack of standard document identification system (naming or numbering documents).
5. Common filing system.
6. Not in Architectural/Construction standard form.
7. Statement of Work not clear or wholly understood.
8. Assumptions not listed.
9. Known unknowns not plainly and noted.

Questions to consider:

1. What is their current version of applicable apps and software?
2. If not the latest version, when do they plan to update it?
3. Are Architectural/Construction forms in use?
4. Do documents go there for a Quality check before issuing?
5. Do you have experience working in advance of the contract signing on previous projects?
6. Do estimates include a list of assumptions as the basis for the forecast?
7. Any issues with documents in previous projects?

8.7.6 Environmental

There are two areas of risk within the Environmental. The first is the existing environment and after the project. The second is the impact on the physical environment during the construction.

1. **Environmental Impact Assessment (EIA)**: This is a comprehensive study that assesses the potential environmental effects of a construction project. It evaluates air and water quality, noise pollution, waste management, and ecological impacts on flora and fauna.
2. **Energy Efficiency**: Evaluating the energy consumption and efficiency of the construction project, including using energy-efficient materials, sustainable energy sources, and design strategies to reduce energy consumption.

3. **Waste Management**: Assessing strategies for proper waste management throughout the construction process, including waste reduction, recycling, and proper disposal of construction debris and hazardous materials.
4. **Water Management**: Evaluating the project's impact on water resources, including water use efficiency, stormwater management, and erosion control measures to prevent sedimentation and pollution of water bodies.
5. **Biodiversity and Habitat Protection**: Assessing the potential impact on local ecosystems, habitats, and protected species. This evaluation includes identifying measures to mitigate adverse effects and protect biodiversity through habitat preservation, restoration, or creation.
6. **Noise and Air Pollution**: Evaluating potential noise and air pollution generated during construction activities and implementing measures to minimize impacts on surrounding communities, such as noise barriers and dust control systems.
7. **Sustainable Materials**: Assessing the use of sustainable construction materials, including recycled content, locally sourced materials, and renewable resources, to reduce the environmental footprint of the project.
8. **Cultural and Archaeological Preservation**: Evaluating the potential impact on cultural heritage sites and archaeological resources. This evaluation may involve conducting surveys and implementing measures to preserve or mitigate potential damage to these sites.
9. **Compliance with Environmental Regulations**: Ensuring the construction project complies with local, regional, and national environmental regulations and obtaining necessary permits and approvals.
10. **Monitoring and Reporting**: Establishing monitoring programs to track environmental performance during construction and post-construction phases and reporting the findings to relevant stakeholders and regulatory authorities.

8.7.7 Existing Environment

Most likely, the client will have environmental information on the property from a consulting firm. This recorded information will be the foundation during the development of the business case. The client wants to know as much as possible about the land to reduce their risk of contaminated soil or endangered species.

Land regulations should be recorded and evaluated for impact on the business case. The local government officials should have a presentation by the owner or consultant of the proposed project.

> Property History Case: The earth only has so much land mass. The chances are pretty high that any plot of land may have been used in various ways over a hundred years, even by nature. For example, a property in the mid-1800s

was a limestone quarry with kilns, barns, outhouses, and buildings. In the mid-1950s, the property, cleared of the most visible quarry operation, was laid out as a subdivision; however, only one house was built. Cost overruns shut the subdivision project down. Today the property has a single home, and sections are overgrown. Just a few feet down are the remnants of the limestone operation and activities on the land. Some features were bulldozed and covered. New Construction presents problems that include archeologists. Construction on a site like this should involve GPR (Ground Penetrating Radar), and a decision would have to be made if that work is part of the client's or the contractors. Because the areas are overgrown, Lidar may also be required. But, again, whose scope is it?

Potential risks:

1. No due diligence on the property – no reports.
2. There are "issues" uncovered during due diligence.
3. Review of regulations not undertaken.
4. Lack of inclusion of government officials.
5. There is a Wildlife regulation in play.
6. Loss of fauna and flora.

Questions to consider:

1. Is there a final report on the existing environment?
2. Is there a final report on the wildlife on the property?
3. Potential costs for restoration.

8.7.8 Construction Impact on the Environment

Construction's impact on the environment is a significant issue for the public. Air, noise, waste, and water pollution are the most common impacts. Requirements will vary from location to location. Most construction firms today have programs in place to handle this pollution. However, consistency among employees and subcontractors will vary. The main risk here is that not everyone follows the procedures. So, reducing or eliminating these risks to the environment is critical.

Each contractor must have a plan, process, and procedure to address the common pollution.

Potential risks:

1. The subcontractor does not have a pollution control plan.
2. An incident occurs.
3. A contractor has multiple incidents.

4. Not being able to schedule evening work.
5. Restrictions to moving heavy equipment by the most straightforward path (e.g., direct route).

Questions to consider:

1. Does the contractor have a pollution control plan?
2. Does a contractor have a history of pollution incidents?
3. Is a particular contractor hired due to past pollution "violations"?
4. What are the local pollution regulations?

8.7.9 Financial

Finances are the heart of any project. Everyone is in it to make money. In construction, this starts with creating an estimate.

8.7.9.1 Estimates

Development of the estimates using the best current information – costs, person-hours, and previous similar projects. Hopefully, lessons learned and closed project files are complete. In addition, several software programs are available for developing estimates and offer annual updates of costs and installation person-hours.

One trend today is using Risk-Based Estimates. Risk-based cost estimation entails developing probable costs for project components and the project based on identified known quantities, fees, and contingency generated from a list of identified uncertainties from both opportunities and threats and their potential impact on the project.[3]

Potential risks:

1. Accuracy of the estimates.
2. Not using current costs.
3. No historical information from previous projects.
4. Assumptions not listed.

Questions to consider:

1. Are estimates generated by hand or software?
2. Is the cost database current?

8.7.10 Force Majeure

"Force majeure" is a standard clause in contracts that essentially frees both parties from liability or obligation when an extraordinary event or circumstance beyond the control of the parties, such as a war, strike, riot, crime, epidemic, or an event described by the legal term *Act of God*, prevents one or both parties from fulfilling their obligations under the contract. In practice, most force majeure clauses do not entirely excuse a party's nonperformance, but only suspend it for the duration of the force majeure."[4]

Financial and schedule are the areas impacted by Force Majeure. Loss of completed work, loss of equipment, and loss of materials at the site. The money to restore the site has to come from somewhere. The schedule now has to include the restore time, returning the site to status the day before the act occurred.

Special note: The significant potential impact of an extraordinary event is the loss of life, meaning affects the families of those lost and the construction family.

8.7.11 Acts of Terror

Acts of terror have to be part of the Risk Assessment. Most government projects face this risk. However, any project that could result in loss of assets and life should address this risk. And not only include it in the design of the completed project but during the construction as well. For example, during the 1960s in Mideastern countries, terrorists were shooting American contractors on job sites.

While it is near impossible to identify that a construction site would become a target of a terrorist, there are some things to consider.

Potential risks:

1. Protesters.
2. Attack on workers.
3. Attack or damage to equipment – storage trailers.

Questions to consider:

1. Is the project a government building?
2. Is the project near a military installation?
3. Is there existing turmoil in the general area of the project site?

8.7.12 Weather

Weather should always be considered a risk, from a few days of rain or snow to monsoons or blizzards to hurricanes and tornadoes.

> Weather Case: During the risk identification phase of a project on an east coast military base, a hurricane making landfall in the area was identified as a risk and summarily dismissed because the place had not seen that storm category for many decades. Risk contingency and recovery

plans associated with hurricanes were not required due to improbability. As fate would have, the site was hit by a hurricane that year during construction. The project suffered an unplanned shutdown of just under 120 days.

If the base of the selected contractor is in South Florida, the project site will be in Wisconsin, and construction will begin in January. Risk Identification starts with the weather and should have a contingency plan.

Potential risk:

1. Severe weather events.
2. Inadequate planning for weather incidents.
3. Insufficient protection and storage in case of a weather incident.

Questions to consider:

1. Are there historical records for the site area?
2. Is there space (somewhere) if equipment needs to be moved?
3. Can shipments be delayed?
4. Is there a plan to protect the site from weather damage?

8.7.13 Government

Government officials are usually helpful with construction projects. As a result, there is an increase in local businesses during construction, and the tax base is positively affected. After construction, the positive impact on the area continues with new employees and increased demand at local businesses.

The local and state inspectors can be a challenge to work with. However, most go by the book on codes and ordinances, and they should, as these are about public safety.

Potential risks:

1. Don't have current Codes and Ordinances for local and state.
2. Contractors that work around codes.
3. Contractors that have a history of conflict with inspectors.
4. Inspectors that inspect to the letter of the code (hard to work with).

Questions to consider:

1. Does every contractor have current regulations and ordinances?
2. Do contractors have a working relationship with the inspectors?
3. How are the city officials to work with?

Notes

1 This Process Safety Management section is provided by Raimund Laqua, Lean Compliance Consulting, Inc. www.leancompliance.ca/. Dundas, Ontario, Canada.
2 Construction section is provided by Steven G. Lauck, visit www.valuetransform.com
3 Risk-Based Engineers Estimate, Jennifer S. Shane, Principal Investigator Department of Civil, Construction, and Environmental Engineering Construction Management and Technology Iowa State University March 2015 Research Project Final Report 2015-10.
4 https://en.wikipedia.org/wiki/Force_majeure#cite_note-1

References

1. P. Ambrose, IATF 16949: 2016 Audit Guide and Checklist, Systems Thinking. Works, 2018.
2. Automotive Industry Action Group, "*Production Part Approval Process*," 4th ed., Detroit: Automotive Industry Action Group Publishing, 2006.
3. K. Pries and J. M. Quigley, "*Project Management of Complex and Embedded Systems, Ensuring Product Integrity and Program Quality*," Boca Raton, FL: CRC Press, 2008, p. 4.
4. K. Pries and J. M. Quigley, "*Project Management of Complex and Embedded Systems, Ensuring Product Integrity and Program Quality*," Boca Raton, FL: CRC Press, 2008, p. 256.
5. C.-T. Hsieh, B. Lin, and B. Manduca, "Information technology and six sigma implementation," *Journal of Computer Information Systems Summer*, 47(4), pp. 1–10, 2007.
6. M. N. A. K. Muhammad Usman Tariq, "*Six Sigma for Risk Identification*," 2011. [Online]. Available: https://core.ac.uk/download/pdf/288023815.pdf
7. M. K. A. Santana and G. Louriro, "Risk Management Approach for Testing and Calibration Laboratories," *Accreditation and Quality Assurance*, 27(6), pp. 313–318, 2022.

Glossary of Terms

- BCWP – Budgeted Cost for Work Performed - the dollarized (budgeted) value of all work actually accomplished in a given period of time.
- CER – Cost Estimating Relationships - mathematical expressions that express cost as a function of one or more variables, used to estimate a particular cost or price by using an established relationship with an independent variable.
- ConOps – Concept of Operations - a document describing the characteristics of a proposed system from the viewpoint of an individual who will use that system.
- CR – Contingency Reserve - a budget allocation or fund that covers unexpected expenses, risks, or uncertainties.
- DSM – Design Structure Matrix – a compact and visual representation of a system or project in the form of a square matrix showing the relationships between the elements.
- ETC – Estimate to Complete - the financial performance index and project management measure that shows you the remaining cost you expect to pay in order to complete a project.
- EAC – Estimate at Completion - the current expectation of the total costs of a project once completed.
- EVM – Earned Value Management - a systematic approach to the integration and measurement of cost, schedule, and technical (scope) accomplishments on a project or task.
- FMEA – Failure Modes and Effects Analysis - a structured way to identify and address potential problems, or failures and their resulting effects on the system or process before an adverse event occurs.
- FRAGNET - scheduling network, that graphically identifies the sequencing of all critical and non-critical new activities and/or activity revisions affected by a Compensable Delay or Excusable Delay.
- FTA - Fault Tree Analysis - a systematic approach that identifies the primary causes of operational and maintenance (O&M) issues.
- IMP - Integrated Master Plan - a top-level document used to help organize, structure, and manage projects.
- IMS – Integrated Master Schedule - a time-based schedule that shows the detailed tasks needed to successfully execute a program or contract.

- MR – Management Reserve - the amount of the project budget reserved for unforeseen work that is within the scope of the project.
- MOE – Measures of Effectiveness – a metric that assesses the ability of a system or person to meet the needs of a particular condition or objective.
- MOP – Measures of Performance - a measure of a system's performance is expressed as speed, payload, range, time-on-station, frequency, or other distinctly quantifiable performance features.
- NGT – Nominal Group Technique - a structured method for group brainstorming that encourages contributions from everyone and facilitates quick agreement on the relative importance of issues, problems, or solutions.
- NPV – Net Present Value - the difference between the present value of cash inflows and the present value of cash outflows over a period of time.
- PoPS – Probability of Project (Program) Success – a holistic view of the overall project or program health in compliance with the program requirements, program resources, program execution plan and external influences
- Payback Period – the number of years required to recover the original cash investment
- POI – Return on Investment - is calculated by dividing the profit earned on an investment by the cost of that investment.
- PRA – Probabilistic Risk Analysis - a systematic method for evaluating risks. It's a system scenario-based risk assessment that uses probability and statistical data to analyze the risk of a system, process, or activity.
- KPP – Key Performance Parameters - key system capabilities that must be meet in order for a system to meet its operational goals.
- MORT – Management Oversight and Risk Tree - a formal, disciplined logic or decision tree to systematically relate and integrate a wide variety of safety concepts.
- RCA – Root Cause Analysis - the process of discovering the root causes of problems in order to identify appropriate solutions.
- KRI – Key Risk Indicators - metric for measuring the likelihood that the combined probability of an event and its consequences will exceed the organization's risk appetite and have a profoundly negative impact on an organization's ability to be successful.
- PDF – Probability Distribution Function - a mathematical function that describes the likelihood of different outcomes for an experiment.
- PRA – Probabilistic Risk Assessment - a systematic methodology for evaluating risks associated with complex engineered technological entities. It can also be used to assess the effects of stressors on the environment.
- RHP – Risk Handling Plan - a document outlining how a team will respond to potential risks.

- Stochastic process – the probability distribution of the random variables Xt for each $t \in [0, \infty)$
- TPM – Technical Performance Parameters - TPM is an evolutionary Program Management and systems engineering tool that builds on the three parameters of (1) Earned Value Management (EVM), (2) cost and schedule performance indicators, and (3) the status of technical achievement
- UFE – Unallocated Future Expense - are expenses related to a company's operations which have not been assigned to any particular segment or project.
- WBD – Wide Band Delphi – am estimation method based on consensus developed in the 1950s and 1960s at the Rand Corporation as a forecasting tool in the presence of uncertainty.
- WBS – Work Breakdown Structure - a visual tool that helps project managers break down a project into smaller components.

Index

For Product Safety Concerns and Information please contact our EU representative GPSR@taylorandfrancis.com
Taylor & Francis Verlag GmbH, Kaufingerstraße 24, 80331 München, Germany

www.ingramcontent.com/pod-product-compliance
Ingram Content Group UK Ltd.
Pitfield, Milton Keynes, MK11 3LW, UK
UKHW020019200926
475702UK00014B/1961
* 9 7 8 1 0 3 2 5 4 5 6 4 6 *